Rethinking Obligation

Rethinking Obligation

A FEMINIST METHOD
FOR POLITICAL THEORY

Nancy J. Hirschmann

Cornell University Press

Ithaca and London

THIS BOOK HAS BEEN PUBLISHED WITH THE AID
OF A GRANT FROM THE HULL MEMORIAL
PUBLICATION FUND OF CORNELL UNIVERSITY.

First published 1992 by Cornell University Press.

International Standard Book Number 0-8014-2309-0 (cloth)
International Standard Book Number 0-8014-9567-9 (paper)
Library of Congress Catalog Card Number 91-55540
Printed in the United States of America
Librarians: Library of Congress cataloging information appears
on the last page of the book.
♾ The paper in this book meets the minimum requirements of the American National Standard for Information Sciences–Permanence of Paper for Printed Library Materials, ANSI Z39.48-1984.

FOR CHRIS

and for the memory of T.,
whose life taught by example

Contents

Preface

IT WAS ONCE SUGGESTED to me that the title and subtitle of this book should be reversed, and there is considerable merit in that idea. This book provides a feminist analysis of liberal voluntarist theories of political obligation, most commonly referred to as consent theory or social contract theory. It reveals that women's exclusion from the realm of the political in modern political theories and practices is attributable not merely to the fact that opportunities for consent, the acceptance of benefits, and other modern indexes of political obligation are effectively denied to some people, such as women and minorities. Rather, it is the very definition of obligation as an exclusively voluntarist principle that makes liberal obligation theory problematic for women and other historically disempowered groups.

But this argument marks a deeper theme, namely, whether and how feminist theory can provide new insights and methods in political theory to keep the latter viable and timely. Feminism, as one of many antimodern, or "postmodern," strategies of the late twentieth century, is an extremely powerful tool for revealing the ways in which the picture of reality represented by state-of-nature theorizing is really a picture of beings of a particular gender, race, and class in a highly specific cultural and economic environment. It provides effective ways of seeing how perspective informs and shapes our conceptions of reality embodied in dominant political theories. I thus take political obligation as a focal point for illustrating the methodological shifts which I believe feminism demands of—and which I am urging on—political theory.

This new methodology requires a reciprocal relationship between

the history of thought and analytical philosophy and between contemporary sources and those of previous eras. Using feminist psychoanalysis to identify the gender bias of early social contract theory, I
explore whether contemporary concepts that derived from the Enlightenment, such as obligation, contract, and consent, contain this
same bias even though we tend to view them as gender neutral. This
gender bias, I argue, is built into the foundation of modern liberalism
and hence constitutes a structural component of contemporary visions of political obligation. Feminist analysis is necessary to revealing
this bias and constructing new theories that can accommodate the
experiences of women and other excluded groups.

It seems somewhat strange to me, though in retrospect it is perhaps
not all that surprising, that in the process of developing this argument, I found that the themes of my book echoed those of my personal life. For me, the task of writing, while extremely rewarding, can
also be so singular, so isolating, that I have often felt quite alone in it
these past several years. I found myself periodically wondering if
Hobbes is perhaps correct to say that relationship is artificial, as difficult to sustain as to create. Yet now, as I call to mind all the people
who have been connected with my intellectual and emotional life during the production of this project, I am reminded of the degree to
which relationship is in fact truly central to our lives.

This book goes back several years, and a number of people offered
crucial help in its earlier incarnations. My general indebtedness to
Richard Flathman, who was involved in this project from its incep-
tion, cannot be overstated. I have incorporated so many of his suggestions that it would be impossible to mention them all. In addition
to stimulating my interest in political obligation in the first place, he
helped me clarify my arguments, and indeed get to the heart of the
problem I sought to grapple with. He also aided me in developing a
voice that allowed me to bring together the often conflicting worlds of
political theory and feminist theory.

Nancy Hartsock has also provided constant support from the project's beginning. She has read the manuscript in its entirety at one
stage or another, always ready to comment on successive drafts. She
often brought to bear insights on points I not only did not see but
would not likely ever have seen but for her assistance. My intellectual
debt to her is evident throughout this work.

Ian Shapiro and Christine Di Stefano each provided careful and insightful readings of the completed manuscript and offered suggestions that greatly improved the clarity and organization of the book.
Rogers Smith also commented extensively on an earlier version of the

manuscript, leading me to several improvements. Sandra Harding provided insights at various places along the way, not only reading key chapters at crucial points in the book's development but also providing access to her own ongoing work. Jane Mansbridge and Julie Mostov offered helpful suggestions on democratic theory, as did Laurie Langbauer on postmodernism. The late George A. Kelly also provided early help and guidance, particularly in my work on Rousseau. Less specific but no less important support came in the form of discussions with friends and colleagues, particularly Chuck Beitz, Liz Bussiere, Jean Elshtain, Jim Kurth, Roland Pennock, and Abby Zanger. Students of feminist theory and political theory at Swarthmore College and, more recently, Cornell University also helped me rethink many of the issues considered in these pages.

Early financial support was provided by the Woodrow Wilson Foundation, in the form of a dissertation grant for research in women's studies. Swarthmore College provided faculty research grants for the summers of 1988, 1989, and 1990, which helped me complete research important to several parts of the book. Cornell University and The Bunting Institute of Radcliffe College provided support during the final stages of preparing the manuscript for publication. Portions of this book appeared earlier in article form in the *American Political Science Review*: "Freedom, Recognition, and Obligation: A Feminist Approach to Political Theory" in vol. 83 (December 1989), and "Feminism and Liberal Theory" in vol. 85 (March 1991). I appreciate the journal's permission to use this material here.

Finally, I thank my family, who have always offered unfailing support for me and my work even when they weren't sure they understood either. Most of all, I thank my husband, Chris Stoeckert, not only for sticking by me during the worst—as well as putting up with me *at* my worst—but for having faith in me when I did not have it in myself. We have been traveling together since this project was very young indeed, and he has seen it and me through many transformations, good and bad, with constancy and good-natured tolerance.

NANCY J. HIRSCHMANN

Cambridge, Massachusetts

Rethinking Obligation

Introduction

POLITICAL OBLIGATION concerns the basis on which states can legitimately exact obedience from citizens, or more precisely the conditions under which citizens are morally required to obey the authority of the state. This statement immediately raises further questions: What do we mean by legitimacy? Authority? The state?

In modern western democracies these questions are generally answered by reference to voluntarist ideology. That is, an *obligation* is a limitation on behavior, a requirement for action or nonaction, which the (non)actor has chosen or agreed to, as opposed to *duty*, which may be a requirement that exists "naturally," or "positionally,"[1] but at any rate is not explicitly chosen by the person who has the duty. It is central to our (western) understanding of obligations that they arise from voluntary and free actions. The paradigm for obligations on the liberal model is the promise and contract, and its political counterpart is the social contract.[2]

Voluntarist obligation theory, loosely dubbed "consent theory," holds that political obligations exist only by virtue of the fact that citizens of a state consent to the authority of the government. Beginning in the seventeenth century, divine right and patriarchal theories of obedience and legitimacy were rejected in favor of new theories that premised legitimacy on individual choice, to greater and lesser degrees. Working from a new conception of human beings which em-

[1]Rawls (1971), Simmons (1979), p. 4.
[2]See Hume, "Of the Original Contract," in *Hume's Moral and Political Philosophy* (1948), and Pateman (1979), for particularly strong statements of the links between the consent theory of obligation, or the social contract, and promising.

1

phasized the independent will and the capacity to make choices, and rejecting the tradition of bonds imposed from (and by virtue of) birth, consent theorists created a new concept of political legitimacy which depended on the will of the governed, not the governors.

This voluntarist notion of obligation has spurred heated and even violent criticism over the past three centuries. Hume, Burke, Godwin, Hegel, and Bentham all rejected consent theory because it went too far, or not far enough. Hume, for instance, rejected it on both descriptive and prescriptive grounds; not only was it a fantastical description of actual political societies in which obligations existed, he argued, but it was also hopelessly mired in illogic and inconsistencies. Obligation, or allegiance, was loosely based on the natural sympathy humans feel for one another, and thus people should support whatever government happens to be in power in order to preserve peace and security.[3] Burke, emphasizing the need for tradition, decried obligation by consent because it took individuals out of their social context—a context defined by hierarchy and inequality, but a context nonetheless.[4] Hegel similarly took consent theory to task and refuted it exhaustively, if not bitterly: the state is the locus of humanity, he said, and therefore we must partake of and support it. The abstract choice provided by consent threatens not only the state but our own humanity as well.[5] The utilitarians rejected the concept of natural rights in particular, Bentham calling it "nonsense on stilts."[6] More recently, critics such as C. B. Macpherson and Carole Pateman[7] have seriously criticized the Lockean and Hobbesian views of consent and obligation; Richard Flathman, Hanna Pitkin, Michael Walzer, and John Rawls[8] have further argued for rejecting consent theory as a legitimate and cogent ground for political obligation, arguing for different conceptualizations of obligation. And theorists such as A. John Simmons and John Dunn[9] have concluded that political obligations do

[3]See particularly Hume, "Of the Original Contract," "Of the First Principles of Government," and "Of the Origin of Government," in *Hume's Moral and Political Philosophy.* See Hirschmann (1989b) for a more detailed account of my reading of Hume's criticisms of consent theory and theory of obligation.

[4]Burke, *Reflections on the Revolution in France.*

[5]See in particular Hegel, *The Philosophy of Right.*

[6]Smith (1985), p. 39. See Bentham, *A Fragment on Government and An Introduction to the Principles of Morals and Legislation.*

[7]Macpherson (1962), Pateman (1979).

[8]Flathman (1972), Pitkin (1965, 1966), Walzer (1970), Rawls (1964, 1971).

[9]Simmons (1979), Dunn (1980), esp. "Consent in the Political Theory of John Locke," pp. 29–52, and also (1969), and (1985). Wolff (1970) should also fall into this category, but I agree with Pateman that it does not. Wolff, in basing his solution on Kant and Hegel, displays an acceptance of the state that puts him at odds with the philosophy of anarchism. Pateman (1979), p. 140.

not exist, perhaps cannot exist, and even that the concept of political obligation is hopelessly confused and should be rejected entirely.

This body of literature would seem to bode ill for yet another analysis of political obligation, and especially for one taking consent as its primary focus. Admittedly there are serious problems with making consent the focus of political obligation. As numerous critics might argue, by now everyone knows that consent theory is implausible. Hume, in effect, said it all. And if he did not, his many successors did. By this time consent theory may be something of a dead horse, or at least a straw man, a point that theorists have been making for decades.

In a sense that is precisely the issue. Why is it that consent theory in particular has been hammered at so long and so hard, with such inconclusive results, if it is so self-evidently implausible? If "self-assumed" political obligation[10] is in fact hopeless, how do we account for its continued prominence as an object of philosophical scrutiny? And why, after all the rejection, particularly of the principles of consent theory, do theorists go to such lengths to salvage the concept of obligation, and even of consent? For in spite of all the literature on the subject, only Simmons, some philosophical anarchists, and possibly Dunn have held that obligations do not exist. Most other critics seek to find an alternative ground for obligation. These alternatives, interestingly enough, generally seek to embody effectively the same fundamental assumptions of "natural" freedom and equality that ground consent theory, indeed that make consent the only possible basis for obligation.

It is my contention that political theory has not been able to advance on the problem of political obligation because consent theory is designed to mask certain assumptions that are nevertheless central to it. As a result, the problems it presents are self-perpetuating and circular. A number of critics have identified the most central of these problems as abstract individualism. The assumptions I mention begin with that but go well beyond it, for while I agree with a great deal of the literature critical of abstract individualism, none of the criticism goes deep enough to articulate the *reasons* for the problems obligation theory displays. It merely addresses the symptoms rather than the causes, with the predictable result that the identical problems recur, albeit in altered form, in the "new" theories developed to replace the social contract. These theories leave unasked the question *why* abstract individualism is so important to these theories. Amid all the

[10]This phrase is used particularly by Pateman (1979).

debate, therefore, "the problem of political obligation" is not resolved; indeed, the problems are merely repeated, recycled, and rehashed.

What is it about consent theory that has tied political theorists in such knots for all these years? What is it about the theory and its contradictions that both attracts and repels? What is it about the critiques that contributes to, rather than resolves, the problem? And how, if these approaches are so problematic, should we approach the question of political obligation? This book is one attempt to explore these questions from a different perspective than has heretofore been adopted.

A Modernist Concept of Obligation

The early social contract theorists—most popularly Hobbes and Locke, later Rousseau, but also such lesser-known figures as Paine and Godwin—varied considerably in their specific conceptions of human beings and of the political society they should inhabit, and hence developed somewhat different notions of consent. Yet these different conceptions share basic characteristics such as an emphasis on individual action, rejection of patriarchy and divine right as formal models of political society, and the attempt to define and execute a particular concept of freedom. So perhaps a silhouette sketch of consent theory can be developed for purposes of definition.

The generic form of consent theory, generally characterized as coming from Hobbes and Locke, begins with their premises that all "men"[11] are naturally free and equal. Equality existed at least in the power people had to pursue their desires; and for Locke, people further had an equal right to appropriate property. They were "free" in that they did not depend on the will of others. This nondependence was essential to a full humanity. As I shall argue more fully later on, freedom was defined in terms of what Isaiah Berlin was to call "negative liberty"; that is, we are free to the extent that external barriers— barriers that exist outside the self—do not inhibit us from pursuing our desires.

This concept of freedom was radical not only in that it was a tremendous departure from the hierarchical conceptions of social life of the previous century, but also in that it was extreme. Autonomy and

[11]In general, I will use *she* as the generic pronoun. In several places, however, particularly in my discussion of social contract and consent theory in Chapters 1 and 2, I appear to use *he* generically and *man* to mean "people." Part of my argument is that the individual in consent theory is a specifically masculinist construction of a masculine self; so when I use *he* in these instances, I am not simplistically referring to males but rather alluding to a masculinized conception of the individual.

freedom required a concept of man as an isolated entity. The only legitimate connections to others are those initiated by the individual or agreed to by him of his own free choice. This abstract individualism involves the notion that the individual can be abstracted from relationships, from social context, and even from qualities of humanness which others—particularly, as we shall see, women, at least historically—have deemed vital, namely the capacity and need for connectedness and for human relationships.

In light of this extreme individualism, the reason for consent lies in the theorists' recognition that some relationships are desirable in the daily course of our pursuing individual needs and interests. That connection is a necessary aspect of human life, even if an inconvenient or possibly dangerous one. But since any relationship is highly likely to involve a curtailment of individual freedom by creating an obligation, such relationships can be tolerated only if they are entered into voluntarily. According to consent theory, no one can determine what relationships are good for someone else and bind that person thereby. Everyone must choose her own relationships. But furthermore, any relationship entered into voluntarily has to be of some value to the partners in the relationship; as Hobbes says, "Of the voluntary acts of every man, the object is some *Good to himselfe*." Locke echoes this sentiment in observing that "no rational Creature can be supposed to change his condition with an intention to be worse."[12] If, in entering a relationship and binding oneself thereby, one gives up some freedom, and if freedom constitutes humanness, then one loses part of one's humanity through that relationship. This humanity must be regained in another way, through that very same act of alienation. This can be accomplished only if an individual's interests are promoted through this curtailment.

Yet such relationships of mutual agreement and gain are often not successfully achieved; that is, although they may be formed for mutual gain, they turn out to be antagonistic and hostile. For various reasons suggested by a number of theorists—greed, an inability to know the laws of nature or to reason, the introduction of money, the lack of a common judge and known law—the state of nature always degenerates into a state of war, that state which Hobbes so famously characterized as "poore, nasty, brutish and short."[13]

---

[12]Hobbes, *Leviathan*, p. 192; Locke, *Two Treatises of Government*, p. 398.

[13]*Leviathan*, p. 186. Because of the complexity involved in citing the various dates of different editions of the works of Hobbes, Locke, Rousseau, and others, these historical sources will be referred to by author and abbreviated title. The bibliography lists the edition from which I quote. Also, all emphasis in quoted material reflects original emphasis unless otherwise noted.

The only way to achieve the peace and order necessary for continued acquisition is to submit to an arbitrative authority, the Sovereign. The Sovereign—whether an absolute monarch or a representative parliament—creates an element of predictability by creating rules that make certain kinds of behavior punishable. It enforces the laws of nature, particularly by enforcing agreements between men and establishing rules of property (what belongs to whom, why, and how). Even though average citizens are generally not involved in governing (with the exception of Rousseau, social contract and consent theorists from Hobbes onward have rejected direct or participatory democracy), they are seen as the source of government, as the foundation for legitimacy. This new emphasis on the self-creative capacities of human beings leads to the notion that they are capable of creating all of their social relationships. Indeed, they *must* create all of their relationships if they are to preserve their human essence, their freedom. Men's relation to government is merely one of these relationships; hence no government is owed obedience unless citizens consent to its authority. Because of the radical and equal freedom of all men, consent is seen to be the only way to create political obligations: it is a necessary condition. Furthermore, on this view, consent is also a sufficient condition for obligation: if people are to respect individuals' capacities for rational decision making, then individuals must be taken at their word when they consent.

This admittedly brief rendering of original social contract theory diverges in several ways from contemporary consent theory, but it provides the latter with its foundation. Although consent theory appears to have lost popularity in theoretical circles in the nineteenth century, it resurfaced as a central issue in political theory in the 1960s and 1970s.[14] Furthermore, contemporary theorists took up consent theory in particular as apparently the central—or at least *a* central—conception of obligation to disarm. This conception of consent was explicitly identified as Lockean. Ironically, perhaps, these theorists often followed Hume's lead, attacking consent on logical, descriptive, and prescriptive grounds.

Even more ironically, however, contemporary critiques can be seen as stressing "even more emphatically than Locke that consent is the sole basis of legitimacy and obligation."[15] That is, while they appeared

---

[14]See introduction, chap. 1, and chap. 2 of Hirschmann (1987). This submersion continues to the latter half of the twentieth century: "Obligation . . . [is] a concept which not so long ago was on one side of the Atlantic virtually discarded as a linguistic anachronism, and on the other treated simply as a behavioralist phenomenon." MacFarlane (1974), pp. 1305–6.

[15]Smith (1985), p. 45, makes this comment about modern consent theory, not about

to criticize and reject consent theory, many contemporary theorists in fact adopted consent as the basis of obligation but transformed the way that consent is expressed, or even the very meaning of consent. For instance, Joseph Tussman, attempting to reconcile the centrality of consent to obligation in the face of the fact that many people do not even think about their consent, suggests that we "assume" that the majority of citizens give their consent and are like "political child-brides" who let others protect and define their best interests.[16] Pitkin, through a creative reading of Locke, develops the notion of "hypothetical" consent: what perfectly free, rational beings would consent to determines what the average unfree, unequal person is obligated to. Flathman argues for a "good reasons" approach, holding that critical reasoning will reveal to us that we have (or do not have) good reasons for respecting the authority of a government. Whereas obligation is a "practice" and must operate within the confines of language—facts that automatically limit what can count as a reason—the final repository is individuals' ability to judge and decide for themselves. He thus gives individuals the same "veto power" over their obligations for which he faults consent theory.[17] Simmons, while maintaining that no existing consent theory accounts for obligations, nevertheless holds that consent is the only possible ground for obligation because it is the only way to preserve individual choice. Similarly, Pateman, who is highly critical of liberal obligation theory, argues for a fully consistent consent theory, which can be realized only in a Rousseauist participatory democracy.[18]

Even within the context of other concepts, obligation still follows the assumptions of consent theory. Rawls's "fair play" principle depends on the active acceptance of benefits within a cooperative scheme. Although a context of justice is important, passive acceptance or nonavoidance of benefits does not generate obligations. This principle is juxtaposed to his concept of duty, which is "natural" and not the product of choice. Both duty and obligation involve "schemes" or ends which are just; but obligation, to be such, must be at base voluntary. Within Rawls's structure, however, if one does not accept the benefits of a just scheme, and hence has no obligation to it, one may still have a natural duty to it anyhow by virtue of its justness; if it is just, then one would have agreed to it in the original

---

modern critiques of consent theory. It is my own contention that his statement holds equally true when applied to these critiques.

[16]Tussman (1960), p. 37.
[17]Flathman (1972), p. 287.
[18]Simmons (1979), Pateman (1979).

position. This fact calls into question the usefulness of Rawls's distinction between obligation and duty, for at least in the case of *political* obligation, my duties require me to do the exact same thing that I supposedly have no obligation to do, namely obey the law.[19]

This highlights a blind acceptance of voluntarism as a prerequisite for obligation even when it does not make theoretical sense. Even theories that challenge the idea of consent as the basis for obligation tenaciously hold on to the guiding assumptions of consent, for most of these theories bend over backwards to bind citizens to their state, and indeed to reassert the centrality and importance of obedience to the state on a *voluntarist* basis even as they reject consent theory. As a result, consent theory was not rejected but rather rewritten: it became implied consent, hypothetical consent, the assumed consent of the "political child-bride," the recognition of good reasons, or the acceptance of benefits. Certainly the differences among these theories are significant; but what is more so is that they all failed to recognize that it was not consent per se that needed to be questioned but the assumptions underlying consent. It is for this reason that none of these theories has satisfactorily resolved the problem of political obligation.

What are those assumptions? As I said earlier, abstract individualism is a basic starting point. What the liberal construction does is reify human will, action, and existence. In asserting that the individual can and does create all of her relationships and all of her obligations, consent theory abstracts people from their social circumstances and ignores the reality that social relationships do in fact influence, shape, and make possible the human capacity for autonomy. Choices exist in social contexts. The fragmentation and alienation of self inherent in the concept of labor and the body as separate from the self, for instance,[20] ignores the fact that self-creative capacities develop within the context of nonconsensual relations, namely a society and family, which an infant does not choose. The social contract theorists wanted, and still want, to deny this and to deny the complex dynamics of human development and social relations in their eagerness to assert man's independence from monarchical rule.

Yet at the same time, and on another level, these theorists also recognized that such denial was impossible. This is an idea that is not often recognized because it is not overt in consent theory; yet it is readily apparent. After all, if they truly believed in individualism, as Godwin did, and perhaps as Simmons does, then why has not anarchism become a more popular doctrine, and why did consent theory

---

[19]Rawls (1964, 1971).
[20]See Macpherson's (1962) interpretation of Locke on this theme.

need to be developed at all? Why not simply declare the freedom and equality of all and conclude that governments are themselves illegitimate? The ostensible answer is the desirability of certain relationships to the end of each individual's pursuit of her own individual interests. This desirability is what gives rise to the idea of consent, to a convention that allows discrete beings to form relationships of agreement and contract.

The deeper answer begins with recognizing that this desirability is in fact considered a necessity. I maintain that the social contract theorists implicitly accepted governmental authority as a fact of human existence, even as they explicitly argued that governmental authority threatened the "fact" of human freedom and individualism. Although government ostensibly is created by, depends on, and derives legitimacy from human choice, in fact humans have no choice: government must exist. This tension manifests itself throughout voluntarist theories of obligation as one between individuality and community, between the "fact" that humans are naturally free, and the "fact" that these free individuals need a common authority if they are to preserve that freedom. Rousseau declared that "man is born free, yet everywhere he is in chains." Consent theorists try not to resolve this paradox but to take it as a given and build their theories on the premise of its irresolvability. In the process, ironically, they end up trying to disguise it, to pretend that it does not really exist.

Of course, a tension between freedom and authority is not necessarily a bad thing; indeed, many see it as the hallmark of democracy. And certainly tensions are a positive strength of political theory. The problem with liberal obligation theory, however, is that the tension is conceived not as a tension per se but as a contradiction. Freedom and authority, individual and community are defined in opposition to each other from the very start. This is where the concept of abstract individualism comes into play: because individuals are seen as so radically separated from one another, the relation between individual and community seems inherently irreconcilable. Abstract individualism requires a conception of freedom as the absence of external restraints, and of authority as one of those restraints. It intimately depends on a concept of the individual that is at odds with community. The problems are thus not the passive product of "human nature" or "divine order" but are the outcome of a particular epistemological framework, a particular way of conceiving, defining, and representing the individual, and indeed the world.

In this portrayal the recognition of the need for authority is masked in favor of the recognition of the "fact" of individual freedom; and the contradiction between freedom and authority is reconciled ostensibly by an ultimate appeal to freedom. Individualism is theoretically more important than authority and order. Hence authority must, at least ostensibly, be based on voluntarism, on the choices of the people who will be subject to the authority. In this way individuals' limitations on choice via the establishment of government and law is really an expression of choice via consent. But this voluntarism is in reality camouflage for coercion; it is not genuine. The theories overtly operate from the claim that authority *should not* win out because of the priority of individual freedom. Indeed, that was the whole justification for this genre of theory. But in reality the need for authority takes precedence over freedom. As a result, almost all of the voluntarist theories of obligation accomplish what Rousseau is singled out and excoriated for, namely forcing citizens to be free. Thus Locke offers "tacit consent," and Hobbes links force and consent. Tussman portrays the majority of citizens as "minors" who need "tutelage." In potentially less coercive terms, H. L. A. Hart talks of a "blind habit of obedience," and Flathman also legitimizes habit as a way of enforcing behavior without making people "feel imposed upon." Rawls tries to get around the problem of people who do not accept benefits by declaring them to have a natural duty to those things to which they supposedly do not have an obligation.[21]

Of course, the consent tradition represents a vital historical move in theories of political allegiance in its initial rejection of authority based on patriarchy and divine right. Nor should we deny out of hand the possiblity that consent theorists recognized some previously obscured human qualities—namely the notion of will, the ability to act voluntarily, and the capacity for self-rule, choice, and self-creation—which I, at least, am not ready to abandon. We must remember, however, that consent *was* primarily a rejection of traditional patriarchal, nonvoluntarist theories of allegiance. Therein lies its primary significance. To assert that all men are inherently free and equal was an important contribution to political thought, for it recognized the self-creative and rational decision-making abilities that humans have. But it is one thing to conclude from this that divine right and patriarchy are illegitimate; it is quite another to conclude that each separate and individual human being must decide for herself which obligations—political and otherwise—she will assume.

Yet to say that these contradictions occur because of the way these theories conceptualize man, society, freedom, and authority still leaves the question, Why do they conceptualize them in this way? That leads us to the heart of this volume. I argue that this skewed

21Tussman (1960), Hart (1961), Flathman (1972), Rawls (1964, 1971).

vision of humans and of the political concepts that define our lives is, at least in part, a product of gender bias.[22] There are several levels to this claim. The first is that, since political theory has been written mostly by men, and "citizens" have always been male until the current century, then political theory must represent a male viewpoint, male interests, male concerns. But of course it goes deeper than this, because the immediate reply is that justice is gender neutral; freedom is neither male nor female (though theorists have long proclaimed the class bias of such concepts).

This deeper level that I speak of is epistemological. It is the central contention of this book that the contradictions and inconsistencies that consent theory displays arise from an epistemological gender bias. Its problems are paradigmatic of the problems of liberalism, for this epistemological gender bias is one foundation of liberal theory as a whole. Although this bias undoubtedly has other dimensions, such as race and class, in the present work I explore how a feminist analysis can uncover the specifically gendered roots of the problem of obligation, how it can reveal these issues to be related to specifically "masculinist" epistemological frameworks, how it can point the way to a more encompassing and adequate political theory, and specifically to a theory of obligation that reflects more accurately the experiences and needs of all human beings.

There are two dimensions to this bias: that is, obligation is not merely *contingently sexist* but *structurally sexist* as well. By *contingent sexism* I mean that cultural biases against women deny them opportunities for consent, and pervert consent theory as a result. This bias, by excluding women from standard means of consenting and by denying them the opportunities for choice afforded men, presents a contradiction to consent theory that it can and should rectify. A fully

---

[22]The issue of essentialism and gender is one I take up later in this book. But I want to say from the start that I have gone to great lengths to avoid being reductive. I realize that gender is an extremely broad category, and that my use of the term does not necessarily encompass differences in race, class, geography and nationality, cultural heritage, historical period, even, as we get further into psychological theory, one's placement in the family (eldest or youngest sibling, whether one has same-sex or different-sex siblings, treatment by parents, including roles they filled, and so on), all of which may have a profound effect on the epistemological considerations I develop in this work. Gender is, however, one important source of the biases of liberal theory, and it is a theme that must be pursued if we are to understand this dimension of liberal theory. Similarly, the approach I take to the analysis of gender is only one possible approach; feminist scholarship abounds with methods and approaches, new ideas and analyses, all of which taken together provide a transformation of most if not all of the current disciplines. For examples and discussions, see Harding (1986), di Leonardo (1984), Di Stephano (1990), Chodorow (1978), Jaggar (1983), Gould (1984b), Trebilcott (1984).

consistent consent theory would allow women full opportunities to choose their obligations.

This type of argument is not uncommon in political theory and in feminist politics.[23] But few have recognized the deeper structural components of this exclusion. By *structural sexism* I mean that the very structure of obligation—the fact that it is defined solely in voluntarist terms, that the concept of a nonvoluntary obligation is something of an oxymoron—is itself reflective of a masculinist perspective, and automatically excludes women from obligation on an epistemological level. In this light, the provision of full opportunities for consent begs rather than answers the question of obligation. By declaring that all obligations, to be such, must be taken on voluntarily, consent theory ignores or denies what women's experience reveals: namely that obligations do in fact exist that are not chosen but rather stem from the crasis and history of human relationships. A fully consistent consent theory would have to include, perhaps paradoxically, the recognition that not all obligations are self-assumed. In ignoring this point, does existing political theory, created predominantly by male practitioners, reflect specifically masculine experience? Does it therefore reflect specifically masculinist orientations toward reality, a specifically masculinist epistemology and ontology? Are the problems that I identify in my discussion of consent theory specific to the historical experience of men, including especially the experience of, and the concern to perpetuate, sexual and gender domination?

These questions should not be confused with the claim that all notions of choice, individuality, freedom, and consent are somehow masculine or male-derived. I seek to establish a more complex and subtle argument that a *masculinist* epistemology and framework underwrites modern understandings and definitions of these notions. *Masculinism* refers to ideas and theories that take masculine experience as the given generic experience, and indeed overvalue men's experience at the expense of women's experience. Or perhaps more precisely, masculinism is an ideology that reifies, exaggerates, and privileges certain aspects of the kinds of material experience that have typically and historically been *associated with* men at the expense of the kinds of experience associated with women. The feminist theoretical framework that I adopt starts from the basic premise that both men and women, masculine and feminine, are socially constructed.

[23]See Jaggar (1986), esp. chaps. 3 and 7. Politically this has been the most common line of attack. From suffrage movements to equal employment opportunity, women have sought entry into traditionally male spheres without challenging the terms and conditions defining those spheres. See Flexner (1959); O'Neill (1969), chap. 8. My point is not to criticize these movements as ineffectual but rather to point out the limitations inevitably imposed on them by structural parameters.

Men are not "naturally" or "essentially" one way any more than women are "naturally" another. In every culture, however, there are certain social continuities and similarities among people labeled "women" and those labeled "men." And an important difference between the social construction of maleness and femaleness has been power: men have historically dominated women and had more (though not complete) control over how they construct both themselves and women. This has resulted in institutions that socially and politically privilege men over women; but it has also affected the structure of meaning and reality by pervading our very categories of knowledge and the ways in which we evaluate criteria. The perspective of this socially constructed masculine experience is epistemologically validated and imposed on women, thus preserving male privilege, or the social practices and structures that enable men to continue to consider their own experience *the* human experience. In the context of consent theory, for instance, attending to women's experiences from a feminist perspective leads to the insight that there are many ways to define choice. Why has it been defined in modern liberal obligation theory in this particular (atomistic) way with other sorts of insights obliterated from public institutions and discourses such as political theory? Part of the answer, I suggest, has to do with the gender of the people who created these institutions and discourses.

Women and Obligation

If the centrality of consent to obligation stems from "man's nature," then a consideration of women and obligation presents a myriad of difficulties on a variety of levels. For although women are human individuals, and are therefore free and equal, they are also declared to have, "by nature," an incapacity to act in public life. This means that they cannot consent, and that their consent is either taken for granted or given by men who supposedly speak for them.

Within the traditional private sphere, of course, women's obligations have been numerous without the benefit of a truly voluntarist basis. The most obvious example is that although women have not had a great deal of choice concerning whether and when to have children, at least until recently (though extreme limitations on women's abilities to control their bodies certainly still exist), they have always been required to care for their children, and indeed such a requirement was considered a natural duty or obligation. At least in early modern Europe, women were considered "naturally" suited to be mothers. That was their function and purpose in life, and social pressure to conform to this role was, to say the least, exceedingly strong. In more contemporary times we like to insist on the wider choices women have, with the availability of contraception and abortion. Yet such choices lie in a context that may often make pregnancy more oppressive than before. The availability of abortion, as Simone de Beauvoir argues and as Carol Gilligan's interviews reveal,[24] can be used by a man to enforce his preference on a woman just as readily as it can be used by a woman to exercise her own choice. The "sexual revolution" may have made contraception more readily available, but it also brought about a diminishing sense of responsibility in the social role of men, as demographics on single and teenage mothers and statistics on the nationwide problem of child support suggest.[25] At the same time, the U.S. Congress has effectively decreed that only women who can pay for abortions may have them, thus restricting freedom of choice for poor women. Antiabortion forces seek to restrict all choice by banning abortion through legislative action and constitutional amendment, and in the meantime by harassment and violence, such as by bombing family-planning clinics. The restriction of abortion coupled with prevalent attitudes about sex leaves women in a serious double bind, particularly poor and young women. As Diana Russell points out, "Sexual liberation without sex role liberation" creates a myriad of oppressive practices and problems for women while enhancing "liberty" for men.[26]

Although these contrary forces might have the potential to collide and cancel one another out (as de Beauvoir suggests, will philandering male politicians ever willingly give up the convenience of abortion?), all of these forces serve to impinge on women and on their ability to choose in ways not experienced by men. Because women have been an oppressed class, it seems easier or more natural to make women (and especially poor and minority women, as doubly oppressed classes) the pawns in the political controversy; it is significant that neither the legal nor the moral controversy surrounding abortion focuses on paternal responsibility. And because women have been the oppressed, they are more sensitive and subject to such forces that would interfere with their ability to choose. A nonoppressed group fighting such pressures, or an oppressed group not fighting such

[24]De Beauvoir (1974), esp. pp. 540–50 and passim; Gilligan (1982), chap. 4.

[25]See, for instance, the following articles in the *New York Times* (entries refer to section, page, and column numbers): October 7, 1986, II, 1:6; October 13, 1986, II, 4:1; October 16, 1986, II, 1:6; November 28, 1986, II, 13:6; December 10, 1986, I, 1:2; December 11, 1986, III, 26:6; December 17, 1986, II, 12:3; December 18, 1986, II, 30:1; January 10, 1987, I, 26:1. See also Moore and Burt (1982).

[26]Russell (1975), p. 208.

pressures, might have a better opportunity for developing and defining a sense of choice on its own terms; but the existence of such pressures seriously inhibits women's chances for developing the sense of self they have been told to deny but which is necessary for choice. And without choice, how can women have obligations within the liberal formulation?

Marriage might seem more promising ground for consensual obligation, for parties choose their spouses and agree to be married. In past centuries, however, women did not choose their spouses; such decisions were made by parents, and the contract was generally one of dower and exchange, or of solidifying kin or clan relationships, between the husband-to-be and the father of the bride. Once in the marriage relationship, the woman, whose prior identity subsisted in her father's, was subsequently subsumed by her husband.[27]

In the late twentieth century in the West such conditions have been altered, but serious sexual double standards still undermine the liberal democratic principle of freedom and equality for all individuals. The law has been exceedingly slow to recognize women as equal and independent legal entities within the marriage relationship. Credit law is one particular problem for many women. A woman's credit is generally based on her husband's income, regardless of her own wage income, the assumption being that the woman might quit her job at any moment to have a baby or to work in the home. If the husband dies, the woman's credit rating dies along with him.[28]

Such nonrecognition of women—or their ascription as nonpersons—contradicts the concept of consent: not only is the wife dependent on her husband in a way that violates the tenets of freedom defined by consent theory; but also, if she is a nonperson, how can she be a party to a contract? On a deeper level, however, the assignment of women to the private sphere as guardians of everything in it, from morality to nurturance to the kitchen and the bathroom, serves also to contradict the consensual nature of marriage. As Carole Pateman argues, what a woman "consents" to is a prescribed role, a set of duties, activities—and, it might be added, even attitudes and feel-

[27]Rubin (1975), Bension (1935), Lockridge (1968), Pateman (1984).

[28]Reagan (1984). In states with equal rights amendments this situation is slowly improving. As Schwendinger and Schwendinger (1983) point out, however: "In non-ERA states such as Georgia, a couple's home belongs to the husband even if the wife paid for it; in several states like Louisiana, a wife can be sued for her husband's gambling debts; and in New Mexico, before the state ERA was adopted, a wife could not advertise for the sale of the family dishwasher without her husband's consent. . . . In many states a housewife still cannot obtain credit apart from her husband. The legal changes that remove such inequities have been uneven, and they have by no means guaranteed independence for women" (pp. 118–19).

ings—determined by the fact that she is a woman, by the fact of her gender. Only women can be wives, and wives are expected to perform certain functions and fill certain roles.[29] Failure in these roles and functions constitutes failure as a woman. Not only is such a formulation inhibitive of free choice, but it is also dehumanizing; indeed, it is *thereby* dehumanizing on the liberal democratic account, since freedom is central to humanity. One is reminded here of metaethical discussions of "good" where criteria for good are attached to a particular object's function; a "good woman" is a "good wife," and a "good wife" performs certain functions. Particularly in marriage, gender roles are so prescribed, especially for women, that to speak of choice and consent is in itself problematic.[30]

Aspects of these roles overlap with the even more serious problem of rape. Because a wife traditionally "consents" to obey her husband and to engage in conjugal relations, it has generally been thought a legal and even logical impossibility that a husband could rape his wife. The problem of consent is particularly keen in this area because the question of whether a woman consents and what she consents to has been understood by laws, courts, and societies to be what men say and think women consent to. In the last decade or so some changes have been made in marital rape laws, although the courts have been ambivalent in the United States and other western democratic countries about the status of married women in relation to their husbands' sexual desires. For instance, in some states, such as Pennsylvania, spousal sexual assault statutes exist; yet under such statutes a husband's rape of his wife is considered a less serious offense than nonspousal rape. In Pennsylvania, spousal rape constitutes a second-degree felony with a maximum sentence of five to ten years; nonspousal rape is a first-degree felony with a maximum sentence of ten to twenty years.[31]

[29]Pateman (1984), esp. pp. 76–79.

[30]Of course, men are also put into roles that may result in their repression, for example, the classic case of the man who quits school to marry and support his pregnant lover. We might argue that men's oppression per se is less than women's because the oppression goes hand in hand with privilege; but the larger point is that feminist theory does not maintain that women are the victims and men are the problem. Rather, we all have the problem, and patriarchy, which defines the way men and women interact, is the cause. In this sense feminism is "the new humanism"; but see Di Stefano (1990), Flax (1986), Harding (1986), and Hartsock (1987).

[31]See Pennsylvania Crimes Code, Pennsylvania Statutes, vol. 18, sections 3128 and 3121. This difference might suggest a holdover of the origins of rape as a property offense, but the court might also have a paternalistic interest in keeping "families" together. It should be noted that if a divorced or separated husband rapes his (ex)wife, the crime falls under the rape statute, not spousal sexual assault. For the property origins of rape law, see especially Brownmiller (1975) and Schwendinger and Schwendinger (1983); for courts' interests in keeping families together, see Daly (1987).

The question of rape in general is particularly important for the issue of women and consent; for while it has long been thought that women were incapable of consent in political terms, it is simultaneously asserted that they always consent to sexual intercourse.[32] From the seventeenth century to Henry Miller, Normal Mailer, "pop" post-Freudian psychology, and the modern-day rapists' legal defense, it is assumed that even when a woman says no to sexual intercourse, she means yes. Rousseau carefully outlined how a woman *had* to refuse sexual relations, and could never actively say yes, in order to repress her animal nature and thus preserve her virtue, thereby safeguarding men's freedom. But at the same time, she had to satisfy the male's desire and so had to develop indirect and flirtatious ways of saying no that really did mean yes.

That myth and image of women persists today. Until quite recently a woman's sexual history could be admitted as evidence in rape cases in an effort by the defense to suggest that the victim had actually consented, the assumption being that a woman who was not a virgin, or who at least had had several sexual encounters, was promiscuous and liable not only to be lying but to have consented to sexual intercourse as well. The most believable evidence generally accepted in court that a woman did not consent to intercourse is that she actively, physically resisted, and the best proof of that is physical injury, such as cuts and bruises. The act of saying no is in itself not sufficient to establish denial of consent, and indeed even resistance is often interpreted as a form of consent. Pateman has noted a defense involving the claim that the defendant "believed" the woman to have consented.[33] The jury is not to determine the fact of whether the woman in fact consented but whether it was reasonable for the man to believe she did, thus placing the burden of proof on the woman to establish dissent and the burden of responsibility on her not to be raped.

The problem of rape brings us closer to a consideration of women's obligations within, or in relation to, the "public" realm. In the past, such consideration was relatively straightforward. Women were not allowed to partake in public life by voting or holding office because their nature made them unfit for such responsibility. They were incapable of making a rational assessment of their interests (read their husbands' or fathers' interests, since they owned no property, not even in their persons) and so were banned from the public realm in order to safeguard it from anarchy and mayhem. But they were equally subject to the law as men and were liable for tortious acts and

---

[32]Pateman (1980).
[33]Ibid., pp. 159–60.

other lawbreaking;[34] for if the purpose of excluding women from the public was to preserve the civil order, it would make no sense to exempt them from obedience to law.

Today the issue of the vote has been, at least superficially, put to rest, with most western democracies having granted the vote to women in the twentieth century (Switzerland as late as 1971). The recentness of female enfranchisement could explain some degree of reticence on the part of new women voters. For example, female voters in the United States in the 1920s usually voted as their husbands told them to, along standard party lines.[35] Although there has more recently been talk of a "gender gap" in policy issues, it has not seemed to play out in votes; even though polls revealed that men approved of Ronald Reagan more than women, and that women disapproved of his policies more than men, the 1980 and 1984 election results did not show an appreciable gender difference between parties or candidates, or at least not appreciable enough to influence policy decisions favorable to women.[36]

It could be argued that women do not have a unified political identity in terms of casting a vote (as opposed to expressing political opinions), or that there is in fact no gender gap. But remarkably low voter turnout in the United States also suggests a compensatory variable. That is, a wider variety of people answer polls than vote, and the conditions for choosing to be one of the electorate may be self-selective for certain attitudes about politics and candidates. Politicians have long recognized that getting the support of public opinion is not as difficult, or as important, as getting the holders of those opinions to vote.[37] Women, like the poor, may feel that there is little reason to express their preferences because they view the system as unresponsive, a suggestion that raises the more relevant issue of whether the vote has been, is, or even can be an effective tool for political equality and power for women. I suggest it is not and perhaps cannot be within the confines of liberal democratic institutions as they are, and that the lack of a gender gap in voting statistics when it exists in the

[34]For instance, in the Connecticut Valley in the seventeenth and eighteenth centuries, women were liable for punishment decreed by law for tortious acts, usually the stocks or prison, although they could not themselves bring suit for tortious acts committed against them, and although their husbands or fathers were generally sued for financial remuneration. See Smith (1961).

[35]O'Neill (1969), chap. 8; Randall (1982).

[36]This is a disputable statement, and scholars have argued both that there was a gender gap and that there was not. See, for example, Abzug (1984), Kelly (1989), Klein (1984). At the electoral level at least, however, this gap has not thus far had a serious impact on who is elected to office.

[37]See, for instance, Parenti (1974), Wolfinger and Rosenstone (1980), Piven and Cloward (1988).

polls may reflect women's belief that this is so. For even with the vote, a de facto exclusion of women from the political realm by the "feminization of poverty"[38] has effectively disenfranchised what voice they have.

The holding of political (and possibly military) office may be easier to pinpoint as a sign of women's continued exclusion. Indeed, the absence of female elected heads of state (queens, of course, are not elected) is remarkable. Margaret Thatcher was the first female head of state in a modern western democracy, in a country where only 28 out of 650 members of Parliament were women. Eastern democratic countries have fared a little better in this regard with Golda Meir, Benazir Bhutto, and Indira Gandhi, although female members of legislatures are few in countries that are in many ways deeply misogynist. Corazon Aquino's 1982 victory in the Philippines is also noteworthy (though her presidency has seemed continually threatened by her male advisers). And although Geraldine Ferraro broke the barrier for national candidacy in the United States in 1984, the U.S. Senate had 2 women out of 100 members, the House of Representatives 22 women out of 435 members.

Susan J. Carroll has argued that this is neither accident nor coincidence. From the results of extensive surveys she concludes that women are systematically excluded from party politics, at least in the United States. She found that parties were very reluctant to sponsor or support women for national seats but were more willing to back them for local offices. Parties were also more willing to support women for multimember seats, for example, a school board or town council, where the party runs a slate of candidates and electors vote for more than one. She also found that when parties faced certain defeat—because a seat was "safe" for the opposing party—the losing party was then more likely to support a woman candidate. What she calls the "sacrificial lamb" would not only thus hurt herself politically but would "save" a male candidate from being hurt.[39]

The fact that women who succeed in public office are the exceptions to the rule points out that women have an anomalous place in politics, not a usual one, and certainly, according to party organizations as well as the electorate, not a welcome one. When male politicians make the laws, women's interests are that much less likely to be represented—not necessarily because male politicians do not sympathize with or like women, but because "women's issues," that is, issues of concern primarily to women, are seen as secondary. Or,

[38]Nelson (1984).
[39]Carroll (1985), esp. chap. 3. See also Mandel (1983) and Mezcy (1980).

perhaps more precisely, it is because male politicians tend to take patriarchal attitudes toward women's interests. Thus, although the majority of Americans favors passage of the Equal Rights Amendment, it is defeated in Congress; although most Americans favor the right of a woman to choose abortion, the Hyde Amendment passes Congress, and states such as Pennsylvania and Louisiana pass restrictive abortion statutes. And thus the failure to address issues of pregnancy leave, federally funded child care, reform in rape laws, equal pay, comparable worth, reform in credit law, pension and social security differentials, and so forth ad nauseam.

Of course, some western democracies have made progress in certain of these areas, and my discussion is obviously biased toward the United States because I am most familiar with it. But that does not mitigate the general political and social attitude that women's issues are considered *just* women's issues, and not broader issues of primary concern to male politicians and their male constituents. Even when the struggle for equal rights is advanced somewhat, it is always couched in terms of allowing women to try to "catch up" with men, rather than in terms of redefining policy goals and initiatives to reflect women's needs as an oppressed and politically excluded group. That reformulation of policy cannot happen while Congress and other representative bodies are not merely dominated by men but are defined in masculinist terms by that domination.[40]

Political Obligation and Feminist Theory

The foregoing shows most obviously that consent theory is contingently sexist, that it is used to promote and perpetuate cultural biases against women to deny them the ability to consent and to further deny them the political and social equality that the full exercise of consent should, theoretically, allow. The problems highlighted by the literature critical of consent theory—the nonvoluntary aspects of tacit consent, the lack of real input and choices in such supposedly participatory acts as voting, the existence of coercive restrictions on political

[40]Kathleen (1986), p. 5, suggests that women and men do express different "attitudinal orientations during the policy formation process," which can have an important impact on the generating of policy helpful to women. This suggests that there may be more hope for women in policy objectives at the state level if the "new federalism" gains momentum and states get more power in setting policy because parties have been more likely to support women's candidacies for state legislative positions, according to Carroll's (1985) thesis. But her thesis also would imply that if state positions become more important because of increased power in policy making, parties would be less likely to support women for those offices.

choice by virtue of economic and political disempowerment—are at least twice as severe in light of women's relation to obligation, consent, and citizenship. To say that women are not free to consent in the way required by consent theory is to highlight women's oppression and exclusion from the political.

But the foregoing discussion has also hinted at the deeper problem of consent theory, namely, its structural sexism. The definition of obligation as only and always consensual ignores or denies the realm of private sphere activity which has defined women's obligations. Whereas women's experience is to a large degree the product of contingent sexism, and what is declared to be "consent" for women is generally not genuine consent, women's experience also suggests that there are structurally sexist components of obligation theory, and these lie in the exclusive conceptualization of obligation in voluntarist terms. For such a conceptualization cannot explain or accommodate many aspects of social relations and bonds that women's experience in particular reveals. That is, it is not just that women's experience is actively excluded from the dominant conceptualization of obligation by unfair and sexist implementation, but that liberal political theory defines obligation so as automatically to preclude women's experience from being adequately encompassed and accurately expressed. It is thus not merely a matter of "bringing women in" to liberal political theory; the only way women can be "brought in" is if they abandon their experience and adopt the public-private split that separates their experience from perceived reality. This is precisely what has happened under liberal feminism in contemporary society: child care becomes a private problem for the "working mother" (itself a significant term); pregnancy becomes a private issue but abortion a public one. Women voters must choose among male politicians, all of whom ignore issues of child care, comparable worth, credit law, and the Equal Rights Amendment.

Women's experience suggests that the liberal definition of obligation needs to be broadened to include some nonconsensual aspects of life. An example may illustrate this notion. I pointed out earlier that women have had little to say about when and whether to have children yet have always been considered obligated to care for them. Is such an obligation invalid without consent? If so, does a woman have a right to abandon a baby whose gestation and care she did not consent to? Certainly, legal authorities in most countries, democratic or not, would deny such a right. But, more significant, many women who have had babies under such conditions might also tend to deny such a right. The obligation to care is not merely imposed by society; it has also historically been recognized by women themselves for a variety of reasons, ranging from strict socialization to enthusiastic and conscious choice. This would suggest, however, that recognizing an obligation is not coextensive with or even the same thing as consenting to it. If a woman has a child against her will but comes to love it, or is influenced or even socialized by her family and other people she loves, she may recognize an obligation without fulfilling the necessary criteria for consent. As we shall see more fully in later chapters, a woman in such a situation is likely to refer to a different set of values in assessing obligation. Love is a particularly problematic element in this scenario. One does not choose to love. One can love against one's will, or in spite of oneself, as it were, and be involved in all sorts of obligations as a result. One can fall into certain responsibilities and obligations. One can have obligations foisted upon one. And one can then recognize an obligation, even when the criteria of "good reasons" fails, or even when one has good reasons *not* to recognize the obligation (for example, when pregnancy results from rape).

It could be argued that women do in fact consent, say, by following a religion that believes that abortion is immoral. But this would be an extremely loose definition of consent, and a rather disingenuous one. At the same time, I do not wish to put motherhood on a pedestal. Babies have been abandoned and even killed by their mothers, and women have asserted the right to abortion in the name of self-interest (though according to Gilligan the decision to abort can also be based on a concept of responsibility and connection; and, as de Beauvoir reminds us, abortions are just as likely to be performed in accordance with men's preferences as with women's).[41] Nor am I saying that history dictates that women should or must raise children, but rather that the historical fact that women have done so suggests the need for an alternative way to conceptualize obligation. Recognition involves the admission of an obligation that *already* exists. Consent theory, by contrast, bases its claims to legitimacy on the notion that consent *creates* obligation. It is precisely this notion of creation that, I am suggesting, women's historical experience challenges.

Some might wonder whether the concept of duty, which refers precisely to bonds that are nonconsensual, which come from nature or God, solves this dilemma. In activities such as child rearing, it might be argued, parents have duties of care. That the social and gender configurations of a particular society appoint particular duties for women (say, daily care of infants and children) and others for men (say, earning wages for the family's subsistence) may indicate unfair

[41]Gilligan (1982), chaps. 3 and 4. Also de Beauvoir (1974), pp. 548–49, 682–83.

structures that should be changed; but duty still remains the proper philosophical concept for describing such bonds. When social norms change, there is nothing to prevent the terms of duty from being negotiated, so, for example, men and women share equally the burdens of both early child rearing and breadwinning. Yet it is not at all clear that such a move is legitimate. My reluctance to invoke duty centers precisely on its gendered history and its dichotomy between public and private. In social contract theory at least (though the case can be made all the way back to Plato), women have natural duties in the private sphere and men have freely chosen obligations in the public.[42] This differential in bondedness and freedom has in part resulted from, and in part contributed to, the overall differences between men and women in personal freedoms and powers, the choices they are permitted to make, and so forth. Furthermore, once we introduce the idea that the content of duties can be negotiated, not only do we problematize and even abandon the normal sources of duty in God or nature, but also duty begins to look more and more like obligation, with a contractual, consensual basis.

Thus the terminology of obligation is central to my enterprise. Rather than merely accept the modern definition of obligation and try to fit women's experiences into it, I view the fit between such experiences and liberal obligation theory as problematic and question why obligation has been defined as it has. I maintain that consent theory does not recognize women's historically nonconsensual bonds as obligations because it cannot; its epistemological framework precludes it. But perhaps it would be more precise to say that it cannot because it does not wish to. It is my contention that the epistemological bias that creates these particular definitions is a specifically gendered bias, that the liberal epistemology underlying consent theory is structurally sexist. Furthermore, a major component of my argument is that liberal obligation theory displays a masculinist psychic dependence on women's political powerlessness and private sequestration. This dependence not only gives rise to a political ideology requiring the separation of public and private, but also is so strong as to create an entire epistemology that supports this ideology as well as definitions of female and male, private and public. This epistemology creates the foundational impossibility of calling a nonconsensual relationship an obligation, and indeed makes unimaginable—except with horror at the sub-

---

[42]See Okin (1979), chaps. 3 and 4. Obviously, in regard to the ancients, and perhaps even the "Atlantic Republicans," the statement would have to be modified to "men have public duties of participation, choice, and direction as political actors." But the basic distinction between choice and public power for men and private bondedness and powerlessness for women remains.

conscious level—the political empowerment of women which such a definitional shift would entail.

This assertion likely appears rather bold to most readers, to put it mildly. Yet when I refer to masculinist psychic dependence, I do not necessarily mean the particular pathologies of individual theorists. Rather, I am speaking of a much more general epistemological and ontological environment—a social pathology, if you will—constituted by the cultural, social, political, sexual, economic, and interpersonal structures of the modern liberal era. Feminist theory does not maintain that men are the problem and women the solution but rather that the problem is patriarchy and we all share it. Thus the goal of my argument is not to put political theory on the couch but rather to develop divergent themes in political obligation theory that cohere with two historically gender-related models, and to use psychological arguments to understand a thematic difference in political theory that coheres with a historical gender difference.

It is thus important to recognize that feminism as applied in this study is not just a political position but, equally important, a method, one that mainstream political theory needs to utilize. While even mainstream political theory is becoming less and less "mainstream"— as a *Political Theory* editorial testifies, the field is recognizing the need to adapt to and borrow from a variety of other approaches[43]—in contrast to other disciplines, such as history, sociology, and literature, feminism has been slow to catch on in political science. This is unfortunate, for the tensions between the public ideology of liberalism (here, obligation theory) and the private practices of women need to be explored in a more complete fashion than has been done, and on a much deeper level of analysis, so that we may better understand both and arrive at a clearer understanding of concepts such as obligation that accounts for the experiences of both men and women. A feminist theoretical approach is necessary for this deeper analysis, for it can bring many methodological and epistemological insights to the practice of political theory. Feminist theory and political theory are often treated as if they operated in two separate worlds; but if they are in two worlds, it is not because they are inherently opposed but rather because there are very few people who speak both languages. Both languages, however, are crucial to the present argument. I hope that this book will help theorists see the ways in which feminism provides an important and revealing critical approach to the political theoretical concepts of mainstream theory, and thereby to transform that theory.

This kind of methodological feminism is highly critical, devoted to

[43]Vol. 16, no. 1 (February 1988): 3–4.

unmasking the myths that liberalism has created and revealing the reality underneath. But in conjunction with this negative side of critique and analysis, feminist theory has a positive, theory-building side as well. If Hobbes's or Rousseau's or Rawls's theories exclude women and are masculinist, then what would a feminist theory of obligation or justice be like? Certainly critiques of liberalism and other theories are necessary if we are to determine whether a sexist bias exists and, if so, how it is manifested. But in such critiques lies the power of creation, and that power is largely untapped. Some attempts have been made to adapt feminist psychoanalytic theories to political analysis, and in a way this work is a contribution. But I also consider the specific relations to substantive political theory, which has not been done to any great extent. *Money, Sex, and Power* by Nancy Hartsock (1984) was one of the first attempts at a comprehensive feminist analysis of a major political concept, namely power. Since then, a number of theorists have added important work to this emerging branch of feminist political thought.[44]

But this more positive side of feminist theory has definitely played a minor role compared with the negative methods of critique and deconstruction. Certainly such theory building is arduous and time-consuming. No one can expect to develop comprehensive feminist theories on all major concepts within a matter of years. After all, theorists working within the traditional frameworks have a vast body of literature to build on, and "new" theories of freedom, justice, obligation, and so forth are possible only because they build on other theories. Whitehead said that all philosophy is a footnote to Plato. This overstatement reflects the truth that theory builds on itself, and that to come up with something truly original and new takes a great deal of time. To this end, feminist theory must progress in a cooperative fashion, each theorist contributing not a self-contained argument but a contribution to a new whole. I believe the present work contributes to the beginnings of a new theory of obligation in the process of deepening the analysis of the old.

But it is more than originality that is at issue. Feminist theory must build its own groundwork; it must lay a new and different conceptual foundation on which to build substantive theories. As a result, building positive feminist theories suffers from another more immediate difficulty, and that is the need to defend so many of its assumptions.

[44]For example, see Eisenstein (1988) on equality, MacKinnon (1989) on the state, Okin (1989) on justice, Pateman (1988) on contract. Most of these works, like my own, are involved in criticizing "malestream" political theories at least as much as—if not more than—constructing feminist alternatives to dominant conceptions of obligation, justice, contract, and so forth; but this latter enterprise is beginning to take off.

Feminist theorists are not allowed to make assumptions the way mainstream theorists do, partly because these assumptions often lie outside the scope of the dominant discourse. Liberal theory has all sorts of assumptions—the priority of liberty, the primacy of rights, the doctrine of individualism—built into it so deeply that we hardly see them as assumptions anymore but rather consider them a definition of the world. This definitional bias limits the criticism that can be made within the structure (for example, obligation just *is* something one consents to; if we define obligation differently, we are necessarily speaking of something else, such as duty or political association). Since these biases are considered natural and self-evident, a claim from without that brings the entire system into question can be easily dismissed on the grounds that it ignores the central facts of the human condition. Feminist theory, then, is caught by the demand to defend its assumptions and to turn them into arguments when they differ from the premises of the dominant discourse. This is the dilemma: within liberalism's framework, feminist theory can go only so far; but by circumventing it and setting up its own assumptions and conceptual framework, feminist theory becomes incomprehensible in the epistemology that liberalism defines.[45] So it is necessary to develop a new conceptual language through the existing one when the latter is precisely the barrier to be overcome.

One way to approach such theory building, which has gained force in the past decade or so, involves an identification and valuation of so-called feminine experience,[46] and a translation of it into theoretical meaning. If there is a gendered bias in existing theory, and existing theory reflects so-called masculine experience only, then what does feminine experience offer us by way of a basis for a new theory? A feminist theoretical approach can help us look at the problem of obligation in a new way, and thus to formulate not just new answers to the old questions but new questions—questions that could not even be conceived of before. By saying that epistemology is created and influenced by material experience, including the experience of being of a certain gender within a given culture, by exploring the ramifica-

[45]It also becomes "trivial." See Marcil-Lacoste (1983), pp. 121–38.

[46]I use the words *feminine* and *masculine* in the adjectival sense (of or pertaining to the female or male). "Female" experience suggests specifically sexual and perhaps even essentialist imagery. I wish to suggest a broader-ranging cultural experience. The experience of cleaning the toilet, for instance, would be part of "feminine" experience in my usage of the term, because it is done by women, although it would not be considered "traditionally feminine." Where the traditional (and more limited) meaning is indicated, I try wherever possible to use that term. The distinction between *male* and *masculine* similarly holds, but the problem is less pervasive, since *masculinity*, though culturally constructed, is generally a term of power.

tions of that gendered psychic development on values and frameworks, we are allowed to question the "universality" of liberal obligation theory. If all men are created equal, is it only because women are their unilateral inferiors?

But even so, why turn to *feminist* theory in particular? If liberal obligation theory is sexist, it is also classist, racist, ethnocentric, and imperialist. Why not turn to marxist theory, or socialism, or postmodernism, or some other body of thought critical of liberal theory that can embrace all of these different biases? My purpose in the critique of voluntarist theories of obligation is not merely to criticize liberalism. If it were, other forms of theory would suffice. But such an undertaking would not be particularly helpful, for there is a specifically masculinist bias to consent theory. Its conceptual foundations do depend on the oppression of people of color and the propertyless laborer, for instance, but they also depend on the oppression of women specifically, and not "merely" of women as members of these other groups. My feminist approach does not preclude analysis by class, race, or other category. Indeed, it welcomes analyses by excluded others as complementary. My argument relies on the recognition of the gendered bias of liberal theory as an important, even a central, aspect, but it is not necessarily the only aspect: the validity of developing a feminist theory does not depend on the claim that the sexual division of labor and experience is prior to other divisions and socially constructed characteristics. But it does require theorists to take seriously what we mean by *gender* and the relation of women to society, history and political thought.

Some—particularly postmodernists—might argue that such a position requires a notion of fractured identities, a denial of the ways in which race, for instance, is not simply another factor to be added to gender but is also part of gender. That is, a black woman does not necessarily have this one part of herself, called woman, which is the same as that part of a white woman, with any differences between black and white women attributable solely to race. If gender is socially constructed, then race, class, age, culture, and so forth, which are also socially constructed, can alter the meaning of gender itself. Thus to talk about gender outside the context of these other things is to engage in as offensive an abstraction as that found in social contract theory's "natural man."[47]

I must confess that this is a view I have some sympathy with. Postmodern theory, as Quentin Skinner suggests, offers a perspective that calls into question the absolutism of "the human sciences" and em-

---

[47]See Spelman (1988) for this kind of argument.

phasizes "the extent to which our own concepts and attitudes have been shaped by particular historical circumstances."[48] Postmodern theory criticizes modernism for representing reality as given and universal when in fact what we call reality is generally a reflection of particular institutions, practices, and events. Modern theories (such as liberalism) are metadiscourses, universalizing and ahistorical ideologies that fictionalize human experience by ignoring individual particularities, or at least reducing them to gross generalizations, which are then proclaimed to be the one and only truth. Hence the argument that the "natural man" of state-of-nature social contract theory is really a wealthy white European male at the dawn of capitalism and industrialism can be seen somewhat loosely as a postmodern type of claim. As Nancy Fraser and Linda Nicholson argue, "The metadiscourse narrates a story about the whole of human history which purports to guarantee that the pragmatics of the modern sciences and of modern political processes . . . are themselves legitimate. The story guarantees that some sciences and some politics have the *right* pragmatics and, so, are the *right* practices."[49] Postmodernism thus rejects universalizing theories as "totalizing fictions." As Jean-François Lyotard says, "Simplifying to the extreme . . . *postmodern* [is] incredulity toward metanarratives." He suggests that dominant discourses produce an image of society as a "unified totality, a 'unicity,'" and articulates the task of theory as resistance to such constructions: "Let us wage a war on totality; let us be witnesses to the unpresentable; let us activate the differences and save the honor of the name."[50]

Feminist postmodernism, of course, is concerned with this approach particularly as it applies to an understanding of women's experience. Thus, according to some, feminist postmodernism differs from mainstream postmodernism in that it is "intensely political." Feminist postmodernism suggests not only that it is acceptable that our theoretical understandings and positive constructions are noncomprehensive but also that such a situation is intellectually (and politically) preferable: "There are as many interrelated and smoothly connected realities as there are kinds of oppositional consciousnesses. By giving up the goal of telling 'one true story,' we embrace instead the permanent partiality of feminist inquiry." Furthermore, the tensions that this "permanent partiality" produces need to be tolerated, even highlighted, by feminist theorists; for it is not ambiguity and tension themselves that pose a threat to women and to all people but

---

[48]Skinner (1985), p. 12.
[49]Fraser and Nicholson (1990), p. 22.
[50]Lyotard (1979), pp. xxiv, 12, 82.

rather "the tensions we long to repress, to hide, to ignore that are the dangerous ones."[51]

Postmodernism obviously has much to offer both to a critique of liberal obligation theory such as I propose here and to feminist theory as well. Yet it is also problematic, particularly from the perspective of the latter. The recognition of human multiplicity that postmodernism affords is a significant political and philosophical move for feminism. As Patricia Hill Collins notes, although black women's experiences share some features with those of both African-American men and white women, the standpoint of black feminism is unique. The construct *black woman* does not merely mean black-plus-woman, because such a formulation defines *black* as male and *woman* as white, with *black woman* simply becoming an odd variation on two basic themes.[52] The dangers of such reductive and biased thinking have been largely responsible for women's oppression, at least in modern history, and have indeed thwarted feminist efforts since the early 1970s to achieve gender equality. As the *Sears* case demonstrated, a concept of equality that is premised on sameness and unity works against women, because it takes men as the standard against which women are measured; but a recognition of women's differences (in this case, reproduction) within modern liberal culture results in their continued institutionalized inferiority. This political Catch-22 dominates in political theory as well, and it is a bind that feminists seek to break out of.[53]

At the same time, however, postmodernism—or at least a certain version of postmodernism which some might call post-structuralism —seriously threatens the present project and feminist theory as a whole. For without the ability to discuss gender in relative if admittedly self-conscious isolation from other factors, we cannot engage in any kind of feminist theory because the term *woman* evaporates. And if *woman* evaporates, then claims to structural sexism in liberal obligation theory evaporate with it: consent theory may be reductive, totalizing, and fictionally universalizing, but there is no special relationship that the people historically labeled women have to these fictions. This is not only problematic for feminist theory but deeply dis-

---

[51]Harding (1986), pp. 194, 247.

[52]Collins (1989). See also Hull, Scott, and Smith (1982).

[53]*Equal Employment Opportunity Commission v. Sears, Roebuck and Co.*, 628 F.Supp. 1264, 39 FEP 1672 (N.D. Illinois, 1986). The EEOC charged Sears with sexual discrimination in its failure to promote women to commissioned sales positions. Sears claimed that women preferred not to seek or accept such positions because they had different values than men. Specifically, Sears argued that women were more oriented toward family responsibilities, which were difficult to reconcile with the demands of commissioned sales. See also Cooper (1986); Eisenstein (1988); and Scott (1988).

turbing to the particular people in history who have suffered from the social construction of their identity as "women." Indeed, such a notion is politically dangerous to women, as it is to other marginalized and disempowered groups, for their identities seem to be evaporating before they can even get a solid grasp on what they are.

To say that a person has different aspects or parts of her identity is not to fracture that identity but rather to allow synthesis to occur. My identity does have different parts, some of which often sit in too uncomfortable a relationship with one another for me not to say that my identity is multiple, even somewhat conflicted. But that does not mean that I do not strive for a synthesis of these parts, to reconcile them so I can live a relatively coherent life. I am not a multiple personality or a schizophrenic. The key to synthesis is understanding those parts as distinct entities. Certainly if I want to understand someone's intense emotional dependence on her children, or her cigarette addiction, I need to locate those parts of her in the context of her personality and personal history as a whole to understand why these aspects exist. But they are also distinct entities, not necessarily connected to, say, her affinity for thinking analytically about social contract theory or her anxieties about computers, and it would be counterproductive to seek to understand them exclusively in those terms. All four aspects may relate to similar sources—for instance, let us say that being a daughter and a middle child in a particular white, northeastern, suburban American middle-class family created both an oral fixation and a heavy reliance on analytical skills in the face of certain stressful life situations—but that does not mean that her smoking can be understood in terms of her skill as a theorist. So although these different parts cannot be seen as entirely separated, because they all exist within her and thus must all be part of the same set of historical experiences and circumstances, they also reflect distinct aspects of the complexity of a human personality, and it would be a mistake to say that we cannot understand one except in terms of all the others.

Similarly, we need to understand that feminists can consider the social construction of gender as not opposed to or more important than race, class, ethnicity, and culture but also as not completely intertwined or coextensive with them. For instance, a white male may feel it is easier to harass a black woman than a white woman, and this attitude is not something that can be broken down into either gender or race (or class) alone. Yet there are distinct gender and race (and class) layers to the problem. Similarly, a black woman and a white woman experience many things differently *as women* because of their race, that is, because their racial differences modify their experience of their gender. But their gender also displays commonalities; that is, they also experience many things similarly because they are women. The fact that gender is a social construction does not address why it is that certain people with particular social and physical characteristics have historically been called women and others men, and what that means. The social construction *black woman* may be unique, but it also *in part* derives from what *black* means in our language and how race is socially constructed, and in part from what *woman* means in our language and how gender is socially constructed. So although I seek to focus on the dimension of gender, that does not require, nor does it mean that I have, a unified conception of what *woman* means, or that other dimensions such as race and class do not at least implicitly affect that meaning.

These postmodern issues of difference and diversity may seem to have little to do with Hobbes, Locke, and Rousseau. But in fact these considerations are very important to my reading of social contract and liberal obligation theory, for it is in the act of bringing in particularity and concrete embodiedness that modern obligation theory is most strongly challenged. The centering of a historically located, economically privileged, and culturally specific white male as "natural man" is central to the structural sexism (and other biases) of liberal obligation theory. It is through locating the historical specificity of this supposedly universal understanding of humans that the door can be opened to the kind of fundamental critique in which the present analysis is engaged. Such an analysis provides the starting point for the epistemological shift which I argue is required to understand what obligation means in the dominant liberal discourse, and what it might mean in feminist theoretical terms.

Chapter 1 begins with a general analysis of the basic problem of political obligation. Here I focus on a critical assessment of the "fathers" of the social contract, Hobbes, Locke, and Rousseau, which I follow in Chapter 2 with a similar analysis of contemporary consent theory. I examine these theories of obligation to reveal the central tension between freedom and authority, and how, despite their ostensible differences, they all approach and resolve the contradiction in similar ways. I further analyze the relation of women to obligation in their theories in the attempt to demonstrate that the place of women is at least a partial cause of the apparently gender-neutral contradictions and conflicts in the theories. I also argue that these problems lie at the heart of contemporary theory's failure to get beyond the problems of the social contract. The theories are all *premised* on the exclusion of women, and yet this exclusion is an important source of the contradictions that make the theories fail. Thus a consideration of women becomes central to making sense of obligation theory, *and* to any hope of maintaining obligation as a viable political theoretical concept.

I then turn immediately to the deeper feminist theoretical analysis and the central argument that the problems just identified are epistemological. I begin the exploration of gender-biased epistemology through the argument from psychology: Chapter 3 is devoted to an explication of object relations theory and the moral psychological work of Carol Gilligan. Nancy Chodorow[54] suggests that women's and men's psychosexual experiences provide them with different orientations toward conceptions of the self, the external object world, and human relations. Gilligan[55] argues that men and women think of morality in ways that synchronize with these different orientations. These two literatures resonate with each other. I draw out the ramifications of the ideas these works suggest for political theory in general but, most important, for theories of political obligation.

The significance of object relations and moral psychology is that they provide a standpoint for developing a specifically feminist perspective on obligation. The approach of standpoint epistemology holds that epistemology is not objective or pure but is the product of specific social relations and experiences. Such a conceptualization is potentially powerful for understanding obligation. Accordingly, in Chapter 4, I explore the epistemological and ontological ramifications of the argument from psychology: if we can identify (nonreductively) different gender-related psychological and resulting moral orientations—and I would hardly deny the controversy surrounding this literature—then what are the implications for knowledge? For the way we conceptualize and develop political theory? For the framework of our analyses of concepts such as obligation? For those concepts themselves?

In Chapter 5 I apply these considerations more particularly to political obligation. I examine the implications of the ideas offered in Chapter 4, suggesting that we need to reformulate both our concept of obligation and our approach to it. One approach suggested by the feminist analysis is to take obligation, as opposed to freedom, as the starting point for writing theory and assessing social relations. From the argument that consent theory and much else of liberal theory works from the premise that freedom is "natural" or a given, a premise derived from a prior, unacknowledged assumption of basic human separateness, I explore the possibilities that arise from taking obliga-

---

[54]Chodorow (1978). And see Chapter 3 for mention of other articles by Chodorow on this topic.

[55]Gilligan (1982). And see Chapter 3 for mention of related articles by Gilligan.

tion as a given (an idea to be distinguished from "natural" obligations), which might result from a basic assumption of human connectedness.

In Chapter 6 I explore the theoretical implications of treating obligation as given and develop more fully what a feminist theory of obligation would actually be. Here I discuss what the argument from psychology and standpoint epistemology can tell us about new methods of substantive political theorizing. The emphasis on new methods is a key to understanding the idea of obligation as given, for it requires us not to conceptualize one static concept forever at the heart of reality but to adopt a much more fluid understanding of social relationships that derives from context. I do not define a complete feminist theory of political obligation in keeping with the modern tradition so much as I discuss the kind of political society that is needed for obligations to be worked out on an ad hoc and interpersonal basis. Drawing on various arguments in the participatory democratic literature which I argue are feminist, though they are not self-identified as such, I attend to the context in which obligations will exist to develop a theoretical understanding of the concept itself.

The theorizing in this chapter borrows much from postmodern insights, yet the enterprise of constructing a feminist theory is one postmoderns vehemently reject as totalizing. My major concern about postmodernism is that it undermines precisely the constructive side of feminist theory. I believe that feminism must engage in such construction or else suffer women's continued disempowerment. Thus in an afterword, I argue that while feminism, including particularly the feminist methods I develop, can and should borrow insights and ideas from postmodernism—and thus create a *postmodern feminism*—there can be no such thing as *feminist postmodernism*, because the latter term deconstructs, and even explodes, the former.

It is here, in these last two chapters, that the argument departs most sharply from more standard methods of modern political theorizing. But these chapters merely make explicit what is implicit throughout the book, namely the narrow path that feminism must negotiate between the rocky cliff of modernism's totalization and the abyss of postmodern nihilism. My argument is modern insofar as it seeks to hold on to a notion of women and gender as a way to understand oppression, and to construct alternative futures for political society and theory that are more inclusive and egalitarian. It seeks to acknowledge that the Enlightenment yielded certain insights about humans at this particular time in history that many feminists—including myself—are not yet ready to let go of, such as the ability to think reflectively and make choices, the desire to be self-creative, the yearning for a notion of justice, freedom, and equality, even as it challenges the particular ways liberalism defines and formulates these abilities, desires, and ideas.

But this work is also postmodern insofar as it rejects the provision of unified and comprehensive theories in favor of the more richly complex enterprises of formulating new perspectives and questions, listening to partial answers, and searching for ideas that are not so much *true* as *less false*. The deconstructionist's metaphor of digging a tunnel accurately represents my approach to political philosophy: in digging a tunnel, one hacks away at rock and earth, carving a hole through a mountainous mass, working one's way through the metaphorical text. But as one does so, one is also building a pile of loosened rock and unpacked earth, and this has meaning, too. So as feminist theorists pull apart and analyze various theories and unpack what is repressed in patriarchal political thought, they reveal a great deal of newly unearthed material which has meaning. My book is engaged in precisely this sort of excavation. Its purpose is to unearth the assumptions underlying our common conceptions of obligation and to let us see that very different questions need to be asked than have been asked previously. But I go further, for these new questions should suggest new kinds of answers as well as new ways of thinking about and formulating those answers.

Although theorists such as Derrida and Foucault would argue that such excavated material in turn needs deconstructing in an ongoing process, and does not provide the basis for some new constructive enterprise, I believe that feminism needs to play around with this debris first, seeing what it can construct by adding new material. It is likely that these new structures will in turn need to be deconstructed; but this effort of reconstructing—absent the arrogant belief that what one reconstructs is the final answer—is an important part of feminist method. And yet, although I believe that this more positive, constructive side of feminist theory is vital, critics may find, and I am willing to concede, that the greater strength of this book lies in its critique and excavation. This does not disturb me. If this enterprise makes the ground we have been walking on for the past three hundred years somewhat less stable, the achievement is significant.

CHAPTER ONE

The Problem of Women
in Political Obligation

IN MAINSTREAM POLITICAL THEORY, and particularly in original social contract theory, contingent sexism is readily apparent. For the most part women are not even mentioned, let alone is their role in politics articulated. Yet the few and scattered remarks concerning women made by the original social contract theorists are powerful and revealing—powerful in the contradictions they display, revealing in the ways in which apparently contingent sexism signals a deeper, structural theoretical dependence on women's exclusion from politics.

Hobbes: Abstract Individualism

Let us begin by seeing how these problems are represented in Hobbes's political theory. Whereas some elements of his theory, such as his extreme version of what constitutes choice (giving a thief your wallet while being held at gunpoint, for instance, would constitute choice for Hobbes), are generally rejected by most other theorists, and some would question whether we can really say that Hobbes has a strong influence on modern consent theory, I would nevertheless hold that the fundamental underpinnings of Hobbes's theory reverberate in modern conceptions of obligation. The picture of Hobbesian man as competing ruthlessly for ever more goods, for example, typifies western capitalist assumptions about scarce resources and naturally acquisitive individuals.[1] Furthermore, the problems of tacit and

---

[1]See Hirschman (1977), Lukes (1973).

hypothetical consent that plagued Locke and modern theorists such as Rawls have their beginning in Hobbes. In *Leviathan* we see a particularly strong reflection of the themes of abstract individualism, negative liberty, and the necessity and sufficiency of consent for obligation. Hobbes begins with a notion of men as free and equal. Their equality is established in the most basic fashion, namely in bodily strength and mental capacity. This corporeal equality provides the foundation for the further equality of right to all that one is able to attain.

This concept of equality is paired with a concept of freedom that is equally absolute and practical. Hobbes's definition in *Leviathan* presents a classic statement of negative liberty. He says: "By *liberty*, is understood, according to the proper signification of the word, the absence of external impediments: which impediments, may oft take away part of man's power to do what he would."[2] And in a later chapter he remarks: "Liberty, or freedom, signifieth, properly, the absence of opposition: By opposition I mean external impediments of motion. . . . And according to this proper and generally received meaning of the word, A FREE-MAN *is he, that in those things, which by his strength and wit he is able to do, is not hindered to doe what he has a will to"* (p. 262).

This condition of freedom and equality guarantees that obligation can exist only by the exercise of will, "there being no obligation on any man which ariseth not from some act of his own; for all men equally are by nature free" (p. 268). Thus, some form of consent is necessary to obligation. The Sovereign can derive authority only from the agreement of subjects to transfer the rights they have in nature (namely, the right to acquire whatever they can) in exchange for the security of civil society, which in turn derives from other members' giving up the same rights. The importance of consent to this construct is logically obvious: a number of theorists have highlighted the epistemological grounding of this importance. Whether methodological, possessive, epistemological, ontological, or abstract, Hobbes's extreme concept of individualism compels him to base obligation on consent.[3]

Yet such consent, according to Hobbes's theory, is in many ways not voluntary in the way we commonly understand the term. Indeed, Hobbes deduces consent by what I call a rational fiat. The social con-

[2]Hobbes, *Leviathan*, p. 189. Subsequent references to this source will be cited in the text.

[3]See, for instance, Macpherson (1962), Hartsock (1984), Pateman (1979). Lukes (1973) distinguishes among these various kinds of individualism. I agree that there are differences, but all derive from and return to the same general idea, and thus can be used more interchangeably than he seems to allow.

tract with the Sovereign is the only way to end the state of war, for only the Sovereign can enforce the laws of nature and ensure that they rule over and check men's unbridled passion. Since the social contract is the only way to achieve the utmost security, then men *must* consent. Or rather, looking at his contemporary society, Hobbes concludes that subjects *must have* consented; that is, given that humans seek to avoid the state of war, and given that free and equal beings cannot be forced to do anything they do not wish to do (and given that anything they wish to do will be of some good to themselves), Hobbes concludes that they must have consented to the current state of affairs.

But this descriptive justificatory account is backed up by a prescriptive account of logical necessity. Given that humans wish to escape the state of war and live, and given that the Sovereign is the only (or at least the most effective) means of achieving this goal, they *had to* consent. It would be irrational for men in the state of war not to consent, for the advantages of doing so are clear and far outweigh the good of the absolute liberty of the state of nature: "The final cause, end, or design of men who naturally love liberty and dominion over others, in the introduction of that restraint in themselves in which we see them live in commonwealths, is the foresight of their own preservation, and of a more contented life thereby" (p. 223). There is no choice, says Hobbes. Or rather, there is only one choice that brings to men the greatest opportunity to fulfill their desires. Since that is what men seek, they consent to the Sovereign. Hobbes can envision no other conclusion, and indeed his premises build to it quite neatly.

Such a theory works well with his conception of people as isolated units with few if any social capabilities. Hobbes presents one of the most extreme versions of abstract individualism in *De Cive*, where he describes men as springing forth, virtually overnight, separate, discrete, and fully formed, like mushrooms.[4] They have no natural relationships and hence no natural obligations. Indeed, it is doubtful that such men, in total control of their obligations and with such disparate and mutually exclusive interests, could even form societies by consent. The only way for such beings to unite is by fiat, rational or otherwise, but always backed up by the sword of Leviathan. Obligation in Hobbes's theory ends up being prudential: one obeys because one wishes to avoid pain and punishment. But because humans' rational capabilities enable them to see that they want to avoid punishment, Hobbes says, such obedience derives its force from citizens'

---

[4]This is particularly pointed out in Di Stefano (1983). See Hobbes, *De Cive or The Citizen*.

consent. That is, people will always consent to whatever it is prudent to do.

So consent would seem to be not only necessary for Hobbes but sufficient as well: his rational fiat ensures that this consent is all that is required. Yet Hobbes is very particular about what it is rational to consent to. For instance, it would be an act of insanity to consent to something as chaotic and dangerous as a democracy. This might suggest a contradiction, or at least an inconsistency. But like all the consent theorists, Hobbes makes some exceptions to what obligates by consent. A prisoner, for example, is not obligated to accept execution as punishment and is free to escape if he can, but a prisoner condemned to a jail sentence is obligated by his consent. If men enter civil society to preserve their lives, then it would be at least a paradox, and perhaps a contradiction, if such action entailed consent to be killed. The exception is still based on what it is rational to consent to.

Yet it would also seem that Hobbesian individuals are incapable of deciding what is rational. Hobbes says that anyone who consents to die "is not to be understood as if he meant it, or that it was his will; but that he was ignorant of how such words and actions were to be interpreted" (p. 192). Just as it is rational for men to join civil society because men are machines seeking to preserve their natural motion, so it is rational to resist death, whether or not the Sovereign decrees it. In both cases the "rationality" borders on a form of compulsion.

The necessity and sufficiency of consent derive significantly for Hobbes from a concept of liberty as negative: if men were not naturally and fundamentally free, and if freedom were not the absence of restraint, then the series of events and conditions that produce the state of war would not come about. This emphasis on negative liberty goes hand in hand with a theory of abstract individualism. Hobbes's conception of liberty as freedom from restraints entails, at least as he sees it, that all individuals are and should be isolated units. If men are to preserve the essence of their humanity, they must preserve their freedom. Relationships threaten that freedom because there is no assurance that the other person will not try to harm you. The natural propensity of all men being to preserve themselves and to gain all they can, any alliance is suspect, and everyone must be on guard against the other person's taking advantage.

Alliances are rational and desirable under some circumstances, of course. Hobbes suggests, for instance, that several people being oppressed by the same person could form an alliance to kill their oppressor. Thus, even a being with superior strength could be killed by a relatively weak individual "in confederacy with others, that are in the same danger with himselfe" (p. 183).[5] But the alliance must logically end as soon as the common purpose is achieved, given mutual distrust; and at any rate Hobbes seems to think that such occasions will not happen often. The more standard representation of the psychology of Hobbes's natural man is the Prisoner's Dilemma.[6] Trust is totally lacking in Hobbesian beings because, he insists, it will always prove fatal. The reason men must submit to an absolute ruler is that trust among men is impossible without the sword of Leviathan hanging over their heads, ready to drop upon the one who breaks a—or *the* (social)—contract, who violates a trust. If the capacity for trust existed naturally in men, Leviathan would be unnecessary; but to speak of such conjectures, Hobbes might say, is pointless.

Citizen Fathers, Invisible Women

Thus abstract individualism and negative liberty give rise to the conclusion that individuals must submit to a Sovereign with virtually absolute power over them. Hobbes's most radical assertion of the separateness and individualism of humans results in one of the most repressive solutions to the problem of reconciling political authority with individual freedom. And it is in his radicalism, as well as in his simultaneously brilliant and disingenuous attempt to reconcile such opposing extremes, that we find the sexism of his epistemological and ideological framework. Hobbes's thought has been characterized as exhibiting "a distinctively masculine orientation to the realm of politics.'"[7] Certainly on the face of it Hobbes seems contingently sexist, as he simply, if somewhat mysteriously, drops women out of civil society. In the state of nature, women are in every way the equals of men. They are men's equals in strength and intelligence, so any sort of "natural" subordination is impossible. Women can be subordinated—like men—only through war; and the laws of nature rule

[5]In this interpretation I am at odds with both Elshtain and Lukes, who declare that all relationships in Hobbes's theory are "accidental." Although I agree with their basic point—that the problem with Hobbes is that he ignores the intrinsicality of relationships—I disagree that he says they are unimportant. As I see it, the problem is that although relationships are necessary, Hobbes still asserts that we always choose them; thus he asserts the myth of choice as a means of controlling something that is in fact not chosen—human sociality.
[6]This model of rational decision making comes from game theory and is by now familiar to most philosophers and political theorists; but see Gauthier (1990), pp. 221–22, for an extremely clear and concise account, and Gauthier (1969) for its workings in Hobbes's theory.
[7]Di Stefano (1983), p. 634

women just as they rule men.[8] Indeed, in some ways they are men's superiors, because of their connection to children. In the state of nature, a mother has ultimate and absolute control over a child she bears—she is its "master"—because only she knows who the father is, and only she has the power of life and death over the child in choosing to "either nourish, or expose it" (p. 254). Children thus owe allegiance to the mother in the state of nature much more than to the father, and in some ways can thus be considered women's allies. Although Hobbes does not acknowledge this, logically the mother could use the child to her own ends for at least the limited time before the child leaves her. Thus the mother and child working together could overcome a man.[9]

Yet in civil society, women drop out of the picture. They become subservient; they lose their ability to consent and hence never can partake in politics; they virtually lose their voice as they disappear from Hobbes's account altogether. Indeed, where mothers in the state of nature are the fulcrum and creators of any concept of family, in civil society Hobbes defines a family as consisting of "a man and his children; or of a man and his servants; or of a man, and his children, and servants together; wherein the Father or Master is the Sovereign" (p. 257). The mother is not merely demoted; she becomes invisible.

Why did Hobbes present this contradiction? The only apparent explanation he offers is a feeble claim that "for the most part Commonwealths have been erected by the Fathers, not by the Mothers of families" (p. 253), as if that answered rather than begged the question.[10] Hobbes does allow that "the naturall inclination of the Sexes, one to

[8]"There is not always that difference of strength or prudence between the man and the woman, as that the right [of Dominion] can be determined without War." *Leviathan*, p. 253.

[9]This, then, would be the one exception to Hobbes's claim that no one can be held as a slave in the state of nature because eventually the slave would be able either to escape or kill the master. Hobbes gets around this problem by declaring that in their dependence children consent to parental authority, "either expresse, or by other sufficient arguments declared" (p. 253). Certainly the mother's "enslavement" of the child could end as soon as the child was old enough to leave the mother; but this denies the psychology of fear which Hobbes so eagerly employs elsewhere, for a child must reach a relatively advanced age before she sees herself as other than the caretaker sees her. Furthermore, as psychological literature (some of which is discussed in Chapter 3) reveals, children form a bond of trust even with "bad" mothers, a fact that would not fit Hobbes's schema. Perhaps this relation is the "natural power" of women which tacitly sits at the heart of Hobbes's need to exclude women from civil society, as I discuss later on.

[10]Hobbes also maintains that men assume a superior role because of the need for unity and swift decision making. Elshtain (1981) holds that this rationale for making the Sovereign an absolute monarch also justifies patriarchal authoritarianism within the family, as Hobbes practically obliterates the distinctions between the state and the family.

another, and to their children" may lead to a contract between men and women to "dispose of the dominion over the Child" (p. 253), thus presenting an important exception to the impossibility of contract in the state of nature, and in fact locating such contract in natural inclination. But he does not indicate that such contracts extend as far as to create families before civil society exists.[11] He even fails to take advantage of the Bible as a "natural" source of female subservience; in Chapter 20, "Of Dominion Paternal, and Despotical," Hobbes devotes several pages to scriptural citation, where he cites subservience of sons and daughters, and even "maid servants," but nowhere mentions wives' subservience to husbands, not even in his references to Adam and Eve (pp. 258–60). Hobbes was a genuine egalitarian; people were equally subservient, yes, but equal nonetheless in both body and intellect, and it was precisely this equality that created the state of war and thus provided the rationale for his construction of the state. So why did he not continue to grant equal status to women in civil society? There was no logical need to exclude women, for they would be just as subservient to the Sovereign as men.

An answer to this question may begin with the recognition that in instituting the patriarchal family in civil society, Hobbes eliminates—by fiat once again—the potential for conflict not just between individuals but between *classes* of individuals, namely, men and women. This poses even more of a contradiction to Hobbes's theory; for if it is women's status as individuals—that is, as appetitive machines—that spurs Hobbes to impose the patriarchal order on them, it is just such action that denies their individuality by treating women as a class. Although consent to the Sovereign implies a perverse equality, the differentiation between groups of individuals based solely on sex— for Hobbes makes no distinctions between economic classes, and race is virtually invisible—is categorically discriminatory.

But that may point to the structural sexism of Hobbes. As Christine Di Stefano argues, there is a "deep structure" of masculinity in Hobbes's work; masculinity forms a "subtext" that interacts with and forms the particulars of his political theory.[12] Certainly the very con-

---

[11]Pateman (1988), p. 49, argues that the patriarchal nuclear family must predate the social contract in order to make sense of the fact that only men participate in the social contract; but she also notes the difficulty of this position. If women's child rearing created a temporary strategic disadvantage that enabled men to subjugate them, it is more likely that infants would be abandoned by women; for when faced with the prospect of keeping the infant and being subservient to a man versus abandoning the infant and maintaining her ability to fight men on equal footing, Hobbesian woman would have to choose the latter.

[12]Di Stefano (1983), p. 634.

cept of the state of nature is structurally sexist in that it denies the historical role of women as child rearers and childbearers. Hobbes's concept of man must depend on such a denial, for that is necessary to radical individualism. If women are indeed the fearful, appetitive creatures Hobbes says "men" are, it is a wonder that the human species was ever propagated. It is as disingenuous to assume that the child realizes the danger to herself and escapes before the mother can inflict harm as it is to claim that children "consent" to parental dominion. Hobbes's epistemology of radical nominalism, or methodological individualism, works hand in hand with the exclusion of women from his political framework. Elshtain further argues that Hobbes's obliteration of all distinction between public and private is similarly a structurally sexist element of his theory.[13] Again, it denies the importance of women's historical work, and denies as well two things that are central to women's historical role: relationships and reproduction.

These responses, however, reject outright the picture of "natural woman" that Hobbes depicts as the equal of man. If we accept Hobbes's conception of natural woman—and I am not at all suggesting that we should for other than interpretive purposes—we are led to the conclusion that women's exclusion must form the basis for Hobbes's state precisely because of the "natural power" they have through reproduction. This power cannot be altered by the social contract in the same way that men's natural power to kill is altered. What Hobbes seeks to do instead is to change the relations of child rearing in ways that parallel the changes made over natural man through the creation of civil society. That is, the institution of the patriarchal nuclear family does for women what the social contract does for men: it takes away their ultimate natural powers. That women have more natural power than men—the power to give life as well as the power to take it away—necessitates a dual structure of restraint. The significant difference, however, is that whereas men would readily consent to the Sovereign through the rational fiat, women would not logically consent to this family. After all, in a Hobbesian framework reproduction presents a threat not to women (or at least not a threat that the family ameliorates) but only to children, whereas the state of war unconditionally threatens all men and women. This threat is what yields the social contract. But if reproduction does not threaten women, they have no need to consent to this second structure, the family; or at the least, they would have no logical need to accept the secondary status that Hobbes gives them.

The most obvious solution to this problem, and one that Hobbes

[13]Elshtain (1981). Obviously I do not entirely agree with Elshtain's analysis, as I argue that the public-private dichotomy is central to social contract theory's structural sexism.

could easily have argued, is that women consent to the social contract, just as men do, out of fear of death and a desire for peace. They
thus, like men, would owe absolute obedience to the Sovereign. The
Sovereign could then command women to obey husbands and fathers—he could, in short, create patriarchy—on the grounds that it is
necessary to establish paternity so as to enhance order and reduce
conflict even further. Indeed, Hobbes notes that the question of familial dominion "in Common-wealths . . . is decided by the Civil Law;
and for the most part (but not alwayes) the sentence is in favour of
the Father" (p. 253). Women would thus "consent" to the patriarchal
nuclear family because they consent to the social contract, much as
men "consent" to their own imprisonment when they break the law
because they have consented to the Sovereign's authority. Of course,
this presupposes that males really do care about claiming ownership
over infants they have fathered. Given that Hobbes seems to believe
that women in the state of nature will not automatically kill a child,
thus implying that many humans will ascribe an object value to children (a view, unfortunately, consistent with seventeenth-century attitudes toward children),[14] and given that the social contract merely
contains but does not transform human acquisitiveness, this is quite
likely. Indeed, as I pointed out earlier, an important natural activity is
to "dispose of the dominion over the Child" (p. 253), and there is
nothing to indicate that the social contract would lessen the desire for
such dominion. On this account, women's reproductive power would
represent an unstable element in civil society because it provides
men with possible grounds for dispute among themselves, that is,
over paternity. And just as an army increases order over male citizens, male control over females reinforces peace in a hierarchical extension of state power.

Of course, if Hobbes had explicitly made this argument, the job of a
feminist theorist would be considerably easier; for this "answer" to
the question of women's subordination in the family displays overtly
the ways in which the social contract is structurally based on wom-
en's exclusion. The question asserts itself: *Whose* order do women
supposedly destabilize? That is, why is paternity important? Why
could not the Sovereign eliminate the problem altogether by creating
a matrifocal society in which fatherhood is not significant? One could
argue that such an ordering ignores the natural acquisitiveness of humans; but it also demonstrates an overt masculinist bias in defining
the world. Why is it women in particular who need this extra layer of

[14]Di Stefano (1991) argues that Hobbes's own childhood, typical of his times, is an
important source of his views of the human condition. See also Clark (1982), Fraser
(1984), and Prior (1985).

authority, unless they are naturally more powerful? It would seem that for Hobbes, to the degree that women are the problem, men provide the solution.

Although Hobbes structures his theory to reveal the logic of men's consenting to give up so much power to the Sovereign, he does not provide a parallel argument why women would want to give up even more power to their husbands. This is not surprising, for in fact it does not make sense to say that Hobbesian women consent to the family in its patriarchal form. It is *Hobbes* who needs women to do this. Indeed, it is Hobbesian man in general who has the need. Hobbes creates and defines "man" so as to require dominance over "woman." That is why Hobbes does not even try to construct an argument that women consent to the family. To do so would violate the logic of his argument, so he merely passes over the issue, knowing that none of his contemporaries—and probably not posterity either—would note the contradiction. There are other ways, such as that provided by the psychoanalytic perspective I adopt in a later chapter, in which Hobbes's structural sexism is revealed, and I will return to Hobbes's structural sexism in Chapter 4. But these arguments demonstrate that the gender bias contained in Hobbes's social contract theory is not merely contingent and therefore changeable. It is not possible merely to reinterpret "man" as "men and women," because his conception of politics and political society requires the exclusion, subordination, and disempowerment of women.

Locke: A "Social" State of Nature

Whereas Locke apparently excoriated Hobbes, in very interesting and important ways Locke and Hobbes share some conceptualizations of individualism, freedom, and authority. Indeed, I would argue that Hobbes provided much of the epistemological groundwork for Locke's theory. What is overt in Hobbes concerning negative liberty, the necessity and sufficiency of consent, and the presentation of coercion as consent is far more subtle and perhaps even diluted in Locke, but is present nonetheless. At the same time—and perhaps ironically —what is deeply embedded and even hidden in Hobbes concerning the place of women in the political structure, and concerning the subtext of masculinity in liberal epistemology, is more open to view in Locke's theory.

In Locke's *Two Treatises* the severity of Hobbes's abstract individualism seems to give way to a more peaceful, perhaps even social, rationalism. In contrast to Hobbes, Locke argues that in the state of nature, men are peaceful because they are rational. The competition for goods found in Hobbes's state of war is at least seriously diminished for Locke because rationality dictates that men desire only what they need, not as much as they can get. Yet Locke shares some central assumptions with Hobbes concerning the meaning of freedom and the reasons why men's "natural" socialness is undermined. Furthermore, Locke "seems to make consent even more essential to political obligation than does Hobbes."[15] These two elements stand in difficult opposition, for they presuppose two conflicting concepts of humanity, one of individualism and one of sociability. Although Locke's theory of obligation embodies an attempt to recognize the limitations on individual choice that sociability yields, such attempts leave him with serious contradictions.

Locke begins with a concept of freedom that is not as starkly negative as Hobbes's, yet might be seen to fit Isaiah Berlin's formulation quite nicely:

> To understand Political Power right, and derive it from its Original, we must consider what State all Men are naturally in, and that is *a State of perfect Freedom* to order their Actions, and dispose of their Possessions, and Persons as they think fit, within the bounds of the Law of Nature, without asking leave, or depending upon the Will of any other Man.
>
> A *State* also of *Equality*, wherein all the Power and Jurisdiction is reciprocal, no one having more than another.[16]

The key phrase is "within the bounds of the Law of Nature." Locke's state of nature is more peaceful than Hobbes's as the latter's physical equality is transformed by Locke into an equality of right. Men are naturally free, and everyone is equally free by the laws of nature. Thus, freedom is limited by equality of rights. The unbridled license of Hobbes's state of nature cannot coexist with a concept of equality of freedom decreed by natural right. Rather, it entails a society of reciprocal respect for one another's rights.

But this limitation on freedom that equality entails is made easy and natural by the fact that humans are rational. Although humans need the things of nature that enable them to live, they neither require nor want an unlimited amount of those things. They do not want more than they can use, for spoilage represents a waste of labor, and hence a waste of property, violating a law of nature: "As much as any one can make use of to any advantage of life before it spoils; so much he

---

[15]Smith (1985), p. 42.
[16]Locke, *Two Treatises*, p. 309. Subsequent references to this source will be cited in the text.

may by his labour fix a Property in. . . . Nothing was made by God
for Man to spoil or destroy" (p. 332). But, given men's rationality, and
"considering the plenty of natural Provisions there was a long time in
the World, and the few spenders" (p. 332), this law, while a moral
maxim, is also a principle that rational beings would naturally use to
guide their actions. Rationality, if not allowing men to see the laws of
nature and follow them as the will of God, at least shows men that
the course of action the laws of nature decree is the best to follow on
its own merits. To gain so much that the fruits of labor spoil is to
waste the property one has in one's person, and is irrational.

Because of this rationality, it follows that the freedom Locke attributes to natural man is a self-determinative, self-creative conception.
Freedom from dependence on the will of another is a vital aspect of
being human. Legitimate limitations on freedom exist, but in impersonal laws, not in the will of a person. The first and most obvious of
these limitations consists in, as previously noted, the "bounds of the
Law of Nature," which include most importantly the idea that all people have an equal right to freedom. Natural law, of course, is not
consented to per se; for though natural laws are moral maxims, they
also represent man's essence, as God has created him. It is as nonsensical to say that one "consents" to natural facts of human existence as
it would be to "consent" to the laws of gravity or to having blue eyes.
Just as Hobbes said it was inconceivable that a man could consent to
die, because life is the essence of humanity, so the laws of nature do
not limit freedom—and hence it is inconceivable to wish to violate
those laws—because they express the essence of man. The duty of
self-preservation is not a law given by God as an arbitrary dictator
might lay down a law. Although we should obey, it is not the case
that we must *merely* obey. The laws of nature are decreed by God as
the definition of humanity, and as the guidelines we must follow to
be human. But this "must" is as much prudential, or a rational fiat, as
it is a moral maxim. Locke can be seen as saying that "no one may"
means "it is inconceivable that anyone would." If someone were to
violate the laws of nature, her actions could not be afforded the assumptions of rationality and rational choice; she would be considered
incapable of directing her life through reason, and therefore not fully
human.

Conventional laws (in the sense of human-made) may also define
the parameters of liberty, but only a particular kind of law may do
this, namely those laws consented to by members of the civil society.
When people decide to leave the state of nature (whether because of
the introduction of money or the lack of a known judge),[17] they are

---

[17]There is scholarly disagreement about why men leave Locke's state of nature. Green
(1986) emphasizes the notion that it is the want of a common judge to resolve disputes

still their own masters in forming the social contract: "The *Liberty of Man in Society*, is to be under no other Legislative Power, but that established by consent, in the Common-wealth, nor under the Dominion of any Will, or Restraint of any Law, but what the Legislative shall inact, according to the Trust put in it" (p. 324). Consent must be given to government for it to exercise legitimate authority; and consent must be given to any constraint, including one of law, on an individual's freedom to pursue her interests. Rules that have been consented to limit freedom, but they do so by an act of free will (consent) and therefore can be seen as an expression, rather than a hindrance, of the will.

The concept of a rule-governed freedom may appear confusing, and might even demonstrate a tension within Locke between the two extremes presented by Hobbes and Rousseau. Like Hobbes, Locke bases freedom on independence from another's will. But like Rousseau, he depicts law as not so much a restriction on freedom as an enhancement of it: "*Law*, in its true notion, is not so much the Limitation as *the direction of a free and intelligent Agent* to his proper Interest" (pp. 347–48). Here we might seem to have a somewhat "positive" notion of freedom: a situated freedom, defined by certain parameters that enhance human abilities rather than limiting them (or, rather, that enhance the productive and good abilities while requiring the limitation or relinquishment of the bad and counterproductive ones). This would seem to contradict my central claim that negative liberty is the cornerstone and fatal flaw of consent theory. All of these rules come from God; even the conventional rules we consent to by adher-

---

that crop up from time to time. He postulates the state of war as these intermittent periods of dispute among individuals and argues that the social contract ends the state of war by providing arbitration. Macpherson (1962) argues that the introduction of money brings about the state of war by allowing men to accumulate more than they can use. The introduction of money changes what it is rational for men to do: just as it is rational before the existence of money to take only as much as one can use, so is it rational after the introduction of money to accumulate as much as one can. But Locke suggests in *Questions concerning the Law of Nature* that not everyone can or will use his or her God-given reason. Equality of right may thus be a safeguard for natural inequalities in reasoning ability. I believe this point brings Green's and Macpherson's theses together. As Green implies, irrational beings would start disputes, and rational creatures would seek relief from irrationality by forming the social contract. And if, as Macpherson argues, Locke believes that the propertied obtain their wealth because of their superior rationality, Locke has a justification for eliminating the propertyless from the electorate. The belief that economic status is a reflection of natural ability to reason, however, contradicts the fundamental assumption with which Locke begins his argument: that all men are naturally free and equal. But if the problem stems *not* from unequal ability but rather from the fact that some men simply "love the darkness," then Locke's argument in *Questions* is circular, for if God gives all reason to start with, it would be unreasonable for any to choose not to use that reason. See esp. Question I.

ing to God-given rationality follow the divine order.[18] Thus, these rules are constitutive of men's humanity and do not—indeed cannot—limit men's self-creative abilities; rather, they enhance them. But this is not a true "positive" liberty, for two reasons.

First, Locke says that I also have "A Liberty to follow my own Will in all things, where the Rule prescribes not" (p. 324). Where God and humans have seen fit to leave discretion to the individual by not decreeing laws, the individual is the sole arbiter of her actions. Although bound by the limits of law, people are still afforded a great deal of autonomy in choosing their actions and fulfilling their desires. Indeed, creating an environment for such fulfillment is the purpose of natural law and should logically be the point of conventional laws.

The most obvious of these are the laws of property; and this brings us to the second reason. The acquisition of property in the state of nature is a law of nature, a formula wherein anyone who adds labor to the things in nature becomes the owner of property. Everyone naturally has property in the person in the form of labor; labor transforms natural objects into property. The purpose of civil government is to protect that property, both in the person and in things. Thus people consent to government; they give up their natural liberty in exchange for a more effective liberty that is defined by rules chosen by the participants to the social contract. The end of these rules in protecting property is to preserve the self, to serve individuals *as* individuals with particular desires and interests, and not merely as God's property.

The centrality of the protection of property to the social contract emphasizes the fact that individuals in Locke's theory, as in Hobbes's, seek their own perpetuation and the gratification of their desires and interests. It is this foundation that justifies the representative form of government Locke endorses; if preserving men as God's property were the only concern, then an absolute monarch would seem better suited to the job of God's spokesman. Without a focus on individual interest and negative freedom, Locke's rejection of divine right does not hold great force. Indeed, Richard Ashcraft notes that the Dissenters, whom he claims Locke followed in his *Two Treatises*, in fact "*had to* assume that individuals were autonomous rational agents with a liberty of will which, however, was not always conformable to reason."[19] But the notion of a "situated" freedom allows Locke to do what Hobbes could not: that is, to preserve a concept of freedom as negative within the context of a civil society, to ensure

[18]Dunn (1980).
[19]Ashcraft (1986), p. 51; emphasis added.

maximum autonomy and self-determination within the confines of government and law.

Thus, even though Locke recognizes the liberty-enhancing aspects of natural and man-made laws, his formulation is much more negative than positive. The key to liberty as Locke defines it is "Freedom from Absolute, Arbitrary Power" (p. 325), power which could easily be wielded by a patriarchal monarch not subject to the laws consented to by citizens and disrespectful of the laws of nature. Locke's emphasis on what has come to be known as the rule of law preserves negative liberty and the ability to pursue interests without arbitrary interference. Law may indeed direct, but more important is the fact that it protects. When Locke articulates freedom within certain boundaries, what is most important is the freedom, not the boundaries. For positive libertarians such as Rousseau or Hegel, it is the boundaries—what they are, how they are established—that are more important than the (negative) freedom.

Locke's conception of freedom obviously ramifies on the role of consent. Locke has said, in the passage cited previously and elsewhere, that "the *Liberty of Man, in Society*, is to be under no other Legislative Power, but that established by consent" (p. 324). Most theorists concede the necessity of consent in Locke's theory. But the grounds of sufficiency are less clear.[20] Obviously, conventional laws inhibit people's ability to consent to certain things. But since those laws originate in consent and are changeable by consent, it would be stretching things uselessly to say that consent inhibits consent. The laws of nature, by contrast, are not "consented" to in this same way,

[20]For instance, although Dunn (1980, p. 33) asserts that "the sole source of legitimate authority . . . [is] the rational consent of individuals," such consent is not sufficient to establish political duty. What is consented to is significant as well. Dunn says, "The practice [to which one consents, namely, a government] must be legitimate itself" (p. 51). "Where a practice is legitimate and a role involves participation in the practice, consent to doing so and hence consent to its responsibilities is axiomatic—all potential doubts are resolved in favour of the practice. But when it is illegitimate the doubts are resolved in favour of the agent" (p. 52). Although legitimate authority is transferred by consent, the standards for assessing legitimacy come from God (p. 52); and presumably man is to know what God thinks of any given practice by consulting and obeying the laws of nature and preserving all natural rights (p. 33). This interpretation of Locke is not far from what other theorists, such as Pitkin, have developed in critiquing Locke (or, as Dunn would say, in misreading Locke), but it bears mentioning here because it is one of the stronger denials of the contemporary idea that Locke placed consent at the heart of obligation: "Consent may explain the origins of political legitimacy. It may indicate how it is that a particular individual at some specific time becomes liable to particular political obligations. But it is simply not the reason why Locke thought most men were obliged to obey the legitimate exercise of authority" (p. 31). The fact that this reading produces a rather Humean theory of obligation should raise suspicions about its soundness, but I am not prepared to enter into that debate here. See Hirschmann (1987), appendix A.

and thus might support the claim that consent is insufficient to create obligations. Locke's theory is problematic on this point. On the one hand, Locke wants to assert the self-creative and autonomous capacities of humans, to assert that freedom consists in an absence of restraint and that people create their own obligations. On the other hand, he wants to limit the capacity to create obligations.

One can resolve this problem by saying that consent is sufficient only within the confines of natural and consensual law, thus preserving an absolute "Liberty to follow my own will in all things, where the rule prescribes not" (p. 324). If a practice does not violate these rules, consent to it is sufficient to bind the consenter. If it does violate them, then consent is not sufficient. This solution is extremely problematic in terms of the social contract, however. In regard to the consent that forms the social contract, the only limitation is natural law, since conventional law does not yet exist; and this is where Locke becomes particularly confusing. Any government that is consented to must operate within the bounds of the laws of nature. It must not be tyrannical, for such a government is a rule of men, not law; it must preserve lives, for otherwise it will be abusing God's property; and it must preserve the liberty of individual consent, which men must be able to exercise in order to pursue their interests and thus preserve themselves.

The confusion arises as to where exactly the line is drawn between the law of nature and men's interpretation of it (or even their ability to see it), which depends on or derives from their self-creative capacities. John Dunn, for instance, asserts that God is the final judge of legitimacy.[21] But who is to judge what God says? Presumably humans are to know what God thinks of any given practice by consulting and obeying the laws of nature and preserving all natural rights. "What [humans] can rationally consent to is limited by their own rights,"[22] which of course come from God and constitute the laws of nature. But this circular reasoning does not solve the dilemma. For who is to judge whether a particular situation in fact violates a law of nature? For example, if the only way to preserve my life—say, in a war, famine, or natural disaster—is to consent to slavery, which law should take precedence? And how am I to judge? Or, who is to judge, if not me? Certainly, in *A Letter concerning Toleration*, Locke was keenly concerned to establish the individual's relationship to God; and, as Ashcraft has argued, such a principle was central to the political struggles of Locke and his contemporaries in resisting the absolute monarchy

[21]Dunn (1980), p. 52.
[22]Ibid., p. 33.

threatened by Charles II's Catholicism.[23] But if, within the parameters that the laws of nature set, all men are free to follow their own will in all things—including the establishment of a government—then why does Locke go to such lengths to bind a majority of the population to civil society by tacit consent, and why does he offer such improbable means for this consent?

These are questions that demonstrate the conflicting character of Locke's theory and the tension between wanting men to be self-creative while also wanting to bind them to a specific form of government. These tensions characterize consent theory in general as it has developed from Locke's theory. These and other similar questions have defined the problems for subsequent consent theorists and have been addressed in various ways, though not entirely successfully. But they fail to raise the most important question: Why do these tensions—and even contradictions—exist at all in Locke's work?

I suggest, as was the case with Hobbes, that they stem from the construct of the state of nature. The concept of a state of nature ontologically and epistemologically depends on a conception of humans as autonomous individuals who spring forth fully equipped with rationality and reason, interests and passions, and the motor and physical capabilities to fulfill their desires. Such individuals naturally owe nothing to anybody for these capacities (or for anything else), least of all to a society that does not yet exist. These premises and this construct can only produce a concept of the individual as isolated. Whether, as in Hobbes, he is warlike and competitive or, as in Locke, relatively peaceful seems to depend largely on the abundance of nature and differing notions of rationality. For Hobbes, the acquisitiveness of rational egoism makes resources scarce, and hence contact between isolated individuals must always take the form of conflict. For Locke, human reason, guided by the laws of nature forbidding waste, ensures that resources are ample, at least before the introduction of money, and hence isolated individuals need have few interactions at all. What contact they do have is generally conflictual (particularly after money makes acquisition without spoilage possible); hence the need for a "known judge." Such individuals can form a community only by an act of free will. Although the law of nature can *prevent* them from consenting to certain things, according to Locke it cannot *make* them consent to others, except through appeals to rationality.

Obviously this conception of persons as abstractly individualistic does not fit comfortably with the peaceful state of nature Locke draws

[23] Locke, *A Letter concerning Toleration*; Ashcraft (1986), chap. 3.

for us. It is more suited to Hobbes's state of war for, logically, unconnected individuals *cannot* form a society by agreement; they need a
sovereign to establish it for them. As Carole Pateman suggests, they
cannot even develop a shared language.[24] Locke uses God and natural
law to remedy this discrepancy. On the one hand, this supports
Dunn's claim that Locke cannot be used by modern theorists to develop notions of political obligation by consent.[25] Probably an important reason for modern misreadings of Locke (if they are misreadings)
lies in contemporary attempts to read God out of Locke, and hence to
eliminate the substantive values that form a crucial aspect of Locke's
theory. As Pateman argues, at least natural law "provides representatives, and their subjects, with criteria to evaluate political decisions.
Contemporary liberalism has only the procedure to fall back on."[26] On
the other hand, the role of God in Locke's theory suggests that Locke
needed an escape route, that he could not logically work his way out
of the necessary corollary of abstract individualism that needs to ac-
company a state-of-nature social contract theory.

The Problem of Patriarchy

Not coincidentally, the role of God is also significant in its betrayal
of a patriarchal belief system, one that Locke sought to refute in his
First Treatise. The links between patriarchy and abstract individualism
have been explored by a number of theorists,[27] but it is most easily
made apparent in Locke if we examine the place of women in his

[24]Pateman (1979), p. 39.

[25]Dunn (1980). The place of God in Locke's thought may, as Dunn suggests, put
Locke into another framework entirely, one that is not appropriate for secular thinking.
But the matter cannot be so straightforward. If natural rights and laws of nature exist,
why must they come from God? If we reject the idea of God, must we reject natural
rights? Dunn might think so (he says that for Locke natural rights come from God and
hence it makes no sense to speak as if they did not), but Tussman (1960) for one
suggests that theorists can adopt the same ideas without God as a base: "The possibility of alternative interpretations frees the theory of natural law from any necessary
dependence upon religion." Tussman concludes that "the theory therefore deserves
further consideration from those who otherwise would get off the train (with me) at
this point" (p. 132). I take Dunn to be saying that this is precisely where contemporary
consent theory went wrong, that one cannot excise God from Locke's theory and then
view the remainder out of its theological context. But if that is what Dunn is saying, I
think he at least overstates the problem; he attributes an extremely patriarchal conception of obligation to Locke and leaves unanswered how the individual is supposed to
be able to determine what it is that God wants. Although I argue subsequently that in
fact Locke's notion of obligation is patriarchal, I disagree with Dunn that this was
Locke's intention.

[26]Pateman (1979), p. 71.

[27]See, for instance, Eisenstein (1981), Elshtain (1981), Hartsock (1984), and Pateman
(1984).

theory. The at least tacit exclusion of women from politics,[28] and their silence in consent, is prototypical of the tension in Locke's theory between "free and equal individuals" and the attempt to obligate people to a government without their consent. Women do not consent immediately to the government by using the roads, or by living within a state (certainly not by owning land or voting); rather, they consent intermediately by virtue of being wives or daughters, that is, by way of their husbands' or fathers' tacit (or perhaps express) consent.[29] Thus women's consent is at one remove even from poor laborers' tacit consent, and it presents a deeper conflict for Locke. Indeed, the problem that women pose to Locke's theory suggests that the tension between freedom and nonconsensual bondage, equality and second-class citizenship, goes beyond anything that invoking God can remedy. It reflects the epistemological and ontological assumptions of Locke's theory, the theoretical perspective from which he wrote. And this perspective persists in our own time as well, in the use of Locke to develop contemporary consent theory.

Locke may be considered an odd entry point for a discussion of sexism in political theory, for he is in many ways among his contemporaries the most considerate of women; some would argue that in fact he was an early feminist.[30] Others would hold that the central problem for Locke is class, not sex, because the crucial distinction he makes is between property-holding express consenters and nonlanded tacit consenters. On this account, Locke has a theoretical foundation for his exclusion of some people from the social contract—namely, ownership of property—that could be seen as sex blind; after all, women are not the only ones excluded from either property or political participation.

---

[28]Smith (1985) and Dunn (1980) both hold that Locke does not say that women cannot be citizens, but the implication is that they are not. Eisenstein (1981), Okin (1979), and Elshtain (1981) all persuasively argue that women's exclusion from politics is a central element of Locke's thought. Smith (1985) also argues that nowhere does Locke say that women cannot think rationally. But Macpherson (1962) points out the differential rationality and power of the propertied and nonpropertied. Since all women are systematically excluded from the institution of property (nonpropertied men can theoretically obtain property through hard work—the ideal of equal opportunity—but women are barred from property except in the unusual circumstances leading to the granting of *femme sole* status), they must also be uniformly irrational as well as politically disempowered. Macpherson further points out that in *The Reasonableness of Christianity* Locke holds, "'Tis well if men of that rank [i.e. laborers] (to say nothing of the other sex) can comprehend plain propositions, and a short reasoning about things familiar to their minds" (pp. 224–25). Among Locke's contemporaries, see George Hickes, *A Discourse of the Sovereign Power* (1682), cited in Ashcraft (1986), p. 236, who explictly notes that the Whigs' exclusion of women from suffrage was inconsistent.

[29]Pateman (1980) makes this point as well.

[30]See Butler (1978).

Indeed, in the *Second Treatise* Locke grants women something close to rights on several occasions when he could easily have ignored the issue. For instance, in "Of Conquest," Locke argues that if the men in society A unjustly invade society B and lose, B has a "right of conquest" over A. This right includes a *"perfectly Despotical"* (p. 435) power over the lives of A's soldiers; but B's right to the property of A's members is limited to reparation. The citizens of B are not entitled to all of A's property because B must leave enough for the women and children of A to live on. They, after all, did not make the unjust attack. Therefore, unlike the male warriors of A, they did not give their tacit consent to the consequences of that attack (p. 437).[31] This limitation on B's right could be seen to derive from the law of nature's requiring us to leave enough for others,[32] or from the notion that fathers cannot consent for their children, rather than from any specifically "feminist" concerns. Nevertheless, Locke could easily have forgotten to consider women, and it is likely that none of his contemporaries would have called him on it.

Indeed, throughout the *Two Treatises*, Locke seems torn between wanting to grant women the status of "free and equal beings" and being constrained by the Bible's description of "women's lot." He grants women a relatively equal status within the family; children owe both parents respect (p. 357); and men and women share authority and common concerns in marriage (pp. 362–65). Locke asserts that the power of the father is limited to "what a *Mistress of a Family* may have as well as he" (p. 366). But he also asserts that the man must have the final word as "the abler and stronger," even going so far as to call the husband the "prince" of the family in discussing how the family may have given rise to political society (pp. 358–61, 369). Thus the "family's" political voice is expressed by the husband/father; women have political expression and representation only through their male relatives.

That women's consent was expressed through their husbands or fathers is problematic in itself, for it suggests a patriarchal basis within a body of thought that has a large investment in the rejection of patriarchy. But a further layer to the dilemma is that the men who "consented" for women by virtue of giving their own consent may in turn have expressed such consent tacitly. If, as Locke suggests, such

---

[31]The reason is that A virtually "consented" to rule by conquest when it launched its attack. Locke argues that this is the only possible situation in which a right of conquest exists. See *Second Treatise*, chap. 16.

[32]Ibid., esp. para. 183 (though this idea would probably have to work from the notion that international relations constitutes a parallel to the state of nature).

tacit consenters were "imperfect members,"[33] women must have been that much more "imperfect"; for if tacit consenters were less bound than express consenters, it would seem to follow that women would be even less obligated than unenfranchised males.

Perhaps that was the reason why theorists, Locke among them, bound women so tightly to their families; for a logical extension of the principles of consent would have led to the recognition that women were obligated to the state very weakly, if at all. Such a condition could threaten not only the state but also men's position in it by threatening the family as well, since a recognition of women's non-obligated status by the standards of consent would have to extend to women's "private" obligations. Such a disruption of the family that this might precipitate could threaten the political sphere because politics rests on the fact that it is separate from the private sphere. In a practical sense, as Rousseau particularly suggests, the existence of a class of people working in the private sphere frees men to pursue other interests in the political sphere. Locke suggests that representatives are needed to free men from political concerns, and similarly women would be needed to free them from domestic concerns as well so that they could get on with the real business of expanding their freedom and enriching their humanity by pursuing their material interests in the economic sphere.[34]

But there is an even more fundamental way in which women's exclusion is necessary, one that derives again from the centrality of property. Protection of property is the main reason the social contract is formed, and it is the primary task of the legislature. But the importance of property also explains why the institution of inheritance is so

[33]Dunn (1980), p. 42; Locke, *Second Treatise*, pp. 393–94. Dunn argues that Locke provides the right of emigration only to tacit consenters; express consenters give up the right to leave, but emigration is the tacit consenters' major opportunity to dissent. Hume pointed out the problematic character of such a formulation: those who would benefit most from leaving, such as the poor, are also generally the least able to do so. Women were even more powerless than such men to express dissent, say, by emigrating or by not using public facilities (for example, fetching water for the daily cooking, using the road to go to the market, cultivating the land for gardening produce), if for no other reason than that they were powerless to create their own roles and activities. What sense could have been made by her contemporaries of a woman's refusal to go to market—or perhaps even to marry—on the grounds that such activity would obligate her to obey the law?

[34]Note here the linguistic turn from a straightforward "public." For Locke, economic concerns and pursuits are definitely private in relation to government but public in relation to home life and women's sphere of existence. The ambiguous character of the marketplace may provide a major source of both the tensions of liberalism and its resilience, but it also may attest to the falsity of the dichotomy that liberalism constructs for itself.

necessary: men want to pursue their interests and develop their property, and that includes passing on that property to male offspring (or the husbands of female offspring in the form of dowry). Since property is linked to political power, however, as a qualification for voting and holding political office, then inheritance is the institution by which men pass the political on to other men.

Mary O'Brien has argued that this idea of "passing on" artificial institutions and practices is a result of men's "historical discontinuity," which in turn results from men's physical alienation from reproduction.[35] She argues that human history is a reflection of men's attempts to overcome this basic alienation. Their first step in this struggle was to create the patriarchal family, within which women were secluded and through which they were disempowered. The purpose of women's exclusion from the public realm, on this account, was to deny women access to sexual relations with other men. Only in this way could a man know for certain that a child was "his."

Although O'Brien's thesis is controversial, and though I think it would be a gross oversimplification to assert that this desire for certainty in male reproduction was the primary reason for the public-private split, her theory does suggest some provocative insights into Locke's theory. The gross denial of rights to women which characterizes Locke's period and his own ambivalence about claiming natural rights for them suggest his acceptance of the status quo of women's inequality. This inequality conveniently supplies property with stability through a patrilineal system of inheritance. Without women's inequality, the verifiability of lineage, crucial to inheritance, is cast into doubt, and hence the sanctity of property is threatened.

But perhaps it is not so much that inheritance is important because of the need for property as that property is important because of the need for inheritance. That is, from a philosophical perspective, inheritance protects the masculine attempt to "pass on," to maintain men's place in history. From a practical, political perspective, inheritance enables men to keep women in subservient roles to the end of maintaining political power. (This would also suggest another reason why property in the person is not sufficient to establish the right to political participation, for it cannot be inherited but exists "naturally" within each person.) If patriarchy is the basis for property, and property is the basis for the state, then is not patriarchy the basis for the state?

This is a key question, for it entirely contradicts the central purpose of Locke's theory of government and obligation. It is this contradic-

[35]O'Brien (1981).

tion that shows the sexism of Locke's theory to go beyond the contingency of simply denying women the vote to a structural requirement that they be so denied. With property as the cornerstone and primary rationale for the state, women's exclusion from that institution does not merely *coincide* with their exclusion from politics but *founds* it. Although nonpropertied males are also excluded, they can theoretically obtain a political voice through the diligent labor that yields them the necessary property; but women are not even allowed this equality of opportunity. Nor is it insignificant that women were themselves considered property, if not explicitly by Locke then implicitly, by virtue of his unwillingness to challenge the historical and contemporary status quo of women's political position. Property, as the central political value and institution of Locke's theory, excludes women; yet it requires women to play a well-defined and central, though devalued, role.

As I indicated earlier, however, the deepest and perhaps most important dimensions of Locke's structural bias relate to the epistemological framework he adopts. Indeed, Locke's more general tension between individual freedom and governmental authority can be seen as a tension between his wanting to situate individuals in a social context and an atomistic epistemology that makes such situation problematic. In *An Essay concerning Human Understanding* Locke holds that, because of the weakness of our senses, on which we are dependent for knowledge, we cannot know the "real essence" of things and of man. We can know only the "nominal essence"; that is, we can know only a thing's nature as it is determined by the way in which we classify it. This classification is manifested in language, which is to a degree arbitrary; that is, words have no necessary relation to the things they represent. Language is a system of contingent or accidental regularities for Locke. It is not the product of rules or conventions. Although it enables us to communicate, this regularity cannot overcome the basic atomism of humans. A word or a name does not give us information to form ideas. One must develop thoughts or ideas directly from the phenomenon. This, of course, means that communication between humans is severely limited in its effectiveness. We will never be able to communicate our perceptions satisfactorily.[36]

Yet at the same time, Locke wishes to situate individuals within a social context, namely, civil society. How can individuals with such severely limited abilities to communicate ever come to agreement on a social contract? The conflict between atomism and sociability is what gives rise to the conceptualization of men as "naturally" free, to the

[36]Locke, *An Essay concerning Human Understanding,* esp. Bk. IV, chaps. 2–6.

problem of inalienable rights, and especially to the problem of tacit consent. It also at least contributes to the central but problematic role God plays in Locke's theory. Locke admittedly limits the effect of empiricism on his epistemology by inconsistently bringing in rationalist assumptions.[37] He talks about the importance of the relations between ideas. He also allows for certainty of knowledge by intuition (which produces knowledge of ourselves) and by demonstration (which reveals God to us); "sensitive" knowledge, he asserts, is the only imperfect knowledge. These rationalist elements could explain the central role of God and the law of nature to the success of the social contract, for if men can be certain only of themselves and of God, one of these must provide the key to forming the social contract; and since men's knowledge of themselves is part of what creates the problem of the state of war, God is the only answer to that problem. But this resolution suggests that the tensions between individual freedom and governmental authority demonstrate, at least in part, a tension between Locke's epistemological atomism and his political values.

These epistemological conflicts have particular pertinence to women. Jean Bethke Elshtain has suggested that the seventeenth- and eighteenth-century epistemological emphasis on the split between public and private was itself a patriarchal doctrine. The contention, central to modernist epistemologies, that we all think alike, even though we feel (that is, desire) differently, creates an image of a uniform public world that is knowable to all in the same way, and a private world that is not only unpredictable but inaccessible to all but the self. This sense of private and public—the privacy of emotion versus the publicity of language and knowledge—coheres to Locke's dichotomy between the home and politics. Since women occupy solely the private realm (in the latter sense), they become the epitome of such unpredictability and the locus of irrationality (privacy in the former sense). This further justifies their exclusion from both senses of the public—they are unfit for political action because they only feel and do not think—as it is, in circular fashion, defined to exclude the characteristics that the private realm is designed to produce in women.

Consent as an expression of this epistemology is thus similarly based on women's exclusion. As Elshtain points out, what makes

[37]Some, however, such as Harding (1986), would say it is entirely consistent: that modernist epistemologies, both of which rationalism and empiricism are, share the same framework and are much closer to each other than either one is to either a standpoint or a postmodernist epistemology. I agree with this point, but I would also argue that it is important to retain the distinctions between rationalism and empiricism within the liberal framework. For Locke, his rationalist assumptions do present an inconsistency with his empiricism.

contract possible, and makes it further an essentially public act, is "that *the same knowledge is shared by all* and that the public sphere is the *only* sphere in which this holds."[38] Contract, as the quintessential public act—indeed, as the very basis for the creation of the public realm in the modern era—is thus the quintessential expression of this exclusion: "The 'voice' of woman . . . of privatized irrational desire . . . [reduced to] cloying sentiment" is absolutely incapable of speaking the language of contract, and hence—since for Locke language is a "system of external signs and symbols rather than a complex social activity that links inner and outer"[39]—of *making* contracts.

As Elshtain's argument about public and private implies, and as I argue later, this exclusive definition of obligation denies the obligations that characterize women's privatized experience. This points to an even deeper aspect of the claim that consent theory is structurally sexist, which Locke's theory reveals: perhaps liberty is defined negatively, and individuals abstractly, despite his tacit recognitions to the contrary, precisely to provide the justification for denying such obligations. That, indeed, was a major purpose of consent in original social contract theory: to justify rebellion against arbitrary authority, to refute any claims to allegiance that were not a result of individual choice, and hence to banish such relations from the realm of what we call obligations. The only way that consent theory has been able to operate throughout history is with and through the public-private dichotomy. That is, consent theory may need, for successful implementation, this specific framework—that is, a public realm totally separate from the private—within which all actions *are* conformable to the model of consent. All things that do not or cannot fit this framework—that is, nonconsensual obligations—are consigned to the private realm. And since that is defined as the realm of the inessential, consent theorists do not have to worry about, or even include, such activities or considerations when thinking about and defining obligation.

These two aspects—the denial of nonconsensual obligations and

[38]Elshtain (1981), p. 118. It might be objected that one contract to which women are party—the marriage contract—is private, not public. But although marriage is and should be a private affair between people, in fact it has always been treated as a public act. Historically it was a contract not between a man and a woman but between the groom and the father of the bride, and the transference of property—certainly for Locke another important public act, since regulation of property is the *raison d'être* of the state—was an intrinsic part of marriage. Anyone who has been involved in the legal intricacies of marriage cannot deny its overtly public character: we need licenses in order to marry and court orders in order to separate and end marriages; marriage is one of the central categories for tax purposes; and so on. See Gould (1984a), for some thoughts on the private and public nature of marriage.
[39]Elshtain (1981), p. 116.

the structural division of public and private—are highly interrelated, for nonconsensual obligations, for instance those that exist in the family, "leak" into other areas of life; in reality, if not in theory, they cannot be totally separated. Given the patriarchal social and political conditions of the seventeenth century, the logical extension of such "leakage" was Filmer's *Patriarcha*. The only way Locke could combat this leakage was to deny outright the legitimacy of patriarchy, to deny the king's right over subjects on the basis that subjects were free and equal, capable of choice. Such free and equal men would choose a representative government that defended their interests. They could not choose a patriarchal monarchy because that would defeat the purpose of Locke's entire argument. In short, Locke said, such free and equal men were natural citizens, not subjects. This was an important step.

But at the same time, this radical rejection of patriarchy rested on patriarchy in the subjection of women to men. Consent theory's inability to allow any nonconsensual obligations is really a fear and a refusal to do so, for the only way it *could* effectively deny such obligations was to segregate them in the private sphere, assign them to a particular group of people—women—and then shut those people off from the light of public day, denying them political voice and hence silencing them and their experience altogether. Thus, the tension between the need for authority and the need to preserve individualism led Locke into some awkward conclusions—conclusions that set the tone and agenda for philosophical debate on obligation for the next three centuries. His recourse to God was not, of course, a disingenuous contrivance but (presumably) a genuine belief; yet it was also a source of some of his contradictions, even as he attempted to draw on it to resolve others.

It is important to note that part of the problem involved in defining the place of women in Locke's theory, and thus in understanding his seemingly contradictory attitudes about patriarchy, arises from the fact that Locke did not explicitly create the values his theory espouses. Whereas Rousseau creates an image of women to fit his construction of the political, Locke works within and reflects the cultural and political framework of his time.[40] Indeed, the degree to which Locke recognizes women demonstrates his attempts to surmount the strictures of his society and culture (and perhaps even religion, al-

---

[40]Of course, Rousseau also works within a sociohistorical framework; that is what made his conception of women acceptable. But Rousseau presents a carefully crafted theory of women that suits very particular political needs. For Locke this is not nearly so apparent, although it is still possible to make a similar argument about Locke's work.

though religion was also the likely source of his ambivalence). But that fact suggests that the problematic place of women in Locke's theory goes well beyond his own personal views and is much more systematic and fundamental. For this same problem of patriarchy is also likely to be found (and indeed is found) in most other theories of the time, which were also shaped by the cultural, social, and theological role of women. Those roles formed part of the backdrop for the theories and helped construct the framework within which such theories were written. The problem of patriarchy that Locke's theory displays is a problem for liberal theory as a whole, and for consent theories of obligation in particular. It demonstrates the deeper dimensions of the structural sexism of liberal theory which I began tracing in my analysis of Hobbes: that defining obligation solely, or even primarily, in terms of individual consent is to a large degree implicitly—and sometimes, as with Rousseau, explicitly—premised on women's exclusion from politics.[41]

Indeed, it is through a discussion of Rousseau that this last claim, as well as the foregoing points concerning Locke, might be made more apparent, for what is subtle and indirect in Locke is overt in Rousseau. And in spite of the fact that Rousseau was highly critical of Locke's theory, they make similar points on several matters, particularly with regard to women's place in politics.

Rousseau: Reconciling Voluntarism and Virtue

Critics of consent theory came to the fore as soon as social contract theories were promulgated. Hume rejected consent theory as an inaccurate description of actual political societies in which obligations existed and as an illogical argument, since basing political obligation on the maxim that we ought to keep promises ignores the fact that promising itself is an artificial convention. He particularly attacked as disingenous Locke's tacit consent, analogizing such citizens, particularly the poor, to a shanghaied sailor who "was carried on board while asleep, and must leap into the ocean and perish the moment he leaves her."[42] Burke similarly rejected the concept of the individual that social contract theory relied on; he argued that individuals are more deeply situated in society and that, therefore, tradition is the source of political obligation. Hutcheson also rejected consent theory

---

[41]For more complete reviews of historical figures, I refer the reader to Okin (1979), Elshtain (1981), Eisenstein (1981), Pitkin (1984), Shanley and Pateman (1990).

[42]Hume, "Of the Original Contract," in Aiken (1948), p. 363.

on such grounds.[43] In contrast, Godwin rejected Lockean theory because it did not go far enough in recognizing individual autonomy
and hence did not preserve the ideals fundamental to true consent.[44]
In the nineteenth century, the utilitarians, basing obligation on the
maximization of utility, argued that consent had little to do with obligation and rejected other aspects of social contract theory—such as
natural rights—as nonsensical.[45] Hegel also argued in his *Philosophy of
Right* that consent theory was flawed in its conception of individuals
as inherently separate and that it misrepresented human action; he
held that individuals are obligated to obey legitimate authority because that is the nature of legitimacy and authority. And T. H. Green
dissected Hobbes and Locke, displaying their innards as convoluted
and self-contradictory, and recast Rousseau not as a consent theorist
but as an advocate of political virtue through emphasis on the general
will.[46]

Indeed, in the work of Rousseau we find a critique of consent that
is no less powerful than, though very different from, that offered by
Hume and others. Some readers may think this an odd claim, in light
of Rousseau's emphasis on unanimous consent and popular participation in his *Social Contract*. In fact, he is generally taught to students of
political theory along with Hobbes and Locke, the differences among
them subverted to the central and allegedly more important similarity
they share, namely, the emphasis on individual consent and the social contract. But Rousseau denied that what Hobbes and Locke called
consent was really so, and rejected the Lockean liberal social contract,
with tacit consent at its core, as mythical and classist. As did Godwin
in a very different vein, Rousseau argued for a more stringent concept
of consent. But in the process he went beyond consent as the basis for
obligation, for at the same time Rousseau rejected the atomistic conception of humans found in Hobbes and Locke, and argued that society is of central importance to humanity. Rousseau thus attempts to
reconcile a more exacting requirement of individual choice with a
more demanding conception of society. Like Hobbes and Locke,
Rousseau was confronted with the tension between the two apparently conflicting qualities of authority and freedom. But rather than
trying to hide this tension, Rousseau attacks it head on. He begins his
Social Contract with the famous declaration that man is "born free" but

---

[43]Burke, *Reflections on the Revolution in France*; Smith (1985), chap. 2; Diggins (1984), chap. 1.

[44]Godwin, *Enquiry concerning Political Justice and Its Influence on Modern Morals and Happiness*; see Pateman's (1979) discussion of Godwin, pp. 134–35, 138–40; and Smith (1985), chap. 2.

[45]Bentham, *A Fragment on Government*.

[46]Green (1986).

is "everywhere in chains," and the puzzle is to determine whether and how that situation can be made legitimate.[47]

It is my contention, in accordance with T. H. Green, though hardly following his line of argument, that Rousseau is miscast as a consent theorist. It is not the case that the state is legitimate because people consent to it; rather, people consent to the state because it is legitimate. Consent and choice play leading roles in Rousseau's construct, but they are subordinate to the more central value of political virtue. This term is problematic from a feminist perspective, because, as Hanna Pitkin points out, virtue has been associated with the steadfastness of masculinity, fortune with the caprice of femininity.[48] Ironically, Rousseau makes women the guardians of virtue in a clever self-policing tactic of restricting their activity to the home. But I use the term here to indicate a double meaning: first, to refer to Rousseau's general idea that there are some things a society needs for its own good regardless of what the majority wills; and second, to acknowledge that Rousseau's particular idea of virtue is skewed toward a specific set of values. Although he contextualizes human choice in social relationships, Rousseau also lets consent play roles that are inappropriate to and even contradict the rest of his theory. So what should be a strength in Rousseau—the situation of choice in contexts of relationships—often becomes a weakness in the form of inconsistency and contradiction.

It is obvious that Rousseau is an extreme communitarian; the good of the society, embodied in the "general will," is far greater than any of the "particular wills" that ostensibly determine it. In practical terms, the general will is defined through majoritarian practice; but Rousseau clearly indicates that not just any majority decision necessarily represents the general will. The general will is "constant, unalterable and pure"; it exists independently of citizens as principles of political right that derive their force from natural law. John Noone argues that Rousseau believed in natural law. Rousseau says, "What is good and consistent with order is so by the nature of things and independently of human conventions,"[49] and indeed *The Social Contract* is subtitled *Or Principles of Political Right*. This independent character of the general will is what justifies Rousseau's infamous "forcer d'être libre"; because the general will is right, it is people's "true" will, whether they recognize it or not. Laws are the expression of that will. Since true freedom consists in obedience to a self-prescribed law,

---

[47]Rousseau, *Social Contract,* in *The Social Contract and Discourses,* subsequently cited as Cole.

[48]Pitkin (1984).

[49]*Social Contract,* in Ritter and Bondanella, p. 105. See also Noone (1980).

when citizens must reassess their judgment and obey the law, they are merely being forced to be free. To many this is the epitome of totalitarianism, the most extreme and worst possible form of communitarianism.

Yet Rousseau also embraces an extreme individualism. Like Hobbes, Rousseau argues that the state of nature is populated by totally unconnected beings who have contact only briefly for sexual relations and cannot even recognize one another afterwards. Even mothers and children form only utilitarian relationships for a brief period, until the child leaves.[50] It is this inherent freedom and independence that establishes the need to base political society on a contract, just as it was for Locke and Hobbes. And as was the case for Locke and Hobbes, the recognition of this independence within the context of a need for authority causes Rousseau to attempt to bind people against their will via consent. Although the general will is more sophisticated and even potentially voluntarist than either Hobbes's rational fiat or Locke's tacit consent, it is neverthless their methodological equivalent.

Rousseau was caught in the dilemma of trying to reconcile his view of the primacy of political life—that it is the inevitable and ultimate end of humanity, the only way to pursue the perfectibility which he discusses in the second *Discourse*[51]—with a view of man as inherently individualistic and free, a view that logically required a voluntarist basis of political obligation to establish the legitimacy of any given political regime. Patrick Riley has argued that this tension was one between modernism and Rousseau's attraction to ancient politics.[52] But it also displays the finer point of Rousseau's theory, his attempt to recognize individuals' capacity for self-creation and agency within the context that humans are social beings. In this sense Rousseau is developing an entirely different concept of autonomy from that found in consent theory. It is a concept of the self that is embedded in relationships, that cannot be abstracted or extracted from community. Rousseau thus serves as an appropriate model for a fuller, more comprehensive conception of obligaton: not just a more consistent version of consent theory, as Pateman suggests, but a different conception altogether.

Of course, in trying to realize the need for people to consent to the right things, Rousseau makes his fatal error in forcing people to consent—forcing them to be free—and thus seems to end up with an even greater paradox than we find in other social contract theorists.

---

[50]Rousseau, *The Origin of Inequality*, in Cole, p. 59.
[51]Ibid., p. 74.
[52]Riley (1970).

What saves Rousseau from wholesale capitulation to the contradictions of Hobbes and Locke—though it also condemns him in the eyes of many to a worse sin, that of complete idealism—is the exacting standards he uses to define his political society. This, too, can help us understand the way in which he reconciles his individualism with communitarianism. Rousseau says, "Undoubtedly there is a universal justice emanating from reason alone; but this justice, to be admitted among us, must be reciprocal."[53] There are standards of good that exist in nature, independent of human will. But these must be discovered, and moreover they must be *instituted equitably*, in order for them to have positive effect. That is, citizens must consent, but only to the "right" things, if they are to be morally free. Both conditions, of voluntarism and virtue, must be present.

The difficulty with this is apparent, and has been the source of much critical scorn. But Rousseau recognizes the difficulties. He asserts that true freedom, or "moral" freedom—"obedience to a law which we prescribe to ourselves"[54]—is difficult to obtain and preserve; but since it is the most valued of all human possessions, it is worth our extreme vigilance. Once the majority becomes unable to see the general will, all hope of freedom is lost. But they will be no worse off than if they had never sought freedom in the first place, since all other political forms produce slavery anyway.

Yet there is more to it than this. Rousseau had to construct a theory that he genuinely thought realizable, and his "Dedication to the Republic of Geneva" which precedes his second *Discourse* conveys his belief that it was realizable, if not in fact already realized.[55] In trying to understand the connection between virtue and voluntarism, or natural law and human choice, we must keep two things in mind. First,

[53]Rousseau, *Du contrat social*, p. 258: "Sans doute il est une justice universelle émanée de la raison seule; mais cette justice, pour être admise entre nous, doit être réciproque." Cole translates the final phrase as "must be mutual" (p. 191); Cress (Rousseau, *The Basic Political Writings*, p. 160) translates "réciproque" as "reciprocal" but translates "doit être" as "ought to be"; and although Ritter and Bonadella (Rousseau, *Rousseau's Political Writings*, p. 105) and Barker (1973, p. 201) translate the final phrase as "must be reciprocal," I find their respective translations of the rest of the phrase rather awkward. I am particular about this passage because the added force of "must" over "ought" is important, and I believe that the idea of reciprocity captures the relationship among Rousseau's citizens more accurately than mutuality. Furthermore, whereas Rousseau may use *reciprocity* and *mutuality* somewhat interchangeably, I do not; see my discussion of these terms later in this chapter and in Chapter 6.

[54]*Social Contract*, in Cole, p. 178.

[55]Alan Ritter and Julia Conaway Bondanella, in a footnote to their edition of the *Discourse* (Rousseau, *Rousseau's Political Writings*, p. 4.), hold that "as a description, the *Dedication* is very inaccurate, since eighteenth-century Geneva was an oligarchy, not the virtuous democracy Rousseau portrays. But, if read as a vision of what Geneva might become, should it follow his principles, the *Dedication* gives substance to Rousseau's conception of a legitimate state."

for Rousseau, reason is not the natural faculty it is for Locke. Rather, it develops dialectically with the passions. That is, it is only when the state of nature approaches the state of war and people's interests clash severely that people come to see the need for society and to agree on a social contract. Thus, people can understand the standards for virtue only after the passions have made natural compliance with them impossible.[56] Reason, then, develops only in a nonnatural context; hence, the justice it develops, though universal, is moral and artificial. As a moral value, justice must apply equally to all. It must be reciprocal, coming from all and applying to all. So these "natural" standards of political morality come to have a real existence only in the artificiality of political society; and furthermore, only in a specific kind of political society, where equality and reciprocity are the keystones, can the good possibly evolve. Hence what we might call natural law is as much a necessary condition of the general will as is voluntarism; but it, too, is not a sufficient condition.

The second—and to my mind, more important—factor is the egalitarian genesis and structure of the social contract. In Rousseau's formulation, equality is a vital aspect of any polity wielding legitimate authority, for "liberty cannot exist without it."[57] Equality is not necessarily an end in itself as much as a means of promoting civil liberty and positive moral autonomy.[58] Reciprocity, mutuality, and equality lie at the heart of morality, justice, and freedom. Total impersonal alienation of each individual member's liberty to every other member of society makes the conditions of society the same for all. There is a reciprocal exchange of power. But this exchange also creates mutuality, a collective awareness that the good of each is tied to the good of all. Additionally, the legislative acts of the sovereign must be general in nature.[59] Laws may address themselves only to matters of common concern, because particular concerns necessarily reflect particular wills. Furthermore, since all laws must be universal, if a law singles out a specific group as the object of legislation, the basic equality and mutuality of the social contract are destroyed, for then some people are placed in a position of greater dependence, being subject to greater force than others. For a law to be impersonal, it must be universal. But a further condition required to ensure a law's

---

[56]See especially *Social Contract*, in Cole, pp. 177–78 and *The Origin of Inequality*, in Cole, esp. pp. 77–83 and passim. See also Noone (1980), p. 164. Elshtain (1981) also argues that Rousseau's epistemology differs from Hobbes's and Locke's in that Rousseau unites passion and reason whereas Hobbes and Locke separate them.

[57]*Social Contract*, in Cole, p. 204.

[58]Levine (1976), p. 167.

[59]*Social Contract*, in Cole, p. 187.

impersonality, as defined by Rousseau, is that its operation must not *lead to* inequality, as opposed to merely *applying* unequally.[60]

Of similar importance, of course, is economic equality. Rousseau does not say that every person must have identical resources but rather that "no citizen shall ever be wealthy enough to buy another, and none poor enough to be forced to sell himself." This economic equality is necessary to true political equality, for it creates a similarity of political consciousness concerning the needs of the community and reduces, if it does not eliminate, the blind insensitivity of the haves to the have-nots by curbing unequal political advantage. Rousseau insists that "laws are always of use to those who possess and harmful to those who have nothing; from which it follows that the social state is advantageous to men only when all have something and none too much."[61] Thus it is that equality is institutionalized, that moral and political freedom and obligation take the place of natural freedom and obligation. It is equality that is at the heart of the positive value of the social contract, the basic limit on the element of voluntarism found in Rousseau's polity.

If everyone has an identical political position, with equal power and relatively equal wealth, laws that must apply to all and are of general concern will affect all equally. If the laws truly affect everyone equally in a material sense, then a bad law—a law not in conformity with the general will—will affect everyone equally and will not stay in place for long. Thus the egalitarian structure Rousseau builds into his social contract would seem to provide safety mechanisms against particular wills and bad laws.[62] People will not have an interest in making a law that does injustice to others, for it would do injustice to themselves as well. This binds people together in reciprocal relationships. In thinking of the good to himself, Rousseau says, each citizen thinks of the good to others and to the society as a whole. The participatory process thus places people in positions in which their interests and well-

---

[60]Noone (1980), pp. 37–38, makes this point as well.

[61]*Social Contract*, in Cole, p. 204, p. 181 n. 1.

[62]It may be argued that this is true in only a limited sense. Laws that make the prosecution of rape difficult, for instance, hurt women more than men. There are many ways to create laws that are general and universal in theory but discriminatory in practice, as many critics of liberalism's procedural due process and formal equality have argued. Rousseau was, of course, one such critic of formal equality, yet his theory fails to account for this problem. Indeed, Rousseau goes one worse in that those adversely affected by the law are not merely required to obey the law but are supposedly preserving their freedom—or being forced to preserve it—through obedience to the law that discriminates against them. That is one reason why I believe Rousseau's requirement of economic equality is so vital to the cogency of his theory: it reduces, if not eliminates, the possibility that a law can be discriminatory. It does not eliminate it because sexual inequality can exist where economic inequality does not (or does not seem to), and Rousseau particularly errs on this account.

being are inextricably bound up with those of others. The relations among those people, then, involve a shared understanding of one another's interests, mutual dependence on that understanding, and a recognition of the reciprocal nature of the political process in which all are involved.

Most important, however, equality yields liberty. Equality is of course a necessary element of natural liberty. In *The Origin of Inequality* Rousseau holds that as soon as relationships of dependence developed, everyone became enslaved. When people leave the state of nature and form the social contract, this basic need for equality must carry over. Everyone must alienate his or her liberty totally, and to one another, thus creating the exact same position of power for all. Without equality, any agreement that is made will by definition favor one party over another, which is to say the agreement is automatically void. Rousseau's contract, in contrast, achieves true freedom—what he calls moral freedom—for the parties to the contract. If true freedom consists in obedience to self-prescribed laws, then a participatory democracy in which all the citizens are themselves the legislators is the only political form in which freedom is possible.[63]

In this social contract, political obligation is basically rooted in obedience to civil or political laws. The motivation for obedience can be prudential (one obeys out of fear of punishment) or moral (one feels compelled to obey a law contrary to private interest when there is ample opportunity to break it with impunity). True political obligation, however, must be moral rather than simply prudential, Rousseau says, for the latter indicates a relationship of inequality and dominance that makes freedom impossible. Since moral obligation, like moral freedom, consists in obedience to self-prescribed laws, for political obligation to be moral, civil laws must be prescribed by those subject to them. In short, what is needed is a political system in which the people as a whole constitute the legislature. One can be morally and politically free in obeying a law for prudential reasons only if one is also part of a moral community that created or assented to the law. That is, individuals may disagree with particular laws and obey them only out of fear of sanctions. But since consent to the original contract is not only unanimous but express, even those who obey any particular law "only" for prudential reasons are in fact being forced to recollect and honor their freely made moral commitments to the community. They are thus being forced to obey their moral will, and hence to be free. It is only within such a context that we can also

---

[63]This sense of "participatory democracy" comes from Pateman (1979, chap. 7), who argues that Rousseau differentiates between this and a direct democracy.

say that the general will is "right," that voluntarism can be reconciled with virtue.

Thus Rousseau's social contract is marked by very specific and sub-stantive values. Without equality and universal justice, consent or contract does not create obligations, moral or political, for there is no force of right behind the agreement. Without equality there is no free-dom; without equality there is thus no legitimate authority, and hence no obligation other than prudential, which of course places us back in a state of nature. These elements are all necessary if we are to make sense of the connections between consent and political right, or voluntarism and virtue. They minimize, if they do not eliminate, the possibility that citizens may consent to the wrong laws. Of course, as Rousseau himself points out, the problem with identifying equality as the fail-safe for this polity is that it presupposes that "the effect would have to become the cause; the social spirit, which should be created by these institutions, would have to preside over their very founda-tion; and men would have to be before laws what they should be-come by means of law."[64]

The most immediate response Rousseau makes to this point is to provide the great Legislator, who can lead people out of themselves so that they can will the good. The Legislator is a problematic political fiction, one that Rousseau could have done without; but it points to a much more reasonable alternative that Rousseau also provides, namely, education. Education enables citizens to see the good so they can and do will it. Rousseau constantly makes reference to the fact that only people of a certain kind can ever possibly achieve moral freedom through his social contract, and one of the defining qualities is that they be educable. In *Discourse on Political Economy*, Rousseau claims: "There can be no patriotism without liberty, no liberty without virtue, no virtue without citizens; create citizens, and you have every-thing you need. . . . To form citizens is not the work of a day; and in order to have men it is necessary to educate them when they are children."[65] To make citizens, a certain kind of education must be pro-vided. People are not innately capable of perceiving and understand-ing the good; they must be taught how to perceive it. Political partici-pation itself has certain educative effects, as Pateman argues.[66] But Rousseau envisions a specific and carefully crafted education to form these citizens, and his explicit ideas on education are central to his theory. They are also central to my analysis, for although Rousseau's theory of education does much to salvage the concept of the general

[64]*Social Contract*, in Cole, p. 196.
[65]Rousseau, *Discourse on Political Economy*, in Cole, p. 135.
[66]Pateman (1979), chap. 7.

will and hence obligation, his ideas also reveal the most significant, and most often ignored, problem of Rousseau's social contract: the inherent contradiction that women pose to politics.

Education, Virtue, and Women

Education, as it is outlined in *Emile*, can give men and women the necessary foundation on which to create and build virtuous political institutions. Reason creates strength in men; it provides firmness of resolve and clarity of sight that enables them to will the good or perceive and execute the general will. It is only from strength that virtue can develop; wickedness comes directly from weakness.[67] So the virtuous man must be strong, armed with the resolve that reason affords. He must be independent of the will of others, a person who considers the public good and then has the strength of his convictions to see that the public good is realized. Education is thus crucial to the making of good citizens.

Yet the education that produces these good citizens is not only sex specific but premised on the exclusion of women from political participation and the public sphere. Jean-Jacques's project is to teach Emile to be a virtuous man and a wise citizen, and a virtuous man must have at his side a virtuous wife. Yet the term *virtuous* is sex specific; it means independence, autonomy, and self-control for men but dependence, servility, and self-inhibition for women. The womanly virtues, like the manly virtues, serve the end of enhancing male freedom. More accurately, Sophie's freedom is realized through the general will no less than Emile's, but her role in achieving this realization is one of subservience and indirect manipulation rather than the direct legislative action of citizenship. Thus in *Emile* we read that virtuous women "must first be exercised in constraint, so that it never costs them anything to tame all their caprices in order to submit them to the wills of others" (p. 369). If Emile is to be free by obeying a self-prescribed law, by controlling his desires and passions to the end of realizing his true will, it is Sophie's job to make sure he is successful in this task; for only if her husband is virtuous can the general will be realized, can he be free, and thus can she be free. Rousseau makes women the guardians of morality, ready to "recharge" their husbands who come home from the Assembly demoralized by the passions of self-interest which are bound to surface whenever men debate the laws. The public

---

[67]Rousseau, *Emile: Or, on Education*, p. 67. Subsequent references to this source will be cited in the text.

sphere, while absolutely necessary to the realization of the highest ideals, also holds the greatest danger of corruption and vice.

Thus privatized woman plays an essential (in both senses of the word) role in Rousseau's construct. Not only is the kind of education boys receive different from girls' education, and not only are feminine virtues different from the masculine, but these differences, and their different valuation, are necessary to the state. Furthermore, Rousseau separates the public and private spheres on parallel principles. The private obligations of women must derive from virtue just as much as the public obligations of men, though these two concepts of virtue differ along gender lines. Just as Rousseau seeks to create male citizens who can see the good and thus will consent to it, so he also creates women who will see the obligations of wife and mother as virtuous and consent to them. Sophie *wants* to be a good daughter and a virtuous wife; she thus listens to Jean-Jacques's advice, she does what her parents tell her, she submits to Emile's desire. There is a parallel between public and private.

But there are specific reasons why it must always be women who are the guardians of morality and men who legislate, and these reasons display the inequality that Rousseau's "separate but equal" rationale is designed to mask. Rousseau asserts: "In everything not connected with sex, woman is man . . . in everything connected with sex, woman and man are in every respect related and in every respect different" (p. 357). This is an ambiguous notion, for whereas men have many important tasks to perform and many nonsexual areas of life in which they must be schooled, women are inextricably bound to their sexuality. "The male is male only at certain moments. The female is female her whole life or at least during her whole youth. Everything constantly recalls her sex to her" (p. 361). Women are primarily sexual beings; their natures are almost animal-like in their enslavement to their sexual passions. (Indeed, they are worse than animals in that animals go through heat, while women constantly and continually desire sex.)[68] Women's constant sexuality makes sexual relations at once vital and life-threatening to men; for in woman's ability to arouse men, she has the ability to enslave them. Rousseau

[68]Rousseau says that for animals, "desires comes [sic] only with need. When the need is satisfied, the desire ceases. They no longer feign to repulse the male but really do so. . . . Instinct impels them, and instinct stops them." In contrast, women have "unlimited desires to which . . . shame serves as a brake." This shame, however, can be preserved only by social institutions that enforce the alleged naturalness of modesty: "Who could think that nature has indiscriminately prescribed the same advances to both men and women, and that the first to form desires should also be the first to show them? What a strange depravity of judgement!" Although "natural," shame can easily be lost without the rigorous reinforcement of social relations. See *Emile*, pp. 358–59; see also Rousseau, *Origin of Inequality*, in Cole, p. 71.

paints this scene in fearful colors, equating sex with violence and danger: "Her own violence is in her charms" (p. 358).

Unconstrained women would overpower and control men, who "would see themselves dragged to death without ever being able to defend themselves" (p. 359). Not only is the lure of sex dangerous, threatening violence in its ability to enslave men, but so are women's social manifestations of sexuality, namely "the modesty and the shame with which nature armed the weak in order to enslave the strong" (p. 358). Although God gave men "immoderate passions, He joins reason to these passions in order to govern them" (p. 359). Women, in contrast, control their "unlimited desires" not through reason but through shame. Where the animal's instinct of cyclical sexual desire fails to limit desire in women, the "instinct" of shame takes over. Yet even this is not sufficient. Shame imposes limits on women's passion, but at the same time it is artfully used by women to stir men's passions to greater heights and thus increase men's dependence on women.

Because of the contrary forces of shame and desire, Rousseau says, women always repulse men's sexual advances, but do so ambivalently, "not always with the same force, or consequently, with the same success" (p. 354). Rousseau's views on rape are singularly misogynist, for he basically asserts that a woman cannot be raped if she does not really wish to be. "For the attacker to be victorious, the one who is attacked must permit or arrange it; for does she not have adroit means to force the aggressor to use force? The freest and sweetest of all acts does not admit of real violence" (p. 354).[69] For Rousseau, women consent to sex even when they say no; indeed, women are constructed in such a way that their natural shame will always force them to say no, even as their natural desires indicate that they really mean yes.

Women's incapacitation concerning consent obviously poses problems for their ability to participate in government and to form a social contract; but it is clear that Rousseau does not merely believe women to be inferior. Indeed, it is because Rousseau sees women as *super*human that he must bring them to the level of *sub*humans in order to balance out and make them equal to men. The separate-but-equal approach is once again a myth used by those who are afraid of losing power.[70] Hence one reason to deny women political power is that, in

---

[69]Rousseau then asserts that the decrease in the incidence of reported rape in contemporary times is due to the public's increasing acknowledgment of women's sexual nature and their "realization" of women's wiles; it is "surely not because men are more temperate but because they are less credulous" (p. 360).

[70]Schwartz (1984) misses this point in his assertion that Rousseau grants separate-but-equal status to men and women. As Franklin (1974) suggests, "Jim Crow" laws are a

their uncontrolled state, they are "naturally" so much more powerful than men. Once women's sexual power over men is gained, moral freedom for men is lost, for they no longer exert control over themselves; they are subject to the cruel forces of nature. This is dangerous for men as well as women, Rousseau implies; men cannot realize the general will if they are subject to their passions. The obvious way to escape women is through activities and goals that men can pursue in arenas in which women cannot participate. At the same time, men must be allowed to express their sexual desires; they cannot be "unmanned." The answer is a chaste yet sexually available wife, and it is not surprising that one of the principal features of Emile's education—which is devoted to turning him into the ideal citizen—involves finding and marrying a virtuous woman. Only through a chaste marriage can he both express and control his desires and be a successful, virtuous citizen. Thus it is only after Emile and Sophie are engaged in Book V that Jean-Jacques can teach Emile the principles of the social contract (pp. 450–71).

Thus women must be repressed so that men can know their true will, and politics becomes an institution built specifically to empower men against women. Yet it is not through the exercise of his own will that the man controls his desires but through the woman's repression of her sexual attraction. Woman "ought to make herself agreeable to man instead of arousing him" (p. 358). She must repress her sexuality to free men and to serve them, for only in this way can she secure both her virtue and her husband's. If women's virtue—gained through sexual repression—is the key to men's virtue, if men's virtue is the linchpin to the general will, and if the general will is the key to the success of the egalitarian, participatory social contract, then it would seem that the oppression and repression of women is fundamental to Rousseau's polity. When Rousseau comments in *The Social Contract* that the liberty of his democracy may depend on slavery, perhaps we need not wonder exactly who Rousseau has in mind to be the slaves.[71]

Education is crucial to Rousseau's theory of political obligation, for through it he can literally create people who will consent to the right things. Equally crucial to both education and political obligation, however, is the public-private split and the exclusion of women from participation in legislation, the quintessential act of moral freedom.

---

powerful example of this type of reasoning, and demonstrate the racial dimensions of structural bias. See Eisenstein (1988) for an excellent discussion of difference, sameness, and equality, particularly as they apply to gender.

[71]*Social Contract*, in Cole, pp. 241–42.

Rousseau's construction of the virtuous citizen and the virtuous political society indicates not only that women do not hold positions of
equal political power but also that they *cannot* do so within this polity.
Their possession of power would completely topple Rousseau's construct. Rousseau's sexism is deeply structural; women can never be
allowed into the hallowed halls of the Assembly without threatening
the entire structure. Only by appointing women the guardians of morality, and by removing their naturally corrupting influence, can he
guarantee that (male) citizens will recognize the general will. The definition of obligation (or, more precisely, the absolute requirement of
consent, for if Rousseau relied on political virtue alone as the basis for
obligation and legitimacy he would not have to create such people,
although he would have other problems to deal with) is thus once
again premised on women's exclusion from politics.

The structural sexism of social contract theory ensures that the
problem of political obligation remains unresolved and indeed cannot
be resolved because it is built in to the epistemological framework of
the theories. Specifically, in all of these theories the public-private
split plays a central role in conceptualizations of man, woman, and
political society, and it specifically resonates in the theories of obligation. Although these theories attempt to reconcile the tension between individualism and authority in a variety of specific ways—
whether by notions of rational fiat, tacit consent, or the general will—
all end up claiming that the (male) individual takes primacy over
community and order. Yet the theories are constructed in such a way
that governmental authority must logically, if not morally, take priority over liberty. Such a resolution cannot be overtly stated, and indeed must be masked through theoretical mechanisms such as tacit
consent, because it contradicts the basic assumptions of individualism
evident in the theorists' ontologies.

This contradiction is deepened even further by the feminist recognition that the separation and opposition of public and private is central to these liberal constructs. The fundamental discrepancy between
public and private is symptomatic—and in turn partially causative—
of a notion of human beings as atomistic and abstract. Through this
overarching ontological premise the tension between such individuals
and their need for social union is ultimately resolved by the separation of authority, or the institutions that exercise it, from the arenas
that are seen as particularly expressive of the (male) individual and
(his) liberty. By asserting that man can achieve his essence only
through independence and material possession, the consent theories
of Hobbes and Locke lodge men inextricably in the private sphere;

and by saying that government is an umpire, created merely for the protection of property, they create a split between government and the rest of life. Men control all of their social relations. Government is one of those relations, and it exists wholly and solely to serve every man's private interests. This division yields the reason why men must alienate part of their liberty to a government, to submit to the will of another in some matters. It is the most efficient way to protect property and to free men to continue their pursuit of their economic interests.[72]

Yet at the same time the private sphere is devalued, particularly in regard to women's activities and interests, and this suggests a fundamental puzzle over which sphere really does take priority. If government serves property, then public is secondary to private; yet women, who are wholly private, are devalued, and this suggests that public activity is more important. Rousseau, one might think, avoids this dichotomy by virtue of the fact that his is a participatory democracy: all citizens are also legislators. But his construction of the general will and political society is similarly premised on a very strict separation of public and private. By locating true virtue in the family, Rousseau too lodges male citizens' essence in the private sphere. Yet men must express that essence through public activity if it is to have any meaning. Furthermore, this separation correlates to a division between the sexes. The question who counts as a citizen in Rousseau's supposedly egalitarian democracy is one that poses serious contradictions for his theory.

Thus the public-private split is a function of and perpetuates a specifically masculinist ontology and produces theories that reflect gender-biased values. In a stronger sense, it creates an entire world view that requires as its foundational premise the subjugation of women and their exclusion from the political. This world view entails a series of conceptual parameters for public and private, male and female, an entire epistemology that defines the world as we supposedly know it—the ideas we can use to frame our understanding of it, the language we can use to describe it.

These deeper conceptual dimensions ensure that women's relation to the liberal democratic state is not only one of historical contingency—or historically developed but presumably alterable attitudes

---

[72]I realize that I must hedge a bit here with Hobbes. For Hobbes, the preservation of life itself was the purpose of the social contract. But of course civil society affords men better security in their lives in the context of their pursuit of private interests. Man is naturally acquisitive, and the pursuit of desired objects is important in Hobbes's civil society. In the text I emphasize Locke's ideas and wording more than Hobbes's because Locke has had a greater influence on the general consent theory; but that does not mean it is at odds with Hobbes's theory.

toward women—but also one of epistemological structure. Women's exclusion becomes part of the very concept of politics—and political obligation—itself, as the terms *female* and *political* are defined in opposition to each other. This structural gender bias means that we cannot merely leave the seventeenth and eighteenth centuries behind when we talk about gender equality in the late twentieth century, for the contemporary conception of equal rights is built on the foundation of such exclusion and nonrecognition of women. Contemporary theory has inherited the bad genes of this bias as part of its basic makeup. The structural sexism of contemporary obligation theory is, as we shall shortly see, masked by ostensible improvements in contingent sexism, but, in a continuum of historical devolution, it is systematically implicated and intertwined in the concepts these theories inherit from the Enlightenment.

CHAPTER TWO

Contemporary Obligation Theory: Renewed or Recycled?

THE PROBLEMS FACED by contemporary obligation theory are not readily identified as gender issues. Rather, the gender bias lies within a broader—and proportionately deeper—context of the conceptual framework inherited from the Enlightenment. Social contract theory, confronted with the problem women posed to the notion of free and equal natural beings, resolved that problem by its political construction of gender, as well as by its gendered construction of the political. Contemporary theory no longer has to wage that theoretical battle. It can merely take for granted a conceptual baggage that is packed so tightly that we lose track of what it contains. An understanding of the gender bias of contemporary obligation theory must therefore be entered through a discussion of what would appear to be gender-neutral problems.

Thus, when we consider contemporary political theorists who have turned to consent theory as an object of analysis, we see that many problems, issues, and dilemmas of social contract theory are repeated. For while ostensibly rejecting the idea of the social contract, modern theorists maintain a strong hold on the same assumptions of natural freedom and equality. These assumptions ensure that consent is in fact the only possible justification for political obligation, and once again this problem manifests itself in a tension between individuality and community, freedom and authority. Although we do not find state-of-nature theorizing in these works,[1] freedom is still consid-

---

[1]We do find counterparts, however, such as Rawls's (1971) original position and Ackerman's (1980) scenario of founding a new society on a previously uninhabited planet.

ered the theoretical starting point. Indeed, whereas the early social contract theorists created the idea of the state of nature precisely to assert the centrality and naturalness of human freedom, modern theorists no longer have to engage in such philosophical constructs: freedom is the given, the starting point for philosophical reasoning.

Taking freedom as given may seem significantly different from saying that it is natural; and indeed I wish to preserve the distinction between these two terms. But within contemporary theory the givenness of freedom derives from the historical tradition of natural liberty. Original consent theory had to defend its starting assumptions about human freedom and equality, and did so by asserting their naturalness; by contrast, modern theorists can take those assumptions for granted. Even in the literature on freedom the question to be addressed is not whether individuals are (innately) free but how we define and identify freedom.[2]

At the same time, the theoretical importance of authority has not diminished either. Philosophical anarchism has few adherents. Most theorists seem to assume, almost as deeply as they assume the givenness of freedom, that government is a necessity. Indeed, this assumption works in direct proportion to the assumption of freedom. That is, just as the original contract theorists' claim for the need for a social contract stemmed from the need to assert humans' innate freedom, so does the modern unspoken assumption of the need for authority stem from the unspoken assumption of the givenness of negative liberty. Naturally unconnected individuals who are concerned primarily, if not solely, with narrow self-interest are innately incapable of coexisting without a government. These assumptions, like that of freedom, are so fundamentally accepted by most contemporary theories of political obligation that they are not seen as needing defense.

Yet in spite of these similarities, contemporary obligation theories are also in many ways quite different from one another. For purposes of the present discussion they can be separated into three groups. The first group takes on social contract theory directly and tries to resolve its dilemmas through the framework of consent theory, either by way of more rigorous adherence to its principles or through its modification to conform more directly to practice. The second group includes the work of theorists who try to provide an alternative to consent as the foundation for obligation but still seek to operate

---

[2]Whether they are being denied the freedom that is their natural right is, of course, another question, one that is discussed in the philosophical literature; but even this question operates from an assumption that the "right" to freedom does exist "naturally." See, for instance, Berlin (1971); the essays in Ryan (1979), esp. Charles Taylor, "What's Wrong with Negative Liberty?"; Taylor (1979b); and Flathman (1987).

within the parameters of liberal freedom and individualism. The third group attempts to move away from the liberal consent paradigm altogether. This last group, which provides the greatest potential for a feminist theory of obligation, considers the possibility of obligations as given.

The Framework of Consent: Tussman, Simmons, and Pateman

Those attempting to work within the framework of consent ironically provide its harshest condemnation, perhaps most directly supporting the claim that consent theory is basically untenable. This is most evident in one of the earliest contemporary books on obligation, Joseph Tussman's *Obligation and the Body Politic*. He declares that consent is necessary for "membership" in the state and at the same time points out "that many native 'citizens' have in no meaningful sense agreed to anything."[3] This presents a serious problem of "shrinkage." But democratic principles, which lie at the heart of consent theory, will not allow the community of citizens to be exclusive and elitist. Thus, ideal and practice collide along parallel lines with freedom and authority: "If it is insisted that only those who have consented are members of the body politic then the body politic may shrink alarmingly. But if all—those who have not consented as well as those who have—are regarded as members, then consent cannot be taken as a necessary condition of membership." Tussman resolves this dilemma by calling nonconsenters "political child-brides" who are obligated without their consent, like "minors" whose "period of tutelage and dependence is unduly prolonged."[4] They may be considered the modern counterpart to Locke's tacit consenters, although Tussman denies that such citizens tacitly consent, since all consent, tacit or express, must be given "knowingly."[5]

Yet Tussman's formulation obviously demonstrates many of the problems of Locke's earlier approach. It presupposes that the state consented to by those who can consent is in fact a "good" state, and it further presupposes that what these "trustees" consider to be a good state is not only desirable but essential. Just as Tussman's initial statement that obligation is consensual reflects his unquestioned assumption about the freedom and independence of all humans, so does his "resolution" reflect the equally strong and unquestioned assumption that the state is necessary for these humans' survival.

[3]Tussman (1960), p. 36.
[4]Ibid., p. 37.
[5]Ibid., p. 36.

Given Tussman's resolution, it is curious that he wishes to retain the centrality of consent: *some* people, at least, must consent to the state for it to be legitimate. Yet, as I demonstrated in my discussion of Locke, the characterization of this construct as founding legitimacy in consent is disingenuous at best. The severity of the conflict between individual freedom and governmental authority and the blatancy of Tussman's solution reflect the depth of his acceptance of these conflicting assumptions. Binding citizens nonvoluntarily within a scheme that is nonetheless proclaimed to be voluntarist is the only possible way to resolve this tension. Or perhaps more precisely it is the only way to maintain the illusion that these inherently opposed assumptions are reconcilable.

For A. John Simmons, in contrast, this tension is entirely dismissed by his rejection of the idea of inalienable rights and his strict hold on consent. Rather than modifying consent theory to meet practical considerations, Simmons urges a stricter adherence to the principles of consent, even if this leads to the conclusion that political obligations do not exist. For Simmons, the basic assumption of consent theory is that people have a natural right to freedom that can be transferred only by a conscious and deliberate action, and moreover, that it is always transferred by such an act: that is, consent is both necessary and sufficient to obligation. Any other consideration such as inalienable rights presents a limitation on consent and "smacks of a paternalism that consent theorists, above all others, have opposed."[6] He criticizes equally the Lockean doctrine of tacit consent and Rawls's theory of fair play as inconsistent with the tenets of individualism and freedom on which they lie; neither theory provides for true voluntarism but rather exact obedience from citizens against their will.

This claim might be undermined by the fact that Simmons does allow that benefaction can generate obligations as well, as long as five conditions hold: the benefit must be the result of "some special effort or sacrifice"; it must be generated voluntarily; it must not be forced on the beneficiary; the recipient must want the benefit (or "would want [it] if certain impairing conditions were corrected"); and he or she must not object that it is provided by this particular benefactor.[7] In allowing for "impairing conditions" (he uses the example of alcoholism), Simmons may seem to be thrown back onto Locke's tacit consent, which he so severely criticizes, as a possible basis for obligation. Yet Simmons allows for the legitimacy of such conditions *only* if the other criteria are met. Thus, I might have an obligation to a good friend who heroically rescued me from dying as a result of my drink-

---

[6]Simmons (1979), p. 68.
[7]Ibid., pp. 176–79.

ing, but I would seem to incur no obligation to someone I detested for doing the same thing, nor would I be obligated to anyone who merely prevented me from driving while intoxicated because such action does not entail any "sacrifice" or "special effort." The conditions Simmons requires seem to preserve the voluntary character of such transactions and so are much more in keeping with the individualism of consent theory than Locke's argument from tacit consent.

Indeed, in his commitment to individualism Simmons offers a highly consistent reading of consent theory, one that reveals the unavoidable logical outcome of the tenets of that theory: if obligations exist by virtue of consent and contract, if individuals are truly independent, free, and equal, then there can be no such thing as an inalienable right, for that would undermine the ability of individuals to direct (or even end) their lives. Simmons believes all rights are alienable, for only in this way can respect for individual sovereignty be preserved. He thus concludes that no theory of obligation fully respects consent, and no state can truly provide for it. That is, he recognizes the contradiction between freedom and authority within liberalism. But rather than gleaning from this that there is something inherently flawed about liberalism, he concludes that political obligation simply does not exist, although there may be other justifications for exacting obedience from citizens. To Simmons, the idea of community is mistaken, for the individual's negative liberty is of primary importance. Thus to the degree that liberal theory tries to save community, it contradicts itself. His discussion of inalienable rights reveals that individualism comes at the expense of community. And according to the compelling logic of Simmons's convincing argument, this conclusion is neither radical nor extreme; in fact, it is the only one consistent with the tenets of consent theory.

But this merely highlights the problematic nature of a completely voluntarist conception of obligation. Simmons draws the conclusion he does because he adopts the consent theorists' assertion of natural freedom. If we begin from such premises, then the problem is inherently irresolvable. Indeed, the only possible response is the one Simmons gives us: to dissolve the dilemma rather than to try to wring out its resolution. Yet the inadequacy of such premises and their resulting conclusion is apparent, particularly in Simmons's views on inalienable rights. Inalienable rights are important to Locke's attempt to reconcile the tensions between preserving the negative liberty of individuals who might consent to all sorts of things and the order and authority over beings who have conflicting interests. Simmons, however, believes that such a doctrine compromises the idea of consent, which requires that all rights be alienable: "Why, for instance, should a man not be free to enslave himself if he so desires, or to allow another to rightfully take his life?" Invoking Hobbes's claim that the object of all voluntary acts must be "some good to [my]self," Simmons asks, "Might it not be 'some good to me' to trade my right of self-defense to my best friend for $100, knowing that he would never try to harm me even though he had the right?"[8]

From the perspective of radical individualism this may sound plausible, but in the context of relationships it is absurd. I may say the words "I give up my right to self-defense" when I receive the money, but that in itself does not necessarily mean that a right is transferred. If this friend will never harm me, then obviously she does not want the right and will not take it. No agreement would exist, and hence no transfer. She might permit me to say the words "I transfer the right" and nod, humoring me, simply to allow me to save face because I need the money and despise charity. But the simple expression of the words does not constitute the transfer. She is not paying me for the right if she has no desire to exercise it; she is paying me for some other reason (for example, I need the $100). But if she *were* specifically buying my right to self-defense, then there would be good reason to assume that she wanted it for a purpose, and hence no reason at all to assume that she would never harm me. By abstracting the actions of this exchange from intention, thought, and a realistic understanding of the relationship between best friends, Simmons has offered an implausible example that does not resolve the dilemma he faces.

Other hypothetical examples that might support the abandonment of inalienable rights are equally problematic. One can imagine situations in which slavery might be beneficial, say if one's economic or social situation as a "free" person was worse than it would be as a slave. Or a woman who cannot otherwise feed her children might "choose" to be a prostitute, and even further "consent" to a pimp's controlling her business. But the conditions that certain people—people of color, women, the poor, the uneducated, the very young and old—endure as not-slaves clearly does not justify consensual slavery, for such conditions involve coercive effects on the consenter. In consenting to slavery, one must have someone to consent *to*. There must be a potential master, and such widely divergent class differentials

---

[8]Ibid. p. 68. I am not sure that Simmons would actually require that we be able to assess objectively that all choices I make yield some good to myself. I could completely destroy myself because I feel totally worthless, and that is a choice I should be free to make, according to Simmons. Yet Simmons also allows for "paternalistic" interference, such as preventing an alcoholic friend from drinking, because such people are not necessarily thinking rationally. Passages such as this support the claim that Simmons adheres to Hobbes's rational egoism.

themselves suggest unjust distributions of power. The individuals are in what might be called unfair bargaining positions, the result of inequalities in power that systematically inhibit some people's ability to consent in the theoretically consistent and politically meaningful way that consent theory logically requires. This is antithetical to both the historical roots and the conceptual heart of liberalism, which lie in the notion that all "should start from equal situations and with equal advantages, as horses do on the turf."[9]

Indeed, Simmons's acontextual and abstract notions of the individual and consent are possible only if one assumes equal bargaining positions. If all are in a position of true equality, then there is little reason to assume that the words "I consent to be your slave" automatically reflect coercion. Yet women, minorities, and other excluded groups do not have the same power as economically privileged white males to control or even shape their context. They exist in a culture created by certain privileged minorities, and this places them in an unfair bargaining position owing to the changeable structuring of socioeconomic conditions. For example, victims of physical abuse such as battered women have far less control over their environment than do their abusers: violence, fear, and shame restrict their movements, their life plans, their self-concept. A woman who was born to abusive parents and has no other conception of life is at a distinctly unfair disadvantage owing to the unjustified use of power by other people. Such a position can readily be seen to detract severely from her self-creative ability, both psychologically (what I think I can do, what I think I am) and politically (my position in the world, the power allotted to me). Such a woman is likely to seek out an adult relationship with an abusive male (who may himself have been similarly abused as a child, and indeed may seek to reassert control over his world by being abusive). Certainly the point in counseling battered women is to help them become aware of their and their abusers' patterns of behavior and reject a self-image of worthlessness. But a woman who is not afforded such treatment and support, or who is not responsive to it, and who then returns to an abusive mate cannot be said thereby to "consent" to her abuse.[10]

The assumption that all people start off formally equal is fundamental to Locke's approach to obligation through the state of nature as well, but he at least implicitly recognizes concrete inequality

---

[9]David Williams, *Lectures on Education* (1789), cited in Kramnick (1990), p. 12. The theme of starting equal in the race of life is one that Kramnick traces particularly in the adaptation of early liberalism to eighteenth-century America.

[10]The fact that both battered women and their batterers are likely to have been victims of child abuse neither excuses nor alters the fact that it is women who are gener-

among citizens and provides at least minimal protection in the provision of inalienable rights. Locke's conceptual contention—that someone who says "I consent to be your slave" is not consenting but is doing something else that may seem like consent—could very well reflect an implicit psychopolitical analysis of power relationships; that is, he could mean that anyone who says "I consent to be your slave" is being forced, at least by circumstances, into such a position and does not freely, truly consent. As Hobbes says about someone who consents to die, "He is not to be understood as if he meant it, or that it was his will; but that he was ignorant of how such words and actions were to be interpreted."[11]

For Locke, a belief in God gave rise to the idea of inalienable rights. One cannot transfer one's right of self-preservation because one's life is not one's own but is God's property. But it is the same implicit recognition of the inadequacy of consent theory when applied to real people in liberal societies that has caused many contemporary consent theorsts to retain the concept of inalienable rights. If the social contract is necessary to continued existence and to legitimacy, but not everyone can be allowed the opportunity to consent, then the provision of a set of absolutes to protect nonconsenters is one way around the problem, for these absolutes provide limits on what express consenters—or Tussman's trustees—can consent to; they ensure that the government that is consented to actually *deserves* consent.

---

ally abused in adult relationships and men who are generally the abusers. There are many reasons and some controversy about why battered women stay with abusive mates, or why they return if they are successful in escaping to a shelter. Gelles (1976), Walker, (1979), Martin (1976). Women often report that they could not leave the house for help because of feelings of shame about bruises and markings. This tendency may be less a product of feelings of deservedness, however, than of learned helplessness; that is, the depression that arises in the victim as a result of repeated abuse leads her to perceive her actions as ineffective and therefore fails to try. Eventually this decreases her actual ability to respond in a self-protective manner. See Walker (1984), Giles-Simms (1983).

The presence of children adds an extra dimension, of course. Many battered women may be unable to support their children, and therefore may be economically dependent on their abusive spouses. In addition, escape is more difficult when a woman has children; she dare not leave them behind, but taking them can pose extra difficulties. Finally, the impact of fear should not be underestimated. Giles-Simms (1983) notes that approximately half the battered women in her study reported a repetition of violence after they had left the women's shelter. The figure was higher for women who returned to the same abusive male after leaving the shelter (57 percent), but even among women who broke from the abusive relationship and found a new place to live, 44 percent were sought out by the rejected male and raped or otherwise assaulted. Although these figures indicate that battered women who return to their relationships are at greater risk, the fear of future violence could induce women not to press criminal charges, and even to return home, for fear of retaliation.

[11]Hobbes, *Leviathan*, p. 192.

Thus a doctrine of inalienable rights is crucial to adapting social contract and consent theory to the inequality encoded into social relationships in modern liberal society. To abandon inalienable rights is to abandon a feature that makes the theory politically tenable, and Simmons's rejection of this doctrine demonstrates an elitism and a blindness to real inequalities of power that makes his theory severely problematic. Yet within the logical framework of consent it is Simmons, not Locke, who is consistent and theoretically correct: if obligations exist by virtue of consent and contract, if individuals are truly independent, free, and equal, then there can be no such thing as an inalienable right. But this conclusion merely brings us face to face with the moral, political, and philosophical inadequacy of consent theory. Simmons's extreme emphasis on individualism is completely consistent with consent theory, but it is possible only at the expense of community. Rather than challenging the way the two conflicting notions of individual and community are conceptualized, he dismisses the latter out of hand.

Carole Pateman rejects such an unquestioning embrace of individualism yet similarly criticizes consent theory for providing not true voluntarism but only a "voluntarist gloss."[12] For Pateman the problem is not consent theory per se but its specifically liberal democratic formulation and institutions. Tying philosophical considerations to an empirical understanding of politics, she compares theories of consent with the practices of democracy, such as voting and civil disobedience. She finds not only that liberal democratic societies fall short of the theory but also that the theories themselves misconceive consent, primarily because of premises of abstract individualism. Naturally free and equal individuals cannot incur obligations without consenting to them; but then the basis for the state is unstable, for consent can be withdrawn at any time. To forestall this possibility, she maintains, liberal theorists do not allow for genuine consent but rather create myths of consent to hide the reality of coercion.

For example, Pateman argues that voting is often offered by theorists as the means by which citizens actively assume political obligation. Yet the consensual elements of voting are frequently inferred, and this presents a problem of circularity. By voting, one consents to the general form of a government; one recognizes the legitimacy of the political process by partaking in it. Thus, regardless of the fact that the proposal or candidate one votes for is not the one that passes or is elected to office, one is still obligated *by consent* to obey that law or to respect the official actions of that representative. This logic leads

[12]Pateman (1979), p. 120 and passim.

to the ludicrous conclusion that someone who voted for the Communist party candidate in the 1988 presidential election consented to George Bush's authority. If voting involves consent no matter what one votes for, does the practice of voting offer any opportunity for dissent? One could simply not vote. Such an action could, in the (non)voter's mind, indicate discontent with the existing structure. Yet it is also claimed, to the contrary, that abstention from voting signifies a basic contentment with the status quo. Furthermore, it is argued, by failing to exercise one's political voice one must thereby be content with the decision of those who do vote. If one forgoes one's supposed opportunity to affect the system, then one gives up any right to complain about the outcome the system produces. Whether one votes or not, then, it seems one consents, and this consent begins to look more like acquiescence at best. To retain a consistent relationship between consent and voting, "citizens must be able to decide when to assume an obligation and their own judgement must decide its content."[13]

Yet Pateman also asserts that social context and political education may reveal that there are some things to which we ought not consent, as well as things to which we should consent. Her solution is a Rousseauist participatory democracy, which would provide for such true consent and resolve the tensions between free choice and knowing what are the "right" things to consent to. Yet in making this argument she falls prey to the very problems for which she criticizes liberal consent theory. Pateman advocates Rousseau's model because he provides for true egalitarian consent. Liberalism fails to recognize that the capacities of reflection, critical thinking, and reasoning—which it touts in theory—must be and are learned within particular societies. Rousseau, in contrast, rejects the idea of natural reason in favor of a highly social and contextual account of political society, freedom, and equality.[14]

---

[13]Ibid., p. 18; see also Piven and Cloward (1988), esp. chap. 1. Similarly, civil disobedience entails a willingness to be punished by the state, and hence a tacit recognition of its authority even as one protests its actions. Pateman (1979), pp. 58–59; Thoreau, *Civil Disobedience*, pp. 415–47. See also Scales (1989) for a discussion of the ways in which civil disobedience is robbed of its public, political character by being characterized as an act of "personal" conscience.

[14]I wish to register a disagreement with Pateman on this point in relation to Locke. Although the idea of natural rationality is extremely problematic, and I reject it, that does not entitle us to ignore the consistency of Locke's assertions in this regard. The qualities that are learned in Rousseauist society are to a large extent the same qualities Locke insists God gives men naturally. Critical reflection, reason, and rationality are God-given abilities; they are part of the divine order of nature. It would thus be pointless for God to create beings who could neither discern nor follow this divine order. It is this that justifies the understanding of freedom as existing within the laws of nature, as I argued in Chapter 1. Lockean men are as capable of reason as Rousseauist men,

Pateman would probably reject my claim that she is offering a more consistent consent theory. She is critical of consent theory because it merely provides citizens with the ability to say yes or no (and sometimes not even that) to governmental policies and actions without having any influence over the content of those actions. She argues that the meaning of consent presupposes that someone else has determined the substance of what one will (or will not) consent *to*. This is fundamentally different from a promise, she would hold, because one can negotiate and fine-tune the content of a promise before actually making it. Pateman is attracted to a Rousseauist participatory democracy because it provides for more genuine individual participation and choice, as citizens have a role in deciding what the content of their obligations is, what it is that they will or will not consent *to*. Indeed, she seems to hold that what Rousseauist participatory democrats practice is not mere consent at all, however meaningful that consent might be, but something much richer and much closer to the actual practice of promising.

Nevertheless, I see her account of Rousseau as the fully developed ideal of consent theory. If the promise is the paradigm of social contract theory, then theoretically the social contract allows individuals to negotiate the terms of the contract. That those terms seem preset in Hobbes's and Locke's theories attests to their belief that their proposed contracts are the only ones that anyone *could* conceivably wish, if they were rational enough. But Rousseau is just as convinced as Hobbes and Locke that he has the right answer, and the content of Rousseau's social contract is just as predetermined as theirs. That citizens supposedly have more active participation in forming the social contract and legislation is part of what justifies the more overt coercion of "forcer d'être libre," which is actually no more or less coercive than Hobbes's rational fiat or Locke's tacit consent.

But, as I argued earlier, if Rousseau offers the only theoretically consistent version of consent, he also offers one that is not self-contained, a concept of consent that is situated. Rousseau's approach to obligation is really an attempt to understand legitimacy. This fact helps open up his theory to other sources of obligation besides consent. Consent theory bases legitimacy on obligation, which derives

---

although since each begins from different premises about human nature, each develops a different perspective on exactly what rational beings will consent to. In a sense, Pateman may fall into her own conceptual argument by defining rationality in a way that allows only for Rousseau's account, as if his account were unproblematic. I believe that it is inequality of wealth among citizens, and not (just) of rationality, that causes Locke to develop his notion of tacit consent. See Pateman (1979), pp. 25–26.

from consent. Rousseau based consent on legitimacy, which founded obligation. Pateman is correct to distinguish between the hypothetical and tacit consent of Locke and the actual, unanimous consent of Rousseau. Nor do I wish to diminish the importance of Rousseau's assertion that consent must be actual and unanimous to form the social contract. But ultimately for Rousseau citizens consent because the state is legitimate. It is vital to remember that the contract Rousseau lays before us—just as Hobbes and Locke declare of their own models—is the *only* one that will yield freedom. It includes some definite and particular procedural criteria, but, moreover, it revolves around some very positive substantive values. Thus Rousseau creates a conception of consent that shifts our focus to what is consented to, to the outcome of consent rather than the procedure. By focusing on the unanimous and express character of Rousseau's consent, Pateman attends precisely to the procedural aspects and minimizes the role of substance.

Pateman recognizes the complexity of these issues; she discusses how we can be subject to our obligations and at the same time superior to them. But she glosses over many of the deeper problems posed by the general will, and she further emphasizes voluntarist features at the expense of considering Rousseau's emphasis on natural law and virtue. She thus maintains that the tensions I have discussed still make Rousseau a consent theorist, and she still holds that the state is legitimate because citizens consent to it. In reality, however, such arguments show how untenable consent theory is. If consent theory is stated in theoretically consistent form, as Pateman argues it is in Rousseau's theory, then it can be realized only in a society that is virtually impossible to achieve, or at least one that requires absolute obedience. Consent theory also, as I have shown, depends on the subjection and exclusion of women, a point Pateman herself has come to recognize in her later work.[15] If it is to accommodate actual political societies, however, as liberal consent theory develops it, with people who might consent to all sorts of bad things, then the powerless— such as women, workers, the poor, racial minorities—become bound against their will, and the practice starkly contradicts the theoretical values it is supposed to embody. Either way, Rousseau does not offer us the definitively democratic and sound theory of consent that Pateman would like it to be. At best he may offer us insight into how we

[15]See Pateman (1985), and essays in Pateman (1989). In some of these she explicitly criticizes her 1979 argument and seems almost to retract it, in spite of its 1985 reissue. See particularly Pateman (1988), where she engages a more radical critique of social contract theory based on women's political and social position. I discuss this topic in the final section of this chapter.

should *redefine* consent and voluntarism in such a way·that they are reconcilable with the idea of political virtue.[16]

The Search for Alternate Foundations: Rawls, Flathman, and Walzer

Like Pateman, most other recent theorists of political obligation ostensibly reject an unquestioning embrace of individualism. They attempt to make genuine resolutions that accommodate both individualism and authority. But because of the assumptions of extreme individualism that underlie consent theory—assumptions that Simmons makes most clear—these efforts to dig us out merely mire us in more deeply. For instance, John Rawls tries to evade the dilemmas of consent and to reconcile individual and community through his theory of "fair play." Under the principle of fair play, obligation turns on the fact that one accepts benefits within a cooperative scheme. "The main idea is that when a number of persons engage in a mutually advantageous cooperative venture according to the rules, and thus restrict their liberty in ways necessary to yield advantages for all, those who have submitted to these restrictions have a right to a similar acquiescence on the part of those who have benefitted from their submission. . . . All obligations arise in this way."[17] Rawls views society—at least as it would be formed under the two principles of justice—as such a scheme.

The two major elements of this theory are that individuals cannot merely passively receive benefits but must actively accept them, and that the venture itself must be just, or in accordance with the two principles of justice. The first principle—that benefits must be voluntarily accepted—demonstrates Rawls's desire to ground obligation in the free will and actions of citizens. Whereas duties can be natural, obligations must be self-assumed; and if they are self-assumed, there must be some indication that the individual, in expressing free will, agrees to go along with the scheme. The passive receipt of benefits that cannot be avoided, Rawls indicates, cannot create obligations:

[16]I say "at best" not because this insight is insignificant but because—as evidenced by my earlier discussion of Rousseau—I am not entirely convinced anymore that Rousseau really offers this insight. Perhaps one could say, as Pitkin suggests in reference to Locke, that consent for Rousseau is an important aspect of the state to which people should or would consent, and it is an important quality of a legitimate regime, but it is not the ultimate ground of obligation.

[17]Rawls (1971), p. 112. Rawls's (1964) theory of fair play was later renamed the principle of fairness in Rawls (1971), but they are basically the same theory. I prefer his term "fair play" because it distinguishes his formulation from a more general use of the word *fairness*, and also because other theorists such as Simmons adopt the "fair play" terminology.

obligations are, by definition, voluntaristic. For instance, if the people in my town decide to build a new well, I have an obligation to help build it if I intend to draw water from it. But if the water comes out of my tap and I cannot avoid this benefit, I do not have an obligation of fair play.

The requirement of a self-conscious action undertaken knowingly and willingly puts obligation on a highly individualistic foundation. Citizens can withdraw from the "cooperative scheme"—that is, political society—merely by not "accepting" benefits. They can receive benefits that cannot be avoided, but as long as they do not voluntarily take avoidable or "open" benefits, they would seem able to withdraw from society, to have no obligation to obey the laws of that society (or at least the laws relevant to the benefits they refuse). As Richard Flathman says, Rawls's theory appears to give citizens a "veto power" over their obligations.[18] To this extent the anarchist problems of consent theory are not resolved.

Yet are there not some differences between acceptance of benefits and consent? Simmons seems to think so. He points out that in the well-digging scheme, for instance, a citizen who refused to participate in the scheme could still sneak out at night and steal water. This citizen could even go "to the well during the day, taking the water while shouting, 'Don't think this means I'm coming into your stupid scheme! I'll never consent to share the burdens of this enterprise!' Certainly under those conditions," Simmons asserts, "to call the taking of the water a consensual act would be ludicrous."[19]

Simmons, however, overstates the force of his claim. People can break their promises just as easily as they can "free-ride," so such a tirade in itself is not sufficient to establish that the action of taking water does not constitute consent. In many ways accepting the water can be seen as constituting consent to the scheme, particularly given the strong voluntarist criteria that surround Simmons's definition of acceptance. The person he describes ("Jones") may say that he does not consent. But to base our understanding of consent entirely on what an individual claims to be doing rather than on what she is actually doing presupposes a radically individualist perspective on consent. Obviously there is a reductive danger here, for such arguments are used against women who "cry rape." But the point is that words as well as actions exist in larger contexts, and patriarchal contexts largely shape the meaning of female rape victims' experience. Simmons's well, in contrast, presents no such dilemma to Jones be-

[18]Flathman (1972), p. 287.
[19]Simmons (1979), p. 127.

cause he has every opportunity to make a genuine choice about the water (if he did not have such choices, then he would only be receiving a "closed" benefit and the problem would not arise). So we could point out to Jones that nobody is forcing him to take the water; we could remind him of his reasons for refusing to join the scheme and argue that his actions indicate a retraction of those reasons; and we would be correct in calling him a free rider and in demanding that he make some sort of restitution, such as monetary payment, for the water he takes. In Simmons's own words, we could argue that by taking the water, Jones "implies" consent (something Simmons distinguishes from tacit consent). Given his actions, it would be "hopelessly stupid" to say that he is withholding consent to the scheme.[20]

But why is this argument even necessary? Indeed, why is active acceptance of benefits necessary? Why cannot mere receipt of benefits obligate? If I cannot avoid the benefits of clean water—let us say that instead of coming from the well, the clean water comes out of the tap—is it not possible that its provision may generate some obligatory force? After all, if I need the benefit, it makes no sense for me to try to refuse it. Such a refusal indicates on my part an attempt to withdraw from my society completely, to be the mythical isolated individual. (Indeed, why cannot Rawls invoke his concept of the original position to determine what individuals in a position of equality want, and define acceptance not by the desires of unequal people in the real world but by the preferences of rational beings behind the veil of ignorance?)

For instance, say the main wage earner in family A loses her job. Families B, C, and D go out of their way to aid family A, which has six children, by having them over to dinner frequently or bringing them food, by giving the children a lift from school when they pick up their own, by letting A use their phone when they can no longer afford their own, and so forth. Members of A, in turn, may mow B's lawn without prior consent, do the tailoring for C's new drapes, provide after-school supervision for D's children. These are not formal exchanges so much as a give and take arising from feelings of indebtedness, gratitude, loyalty. A context of relationships of give and take allows for the passage of benefits from B, C, and D to A, and this context disables A from saying, "I didn't ask for your help, so I don't owe you a thing." If people adopted the fair play perspective which focuses on acceptance—or if it were the case that fair play actually characterized our dealings—relationships like these could not go on. If A merely received and received without some attempt at return (and the return would not necessarily need to be commensurate in

[20]Ibid., p. 89.

many cases), the relationships would not last long. As a result, A's survival would be more difficult and would perhaps result in drastic consequences (such as in their having to sell the house, being forced to move, perhaps even breaking up the family).

One response to my description could be that such exchanges are not really accounts of obligations. These people choose to make these exchanges, and they may feel all sorts of magnanimous or petty things about them, but that does not mean they have obligations. If a person makes a return on benefits merely received, she does so because she wants to, and wanting to do so precludes obligation, which is a requirement to do what one would not ordinarily want to do. Such a response, however, involves a denial of the complex inter-workings of relationships in the interest of a "clean" theory. That is, it constructs theory (and examples to fit the theory) that purposely exclude such murky examples as this one for the purpose of defending a concept of humans that it has a vested interest in supporting. This circularity, however, obviously belies the usefulness of the theory. (It also displays at least a contingent gender bias, since women have historically been the participants in such informal, give-and-take relationships; but this point will be taken up later.)

Thus the requirement that benefits be actively accepted builds an inappropriate voluntarism into this account of obligation. The second principle that Rawls builds into fair play—that the scheme itself (or, in the case of political obligation, the society) must be just—demonstrates Rawls's simultaneous yet opposing tendency toward non-voluntarism. Specifically, any society in which citizens can incur political obligation through accepting benefits must accord with the two principles of justice: political obligations arise in part by virtue of the quality of the regime. This tension between voluntarism and virtue Rawls shares with Rousseau and to a lesser degree with Locke. As we have seen, limitations on consent (the general will, natural law) are not limits per se but background conditions that define the parameters of consent to the end of enhancing freedom. For Rawls, too, background conditions of justice enhance liberty by ensuring that individuals do not become obligated by accepting benefits from tyrannical or otherwise evil governments.[21] Thus, where benefits are not accepted but merely received, the justice of the scheme or society would indicate a natural duty to obey.

This second principle demonstrates a problematic role for obligation; for if my duty is to perform the same actions that would be required by my obligation—that is, obedience to law and govern-

<hr>

[21]Rawls (1971), p. 112.

ment—is there any significance to the distinction? Would my being bound by duty rather than obligation entitle me to certain advantages or rights out of consideration of the nonvoluntary nature of my contributions? It would seem that, given Rawls's commitment to the two principles of justice and his declaration of the natural duty that derives from the hypothetical consent of citizens behind the veil of ignorance, political obligation is a superfluous principle. Indeed, Rawls claims that most people will not be obligated to the state: "The better-placed members of society are more likely than others to have political obligations as distinct from political duties. For by and large it is these persons who are best able to gain political office and to take advantage of the opportunities offered by the constitutional system."[22] As is the case with Locke, only an elite has obligations in the strict sense, and this seriously threatens the democracy of Rawls's theory— the requirement that the theory must apply to citizens generally.

Rawls thus structures a two-tiered hierarchy of differential obligation. Those who accept benefits are "bound even more tightly to the scheme of just institutions"[23] than most citizens are under the natural duty of justice. But again, what does it mean to say they are bound more tightly? Locke provides imperfect members with the right to emigrate. This "right" is at best dubious on a practical level, but at least it yields an answer consistent with the rest of Locke's theory. Rawls, in contrast, can only respond that the majority of nonobligated people must still *fully* comply with the rules of the state by virtue of their hypothetical agreement to the two principles of justice in the original position. Rather than asserting that natural laws are created, executed, and enforced from above by God, Rawls postulates that individuals of a society, by entering an original position of equality, choose the two principles of justice that he outlines. By hypothetically choosing these principles, they are bound to observe them.

This choice is essential to Rawls's formulation. Otherwise he could simply assert the two principles and declare our duty to obey them on the basis that they are in fact just. Their justice, of course, is the obvious basis for allegiance to them. Given Rawls's structure, he maintains that individuals in the original position could not possibly choose unjust principles, or in fact any principles other than the ones he outlines. But like Locke, and to a lesser extent Rousseau, Rawls seeks to ground this political virtue in a problematic construction of voluntarism. As with Locke, this voluntarism is largely hypothetical; as with Rousseau, it is absolute and irrevocable, embodying the high-

[22]Ibid., p. 344.
[23]Ibid.

est principles of political virtue. And, like Locke and Rousseau, Rawls similarly founders in the attempt to reconcile the two conflicting needs for individual choice and community and ends up binding people against their will through the elaborate construction of a falsely voluntarist structure. Yet this disingenuous emphasis on choice and its convoluted relation to justice clearly threatens any meaningful distinction between obligation and duty. The idea that obligated citizens are "bound more tightly" is lost. Fair play may be important on an interpersonal level, and hence may be a source for some social or personal obligations, but for Rawls the justice of a society is enough to generate a natural duty of obedience. As a result, *political* obligation falls out of the picture.

Rawls thus solves neither the authoritarian problems of obligation theory—how free individuals can obey and still be free—nor the anarchistic problem of how free individuals can come to be subject to any authority in the first place. Like other theorists discussed here, Rawls is uncomfortable with nonconsensual obligations, but he recognizes that individuals can consent to all sorts of wrong things that may compromise justice. The theory of justice would seem to work primarily from a concept of community; but Rawls seeks to achieve this community by working primarily from premises of individualism and individual choice. As a result, his theory of justice is premised on the most radically abstract individuals: beings in an original position, behind a veil of ignorance, who know only the most general things about themselves and one another, who have no place in history, no social context. Such individuals have little capacity for social interaction except on the most abstract level. Yet they end up in absolute agreement about the two principles of justice. Their lack of a concrete common background gives way to principles that will form a formal or abstract common foreground, that is, principles of justice to which all will—indeed must—agree.

A second theorist who attempts to travel beyond the confines of consent altogether but ends up entangled in it is Richard Flathman. He is highly critical of consent theory, asking in Humean fashion whether we can ever produce any "warm-bodied human beings" who have consented to modern democratic states. Defining obligation as a practice, he rejects consent theorists' notion (and he includes Rawls in this rejection) that we can point to a single, unified, identifiable act performed by citizens, such as a social contract, that generates obligations. Flathman points out that obligation is a rule-governed activity. As practices, obligation and authority have certain definitional bounds that limit the kinds of questions one can ask intelligibly. That is, "obligation" is in part governed by "constitutive rules" where "the rule itself constitutes a reason for acting in the manner specified by the rule."[24] For instance, the rule that promises should be kept can be seen as a constitutive rule; to make a promise involves the requirement that one does what one says one will do.

But these rules themselves are insufficient without the critical reflection of humans about whether the rules should be followed. Obligation is "decidedly in the realm of human action." In particular, it is based on citizens' ability to cite "good reasons" for obedience. Hence obligation involves precepts or instruction rules as well. These are implicitly normative because they "are guides to conduct, not merely stated regulations"[25] working within the confines of a practice. Thus, the question "Why should I (ever) obey the law?" is answered in part by appealing to the practice of obligation in a constitutive manner. That is just what obligation means; it is part of the meaning of legitimate authority that it be obeyed. But it also appeals to citizens' membership within a society that depends on the acceptance of rules of obligation, on their evaluation of the practice of obedience to a particular government as well as to government in general. This acceptance is both practical and normative: accepting the rules of language to a large degree simply means that one cannot reject them if one wishes to be understood. But at the same time, citizens are capable of engaging in a critical assessment of the rules governing obligation and authority; we can identify "good reasons" why we should follow the rules governing obligation and authority.

So, on Flathman's account, obligation is not the cut-and-dried concept that consent theory makes it out to be but a practice in the full sense: an activity that humans engage in to the end of living together and to making living together a fruitful and meaningful experience. This activity is rule-governed, but not all—or even most—disputes or questions can be settled definitively by appealing to one particular rule. Flathman points to the *Crito*, in which Socrates refers not to just one source of justification for obedience—not to consent, or the lack of emigration, or the acceptance of benefits—but rather to a variety of possible sources which, particularly when taken together, constitute "good reasons" to conclude that he accepts (and is obligated to obey) the authority of the state. Thus, questions of obligation can be resolved only in less conclusive ways that will leave them slightly unsettled for some people but that nevertheless have meaning for us all.

This position would certainly seem to be an improvement on consent theory; but even this gets us only so far because it still operates

---

[24]Flathman (1972), pp. 209, 82.
[25]Ibid., p. 85.

from assumptions of liberal individualism. Flathman is not philosophically comfortable with the idea of nonconsensual obligations. But how are "good reasons" to be determined? Flathman holds that an appeal to self-interest is not legitimate as a "good reason" except "in a derivative sense"[26] because of the centrality of community to human life. He also conceives of politics as a common enterprise. But such a conception cannot be fully reconciled with the individualist method he adopts. Many would hold that once their capacity for critical reflection was unleashed, racial minorities, women, groups whose rights and interests are not addressed by the liberal democratic state, might reject the rules governing obligation and authority and thus reject their obligations. Although this might not be a bad thing, it does not advance us beyond consent theory, for once again individuals can choose wholly by themselves where their obligations lie. To use Flathman's phrase, citizens still have a "veto power." Do we still still have a problem in finding "warm-bodied human beings" who have actually accepted the rules? And if some reasons are better than others, by what criteria should we make our judgment? Flathman does not make use of political education as a means to help average citizens develop their capacities to reflect critically without appealing to self-interest; and language is insufficient to forestall the question why we should obey any particular law or even law in general.

His appeal to Socrates begs rather than answers the question. From Locke onward (with the possible exception of Jefferson),[27] theorists have doubted citizens' capacity to make rational assessments of the common good without falling prey to considerations of self-interest. Indeed, the conviction that most people do not have or display such wisdom is precisely the motivation behind the common attempt to bind citizens nonvoluntarily through allegedly voluntarist means such as use of the roads. Can average citizens critically assess the laws the way Socrates did? Do the questions that he poses enter most people's minds? Perhaps not, we might say, but they should, and participatory democrats often hang their hopes on the educability of the people. But Flathman does not necessarily agree. He makes no mention of political education, which seems so vital to other theories, such as

---

[26]Ibid., p. 297.

[27]Thomas Jefferson argued that the concept of citizen should be understood in the full sense and held that even though certain citizens could not vote, they should be expected to participate in government in a variety of ways, most obviously by rebelling and otherwise breaking the law for a higher good (see, for example, letters to Edward Carrington, January 16, 1787, and James Madison, January 30, 1787, in *The Best Letters of Thomas Jefferson*). But at the same time, Jefferson did not advocate universal suffrage, and he also believed in a "natural aristocracy" (see letter to John Adams, October 28, 1813, ibid.).

Rousseau's or even Barber's,[28] that depend on the critical reflection of citizens. And because individuals, like Socrates, engage in reflection as individuals, Flathman provides no common political arena, such as Rousseau's Assembly, in which citizens can talk and learn from one another in the effort to reach a common will. On the contrary, he holds that "habit, impulse, mindless acceptance of the status quo, serve to bring about obedience without a sense of being imposed upon."[29] This assumption threatens Flathman's theory with the same problem found in Tussman's and Locke's, namely, the assumption that people will just go along with the government, and that this does not threaten the criteria of human choice. The reason this is particularly problematic for Flathman, however, is that his dedication to liberty and voluntarism (that is, his emphasis on human action) would seem to require rejection of such acquiescence.[30]

Furthermore, although it is true that individuals exist within "forms of life," Flathman's formulation does not provide for the fact that certain forms of life can not only be oppressive or unjust but can also enmesh people so deeply in them that they are prevented from seeing the injustice. Human life takes place within language and community, but so does our capacity to think about and critically assess that life. This can provide certain absolute limits to our ability to see exactly what is wrong with our form of life and prevent us from being able to offer or even articulate "good reasons" for disobeying or even changing it. This problem has obvious implications for an analysis of epistemological bias, for it can result in the endless perpetuation of certain injustices—against women, for example—that are built into the structure of our society and language. Values of care, connection, and relationship, important to women's historical experience, are systematically obliterated from political obligation because they are not considered part of "our" form of life and hence do not enter the discourse.

Flathman sees the necessity to situate choice within the need for community and political authority. But he does not see this need as further entailing nonconsensual obligation. By trying to emphasize individual choice and voluntarism within a basically communitarian conception of obligation, Flathman is left with a theory that, like Tussman's, Locke's, and Rawls's, declares the importance of individual action and agreement while in fact allowing for the active involvement of only a few, obligating the remainder of the citizenry nonvol-

---

[28]Barber (1984).
[29]Flathman (1972), p. 197.
[30]The concern with freedom is evident in all of Flathman's works, but see especially Flathman (1987).

untaristically. Like Rawls, Flathman makes some significant advances over consent theory. Just as Rawls's commitment to the need for society brings about his emphasis on justice, Flathman's recognition that obligation and obedience take place within forms of life stems from his realizing that community is central to language. But both suffer from the attempt to retain the integrity of liberal individualism, Rawls through the acceptance notion, Flathman through the individualism of critical reflection. The reluctance to recognize the incompatibility of their communitarian concerns with the concept of the individual as liberal theory develops it bars them from envisioning a new understanding of the individual as existing in the context of community. Such an understanding could be achieved through their theories, I believe, if they were able to envision this different individual.

Such a notion of the individual, it could be argued, is at least implicitly evident in the work of Michael Walzer. This might seem a surprising claim, since Walzer could also be categorized as one of the theorists who seek a more consistent consent theory. He accepts the "commonplace of consent theory that obligations can only derive from voluntary commitments.[31] "I am simply going to assume of the many obligations I discuss that they can have no other origin" (p. x). He "takes seriously" the notion of "government by consent of the governed." Like Pateman, he seeks to make consent more consistent as well, holding that "civil liberty of the most extensive sort is . . . the necessary condition of political obligation. Liberty must be as extensive as the possible range of consenting action" (p. xiv). He also seems to agree with Flathman's warm bodies critique, as he never assumes consent "without looking for evidence that it has actually been given" (p. x).

Yet ambiguity pervades Walzer's work. He appears to wish to hold on to tacit consent, his criticisms of it notwithstanding (pp. 100, 117).[32] Similarly, he both endorses and rejects the acceptance of benefits as a ground for obligation: "The description of citizens as passive recipients of benefits is inadequate" (p. 210), even though residence in and of itself generates obligations "in part because of the benefits that are necessarily accepted along with residence" (p. 28). Like other consent theorists, Walzer identifies obligation as "a procedural rather than a substantive ethics" (p. x). Yet his communitarianism pulls him in a different direction, for a key element of "membership" is the "communal provision of security and welfare."[33] His linking of "member-

---

[31]Walzer (1970), p. xiv. Subsequent references to this source will be cited in the text.
[32]See also Pateman (1979), p. 93.
[33]Walzer (1983), p. 64.

ship and need" requires him to attend to outcome and substance, because need is varying, contextual, and highly substantive. Procedures are problematic precisely because they can ignore individual particularity and personal need. And in spite of his emphasis on participation, civil disobedience, and individual choice, a distinct thread of elitism runs through Walzer's work. He suggests that "coercion is only necessary in practice because some minority of actual people don't understand, or don't consistently understand, their real interests. Only the reckless and the improvident need to be forced to contribute—and it can always be said of them that they joined in the social contract precisely in order to protect themselves against their own recklessness and improvidence."[34]

This "democratic elitism,"[35] which Simmons decried as paternalism underscores what I have identified as the unifying if fatal flaw of contemporary consent theory. Specifically, Walzer is unable to get beyond the liberal conception of the individual, even though that contradicts his own vision of politics and society. What appears to be vacillation in his work is really just an impossible fit between the Lockean view of human nature Walzer adopts—that citizens will participate only on a basis of self-interest, that politics is not inherently interesting, that democracy would take "too many evenings" (p. 230)—and his rather Rousseauian view of politics, wherein "political activity . . . is not the price of liberty; it is liberty manifest" (p. 212).

This tension between Walzer's two visions—of human nature and of politics—is not entirely obvious in his work. Indeed, as I have suggested, his approach to obligation initially promises to cast off a liberal framework. Even as he declares *Obligations* to be "essays in consent theory" (p. ix), Walzer, like Flathman, seeks to develop a more complex and sophisticated notion of obligation than that found in consent theory. He seeks to make concrete what consent means by pointing out the complexities of our social relations and how these complexities make consent much more than a simple yes-or-no response to questions posed by the state. Thus, consent as a social practice is multiple, serial, and incremental: "Our moral biographies are constituted in large part by trains of consents—consents of many different sorts, to many different people." Consent is often signified "by a series of acts" as "we commit ourselves very often by degrees," and "consent is given over time" (p. xii). Consent is not a singular, individual act with precise outcomes. Rather, like Flathman, Walzer insists that one consents to, or within, something like a Wittgensteinian

---

[34]Ibid., p. 81.
[35]Bachrach (1967).

form of life. "By our acts of consent, we communicate to others that we are persons of a certain sort, who hold certain opinions, and will conduct ourselves in a certain manner. We entitle them to expect things of us, to rely on us, to plan their lives with us in mind as friends, colleagues, allies, or whatever. We give them rights against us and their rights henceforth define our obligations. . . . Obligations . . . are other people's resources. And all social organizations are funded, as it were, through the commitments their members make to one another" (pp. xi–xii).

Walzer thus seeks to locate consent within a context of social relations. Central to his conception of obligation is community: "Obligation . . . begins with membership . . . in the broadest sense" (p. 7). He seeks to focus on a "horizontal" relationship among citizens rather than a "vertical" relation between individual citizens and governments. It is in the context of such membership that Walzer's declaration that "the best expression of consent available to the resident of a democratic state is political participation after coming of age" (p. 111) is more than the empty cant that Pateman rightfully charges it often is in liberal democracy. Walzer argues that "if the citizen is a passive figure, there is no political community" (p. 210).

The social contract can thus be redefined by Walzer as "an agreement to redistribute the resources of the members in accordance with some shared understanding of their needs, subject to ongoing political determination in detail."[36] In this light, procedure and substance come together as individual members, through a procedure of equal participation, are able to forge common solutions. But what *kind* of participation is Walzer endorsing? Pluralism is his starting point: citizens incur political obligations through their voluntary membership in smaller organizations within the state. "Citizenship . . . is possible only if there are other groups than the state within the state, and it is fully accepted only by joining other groups along with the state" (p. 227). Their activities in these organizations help constitute political activity in the state. And indeed, at its most meaningful such membership requires resistance to the state. Such resistance is the measure of popular consent and obligation: "Only if the possible legitimacy of countergroups with limited claims is recognized and admitted can the state be regarded as a group of consenting citizens" (p. 19). If active dissent is a real option, that is evidence of a participatory, consensual structure, because it suggests that minorities and people not in official positions have genuine access to democratic debate. Furthermore, if dissent is truly possible, then its absence can also indicate consent.

[36]Walzer (1983), p. 82.

Yet even apart from the problems of civil disobedience as consent—the circularity of the fact that the state itself decides whether a claim is "limited" (and hence "legitimate"), the problematic personal cost that resistance may exact from some members but not others[37]—such a conceptualization would require a profound reconceptualization of the state and politics, which Walzer seems neither to foresee nor to desire. Although he sometimes speaks of the activist and potentially transformative qualities of such groups, he also speaks of them as liberal interest groups which, à la David Truman,[38] give members a kind of input and representation that supplements the work of Congress (see, for example, p. 227), and at others they seem like William Whyte's "organizations,"[39] within which claims to individual effectiveness would be disingenuous at best. Walzer also fails to address how these groups would interact with one another within the larger membership of the state, as well as what the mechanisms and processes would be for transforming resistance into positive action or dissent into consent.

Most significantly, Walzer seriously undermines his account by displaying a profound pessimism about political participation. Citizens are in large part Lockean when it comes to politics: "Citizens are driven into action by their particular interests, chiefly economic. . . . They are Lockeian men" (p. 215). Perhaps even more problematically this self-interest does not always, or even generally, cause people to be active in "*politics,* nor are all political questions matters of interest to them unless they have a sense of the whole over and above their sense of themselves as particular persons" (p. 215). Although Walzer believes that "it is upon some such sense of the whole that the idea of citizenship rests," he also appears pessimistic about the possibility that this idea can be realized: "Citizens by and large do not do that work [of political activity] *and probably cannot* (p. 215; emphasis added). They "cannot" not because they are uneducated or feeble-minded but rather because their orientation toward the world as individuals militates against the necessarily communitarian activity of politics.

Understanding Walzer in this way helps us make sense of his work as it is concerned with the tension between what obligation is—its ideal realization—and what is has come to mean in the modern liberal state. This tension derives from a basic contradiction within the mod-

[37]Pateman (1979), pp. 58, 95, makes this first point. As to the latter, one might want to ask whether a single working mother of four can really be expected to go to jail for her beliefs; and if she cannot, can we then truly take her acquiescence as a sign of consent?

[38]Truman (1959).

[39]Whyte (1956).

ern state between "our alienation from all that is public and common"
and "an ideological mask of that alienation or a vain (and possibly
dangerous) fantasy of its transcendence" (pp. 217–18). We are caught
in a circular problem, Walzer seems to say. He decries what we have
become by virtue of the liberal state, namely, possessive individuals
who can no longer survive without that state. He simultaneously rejects the possibility that the liberal state can meet the criteria for obligation, and yet he sees no alternative. While holding onto the ideal,
he believes that we have become a people who can no longer realize
the ideal. There is thus no way to get from here (liberalism) to there
(democracy), or so Walzer seems to maintain. And indeed it is not
entirely clear that he really *wants* to make that journey, for it would
jeopardize (his notion of) the individual. That notion is inherently
antithetical to the concept of community he wishes to promote, but
he refuses to recognize this; or perhaps it would be more accurate to
say that he takes individualism as a given and refuses to pursue the
option of exploring alternate conceptions of the individual. The problem is thus once more seen as inherently irresolvable because of the
way the individual and the community are conceptualized.

Walzer's communitarian orientation should lead him to conclusions
about obligation that problematize consent; but instead he holds on
firmly to consent and attempts to deepen our understanding of how
and when consent can be said to be given. But when forced to face
the unacceptable conclusions that consent theory presents, he retreats
to a communal vision of politics. His resulting inconsistencies, or at
least ambivalence, thus have him critiquing the very ideals he ends
up implicitly embracing while overtly endorsing ideals he is implicitly
compelled to reject. Walzer's attempt to reconcile the individuality of
consent with the sociality of obligational commitment is certainly ad-
mirable and has a number of insights to recommend it. But ultimately
Walzer is drawn into the kinds of contradictory and vague propositions that merely demonstrate an inability to come to terms with,
much less identify, the basic contradiction he has set up.

Alternative Frameworks: Fishkin and Pitkin

Obligation theorists in the third category attempt to transcend the
contradictions of liberal individualism, though it could be argued that
both contemporary theorists I discuss—Hanna Pitkin and James Fishkin—still seek to remain within a liberal framework. Central to both is
a notion of given obligations. In *The Limits of Obligation*, for instance,
Fishkin begins with the assumption that "general obligations" exist as

a facet of our common moral lives. Under what he calls the "principle of minimal altruism," we are obligated to help others in dire need when we can do so at little cost to ourselves. Such general obligations do not depend on consent or other forms of voluntarism but exist independently, as requirements on everyone to anyone. As such they are a product of the requirement of impartiality found in liberalism.[40] At the same time, Fishkin says, calling them obligations threatens the basic structure of individual morality found in liberalism. This leads him to assert that we must "rethink, in a radical way, the obligations of individuals for the solution of large-scale problems" (p. 7).

Although Fishkin's approach to obligation is hardly illustrative of consent theory, the dilemmas by which he is confounded are nevertheless symptomatic of the value presuppositions of liberal theory. Like consent theorists, he reconciles the tension between individuality and community—or, in his framework, individuality and the impartiality that is crucial to making liberal community possible—in favor of the individual at the expense of community. Fishkin is certainly not advocating the dominant mode of liberal ethics; otherwise he would not be able to declare the existence of general obligations. But his deep commitment to liberal principles—he argues that we should not want to reject any of the incompatible assumptions of liberalism, and he attempts to reconcile them—is what causes him to conclude, as in social contract theory and its modern revisions, that the dilemma is inevitable.

Fishkin divides actions into three zones. Those involving already decided questions of right and wrong, which he calls the "zone of moral requirement," clearly set forth obligations. The "zone of supererogation," in contrast, is the gray area where we cannot find moral blame for failure to act. It is delimited by the "cutoff for heroism"; that is, although we can be required to be minimally altruistic, there is a certain point beyond which our actions are no longer obligatory but heroic (for example, a passerby's rescue of a child from a burning building).[41] Finally, the "zone of indifference" involves no moral ques-

---

[40]Fishkin (1982), pp. 7–8. Subsequent references to this source will be cited in the text. General obligations are similar to what other theorists (most obviously Rawls) have called duties, but Fishkin's use of this term indicates a stronger meaning of bondedness than *duty* implies. As I argued previously, Rawls's emphasis on duty takes him away from a liberal framework. This straying may be what causes him to reaffirm liberal individualism through obligations of fair play. But as something that is by definition not consented to, *duty* has extremely weak force in contemporary liberalism. In contrast, not only is a general obligation required, but it is wrong not to discharge it; and one presumes that if we could resolve the problems Fishkin raises, we could even legislate general obligations (for instance, "good Samaritan" laws).

[41]Since this level is heroic, it cannot be obligatory, as an action can belong to only one of these two categories. Fishkin (1982), chap. 2.

tions at all. This zone, Fishkins maintains, is "robust," for a very large number of activities are immune from moral considerations, and the points at which our lives touch on moral questions are relatively few. For instance, it may be generally obligatory not to torture a helpless cat, but eating meat is not a moral issue in most circumstances, according to Fishkin (chaps. 3 and 4).

The main problem to which these assumptions "inevitably" lead us is "the problem of scale." The principle of minimal altruism will always slide down a "slippery slope" past the cutoff for heroism. For instance, Fishkin suggests that five dollars will keep a starving Ethiopian[42] alive for a week. Five dollars is a small, nonheroic amount for most people in the West, so the principle of minimal altruism indicates a general obligation to contribute. But what about the thousands of other starving Ethiopians each of whom could be kept alive for a week for an additional five dollars? And why just one week? Why not several weeks? The problem, Fishkin says, is that the principle of minimal altruism obligates me incrementally for additional five-dollar contributions—because each additional five dollars is in itself a small contribution and nonheroic, and is therefore obligatory under the principle of minimal altruism—until I am sending thousands of dollars to Ethiopia. And even then an additional five dollars could not make that much difference to me, so why not keep contributing until I am as impoverished as the Ethiopian? This presents a seemingly insoluble dilemma about our system of moral reasoning:

> Our usual criteria for differentiating obligations and supererogatory acts of heroism are inadequate for this kind of case. Yet, these same criteria are adequate when smaller numbers are involved. A small number of minor sacrifices would not add up to anything significant. And if the sacrifices were more than insignificant to begin with, then a principle of only minimal altruism would not obligate us to make them. It is only when the numbers are large enough that a principle as weak as merely minimal altruism can entail requirements for sacrifice so great that they add up to heroic proportions.   (p. 7)

Fishkin's example, however, seems unavoidably subject to the "slippery slope" because it focuses on one hypothetical individual abstracted from his or her particular circumstances and society at large. Fishkin and the tradition he writes from misdirect our attention to the obligations of individuals when the dilemma he poses is a social obligation. This produces problems in two opposing directions. The first

---

[42]Actually, Fishkin says "starving African." My alteration may be little more than a token tribute to particularity, but the generalization implicit in "starving African" is one I am uncomfortable with.

involves charging one individual with bearing the responsibility for many people's obligations. It is most likely that if a person in society A has adequate funds to contribute something to society B, whose inhabitants are starving, it is because society A as a whole is more prosperous than society B.[43] If an individual in society A has a general obligation on Fishkin's theory to contribute to ending hunger in Ethiopia, then so do other members of society A. If we look at the obligation in a collective manner—not abstracting the hypothetical person out of social context—the obligation becomes more manageable. In this context the *necessity* for contributing each incremental five dollars diminishes. For example, if $10 million is needed, and there are 100,000 people in the society, then an average contribution of one hundred dollars is all that is needed. From this general formula we would then adjust for individual circumstances; some could afford only one dollar, others could afford one thousand dollars or more. But the point is that when we look at general obligations in a collective manner rather than focusing on the obligations of individuals, the "inevitable" dilemmas Fishkin poses are revealed as created by a specific philosophical orientation that does not reflect the realities of human social life.[44]

In the exact opposite direction, Fishkin's formula absolves the individual from the group's immoral actions through the cutoff for triviality, the level below which the harm I do (by neglecting or even acting in direct violation of a general obligation) is so small as to be completely negligible. Fishkin argues that this cutoff must be preserved to maintain a robust zone of indifference (p. 88). For instance, if I belong to a group of bandits who steal the lunches (which consist of one hundred baked beans each) of one hundred herders,[45] but I take only one-one hundredth of each herder's lunch (as do each of my ninety-nine fellow bandits), then I am not morally responsible

[43]Certainly this might not always be the case. We often find gross differences between the wealthy few and the hungry majority. In these instances, of course, it would be more incumbent on the wealthy few to help their poverty-stricken compatriots, and it is not a coincidence that we view such societies as unjust and the wealthy as taking unfair advantage of the poor.

[44]Thus the possibility that Singer (1979) raises—giving until I am reduced to the situation of a Bengali refugee—is likely an artificial scenario. Fishkin recognizes this when he notes, "We must rethink . . . the limits of individual responsibility for problems that should more appropriately be placed in the sphere of *social* choice" (p. 9). Yet he does not bring this recognition into his analysis. Admittedly his stated purpose is not to show *how* that can be done but to show that it *needs* to be done because of the inevitable breakdown of mutually incompatible elements of our commonly shared moral sphere. Yet ultimately he fails to address even this question because his overly strict adherence to the conflicting principles prevents him from providing a critical understanding of that conflict.

[45]Actually, Fishkin uses the term "tribesmen" as well as the masculine pronoun "he." I have chosen *herders* as a more gender-neutral term.

for the collective harm—one hundred stolen lunches—because I took so little. Fishkin addresses this problem by discriminating between causal responsibility and moral responsibility. He suggests that we consider causal responsibility as the main focus of our inquiry and then base our judgment of moral responsibility on considerations of the causal effects rather than tying moral responsibility automatically to causal responsibility. This "would not permit us morally to condemn a bandit who stole so few baked beans that it added up to an amount below the threshold [although] we could still attribute *causal* responsibility for their disappearance to the bandit" (pp. 94–95). This would allow us to maintain the threshold for triviality. So a bandit who stole only one bean from each herder during the raid would contribute causally to the theft of the lunches but would not be morally blameworthy.

Fishkin's idea of basing judgments of moral responsibility on assessment of causal responsibility and the total effect is important, for it avoids a blind morality that limits itself strictly to rules that disregard context. It enables us to step back from a narrow individualist focus that can obscure the larger picture of harm perpetrated by the bandits. It allows Fishkin to recognize that the herders form a group. In criticizing the assumption that "a person cannot harm a group unless he harms some identifiable individual within it" (p. 95), he thus (rather ambivalently) rejects the conclusion that no moral harm was done to the herders.

But the problem is still intractable for Fishkin. Although moral harm was done, who was it done by, if each bandit remains below the cutoff for triviality? This is where Fishkin claims the problem flounders, where the assumptions of liberalism become irreconcilable. But I maintain that the problem is seen as irreconcilable only because Fishkin does not make the parallel recognition that the bandits, too, form a group. Each knows what the other bandits are doing; each knows the final result is taking one hundred lunches. The fact of collective action and members' knowledge of it transcends individual actions and the responsibility that results. What this points to as well is that a consideration of context is essential to any determination of harm and obligation. Are the herders oppressing the bandits by keeping all the land and starving them into a life of banditry? Do the bandits just think stealing is an easy way to make a living? Or do they simply enjoy keeping the herders in perpetual fear? These and other considerations will help determine the moral blameworthiness of the raiders and the direction of obligation: Who is really harming whom and thus violating the principle of minimal altruism?

Fishkin opens up promising avenues of discussion by making his distinction between causal and moral responsibility, but then he fails to utilize this distinction to resolve the dilemma he defines. His approach conceives of obligation as a linear series of chronologically subsequent occurrences that build upon one another rather than a large picture that one must step back from in order to understand it fully. Just as Fishkin denies the bandits' collective identity, my contributions to famine relief slide down the slippery slope because he treats each incremental five dollars *not* as an increment but as a total contribution. He does not allow us to see the event in context but rather exhibits—and requires—tunnel vision. If we considered the entire picture of my donating money to Ethiopia, we would need to take in all aspects of my context: how much I have given already, my level of income, other more immediate obligations such as caring for my children, and most important, my society and its capacity to give as well as what other members are giving. Such an analysis would involve placing me within a web of relationships and connections, and a stepping back to see more clearly these connections and the network within which I am situated. If we adopt this more contextual approach, the problem of considering multiple aspects of my situation, something liberal theory avoids in its focus on hypothetical individual action, becomes manageable and achievable.

The concept of general obligations presupposes that some obligations are beyond our choice, and the problem for us is to determine *how* to meet our obligations, not *whether* we have an obligation. The former question requires that individuals be situated in their social context. And the question of *how* to meet an obligation helps determine the answer to *how much*—that is, the extent of an obligation for a particular person. In spite of his support of general obligations, it is ultimately Fishkin's orientation to the question of *whether* that produces the so-called inevitability of the slippery slope. For as long as that question remains the primary focus of inquiry into political obligation, our ability to advance our understanding of obligation and to develop our political society will be diminished.

Hanna Pitkin's work on obligation embraces the attention to *how*. She also rejects the strict consensual view of obligation and adopts the notion that certain obligations may be given. But whereas Fishkin's theory falters on the attempt to salvage liberalism's foundational premises, Pitkin sees that these premises are precisely the barrier to a consistent theory of obligation. The reading I propose here goes beyond what is explicit in Pitkin's formulation. These are reasonable conclusions to be drawn from her arguments, but I have drawn them

within the context of my own theoretical perspective.[46] My interpretation reveals an aspect of "Obligation and Consent" that has not been
developed because the assumptions underlying prior interpretations
block perception of it.

Pitkin's claim that Locke's tacit consent is really a theory of "hypothetical consent"—that what truly free, equal, and rational men
would consent to determines what the average unfree, unequal, irrational person, who might consent to all sorts of things, is obligated to[47]
—leads her to conclude that the quality of the government, and not
the actual consent of individual citizens, provides the basis for obligation.[48] Her analysis shifts emphasis from a sphere of negative morality
(no one may) to a positive one (one ought to do X). She takes the
traditional idea of inalienable rights and, in asking *why* certain things,
such as slavery, are prohibited, shifts our focus to the principles underlying these prohibitions. She then suggests that there are values
that must be positively promoted if we are to make sense of inalienable rights. Opportunities for consent and participation are likely indications of a "good" government, one to which citizens owe obligations, and "hypothetical consent" might be a useful theoretical device
for establishing the criteria a legitimate government must meet. But
consent itself is not the basis for legitimacy. Legitimacy, however, is
the basis for obligation.

In this shift lies a fundamental challenge to the liberal epistemology
that frames consent theory. Pitkin takes a philosophy-of-language approach to obligation: humans conduct their lives within the confines
of language, and language determines meaning through the use and
application of rules. These rules set limits not only to the questions
that we can ask and the ideas we can develop but to action as well.
Given the meaning of obligation, authority, and legitimacy in our lan-

[46]In fact this is a modest understatement. I believe there is textual justification for my
reading. Although language is her ostensible concern, in "Obligation and Consent"
Pitkin (1966) indicates that this concern may be a less central aspect of the argument
she says needs to be made. She moves away from that argument to engage in what she
calls the "more limited and less affective" argument about language; the wider meanings she alludes to "would require a discussion of the nature of philosophical puzzlement far beyond the scope of this essay" (p. 46). This "puzzlement," I am suggesting,
constitutes the question of ontology. From this perspective her claims take on a more
consistent and certainly deeper meaning.

[47]Pitkin (1965), p. 996. Pateman also uses the term "hypothetical voluntarism," but
seems to consider it implied consent, a very different meaning from Pitkin's, as we
shall see. See Pateman (1979), chaps. 4 and 6. I find Pitkin's development more useful,
and I follow her lead here.

[48]This is supported to some extent by Dunn (1980), who, while disagreeing with
Pitkin (p. 52, footnote), at the same time recognizes that for Locke, "the practice [to
which one gives consent] must be legitimate itself" (p. 51) for consent to create an
obligation.

guage, she argues, it does not make sense to ask why we should obey a legitimate government. The meaning of "legitimate authority" is that it deserves obedience. Pitkin accepts the questioning of illegitimate government in supporting the right to rebel, even calling it a duty. But consent theory entails a radical questioning of even legitimate government. Its central inquiry is, Why should I ever obey any government at all? The only answer that is acceptable to the consent theorist is that I have agreed or chosen to obey, for then I am still acting as I wish, as obedience becomes an expression of free will. But Pitkin holds that this answer depends on a skewed conception of what it means to be an individual operating within language.[49]

That is, to ask "Why are you ever obligated to obey even legitimate authority?" is "a symptom of philosophical disorder, the product of a philosophical paradox."[50] The questioner misunderstands and misuses language, and thus the question takes place outside the scope of lived reality. While it is therefore acceptable to question particular laws, to determine whether they are in accordance with the goals the government is supposed to meet, overriding challenges to legitimate government (when it is acting legitimately) are not acceptable. Certainly, she says, such challenges are possible; but philosophers should not be spending so much time paying attention to such invalid questions. Or, perhaps more precisely, she is suggesting that the fact that philosophy does pay so much attention to such questions reflects that philosophy itself is disordered.

In this I contend that Pitkin is talking not just about language but about the ontological and epistemological framework of consent theory. That is, she is not advancing a merely semantic argument, or even one about accepted practices; rather, she is arguing that the *foundation* on which the question rests—not the question per se—constitutes the problem. Her concern with language can be taken in part as an entry point for the dissection of the ontology of consent theory and its unveiling as faulty and misrepresentative. Indeed, Pitkin points out that "a concern with language can stimulate or support" this larger ontological issue, for the concept of the individual as an

---

[49]Flathman holds that Pitkin goes too far in this claim. He asserts that one cannot get from the premises of the centrality of language itself to political obligation without some intervening premises that justify a specifically political form of society. That is, "obligation" and "political obligation," while not mutually exclusive, demonstrate important differences that Pitkin does not take into account. Political obligation operates from the premise of a state; and the state, according to (at least most) liberal theories, by its nature continually presents a potential danger to citizens' freedom. This is a significant concern, and not one to be reconciled by the conflation of language, obligation, and political obligation. As should be clear, however, I believe that the interpretation I give of Pitkin reveals that this objection ignores her epistemological argument.

[50]Pitkin (1966), p. 46.

"ineluctably *separate* unit" is, according to Pitkin, the ontological foundation for consent theory and its primary basic flaw. Rejecting the
liberal atomistic vision of humans, Pitkin argues that people are embedded in social relations that shape the context for consent, which
indeed set the parameters for its meaning:

> In truth, there is something profoundly wrong with the consent theo-
> rist's picture of man. Every free, separate, adult, consenting individual
> was first shaped and molded by his parents and (as we say) society. It is
> only as a result of their influence that he becomes the particular person
> he does become, with his particular interests, values, desires, language
> and obligations. The only thing truly separate about us is our bodies; our
> selves are manifestly social.[51]

And in *Wittgenstein and Justice* she argues: "We become persons, become who we are, only by internalizing (some of) the norms, standards, and patterns of our society. We do not agree contractually to do
so; we grow into them. Thus our concepts of promises and contracts
are learned, not chosen. And even individual self-interest is very
much a social product, taking quite different forms in different times
and places."[52]

The faulty ontology of consent theory has epistemological dimensions as well, for only an individual who did not understand that
language is a "model of membership,"[53] only an individual who abstracted the self from social context could question obligations to a
legitimate government, could understand the term *obligation* in the
way described by the social contract. It is because of basic human
connectedness that the unconditional, noncontextual challenge to legitimate authority is philosophically disordered. It is not simply that
the problem of consent theory lies in a faulty articulation of a basically
sound principle; the principle itself must be unsound because it is
based on a faulty ontology. Consent theory does not merely use the
language incorrectly; its construction of human relationships and of
social life is incorrect, misguided, is itself the source of the disorder. If
we begin from a premise of connectedness and relationality, however, as Pitkin seems to argue, it becomes apparent that a different
concept of obligation unfolds. Although it is certainly still possible to
imagine a construction such as the state of nature, it is difficult (if not
impossible) to attribute serious consideration to it as a model for an
actual, lived form of life. Since political theory supposedly describes

[51]Ibid.
[52]Pitkin (1972), p. 199.
[53]Ibid., p. 194.

and prescribes our political and social life, its adoption of such a construction is deeply problematic.

On this view, the confusion would lie not in the notion that the question "Why am I ever obligated to obey the law?" is not allowable, or even possible—for these would be matters of language—but only in that it is (philosophically, politically) unimportant, an artificially constructed dilemma made possible by particular institutionalized social relations. What we need, Pitkin says, is "an account of why the philosopher is driven to ask the question in the first place,"[54] and of why the question is granted such prominence in philosophical discourse.

Of course, neither this nor Pitkin's argument leads, as some critics have suggested, to the conclusion that we should never ask questions about our obligations. After all, premises of connectedness can still give way to "illegitimate" forms of life, or societies with evil governments. Questioning our obligations can provide the necessary function of helping us evaluate the merits of a government so we may refuse our obedience and compliance to pernicious laws and evil regimes. Furthermore, it can lead us to considerations of the general needs and character of humans and social relations, the character of our institutions and our social life in general; it can help us understand and respond to our lives together as social and political human beings. That consent theory produces answers that belie the realities of these relations does not in itself make the endeavor totally worthless, and it is not Pitkin's intent to say that this is the case. Rather, her point is to reformulate inquiries into such matters, to redirect our efforts away from attempts to solve the presumed paradox the question poses and toward a realization of what the question suggests about the theories that ask it.

This perspective helps prevent reductive misreadings of theories like Pitkin's; for her solution, in fundamentally challenging the assumptions of consent theory, seems to give a relatively weak role to human choice, and at the most drastic level it may make us vulnerable to the dangers of totalitarianism. The criteria of "good" government can be controlled and manipulated. Who is to decide what is good? By overtly reconciling the problem of political obligation in favor of the need for authority, Pitkin may seem to threaten our common conceptions of freedom, of democracy, and even of the individual.

---

[54]Pitkin (1965), p. 49. I anticipate my argument here; for this account, it may be argued, is precisely what object relations theory tries to provide, as I show in subsequent chapters. Indeed, it is significant that Pitkin chooses the word "driven," particularly in view of her later psychoanalytic work on Machiavelli (Pitkin 1984).

Yet if Pitkin seems to present the potential threat of the totalitarian menace, perhaps that is a problem of perspective. In all these years of liberal political theorizing we may have been looking at social relations through the wrong end of the telescope. If we turn it around, we will gain a new perspective that broadens our view and includes a wider variety of experience. By rejecting out of hand many of the assumptions of consent theory, she makes important advances in our understanding of political obligation. In the rejection of abstract individualism lies the potential for a recasting of the terms in which the problem of obligation is described. We may not wish to resolve the problem of obligation by a Burkean claim to preserve the status quo, or by a Hegelian absolutism; but perhaps we do need to loosen our grasp on the assumptions of liberalism about the priority of freedom and the idea that individuals are free, equal, and unsituated. In loosening this grasp we become able to explore obligation from a different perspective—the perspective of a given, the perspective that community and individual freedom are not mutually antagonistic but are mutually involved in constituting each other's meaning.

Women and Obligation: Contemporary Replay

The theories of Fishkin and Pitkin are interesting to feminist analysis because they challenge the dominant liberal vision while ostensibly attempting to work within liberalism. Both try to bring together the apparently antagonistic forces of individual and community by attempting to redraw each. Both also may ultimately fail to sustain that tension. In the end, despite his claims to the contrary, Fishkin at least implicitly appears to abandon general obligations by declaring the tension too insurmountable within liberalism, whereas Pitkin appears to abandon liberalism by perhaps dismissing the tension too quickly. Neither fully acknowledges the epistemological reconceptualization their arguments require. Indeed, if they were able to acknowledge more explicitly the profound alteration in thinking about individuals, community, liberalism, and obligation that their arguments implicitly advocate, they would find more satisfying answers to the dilemmas they so thoughtfully identify. Yet both theorists present an alternative approach to the problems posed by liberal obligation theory. In the process they provide an entrée to a feminist theory of obligation, a link between the mainstream theoretical approach to obligation and the critical strategies of feminist theory, by opening up spaces within liberal obligation theory for problematizing and questioning the conceptual categories those theories utilize.

In contrast, the contemporary consensual theories of obligation in the first two groups of theorists I identified in this chapter demonstrate a severe tension, comparable to that found in original social contract theory, between the natural freedom and equality of individuals and the equally compelling givenness of authority and political society. The basic contradiction between the assertion that humans are inherently individualistic on the one hand and that they are dependent on social institutions and practices for the satisfaction of their individual desires on the other is fundamental to contemporary consent theories as well as to their critics. This aspect reveals specifically gendered dimensions on several levels, beginning with the fundamental discrepancy between public and private that is both symptomatic and causative of the theories' atomistic and abstract notion of human beings. Although this concept of individuals provided a source of many of the problems of social contract theory, and even though some contemporary theorists ostensibly criticize it, it nevertheless defines the ontological framework of contemporary obligation theory. Theorists are so concerned to preserve individuals' control over their obligations that they ironically develop devices which, while apparently asserting individual sovereignty, in reality merely camouflage the degree to which such obligations are not in fact voluntary at all.

Yet it is not the deep acceptance of these assumptions per se that causes this paradox to persist. Theories such as Simmons's which reject outright the need to accommodate authority through obligation are just as flawed as those that accept and mask it. Rather, the problem lies in the way authority and freedom, community and individual are conceptualized. The ways they are defined, their ontological and epistemological assumptions, give rise to a concept of human beings that ensures that only consent appears to resolve the dilemma. So theorists struggle to create an image of consenting citizens even at the cost of internal theoretical contradiction and political hypocrisy. This construction of a "resolution" does not resolve anything; indeed, it only makes the dilemma irresolvable.

Thus, Pateman ostensibly recognizes the faultiness of the liberal ontology of abstract individualism and argues for democratic community, but then proceeds to utilize a concept of consent that operates at least in part from that very same individualism. By urging "full" consent through her invocation of Rousseau, she inadequately addresses the fact that the context of virtue makes consent at best problematic. Rawls similarly tries to create a community of justice, but in seeking to bind citizens completely to the state he begins from a premise of radical and abstract individualism. Because this premise threatens the universality of justice, however, he creates a mechanism through which these individuals hypothetically consent to his two principles of justice and then actually obey them through a "natural duty." Flathman, who perhaps demonstrates the least severe tension, also recognizes community and situates individuals within the social context of language; but his theory, too, in its emphasis on individual assessment of "good reasons," presupposes an individualism that makes obligation inherently problematic. Citizens either obey out of habit or else must engage in a formalized Socratic discourse to provide "good reasons," with the at least implied understanding that there are definite, even predetermined limits on what kinds of reasons count as good ones. Walzer's inability to let go of liberal individualism even in the face of his own explicit critique of it causes him to abandon the notion of community which he otherwise argues is so central to political life and political theory.

I have suggested that these problems cannot be resolved in the terms of the current discourse. The relationship between freedom and obligation has been miscast in mutually exclusive terms because of the concept of the individual from which it works. As long as individualism informs our understanding of individuals, the tension between individuals and government will always be seen as a conflict, even a contradiction, and this contradiction cannot, by definition, be resolved. But even more particularly I maintain that the apparent irresolvability of the contemporary dilemma can be traced, at least in part, to the same epistemological gender bias demonstrated in my discussions of Hobbes, Locke, and Rousseau. Certainly, unlike these three theorists, all of whom make explicit if infrequent and rather unflattering references to women, contemporary obligation theorists rarely even use the word *woman*. Hence, the "problem of women" does not appear to surface very often in this literature. The ostensible reason, presumably, is that modern theorists include women in their usage of *citizen* and even *man*. A popular claim in the early 1970s amidst the burgeoning women's liberation movement, was that since women could vote (despite the fact that they could not in fact vote in a number of supposedly democratic countries when many of these theories were written), all of the arguments of democratic theory could and did apply to women just as much as they applied to men. Hence the term *citizen* could be used in a gender-neutral sense.

Yet this ostensible equality—the formal equality that is the hallmark of liberalism—denies and displays both a contingent and a structural sexism. Tussman's characterization of the non–fully participating citizens of both genders as "child-brides" supports the at least implicit notion that women are considered by contemporary theorists to be incapable of true participation in the social contract, and that such inability is nothing to be alarmed about. At the more empirical level, one can argue that a myriad of restrictions on women's lives stemming from legislative action and inaction—restrictions on abortion, the lack of state-funded child care, economic and employment discrimination, erosion of affirmative action, the rarity of adequate maternity leave and its noninclusion in social security and other employment benefits, the even greater rarity of any paternity leave at all—serve a masculinist state's interests in keeping women totally occupied with the concerns of the private sphere and hence de facto safely eliminated from the political realm.

Affirmitive action may be seen as one attempt to recognize and redress this situation by equalizing opportunity in substantive ways; and it is significant that a major objection to it is that it interferes with the market. Thus Allan Bakke charged "reverse discrimination" on the basis that he was more qualified—defined as having better test scores and grades—than minority candidates granted admission to medical school over him.[55] "Equal opportunity" is violated by the failure to allow the market free rein: but whose opportunity? whose equality?

In a more general sense, the phenomenon of unequal starting points or bargaining positions raises serious problems for consent theory that go beyond gender to race and class. Since liberal consent theory works from stated premises of formal equality, gross substantive inequality will ensure political inequality, not only in political voice in determining the laws but also in the ways the laws apply to people. As Rousseau argued (although he did not see the application of this principle to gender or race), laws apply unequally to those who are unequal. Because equality is defined in the liberal contract in formal terms, this inequality can never be redressed. The dominant political group has already been able to structure social institutions, as well as conceptual definitions, to benefit itself, and it will always be ahead as long as freedom, equality, and obligation are defined abstractly and negatively because such conceptions leave it to the worse-off individual to pull herself up by her own bootstraps.

Yet the problem also has specifically gendered dimensions that extend beyond questions such as why Tussman chose the "child-bride" imagery and why Rawls asserts that the people in the original position are heads of families, and specifically male heads of patriarchal nuclear families.[56] These assertions, one could argue, reveal only con-

---

[55]*Regents of the University of California* v. *Allan Bakke,* 438 U.S. 265 (1978).
[56]Rawls (1971), p. 128. See Okin (1989), pp. 94–96, for a discussion of this point.

tingently sexist values which could be altered without challenging the structure of the theories. Yet such seemingly limited phenomena betray a more systematic sexism in modern obligation theory, one that is again structured into the definition of obligation, and which once again turns on the central assumptions of the public-private split. For the denial of the relevance to political obligation of the activities of the private sphere, such as child care, affective relations and production, and reproduction in all its variety, at least implicitly indicates a masculinist ontological and epistemological framework.

This is most obvious in the second group of theorists discussed in this chapter, those who seek to establish alternate foundations for obligation but strive to remain within a liberal voluntarist framework. Walzer's notion of community depends on the idea of shared conceptions—of justice, and hence obligation, which he sees as deriving in part from justice—but the relevant question is, Who shares them? Not only does the power of white patriarchy make the voices of women and other excluded groups practically silent; not only does it exclude women from the circle of sharers whose conceptions count; but also as I argued earlier about Flathman, certain conceptions, or forms of life, may be so deeply entrenched that we cannot envision any other options.[57] In discussing obligation as a practice, Flathman fails to include practices of the private sphere in his calculations; the "good reasons" approach involves the assessment of public criteria only. His invocation of "good reasons" fails to recognize the degree to which the criteria for determining which reasons are good already betrays a bias toward masculinism in a society in which public ideology is defined by male domination.

This type of epistemological hegemony is one of the strongest and yet most troubling aspects of structural sexism because it predetermines the silencing of marginalized groups, such as women, and systematically excludes their voices from the realm of political philosophy. For instance, whereas Walzer argues that democracy is incompatible with the family because it brings out particularism and favoritism, he also takes the family as a model for the reconciliation of free choice and social embeddedness. The basis for romantic love, and hence the modern family, he asserts, is free and equal choice. Yet such free choice between equals also entails a range of obligations which are not explicitly taken on: "Though I freely choose my spouse, I don't choose my spouse's relatives, and the further obligations of marriage are always culturally and not individually determined. Nevertheless . . . the man and the woman are not only free but equally

---

[57]See Okin (1989) pp. 62–68, for similar arguments.

free. The feeling must be mutual, it takes two to tango, and so on."[58] This description of free choice existing in a context of social relationships which entail bonds and obligations not of an individual's own making is a rich and complex advance over both the radical individualism of consent theory and the simplistic communitarianism of many participatory democratic approaches. Indeed, it might locate Walzer in the third group of theorists with Pitkin and Fishkin.

Yet Walzer's account is simultaneously blind to the fact that women are generally not in fact equally free because of social pressures to marry and reproduce. It ignores social limitations on women's options that often make marriage a means of escaping parental domination and economic hardship. And it denies the systematic cultural undermining of women's self-worth which results in many women's "choosing" to remain in abusive relationships. His characterization of "the family as a kind of welfare state, which guarantees to all its members some modicum of love, friendship, generosity, and so on, and which taxes its members for the sake of the guarantee," dismisses domestic violence against both women and children. Similarly, his remarks on "dating" and laws against adultery as "efforts to defend social goods: the 'honor' of a woman and her family, for example, or the value of marriage or of the exchange or the alliance that marriage embodies"[59] rely on, and yet completely obscure, the treatment of women as property on which such conceptions depend.

Walzer's masculinist bias is thus revealed as an offspring of that found in early social contract theory—a bias that forms a fundamental framework of epistemological assumptions and yet is simultaneously denied and obscured on the more conscious level of theoretical prescription. If the "liberal family" that Walzer describes is a model for making sense of this attempt to bring out the complex interweaving of choice and relationship, then Walzer's notion of obligation is deeply patriarchal. The tortuous contradictions of liberalism are clearly revealed: it claims freedom and equality for all, but this claim is in fact premised on the unfreedom and inferiority of many. Perhaps one reason Walzer is so ambiguous and ambivalent in his thoughts on obligation is precisely the fact that his framework of assumptions is fundamentally elitist and exclusive, in contradiction to his declared "solidarity with the oppressed."[60] Recognizing this would force him either to revise his theory or to acknowledge his assumptions.

This sort of ambivalence similarly highlights Rawls's theory. I earlier argued that it was Rawls's refusal to let go of voluntarism that

---

[58]Walzer (1983), p. 235.
[59]Ibid., p. 238, 237.
[60]Walzer (1970), p. 190.

created contradictions for his theory and produced a notion of political obligation that was problematic, if not superfluous. The question then becomes why he gave up consistency, if not for a desire to hold on to a liberal conception of the individual. He similarly wishes to hold on to liberal conceptions of family and contract. As numerous critics have pointed out, gender is a problematic category for Rawls. His silence on gender in the original position leads to almost contradictory conclusions that gender is invisible and at the same time decided, if not overdetermined.[61] Rawls both desexualizes and disembodies people in the original position and yet assumes that sexual difference—and sex itself—exists in his reliance on families not only to reproduce future generations (the just savings principle would otherwise be unnecessary) but to produce people in this and every generation with a "sense of justice."

This approach is revealed to have specifically gendered dimensions when we recall that the liberal family is patriarchal and that Rawls makes no attempt to challenge, let alone change, this family structure. Rawls's identification of people in the original position as heads of households, his remarks about housewives, and other indications critics have noted suggest that the "individual" Rawls relies on is specifically male. His notion and treatment of the family disallows for justice within families, which would require at least an assessment of the sexual division of labor.[62] From the perspective of such an assessment, however, his notion of justice is structurally gender biased. Certainly his conception of justice is incompatible with the idea of fairness that must be adopted by women in their historical position as caretakers and nurturers of children and other family members. The notion of distributive justice utilized by Rawls is of questionable relevance to a "maternal practitioner" who will most likely be required to attend to need rather than rights in "distributing resources." Indeed, the assumption of Rawlsian justice that resources are finite, fixed, and quantifiable is itself highly problematic from the perspective of mothering.[63]

This systematic obliteration of women's historical experience similarly pervades the methodology Rawls adopts. The disembodied view from nowhere of the original position raises the question whether there are people behind the veil of ignorance, much as Hobbes's metaphor of the mushrooms raises questions about whether people really populate the state of nature. Although both seek to develop principles to rule humans, Rawls envisions man as disem-

---

[61]See Pateman (1988), p. 43; Okin (1989), p. 108.
[62]See Young (1990), p. 21; Pateman (1988), pp. 41–43; Okin (1989) chap. 5.
[63]See Young (1990), pp. 24–30; Ruddick (1989).

bodied reason just as Hobbes envisions him as machine. As Seyla Benhabib holds, an abstracted "generalized other" is the only concept of humanity that can operate in the original position. Such conceptualizations systematically deny space to women's historical construction of individuals within affective relationships as "concrete others." The abstraction of the original position denies the concrete realities of "affective production."[64]

Thus Rawls's method—of individualism and rational choice—itself betrays a masculinist bias. But according to Susan Okin, what is even more puzzling is that Rawls actually fails to meet the appropriate theoretical criteria for rational choice. Indeed, she claims that empathy and care are central to the workings of his theoretical mechanism.[65] Although I disagree with Okin's claims for empathy in Rawls—the point of the veil of ignorance is to ensure that self-interested reasoning in the original position will result in decisions that may *appear* benevolent or empathetic once the veil is lifted but are not themselves motivated by empathy behind the veil—her critique of Rawls's rational choice is powerful and shifts our focus. The question is no longer why Rawls insists on utilizing rational choice and ignoring qualities of care that have been central to women's experience but rather, given that Rawls does include care, why he insists on calling it rational choice. This shift parallels my question about obligation: Why does Rawls insist on fair play when those who do not accept optional benefits and receive only unavoidable benefits are still bound to obey the laws through natural duty? What purpose does it serve to hold on to voluntarist obligation?

One answer is that Rawls, like Walzer, wants to retain liberal individualism even when doing so problematizes the rest of his theory. Why they are so reluctant to let go of liberal individualism is, of course, another and larger question. But by understanding the intellectual framework of obligation that these theories reveal, we see that the claim with which I opened these chapters makes more sense. That is, the oppositional definition of individual and community, freedom and obligation, which characterizes liberal obligation theory itself betrays masculinism because it obliterates women's history. The values and methods of consent theory reveal their structural gender bias in a dependency on this obliteration. I argued that Hobbes, Locke, and Rousseau could construct a public realm of male consent only at the price of a private realm of female disempowerment. Their notions of political obligation and contract were thus sustainable only if

---

[64]Benhabib (1987), p. 90; Ferguson (1984).
[65]See Okin (1990).

women's historical experience was made invisible to the public eye. This same systematic and structural gender bias informs contemporary notions in the often counterintuitive ferocity with which theorists hold on to the public persona of the liberal individual and deny the aspects of human life that continue to be relegated to the private sphere, the sphere of the so-called inessential—the sphere of women.

Simmons, for instance, denies that any concept of relationship, such as familial relations, produces obligation. Although certain relationships of benefaction may generate obligations, as I discussed earlier, it is clearly not the relationship per se but the transaction of benefits that grounds the obligation. And such transaction, as I showed, must have a voluntary character, according to Simmons. Children therefore do not have obligations to their parents, for instance, because they did not consent to be born to them. Or even if they do "accept," parents' provision of benefits is still a shaky ground for obligation because "the parents have themselves *created* the needs these benefits satisfy (by creating the child who has them)." There may be other reasons why children might choose to or should care for their parents, but they are not required to do so via obligation unless they engage in some consensual practice, such as actively accepting "significant" benefits under the principle of fair play. In contrast, parents' obligations to children stem from the consensual nature of the marriage relationship and reproduction—not only "the voluntary acceptance of responsibility that sometimes accompanies procreation" but "the special responsibilities as well for even the accidental or unwanted consequences of our actions." The degree to which such relationships entail obligations, then, stems from the voluntary factors at work in the relationship. Simmons categorically denies "that moral obligations are generated by mutual caring (love, friendship, etc.)." The "care" account of obligation is flawed because humans have "no firm control" over feelings. "It is precisely when feelings have died that the point of ascribing moral obligations seems to come most clearly into focus. Where love or friendship flourishes, individuals give of themselves without any feeling of obligation or moral complusion."[66] Thus care and obligation, feeling and reason, are once again clearly delineated, indeed dichotomized.

Simmons's uncompromising—and, to my mind, most consistent and accurate—presentation of consent theory shows that its foundational premises require the rejection of a concept of obligation as embedded in a preexisting network of personal and social relationships. Yet it is precisely for this reason that consent theory provides an inad-

[66]Simmons (1981), pp. 11, 8, 9.

equate account of human life. Practices such as child care and affective production, which are not particularly contractual except in the
most general and disingenuous senses, are ignored by liberal obligation theories. Other practices such as marriage are viewed as completely contractual without a simultaneous recognition of the nonconsensual and even coercive elements of such practices. Thus Rawls can
talk of the family in contractual terms and justify the head-of-house-
hold concept of citizenship. In his discussion of fair play, Rawls, like
Simmons, asserts that benefits must be actively taken, and he rejects
the idea that they can be passively received. Therefore relationship,
needs, dependency, and affection, all of which might generate a fab-
ric or network of benefits that cannot easily be avoided but make life
richer or more livable, have nothing to do with obligation proper.
Walzer, while making specific acknowledgment of family, the private
sphere, and the "woman question," locates his vision of politics in
such an implicitly patriarchal view that women's experiences are
made virtually invisible even as they are supposedly acknowledged.
Flathman's "good reasons" approach could be made to work for families; members could interact relationally and together discuss what
reasons are valid for obeying or disobeying parents, honoring or alter-
ing commitments to children. But the criteria for reasons as located
within existing language games and forms of life reveal a covert orientation toward the patriarchal status quo.

Pateman admits that a focus on consent can be problematic for
women. In her 1985 afterword to *The Problem of Political Obligation*, she
criticizes her own previous work for ignoring the dimensions that
women's experience contributes to the need to rethink obligation fundamentally. And in *The Sexual Contract* she explicitly argues that the
social contract rests on a prior and patriarchal sexual contract wherein
women supposedly trade their freedom for male protection. In the
rejection by Locke and others of father patriarchy as a basis for political right through the establishment of the social contract, Pateman
argues that the foundation of patriarchy was not eliminated but
merely transformed into "fraternal patriarchy," whereby the "brother-
hood" of men as a group rules over women. Contract is thus "the
means through which modern patriarchy is constituted," and the sexual contract founds civil right.[67]

Particularly within the Lockean framework that informs contemporary consent theory, the idea of property in the person enables con-
tractarians to assert that those who are in subordinate positions are
there by choice; and since their positions are a product of choice, they

[67]Pateman (1988), pp. 2, 108.

have expressed their freedom rather than limited it by joining in the employment, slave, or sexual contract. This myth of contract must be preserved because it allows liberalism to safeguard the subordination of nonwhites and women. Thus "the 'individual' is a patriarchal category."[68] The individual as owner of property in the person who can contract out that property—and, indeed, finds meaning as an individual only through such contracts—is a conception that derives from institutionalized relations of oppression disguised as freedom. Accordingly, modern political societies based on social contracts do not merely exclude women and people of color but indeed preclude them as conjugal or sexual right becomes a central source of men's political power.

Pateman's arguments truly challenge the positivist underpinnings of liberalism. But they simultaneously problematize her earlier remarks about obligation and her advocacy of Rousseau's social contract as a model for an egalitarian participatory democracy. Rousseau, as we have seen, is a primary perpetrator of the sexual contract as the basis for the social contract. Sophie's sexual and social subordination to Emile is essential for the discovery of the general will. These insights, however, do more than suggest that Pateman's earlier arguments do not go far enough; rather, they require a profound shift in the epistemological framework used to evaluate consent theory. In spite of her excellent critique of liberalism and consent theory, Pateman seems to fall back on similar solutions. Perhaps the reason is that she is caught in the same epistemological framework as liberalism. Or indeed, to the degree that she utilizes an alternate epistemology, this is never explicitly recognized, and even implicitly fought against, with the result that she is subject to some (though not by any means all, and perhaps not even to the same degree) of the same concerns for which she so rightly and effectively criticizes liberal theory.[69] The question that Pateman seeks to address is, How do we get real choice? Thus, in spite of her critique she implicitly accepts the liberal premise and seeks a more consistent solution. In contrast, the question that needs to be asked is, If obligation, authority, and community are really so necessary to human life that even the most radical consent theorists slip them in as unspoken assumptions, why is it that the theorists ostensibly claim such an important role for choice? And why is choice constructed so abstractly? Although choice is extremely important to feminists, what choice means needs to be reformulated.

Of course the point of the foregoing critique is not to make a simplistic endorsement of women's historical lack of choice as to their "obligations." Rather, it is to highlight the necessity for all humans to

[68]Ibid., p. 168.
[69]Hirschmann (1990). See also our exchange in Pateman and Hirschmann (1992).

take care of the activities traditionally assigned to women which do not neatly fit the contract paradigm. Indeed, in institutionalizing the public-private dichotomy and assigning women to such activities— and conversely restricting such activities to "women's sphere"—these "obligations" are doubly coercive for women. That is, to cover over the fact of their coercion, social contract theory denies that women have the capacity to engage in consent. This conveniently frees such theorists from having to worry about the fact that women have not consented and allows them to sweep the entire issue under the rug.

Because the public-private dichotomy so prominent in the theories of Hobbes, Locke, and Rousseau does not seem to be overtly incorporated into modern obligation theory, it may be more difficult to discuss the role of women in the theories of Flathman or Simmons or Tussman. But the dichotomy provides a fundamental context and basis for these theories, an assumption so deeply embedded in them that it requires no overt mention. The greater subtlety of the split merely establishes its greater perniciousness. In construing obligation in such a way that the concept of given obligation is an oxymoron, consent theory effectively obliterates from theoretical discussion the aspects of life that are not so clear-cut, and it imposes an exaggerated and even false clarity on the rest. A feminist analysis reveals that this dichotomous situation, like the public-private split itself, is a function of and perpetuates a specifically masculinist ontology and epistemology and produces theories that reflect gender-biased values.

That a feminist theoretical approach is needed to conduct this deeper analysis of the problems of liberal obligation theory is significant, just as it is not coincidental that one important challenge to the relevance of consent theory lies in women's experience. This claim may best be supported at this point in my argument by an example. A woman is raped and becomes pregnant. She does not want this child, but abortion is not available to her, for any number of reasons: perhaps she is very young and is ignorant that such a thing is possible; perhaps it is against her religious and moral beliefs; perhaps she cannot afford one, and public funding is not permitted; perhaps abortion is not legally available (contra Hobbes, I do not consider a "back-alley butcher" as constituting a real choice because the option is so life-threatening). Let us also assume that adoption is not a possibility either, again for a variety of reasons; in earlier days, orphanages were deplorable institutions, and perhaps this woman would feel such abandonment to be immoral, that two wrongs don't make a right. Today, given contractual adoptions and surrogate motherhood, infants of color and handicapped infants have a more difficult time being adopted than white, physically and mentally healthy infants and thus may suffer considerably from being put up for adoption. Or perhaps, as women in Carol Gilligan's abortion study explained, giving the baby up for adoption would be so painful as to ruin the woman's life.[70]

We would have to agree that in this case the woman is not free to choose. She did not choose to engage in sexual intercourse, so we cannot even say that her actions implied consent to a possible pregnancy (although the patriarchal dictum that a woman who was raped was "asking for it" tries to get around the problem through this transparent device). Certainly I do not mean to imply that all choice is foreclosed for all women; women have had numerous options throughout history, indeed it is doubtful that women could have survived without some choices being available to them. But it is also necessary to acknowledge that, at least when compared with men's options, women's have often not been of their own creation; rather, they are frequently loopholes in patriarchy rather than windows of opportunity in a sexually egalitarian world. And certainly the particular history and possibilities of women's lives generally foreclose the unconditional if not radical choice that liberal theory demands for male subjects. So although my construction of the example in this choiceless way may seem to resemble the common philosophical tactic of creating an abstracted situation (the archetypal man on the desert island), it should not be considered in this light. If I have not made my example concrete by focusing on particular historical, racial, and social descriptions, it was not to obscure realities but to highlight the fact that a myriad of factors can limit or remove choices—and have done so—for women of many different backgrounds. The circumstances I have suggested are an apt description of the actual situation of many women of different racial, historical, and social experiences who have been faced with unsought and unwanted pregnancies. That it is not necessarily a description of all women in all conditions is not a sufficient objection.

Hence, back to the example. During the course of her pregnancy, as the fetus becomes a viable being the woman feels it move and comes to think of it as a person as well as a part of herself.[71] When it is born, she comes to love the child, and so she meets her "obligations" of caring for the child with less hostility than she feared she would feel, and perhaps even a measure of satisfaction. Does this constitute a case of being obligated against one's will? She was not free to choose her situation. But would we say she is unfree? If she loves the child, then we would not say that she is enslaved (bound against her will) to it or its upbringing. Yet this love cannot negate the absence of choice and free will. It is still true that she did not choose

[70]Gilligan (1982), chaps. 3–4.
[71]See Rich (1976).

to have the baby and may (indeed, very likely will) suffer because of this unsought responsibility. And certainly one does not "choose" to love. The question of freedom and free will would seem to be of questionable relevance to this woman's situation; at the least, freedom is not the primary conceptual issue. Another concept and framework are far more important to this experience and serve as the operative concept for her actions: the givenness of obligation itself.

I must here suppress the desire to qualify this last sentence—explaining what I mean by "given" and how that is different from "natural," highlighting the social construction of this givenness through the social and historical construction of femininity, reminding the reader that my use of the terms *feminism* and *masculinism* operates from this social construction of gender—because such qualifications will keep me from my argument and should become apparent anyway as that argument unfolds. The gender-related grounding for these concepts of obligation and choice is a theme to be pursued in the remainder of this book, and it is one that is, to put it mildly, controversial, for it establishes a set of difficult issues and questions that challenge political theorists' fundamental understanding and construction of obligation as a political concept in the modern world. Yet these challenges are the necessary outcome of the foregoing analysis. If the entrenchment in liberal theory of the public-private dichotomy guarantees the obliteration of women's experience from our ordinary-language understanding of political obligation, and if gender bias relates to the very epistemological framework that defines the conceptual terminology in which theories operate, then any analysis of the "problem of women" within the boundaries of existing theories of obligation will be able to go only so far. Such analyses will have only limited depth by definition, because our conceptual vocabulary is itself biased. And if it is specifically women's exclusion that founds these frameworks, then a feminist analysis is required if we are to understand fully the epistemological dimensions of liberal obligation theory. Indeed, an entire feminist theoretical framework—a methodology, an epistemology, an ontology, perhaps even to some degree a language—must be developed so we may articulate how women's experience challenges liberal theory. By developing a specifically feminist analysis of the ontology of liberal obligation theory, and how that creates its epistemology, we will be able to gain a much deeper and more comprehensive understanding of the structural sexism of liberal obligation theory. Through this understanding we will not only gain a better sense of what is problematic about political obligation but perhaps understand how to remedy its deep-rooted flaws as well and construct a new, feminist theory of obligation.

CHAPTER THREE

The Argument
from Psychology

THE PROBLEMATIC relation of women to consent suggests that liberal theories of political obligation themselves need to be fundamentally rethought. The structural sexism of liberal political theory reveals a particular ontological and epistemological framework that is premised on women's exclusion from politics, their representation as less than human, and an entire construction of gender as a dualistic hierarchy of male over female. And yet the gender bias of these structures cannot be fully revealed as long as we remain within the boundaries of liberal political theories of obligation, for their frameworks are designed to mask the very assumptions from which they operate. More specifically, the notion that concepts such as natural freedom and equality are assumptions, as opposed to objective truths, is obscured.

Feminist psychology and psychoanalytic theory are particularly helpful in the work of analyzing the structural sexism of liberal obligation theory, for they reveal "how . . . gender and sexuality develop and are reproduced in the individual and thereby in society."[1] And yet gender psychology can be dangerously subject to misinterpretation and misreading. I believe this problem stems from the empirical science dimensions of psychology. At the empirical level, gender psychology could be used to affirm that women are different from men, and since men have written most of the political theory, the values and perspectives that reflect women's "difference" have been left out. This literature could thus provide insight into some of the ways in which "natural man" resonates with the notion of male psychosexual

[1]Chodorow (1989), p. 178.

development. In this light, structural sexism has a concrete component.

This empirical aspect of gender psychology is deemphasized in the present work, however, in favor of a deeper level of interpretation and symbolization. Psychology and psychoanalytic theory provide valuable insights into why certain so-called masculine characteristics—characteristics historically associated with men, but that pertain neither necessarily, exclusively, nor universally to any given flesh-and-blood male—dominate in western cultures, the cultures within which consent and social contract theory were created and still thrive. It is increasingly clear that "natural man" is not the universal creature theorists such as Hobbes and Locke assumed him to be. Works from anthropology and sociology reveal significant differences in other cultures. The question then becomes, Why has our culture embraced this particular notion of man? How does it draw from specifically western forms of masculinity? Why has this masculinity gained such ascendancy? What are the ramifications of these characteristics for politics and political theory?

Thus feminist psychoanalytic and psychological theory as I use the terms are less empirical sciences than interpretive frameworks. In using gender psychology I do not seek to psychoanalyze individual theorists but rather to highlight some of the ways in which particular aspects of political theory reflect the cultural-psychological embodiment of masculinity. Certainly, any study utilizing gender psychology—except perhaps a Lacanian approach that focuses exclusively on language[2]—must work from the more empirical level to some degree. Part of the logic of psychology and psychoanalysis is the attempt to understand the meaning that adheres to real social relations; hence its reliance on case studies and interviews. But rather than using this framework to explain why Locke and others developed social contract theory per se, I use it to understand the problem of meaning: not just what kind of meaning these theorists intended, for the history of patriarchy is rife with good intentions, but also what kind of meaning *readers* have derived from it in carrying forward the social contract tradition, what kind of meaning it has come to embody in the modern world. Gender psychology thus provides a symbolic language that can help us begin to understand these meanings in a new way by offering a larger theoretical framework: larger because it allows questions that a liberal framework forbids, symbolic because the unconscious gains its most important expression at the cultural level, in the

[2]Lacan (1985), Kristeva (1986).

symbols and structures that a culture adopts. I am suggesting that social contract theory is one such cultural embodiment.

Yet at the same time, I am not claiming that mother-only child rearing "caused" liberalism; that would be reductive and simplistic, at the least because mother-only child rearing has existed in nonliberal societies as well. Rather, mother-only child rearing is part of, and in turn contributes to, patriarchy in its various forms, including liberalism. Thus, to understand liberalism, we need to explore its various dimensions, and mother-only child rearing is one of them. Indeed, the confluence of liberalism, patriarchy, and capitalism makes my analysis possible. I am therefore not engaged here in a simplistic exploration of the "causes" of male domination or patriarchy, any more than I am interested in the reductive effort to locate a "cause" for liberal obligation theory. As with most controversies of this sort, it is probable that mother-only child rearing lies somewhere between a "pure" cause and a "mere" effect, and that the roots of male domination rose simultaneously and reciprocally with an increasing sexual division of labor; but we need not enter that debate here. Rather, I am interested in the effects of one on the other, of patriarchy on consent theory. If there *is* any singular cause for social contract theory that political theorists could point to, one would most likely have to identify the historical and political events surrounding the writing of a particular theory, the intellectual influences on a writer, and so forth. These points are obvious and not disputed here: Locke's *Two Treatises* were written in response to specific historical events.[3] But that begs the question being posed here. There were many ways to respond to divine right, the exclusion crisis, civil war, and so forth. Why did theorists respond in the ways they did? Even given the important political advances that social contract theory makes toward humanist democracy, why did consent and choice, freedom and equality, contract and authority get defined in the particular ways they did? Further still, why did these theories, as opposed to others that have until recently been considered minor, gain such ascendancy in both scholarly and popular discourses of obligation?[4]

[3]See, for instance, Dunn (1980), Aschcraft (1986), Macpherson (1962), Kramnick (1990).

[4]For instance, although Pocock (1975) and others argue that the theorists of the Atlantic Republican tradition are more influential than liberals such as Locke, this would hardly explain why consent theory still has such philosophical and political force in contemporary literature; nor would it explain why popular conceptions of obligation, for instance in the United States, derive from individualist principles of government by consent of the governed rather than a quasi-communitarian duty to preserve the republic. See Hirschmann (1987), chap. 2, for a fuller discussion of this problem; see also Kramnick (1990) for a similar response to Pocock.

While I will elaborate on this theme of interpretation versus science at appropriate points throughout the book, it is necessary to highlight it from the start to provide a context for the present chapter and indeed the rest of my argument. I say this because in this chapter I primarily attempt to represent the arguments presented by Chodorow, Gilligan, and other feminist psychologists, a considerable task in itself, given most political theorists' unfamiliarity with the literature. But this means that my exploration of the interpretive potential of these works is not fully undertaken until I apply gender psychology to epistemology and political obligation in the chapters that follow. The result may be that the literature discussed here would *seem* to be identifying itself as more empirical than interpretive in its notion that women, because of their psychosexual development as daughters and their role in that development as mothers, exhibit a different orientation from men toward self and relationships, a different perspective on goodness and truth. Indeed, the literature I discuss herein has been commonly criticized precisely because it appears to make essentialist generalizations about what males and females are "really like."[5] But I believe that such readings are reductive, and that symbolism and interpretation are far more important to a feminist reading of gender psychology. Chodorow herself in more recent work confirms this. She implicitly attributes such misreadings to the failure of critics to understand the special methods of feminist "social scientists, who stand epistemologically between the empiricist scientism of psychoanalysts and the interpretive relativism of humanists." Yet she also challenges this scientism by calling psychoanalysis "a deeply embedded cultural discourse."[6]

I agree with this challenge. Although there are elements of empiricism in the psychological works, there is also a great deal of interpretation. Indeed, their primary contribution from a feminist theoretical perspective is precisely to point out that what has been taken to be "true" in fact represents a particular masculinist reading of primarily masculine, and secondarily feminine, experience. Not surprisingly, given that my subject matter is political theory, my own analysis may display greater affinity for what Chodorow calls the humanities than social science (though my approach to political theory makes me as much a "social critic" as a "literary critic").[7] So in the discussion that follows, even when gender psychology appears to be most important in claiming to present new "facts" about females and males, I find its

---

[5]See Bart (1984); Bordo (1990), pp. 137–39; Flax (1990). Fraser and Nicholson (1990), pp. 29–34; Chodorow, Dinnerstein, and Gottlieb (1984); Spelman (1988), chap. 4.
[6]Chodorow (1989), p. 179.
[7]Ibid., p. 192.

primary significance to lie in the ways in which it challenges previous assumptions about what a "fact" is. What are the criteria for claiming something is a fact? What constitutes evidence of truth and knowledge? These questions of interpretation and evaluation represent not merely a shift of focus within a unified field of inquiry but rather a shift in the discourse itself.

Object Relations and Gender Construction

Object relations theory holds that men and boys experience different psychosexual development, gender identification and self-identification, and consequent views of and relations to the world than do women and girls, and that this is due to the nearly universal social fact that women have primary (if not sole) responsibility for the care of infants and young children while men are usually totally absent from early child rearing. The central tenet of object relations theory is the notion that "human beings are created in and through relations with other human beings."[8] It shifts psychoanalytic focus from the Freudian oedipal period to the preoedipal period (birth to three years) as the period of primary personality formation.

During the first three years of life a great deal goes on, such as perception of the self as a real entity and the development of self-other conceptualizations and gender identity, all of which "can only occur in and through social (object) relations."[9] At an early age—approximately three months—the infant realizes its absolute helplessness, and it comes to recognize its caretaker in recognizing its helplessness and dependence. This means that the infant forms an intense attachment—a symbiotic one from its perspective—to the caretaker. Formation of this attachment is "the most important task" of the infant's first three years.[10] Since in our society and most others a woman is generally the sole caretaker, this attachment is almost always to a

---

[8]Flax (1983), p. 250.

[9]Ibid., p. 251. The works I primarily rely on for my understanding of object relations theory include standard ones such as Klein (1950, 1975); Mahler (1968); Mahler, Pine, and Bergman (1975); and Winnicott (1965, 1971). But even more important are feminist theorists who have pulled out the specifically political potential of object relations theory and explored the interaction between gender difference and patriarchy. Chodorow (1978) is particularly relied on here; see also Chodorow (1974, 1979a, 1979b, and 1989); Flax (1978, 1980, 1983, 1990); Benjamin (1980); Keller (1985); and Dinnerstein (1976). For a comprehensive view of object relations theory, see Greenberg and Mitchell (1983).

[10]Flax (1983), p. 251. My referring to the infant as *itself* is one example of the potentially objectifying qualities of object relations parlance; but I self-consciously retain the neuter to avoid clumsy construction and confusion, since my use of *he* and *she* in this section are specific references to male and female. Also, *it* refers to genderless con-

woman. A woman thus provides the infant with the most meaningful relationship it is ever to experience, and "the infant develops its sense of self mainly in relation to her."[11]

Because of its focus on the mother, this school of psychoanalytic thought has lent itself readily to feminist analysis. The institutional significance of the social relations of child rearing has much farther-reaching ramifications than the concept of personality might allow. By recognizing the importance of the role of women in the formation not only of personality, which is seen as individual, but also of gender, which is cultural, object relations theory highlights the nexus of the two and hence women's role in creating gendered individuals, or cultured personalities. Feminist theorists such as Nancy Chodorow, Jane Flax, and Dorothy Dinnerstein have deepened the arguments of the original object relations theories of Margaret Mahler and Melanie Klein by analyzing the specifically cultural and even political dimensions of personality development. What has been assumed to be an individual phenomenon is revealed to be cultural and institutional. Through theoretical and clinical analysis these theorists argue that the experience of being raised by a mother only[12] creates gendered differences that perpetuate the patriarchal sexual division of labor which made them possible. It does this by reproducing gender-specific self-conceptions and epistemological frameworks. Patriarchy thus reproduces itself through the sexual division of labor by producing personalities that are inclined to replicate existing gender-based structures and perceptions of social relations.

This social structure of child rearing produces significant differences in feminine and masculine personality development, according to this body of thought. By the age of three, children have formed a sexual or gender identity. Or, more precisely, they have formed an identity—that is, they see themselves as a self—of which gender is a central aspect, having been "with rare exception firmly and irreversibly established for both sexes" by age three and often as early as

---

cepts, and that is appropriate to my discussion of the infant before his or her gender is learned. That it also exclusively refers to objects and that we are offended by the use of this term in reference to people is testimony to how much we are in thrall to identifying gender, and doing so in oppositional terms.

[11]Chodorow (1978), p. 78.

[12]I prefer my own term *mother only* to "mother-monopolized" (Balbus [1982]) or "mother-dominated" or "mother-dominant" child rearing (Dinnerstein [1976]), for fairly obvious reasons: their vocabulary of Hegelian struggle and capitalist hierarchy is inappropriate. *Mother only* avoids the imagery that women have consciously created the current relations of child rearing for their own benefit and for the oppression of men, while also emphasizing the active roles both parents play (mothers through presence, fathers through absence) and avoiding the implication that women (and men) are merely passive victims.

eighteen months to two years.[13] It is important to note that gender
identity is not a "natural" development on this reading but a cultural
one: it "receives its major input from social ascription of sex that
begins at birth and is cognitively learned concomitantly with language."[14] Physical experience, and a child's perception of his or her
genitals and body, help to create a gendered body ego, but the social
relations of child rearing and the gendered quality of social relations
in general are far more important to gender identity formation. Although one experiences one's body in a certain way, that experience
cannot automatically translate into a social category—gender—without a learned conceptual framework about what that category means.
The fact that one has a vagina or a penis becomes significant as female or male insofar as those concepts exist in a particular relation to
one another in a particular culture, language, and social-conceptual
framework.

The intensity and exclusivity of mother-child relations means that
gender identity is formed in relation to the mother; girls thus identify
with her, in recognizing sameness, while boys identify "against" her,
so to speak, in recognizing a profound disparity. Again, this is not
because gender is "natural" but rather precisely because it is a cultural
category of meaning and value which children learn through their
acquisition of language. But the central elements of exclusivity and
intensity carry this constructed difference even further; for the mother
represents for the infant not just a particular gender which one either
identifies with or differentiates from but also the entire outside world,
that is, the world outside the infant's self. Hence, if a girl identifies
with her mother and perceives a basic definitional connection and
continuity between herself and her mother, she also sees the world
itself, as represented by her mother, as continuous and connected
with her. Her "other"—the not-me, the boundary of the self—is very
much connected to and part of the self. Both self and other are female, a crucial factor at this point, since gender identity has such
importance in the conceptualization of the self. The self is thus identical (or at least extremely similar) to the other. The self-other dichotomy is not a dichotomy after all for a girl but rather a continuum, a
movement from the core self to external objects which she perceives
as connected to herself. In a sense her self *is* the other.

In contrast, the boy, lacking gender identification and self-identification with his mother—who for him, as for the girl, represents,
embodies, *is* the outside world—perceives a fundamental difference,

---

[13]Chodorow (1978), p. 150. See also Flax (1983), p. 251, and (1978), pp. 171–89;
Money and Ehrhardt (1972).

[14]Chodorow (1978), p. 150. See also Fried (1982), pp. 47–69.

a basic disjunction, between himself and that outside world. Similarly, the "other" is more radically separated and different from the self: "other" is female, "self" is male. Whereas gender identity requires the girl to feel connected to the (m)other, the boy's blossoming gender identity requires him to feel radically separate, to view his differentness as a dichotomy between self and other. Hence, Chodorow argues, "because of their mothering by women, girls come to experience themselves as less separate than boys, as having more permeable ego boundaries. Girls come to define themselves more in relation to others."[15]

The key to understanding the genesis and character of this gender difference is the infant's movement from primary identification into the process of separation and individuation, which begins to take place at approximately six months. It involves the infant's growing perception of a demarcation between the self and the other, specifically the mother. "An essential task of infantile development, it involves the development of ego boundaries (a sense of personal psychological division from the rest of the world) and of a bounded body ego (a sense of the permanence of one's physical separateness and the predictable boundedness of one's own body, of distinction between inside and outside)."[16]

Under ideal conditions (referred to as "good enough social relations" by object relations theorists), the period of separation and individuation (six months to two years) is a period of recognizing motor skills and developing autonomy within the context of the secure caretaker relationship. As the child practices its skills, it quickly comes to realize its limits and also learns that its mother is not all-powerful. Because of the child's internalization of the relationship with the mother, this recognition produces ambivalence between the desire to return to symbiosis and the desire to be fully separated. The ideal resolution is an acceptance of connection *and* separateness, a letting go of "the early bond without rejecting the other."[17]

In mother-only child-rearing practices, however, this resolution is often not attainable. Because his primary identification is with a woman, the boy—in order to feel "adequately masculine, distinguish and differentiate himself from others in a way that a girl need not—must categorize himself as someone apart"[18] to assert his separateness from his mother and establish a gendered, adult secondary identity. In doing this the boy defines his masculinity "negatively, as that

---

[15]Chodorow (1978), p. 93.
[16]Chodorow (1979a), p. 54.
[17]Flax (1983), p. 252.
[18]Chodorow (1978), p. 174.

which is not feminine and/or connected to women, rather than positively. This is another way boys come to deny and repress relation
and connection in the process of growing up."[19] Boys define themselves, as it were, in relations *against* others, most prominently as not-
female.

The father's absence means that both girls' and boys' primary identification is with a woman; but it produces problems for identity development after the primary period as well. For a boy, most basically
it means the lack of an active role model. If the father is absent, the
boy must identify with abstract notions of an idealized image, in fact
partly created by his mother. He most likely will also identify only
with particular *aspects* of the male role, thus fragmenting his self-conception of his gender identity. The only concrete self-knowledge he
has is that he is different from his mother; he is not-female. The boy
can develop only a "positional identification," which involves identifying with only specific aspects of another's role and usually does
not involve internalizing the other's values and personality. It is resorted to as a second-best choice when "personal identification,"
which grows out of a personal, concrete relationship involving a diffuse identification with someone else's general personality, is not
available or possible.[20]

In contrast, a girl's gender identity is more positive. It is formed by
a concrete, affective association with her mother as she develops her
own "personal identification." Her identity and role are learned
through active observation. Her mother is there with her for much of
the time. She does not have to imagine or abstract her identity. Yet in
calling her identity positive, we should recognize that there are still
severe difficulties for girls, as Mahler notes in her theory of the three
stages of preoedipal development: symbiosis, practicing, and rapprochement. The gist of her theory is that because mothers are less
available emotionally for forming an early symbiotic bond with
daughters and more ambivalent about daughters' move to the separation stage, mothers may inhibit that move, or at least not give daughters the necessary push all children require. The daughter emerges
from this period feeling somewhat confused and tied to the mother's
own psychosexual feelings in an intense and ambivalent way. The
inadequacy of this phase for girls creates further inadequacies in subsequent developmental phases and reverberates throughout the girl's
life. For instance, in the practicing stage, the girl feels less free than a
boy to leave the mother to explore her developing powers over the

---

[19]Ibid.
[20]Chodorow (1978), p. 175. The concepts of personal and positional identification
come from Slater (1961), Winch (1962).

world. In rapprochement, where gender enters most explicitly into psychic development, the girl finds it much more difficult to complete her separation from her caretaker and turn to a secondary, adult identity.

Thus, the very process of identification for girls is relational, whereas for boys it tends to deny relationship and emphasize abstraction and fragmentation. "A tie between affective process and role learning—between libidinal and ego-development—characterizes feminine development. . . . For [boys], the tie between affective processes and role learning is broken."[21] The boy's shift from primary to secondary identification is a shift from a person to a position, a role, an abstract idealization—basically to something that is vastly removed and separate from the self, which is a concrete entity. In direct contrast, the girl must make this shift to the very same person, her mother. That is, she must move out of one kind of relationship with her mother into a new kind of identity relationship, exhibiting new dynamics and a new concept of self, with the very same person.[22] Just as the boy's identification with an abstraction makes it difficult for him to maintain connection and trust in later life, so does the girl's difficulty in breaking away from her primary identification inhibit her sense of separateness.

Moreover, the girl's situation is compounded by the fact of her father's rejection, his refusal to be available for secondary identification. As a microcosm of the universal cultural devaluation of women, this rejection makes her secondary identification problematic in an additional way. The process of developing a self-identity requires feeling that one's self is valuable; but the girl must identify herself with, indeed is told she is, someone of relatively little social value.[23] She be-

---

[21]Chodorow (1978), p. 175.

[22]Ibid., p. 177.

[23]The issue of sexualization should perhaps be disussed here, as it highlights another difference the absence of the father produces. Chodorow and others assert that the mother "sexualizes" the son, that is, puts him into the oedipal relation at an earlier age than the daughter. Chodorow (1978), pp. 107, 134, and passim. Although Chodorow is unclear on this point, such sexualization involves the recognition of sexual identity and hence of the potential for adulthood and autonomous independence. The mother does this not only because she perceives her son as different from herself but also because it is a cultural expectation and a characteristic of the social gender landscape; the expectation that a boy will be separate and independent is a self-fulfilling prophecy. Indeed, the mother recognizes her son as a member of the socially superior gender. Mothers do not recognize daughters' sexual identity and potential for adulthood for parallel reasons: mothers do not wish to help daughters out of the preoedipal relation, as Flax indicates (see discussion in text). Perceiving her daughter as like herself, she treats her as such, thus both replicating her own feelings of continuity with her own mother and complementing her daughter's identical preoedipal feelings.

In contrast, fathers often sexualize daughters, and at an even earlier age than

gins to become conscious of social gender differentiation and devaluation of the female and suffers "a gender specific lessening of self
esteem as well."[24] Finally, she usually cannot turn to the father for
psychic help in this period, since he is less available to her than he is
to the son. Thus the girl is "thrown back on the very person from
whom she was unable to differentiate completely" in the first place.
Whereas the boy's complete turn to the father, the "figure of social
authority," provides the basis for his own sense of social power, the
girl "cannot repress the female part of herself and totally reject the
mother, because it is precisely at this stage that she is coming to an
awareness of her own femaleness, that is, her gender."[25] The girl is
thus dependent on her mother—a person who is herself plagued by
the same personality problems and deep-seated belief in her own and
her daughter's imperfection and inferiority—for the approval and
sense of self-worth necessary for forming an identity, when this kind
of dependence on her mother is precisely what prevents the girl from
developing a fully separate identity.

It should be obvious at this point that differences in boys' and girls'
relationality are compounded not only by the father's absence but
also by the mother's differential treatment of sons and daughters. Although the possibility of blaming the mother is one of the most troubling aspects of object relations theory from a feminist perspective, it
is necessary to note how daughters become constructed through gender into adults who reproduce the patriarchal cycle of mother-only
child rearing. Flax argues that a mother unconsciously views her relationship with her daughter as a means to resolve preoedipal issues
left over from her relationship with her own mother, issues left unre-

---

mothers do sons. But the situation is not parallel, and the daughter suffers rather than
benefits from such sexualization for two reasons. First, it does not push the daughter
out of the preoedipal relationship, since no such relationship exists with the father.
Second, and more important, the content of fathers' sexualization is far more abstract
and objectifying than that of mothers' sexualization of sons. For instance, fathers emphasize dressing their daughters in traditionally "feminine" clothing far more than
mothers; they encourage, reward, and often respond only to flirtatious behavior from
daughters. Chodorow (1978), pp. 118–19; Macoby and Jacklin (1975), p. 329. This difference in sexualization reaches its most grotesque proportions in the fact that fathers
rape daughters and commit other forms of incestual abuse with far greater frequency
than mothers do with children of either sex. Although such behavior is far from the
norm, it indicates certain cultural notions of femininity and masculinity that allow and
even encourage fathers to sexualize daughters in ways that emphasize an abstract femininity rather than treating sexual identity as an indication of personhood. And in seeking to turn to the father for a secondary identity, the girl receives the paradoxical message that, in order to receive her father's attention and approval, she must seek a
secondary identity through her mother: she must be "feminine."
    [24]Flax (1978), p. 177.
    [25]Ibid., p. 178.

solved because her mother unconsciously used her for the same purpose.[26] This produces a greater internal conflict for mothers of girls by
repeating the woman's unresolved wishes concerning her own
mother, thus resulting in confusing, unconscious expectations for the
daughter to "mother" her mother. And as I noted earlier, according to
Mahler this conflict in the mother means that the first symbiotic stage
of infant development is fraught with confusion and is often never
satisfactorily achieved for a girl. Because of gender difference the boy
is more likely to achieve a satisfactory symbiosis and hence to have all
the resources needed for adequate development of self in later stages.

This situation obviously produces confusion for the girl—Has she
really left her primary identification behind? How can she know that
she has if there is no break but only a fluid continuity?—and greatly
interferes with her ability to develop a separate sense of self. Her later
development is suffused with preoedipal issues, and her adult identity is deeply entwined with feelings about her mother. As a girl is
thrown back on her mother, she fails to complete the separation
process. Her mother, as a not fully separated person herself, sub-
consciously perceives her daughter's situation and is able to continue
to experience her daughter as like herself, as continuous, on a deeper
level: they are sisters in diffuse identity as it were. Thus the daughter,
in a continuous cycle of attempting to leave the mother and being
pulled back by the proverbial twitch upon the thread, "continues to
experience herself as involved in issues of merging and separation."[27]

Although such an experience has its obvious difficulties for daughters, its disadvantages are exacerbated by a context of patriarchy that
predetermines its denigration. Such an experience of relationship and
personal identification provides the basis for a strong sense of self,
but only if we redefine the atomistic self of masculine autonomy to
reflect an idea of self-in-relationship, a self that draws strength from
connection. From this perspective the strengths of girls' experience is
revealed. In particular, Chodorow says:

> Girls emerge from this period with a basis for "empathy" built into their
> primary definition of self in a way that boys do not. Girls emerge with a

---

[26]Flax (1978), esp. p. 174, says that mothers tend to identify more strongly with their
infant daughters than sons: "They do not seem to have as clear a sense of physical
boundaries between themselves and their girl children" as in their relationships with
their sons. Similarly, clinical evidence reveals that female therapy patients commonly
express a lack of "sense where they end and their mothers begin, even in a literal,
physical way." This does not happen to boys, Flax argues, because the "fact of gender
differences with boy babies enforces, on the mother's part, a sense that the child is 'not
me,' is other than me."

[27]Chodorow (1978), p. 166.

stronger basis for experiencing another's needs or feelings as one's own (or of thinking that one is so experiencing another's needs and feelings). . . . From very early on, then, because they are parented by a person of the same gender (a person who has already internalized a set of unconscious meanings, fantasies, and self-images about this gender and brings to her experience her own internalized early relationship to her own mother), girls come to experience themselves as less differentiated than boys, as more continuous with and related to the external object-world and as differently oriented to their inner object-world as well.[28]

Feminist object relations theorists hold that such an experience and definition of self is a source of strength, and may even provide an advantage over masculine experience. For at the same time, because the boy "has engaged, and been required to engage, in a more emphatic individuation and a more defensive firming of experienced ego boundaries," his separation is exaggerated. Because they are pushed out of the preoedipal relationship, boys are forced to curtail the empathic tie with the mother, and hence lack this basis for empathy. For the boy, oedipal issues have become fused with preoedipal issues, and "issues of differentiation have become entwined with sexual issues." The understanding of love between two people becomes confused with the fear of loss of self. The resolution of this odepial crisis is repression, specifically and most centrally the repression of the need for relationship.[29]

From the feminist perspective that relationship is of central importance to humans, such repression is deeply problematic. Indeed, the idea of connection raises the question as to how the boy *can* deny relationship if it is so central to his self-identity. But again, patriarchy provides the answer: dichotomous gender difference under patriarchy allows the boy to project all frustration from this early period onto his mother and then to split off this "object" from himself. In becoming not-female and turning to the father (or, more precisely, the father's role), the boy develops his autonomy and deals with ambivalence "by denial (of having been related), by projection (women are bad; they cause these problems), and by domination (mastering fears and wishes for regression by controlling, depowering, and/or devaluing the object)."[30] The girl cannot engage in such repression and denial because it is precisely at this age that recognition of her gender identity becomes important; she is thus dependent on a close psychic tie

[28]Ibid., p. 167.
[29]Ibid., pp. 166–67. Chodorow goes so far as to assert that men "look to relationships with women for narcissistic-phallic reassurance rather than for mutual affirmation and love" (p. 196), though I believe she overstates the case.
[30]Flax (1983), p. 253.

with her mother even as the boy's identity depends on severing that tie. The cycle thus repeats itself, as patriarchy contributes to the construction of gendered identities and social relationships that in turn reproduce patriarchy.

Thus, although all children proceed developmentally from symbiosis to autonomy, it might appear that males achieve more success in achieving autonomy while females tend to remain in a more symbiotic relationship with the primary caretaker and their own primary identity. But such a claim is already biased in favor of the masculine model of separation. In reality, the differences in masculine and feminine experience can be seen to turn on two different conceptions of autonomy, just as they turn on two different senses of self. In the masculine model of development the sense of self and autonomy are conceptualized "reactively," that is, as a reaction against the mother. Reactive autonomy "confuses autonomy with separation and independence from others." Reactive autonomy is thus "static autonomy," in Evelyn Fox Keller's terms, because it is locked into a reductive and negative conception of the self as not-mother. If autonomy is defined as "the psychological sense of being able to act under one's own volition instead of under external control,"[31] and turns on individuality and the integrity of the self, then reactive autonomy is self-defeating; it in fact *robs* the individual of self-creative agency, for such autonomy is premised on an artificial separateness that cannot be sustained without repression, and on abstract roles and rules, which are external to the self, for identity. Reactive or static autonomy "precludes the creative ambiguity without which neither love nor play, nor even certain kinds of knowledge, can survive."[32] This masculine, reactive conception of agency "manifests itself in self-protection, self-assertion and self-expansion . . . in the formation of separateness . . . in isolation, alienation, and aloneness . . . in the repression of thought, feeling and impulse."[33] It thus reveals "not so much confidence in one's difference from others as resistance to (even repudiation of) sameness, not so much the strength of one's own will as the resistance to another's, not so much a sense of self-esteem as uncertainty about the durability of the self—finally not so much the security of one's ego boundaries as their vulnerability."[34]

"Relational autonomy," in contrast, operates from a notion that the self is conceived in terms of, and draws strength from, relationships

---

[31]Keller (1985), p. 97.
[32]Ibid., p. 98.
[33]David Bakan (1966), cited in Chodorow (1974), pp. 55–56.
[34]Keller (1985), p. 102.

with others. Although David Bakan may go too far in saying that the "communal" personality he attributes to girls exhibits "the sense of being at one with other organisms . . . the lack of separateness . . . contact, openness, and union . . . noncontractual cooperation . . . the lack and removal of repression [of thought, feeling, and impulse],"[35] it is clear that relational autonomy, or what Keller calls "dynamic autonomy," "is a product at least as much of relatedness as it is of delineation" and "reflects a sense of self . . . as both differentiated from and related to others."[36] Many psychoanalysts and psychologists—and particularly object relations theorists—construe this model of autonomy as preferable because it more accurately reflects the reality of how we have come to be the individuals that we are, that is, through intimate relations with particular persons. Indeed, D. W. Winnicott describes this as "the true self."[37] Hence, as Keller argues, dynamic or relational autonomy "gives rise to a sense of agency in a world of interacting and interpersonal agents with whom and with which one feels an essential kinship, while still recognizing, and accepting, their independent integrity." Agency thus derives from recognizing "the differences between oneself and another" and yet also "acting on others more or less like oneself."[38]

In light of reactive and relational autonomy, then, it can be seen that object relations theory, and particularly a feminist reading of it, provides a very different way of conceptualizing the individual, one that argues against the concept found in liberal obligation theory. There, relationships need to be justified. Separation and individualism are taken not only as givens but as the most desirable, most "human" forms of life. Object relations theory challenges the hegemony of this notion of the individual by revealing the pathologies of these forms. While object relations recognizes the problems of overidentification typically found in women's development, it also reveals the strengths of the relationship orientation found in this feminine model. Indeed, although I have tried to highlight the problems of both models, a feminist reading of object relations theory is not *merely* engaged in an argument that feminine and masculine models of development are simply separate but equal (that is, equally problematic). Rather, it reveals that the masculine emphasis on individuation and separation is more problematic than women's connectedness, partly because it has caused relationality and connection to become subverted in the modern world. The weaknesses of the feminine model—particularly the so-called failure to separate adequately—are

[35]Cited in Chodorow (1974), pp. 55–56.
[36]Keller (1985), p. 99.
[37]Ibid.; and see Winnicott (1971).
[38]Keller (1985), pp. 99–100.

weaknesses predominantly from the perspective of masculine experience. By problematizing that experience, and revealing that many of its pathologies can be addressed by feminine experience, object relations "emphasizes not only that separateness, not connectedness, needs explaining, but that intersubjectivity and the mutual recognition of the other and the self are fundamental to satisfactory development."[39] This kind of feminist psychoanalysis provides a cultural location for the modernist conception of the individual as masculine, and suggests that a reconsideration of the historically devalued feminine can help produce a notion of the self that is richer, more complex, and perhaps more balanced than the reductive models of public man and private woman that pervade a social contract conception of politics.

Furthermore, this shift in notions of selfhood and the individual brings with it new concepts of morality, value, and even knowledge. If boys and girls develop different self-conceptions, orientations toward the object world, and conceptions of it, it is likely that contrasting value judgments will follow from these differences. Therein lies the first key to understanding the significance of object relations theory for political obligation: it suggests that ontology can influence, or even create, moral values and a moral perspective. A grounding in a particular moral perspective will likely give way to the construction of political theories that utilize those perspectives. If these moralities are redefined—say, away from one that takes the individual as separate and hence morally privileges the individual over society, to one that takes the individual as connected and gives moral primacy to relationship—then the vision of politics that is created to support that morality must also change.

Moral Psychology and Women's Voices

This claim may seem puzzling. On what grounds can it be asserted that morality will arise from personality and from these experiences? If morality were merely a question of personality, then morality would be different for every person. Am I defending moral relativism and subjectivism? There is an important difference between saying that morality is shaped by personality and saying that it is shaped by personality development. The latter involves the structural and institutionalized dimensions of culture within which the former can take place; it highlights the cultural practices and contexts within which individuals come to see themselves and others as such.

[39]Chodorow (1989), p. 185.

Within a psychoanalytic framework in particular, morality and the moral sense develop with and through the emergence of the superego; and superego is formed by the introjection of the "admonishing parent."[40] In a broad sense, introjection of the mother in the formation of the superego, and hence of values and ideas that guide moral decision making independent of consciously learned values, will necessarily involve very different things for girls and for boys under mother-only child rearing. Specifically, boys would introject a concept of difference, of decisive boundaries, in introjecting a mother who is different, "not-me." In this, admonishment—ranging from withdrawal of the breast during feeding to inhibition of masturbatory action to facial expressions and, as the child gets older and acquires language, harsh words and physical punishment—would appear to the boy to originate from a source completely distinct from the self. The superego is hence the introjection of externality. A girl would introject an entity to which she feels strongly connected. Admonishment comes from a source that is as much "me" as "not-me" (or even more so). These differences would likely be compounded by—if they do not partially cause—social customs that censure girls for separation, boys for attachment.[41]

Thus, if the superego is formed out of these infantile experiences, we find a superego in girls that is likely to value relation and connection, one in boys that is more likely to value separation and rules. And if there are systematic cultural variants that tend to create similarities among girls and boys, superego development is not merely personal but cultural and institutional as well. Accordingly, moral systems, which are created by humans, should reflect the systematic

[40]Chodorow (1978), p. 43.

[41]For instance, the epithets "sissy," "mama's boy," "tied to his mother's apron strings" reinforce male values along these lines. Modern western society tends to scorn or be suspicious of grown men who live with their mothers, as well as "henpecked" and "pussy-whipped" husbands, for such men cannot and do not retain control over women. As Rousseau argued in *Emile*, men must either dominate women or be "dragged to their deaths." As to women who assert separation, the old double standard—"he's aggressive, but she's a bitch"—is echoed in Gilligan's discussion of Thematic Aperception Tests (see my discussion later in this chapter), in which men are rewarded for success but women are punished because of the disconnection entailed in being at the top of a hierarchy. And certainly the incidence of violent rape and the concomitant difficulties for female victims in prosecuting and securing conviction is only one frightening manifestation of cultural sanctions against women who venture into the public realm alone. Indeed, these gender differences can be seen to compound one another. In object relations terms, the working out of the male's subconscious aggression against the mother which is the source of the male's fear of connection creates a social phenomenon (violence against women) that reinforces the female's fear of isolation, which derives initially from her relationship to her mother. Socialization and social practices thus interact with and support the psychic effects of mother-only child rearing.

differences between male and female development. Since men have for the most part been the authors of moral theories and codes, these may well reflect, at least in part, their culturally and institutionally influenced superego development.

In a parallel vein, if women's personality and ontological perspective revolve around connection, empathy, relationship, and merging, a theory of morality based on that experience would reflect these characteristics as values. A moral perspective arising from women's psychic experience would take as its basis the notion that people are ineluctably connected, not separate, and that relationships are of primary importance. Women's ways of experiencing the world would thus become translated into prescription, just as the dominant ideology of individualism, rights, and property can be seen to reflect masculine hyperdifferentiation (where the object's subjectivity is denied), positional identification with aspects of an abstract role, and fragmentation of that identification. This would point toward a moral schema that emphasizes empathy, or emotional inner connection based on perceived similarities and concrete relationships, rather than formal agreements between abstract individuals. Such a morality would be likely to embody principles of care, responsibility, and human connection. It would also emphasize individua*lity* in relationship and reject abstract individua*lism*. That is, it would embrace relational autonomy, or a strong sense of self that recognizes, and does not feel threatened by, inescapable and intense connections to others; and it would reject reactive autonomy, an exaggerated conceptualization of independence that is a reaction against the (m)other.

In the masculine model of development, in which the notion of separation is primary, the formation of the superego involves introjection of externally created standards and rules that have been articulated and explained, and which are conceived and applied universally and impartially, regardless of relational contexts. For the feminine model, it would seem that it is not what the rules say that is important but whether following a certain rule or performing a particular action displeases the mother. There is an evaluation of the rules based on relationship, which is seen as prior to the rules. Thus a morality derived from a feminine orientation would eschew rigid reliance on rules as the externalized superego and, accordingly, the principle of abstract rights. It would rely instead on inductive reasoning that refers to contextual considerations and that flows from a stronger, more solid superego that is flexible and willing to adapt to change. It would begin from an assumption of social connection and obligation, not from an assumption of isolation and "natural" freedom, and it would give priority to human relationships.

Carol Gilligan has argued for just such a construction of a so-called feminine moral schema.[42] Gilligan's work traces gender differences in psychology and moral development. It began in an examination of case studies and tests done by Lawrence Kohlberg, whose studies of children's moral development have contributed significantly to contemporary beliefs that girls' morality is retarded.[43] Gilligan offers a reinterpretation of Kohlberg's findings and discusses the results of her own tests. She rejects the notion that women's moral perspective and methodology are regressive, arguing instead that women have developed and maintained their own moral logic that is in many ways more consistent than the dominant moral discourse of rights dialogue.

The foundation for this difference is based on self-other conceptualizations. Like Chodorow, although on a different basis, Gilligan found that women emphasized relationship and connection and feared isolation, whereas men emphasized individualism and feared loss of self in connection. For instance, in Thematic Aperception Tests given to college students, significant sex differences were noted in the location of danger in connection and separation, with men perceiving danger to themselves in pictures indicating closeness and relationship, while women perceived danger in situations of isolation, whether in a dark alley or at the top of a hierarchy.[44] For example, in response to a picture of trapeze artists performing, women explicitly created safety nets where none existed in the picture, insisting that maintaining the safety and well-being of the artists and keeping the group together were more important than the prestige afforded by working without a net. Men, by contrast, created stories in which, for example, the woman trapeze artist is purposely dropped by the man because she has been unfaithful to his friend. Both males and females

[42]Gilligan (1982) is the primary focus of this discussion, but the essays in Gilligan et al. (1988) and Gilligan, Lyons, and Hamner (1990), as well as Belenky et al. (1986), also influence my understanding and application of this kind of gender psychology. This work has been the center of a great deal of controversy, which I do not wish to ignore; see Tronto (1987) and Kerber et al. (1986). But, as will become clear in my argument, I am not invested in any sort of reductive notion that men and women think differently; rather, I am interested in locating possible sources of difference—not necessarily differences between men and women but between liberal obligation theory and nondominant voices—and in determining what those differences are.

[43]See Kohlberg (1984) for a recapitulation of the Heinz dilemma and other tests initially conducted by Kohlberg.

[44]Although expectations of violence stemming from isolation may be grounded in actual fact, this does not change the theory of morality. A woman may be afraid of being alone because of the evidence of real violence against women, but that does not deny the validity of the claim that women do fear isolation. Gilligan cites Chodorow's work as a reasonable source of gender differences, but she maintains no investment in such a reading and would allow for other sources of the differences she mentions.

created stories not self-evident in the pictures, and both identified violence or its potential, but they located it in different ways: females feared the violence (death) arising from the separation implied by the lack of a safety net, whereas males linked death to love.[45]

This different relational schema lends itself to different moral outlooks. Gilligan's findings indicate that males, when thinking about moral issues and questions, tend to think primarily in terms of rules and general principles, rights that pertain to the individual as such, and legality; they tend to disregard the relational context of a particular moral dilemma and attempt instead to refer to or establish general rules and principles to guide their moral decision about what the correct action would be in a given dilemma. They are concerned with exhibiting the formal constraints of logic and rational thought in their attempt to arrive at a conclusion that anyone with the same information could reach. In contrast, she argues, females, when thinking about moral problems, are typically more concerned with relationships, responsibilities, and the contextual factors of a particular moral dilemma. For females,

> the moral problem arises from conflicting responsibilities rather than from competing rights and requires for its resolution a mode of thinking that is contextual and narrative rather than formal and abstract. This conception of morality centers moral development around the understanding of responsibility and relationships, just as the conception of morality as fairness ties moral development to the understanding of rights and rules. (p. 45).

The notion that men and women follow these two different lines of moral reasoning is certainly not contradicted by her predecessors.[46] Gilligan's point, however, is to challenge their belief that the rights model (alternatively called the "justice conception" by Gilligan) is the only one that is correct and that the relationship model (or "care conception") is deficient and confuses morality with other things, such as love. Quite the opposite, Gilligan says: for the girls and women she studied, morality and love are not confused; they are related in im-

---

[45]Gilligan (1982), p. 44. Subsequent references to this work are cited in the text. It is interesting to note that in both the men's and women's stories reported by Gilligan, violence is always the woman's "fault"; she has deviously ruptured a relationship with a man and then pays the price. Even more interesting, this blame is sometimes taken on by women respondents as well. In response to a picture of a woman scientist at work, one woman wrote a story in which the woman, at the top of her medical school class, is maimed by her jealous fellow students. In setting herself apart from her colleagues, she "asks for it."

[46]See, for example, Freud, *Three Essays on the Theory of Sexuality*; Piaget (1965); Kohlberg (1984); Bull (1969). See also Chodorow (1978), p. 173.

portant ways.[47] Rather than being unable to understand the concept of a rule, or being morally deficient because they do not "see" that rules guide morality, Gilligan asserts, following Piaget, that girls are "more tolerant in their attitudes towards rules, more willing to make exceptions" (p. 10) according to the human needs in a given situation.

Piaget concluded from his observations that girls lacked the "legal sense" and hence were deficient in moral reasoning ability. Gilligan concludes instead that girls are merely centered in a different perspective and that this flexibility is a source of moral strength. She argues that females tend to use caring as a standard for morality: they "judge themselves in terms of their ability to care" (p. 17). This care conception is far from regressive, however; it has integrity and consistency, and it reveals and accommodates much that is significant about our lives that the rights model denies or ignores.

Two studies make this point particularly clear, the "Heinz dilemma" and Gilligan's abortion study. In the former, originally one of Kohlberg's studies, eleven-year-old children of both sexes were asked to respond to this moral dilemma: Heinz is a man whose wife is fatally ill. The medicine she needs to help her is too expensive for him to buy. Should Heinz steal the drug? Gilligan selects for discussion the responses of a boy and a girl that elucidate most brilliantly the problem of interpretation and the significance of women's voice.

The boy, Jake, maintains unequivocally that Heinz should steal the drug because "human life is worth more than money" (p. 26). Seeking to establish and follow general precepts and principles in applying this case to the rules, Jake emphasizes the need to arrive at the solution "rationally," so that any other person will be able to reason to the same conclusion. Heinz is justified in breaking the law on this basis; although laws are important, they "make mistakes," which can be corrected in a court of law by a judge using the same process of rational deduction. Hence, a judge trying Heinz's case "should give Heinz the lightest possible sentence" because his action was "the right thing to do" (p. 26). In contrast the girl, Amy, maintains that Heinz should not steal the drug but rather should seek some other form of action, some other means to solve the problem; for if he does steal and goes to jail (as he most assuredly will), "his wife might get sicker" (p. 28), and the jailed Heinz would be unable to help her further.

Amy's allegedly naive response highlights several deficiencies in Jake's reply. First, the wife is brought into the picture and recognized as part of a triangle of people rather than considered as Heinz's

[47]Gilligan (1984).

"property" to be balanced against the druggist's property (the medicine or the money to be gained from its sale) and found more valuable. Second, the marriage relationship is dealt with realistically. The problem is not abstracted out of the context of the woman's continued need for her husband's help. Rather, the assumption is that relationships are a continuing need and a central aspect of human life. Quality of life is as important as living itself; and perhaps the woman does not wish to risk her husband's incarceration. Third, rather than seeing the right to property and the right to life balanced in formal mediation (Heinz steals the drug and a judge decides it is a right action), Amy finds the solution to this problem in consultation and discussion, with all parties being considered and a compromise being reached: perhaps Heinz could "pay back the money later." If Heinz and the pharmacist had talked the problem out long enough, she insists, they could have agreed on "something besides stealing" (p. 29).

Although an approach of this type has been viewed traditionally as regressive by the standards of psychological testing as well as in moral theory, precisely because it does not use logic and standard formal categories of thought, in fact Amy's response is remarkably sophisticated, displaying a rich understanding of the complexity of the dilemma and of the relations among the people involved. Beginning from a framework that logical reasoning is a given shared by all, Jake assumes that logic will produce a clear answer. Amy, believing that connection is universal, is equally sure that communication will provide a solution.

The problem for Amy, however, is compounded by the fact that the questioner does not share her perspective and hence cannot hear her answer:

> Amy is answering a different question from the one the interviewer thought had been posed. Amy is not considering *whether* Heinz should act in this situation ("*Should* Heinz steal the drug?") but rather *how* Heinz should act in response to his awareness of his wife's need ("Should Heinz *steal* the drug?"). The interviewer takes the mode of action for granted, presuming it to be a matter of fact; Amy assumes the necessity for action and considers what form it should take. (p. 31)

The bias toward the masculine response is built into the questions themselves and is part of the evaluative framework the interviewer uses in assessing all responses. This creates a cyclical problem as the interviewers find what they want to find because of the structure they give the inquiry.

This bias is the same as in liberal theory. Indeed, Kohlberg explic-

itly allies the stage theory of moral development with the development of the liberal conception of justice. His fifth and sixth stages—
what he calls the "post-conventional level," the highest level one can
achieve—rely centrally on the concept of the social contract. At stage
five, one exhibits a "concern that laws and duties be based on rational
calculation of overall utility." At stage six, the individual moves to a
"justice" conception of morality, defined as "equality of human
rights" or as "reversibility," following an explicitly Rawlsian understanding of justice.[48]

Whereas Kohlberg's stage theory would seem to put at least one
great moral controversy to rest—utilitarians are not just wrong but
morally undeveloped—it actually highlights the bias of his theory toward a preconceived notion of justice and of moral development. Indeed, he goes so far as to say that social contract is an aspect of all
facets of our lives. His criticism of Gilligan and Nona Lyons points
this out. He argues that "the care and response orientation was directed primarily to relations of special obligations to the family,
friends and group members, relations which often included or pre-
supposed general obligations of respect, fairness and contract."[49] Yet
the characterization of such relationships as contractual and based on
"fairness" (read formal justice) is itself masculinist because of its complete denial of women's perceptions and experiences of such relationships. Contract hardly characterizes women's historical roles as
mothers, nor is "justice as reversibility" particularly appropriate to a
mother's assessment of her children's needs in "distributing resources."

Its inappropriateness is particularly striking in Gilligan's study of
women contemplating abortion. Not only is this dilemma specific to
women's lives, but it is one that highlights in a concrete way the fact
of human connection. Interestingly enough, when this dilemma enters the realm of public policy, it is considered in the legal terminology of conflicting rights by legislators, courts, and even women's
lobby groups. Yet this conceptual language is not the primary consideration for many women going through the agonizing process of deciding what to do about an unexpected and unwanted pregnancy.
This dissonance presents a stark contrast between the two models
and affords us an understanding of the ambiguity of concepts such as
responsibility and choice.

Because of the specificity of pregnancy for a woman, the choice to
continue or terminate it is ultimately hers.[50] Yet because abortion as a

[48]Kohlberg (1979), pp. 347, 348.
[49]Ibid., p. 349.
[50]Gilligan (1982), p. 19. I agree with Tronto (1987) that men faced with the abortion
dilemma might also refer to concepts of care and responsibility rather than rights and

moral dilemma is one that concretely demonstrates deep involvement in relationships, her choice is subject to the extremely powerful influence of demands from those she is connected to: family, the father, the potential infant. It is thus not the case that she can make her choice in an isolated context, and the choice itself can never be abstracted from others. The moral dilemma in abortion is painful and difficult precisely because the recognition of connection all around ensures that there is no right answer, that is, no solution in which no one will be hurt. The women in Gilligan's study often perceived themselves in a no-win situation, having to choose the lesser of two evils or to decide who would be the sacrificial victim.

Rather than echoing a rights dialogue, then, the moral language engaged by the women in this study centered on notions of selfishness and responsibility. Such a conceptual framework, which assumes relationship, defines the moral problem for these women as one of an "obligation to exercise care and avoid hurt." Responsibility for these women was understood primarily in terms of care, particularly of not hurting, and was directly opposed to selfishness, which "denoted a morally problematic separation of others from self."[51] Some saw the pregnancy as hurting family or lovers and felt that was of primary importance. But for most of the women the question of being able to care adequately for the child, of giving it a bad life or an unequal chance in life, was a central consideration. Having the baby, in this light, might have been considered selfish, an act of inflicting harm: "How can you bring a child into the world," one woman asks, when one cannot care for it adequately, in order to "assuage your guilt [about taking] responsibility for taking a life?" (p. 118). Responses such as "It would have been hell for that poor kid and for me too" (p. 120) pervade the study in the women's expression of their moral reasoning.

The moral considerations on each side of the decision are extremely weighty but turn on issues that pertain to the concrete conditions of women's lives and not on an abstract right to choose. Thus a woman in the abortion study couches the Heinz dilemma in terms of "who is going to be hurt more" (p. 75), considering not a logical priority of rights but an assessment of actual consequences revolving around a

---

rules. But I believe this oversimplifies in two ways. First, it ignores that men do in fact play key roles in Gilligan's abortion dilemma; several of the women report that their lovers were demanding they have abortions or were making the decision de facto by refusing to commit to the pregnancy. Second, the choice and responsibility *are* ultimately the woman's in a way they (probably) never could be for a man, simply because she is the one who is pregnant.

[51]Gilligan (1986), p. 4.

definition of morality as not causing hurt. Similarly, one Catholic woman, pregnant again two months after the birth of her first child, frames her choice in terms of concrete effects and material realities, not in terms of priorities of rights. She believes that having an abortion is "taking a life," a realization she "can't cover . . . over," yet she has to think of lives, "mine, my son's, and my husband's" as well, which she feels would be unfairly strained financially and emotionally by the birth of another child (p. 83). Her understanding of morality and goodness exhibits at once a strength in perceiving the real effects of her decision and an apparent confusion about what morality is: she says she cannot be "so morally strict as to hurt three other people with a decision just because of my moral beliefs" (p. 84). That is, being "moral" in acting on her belief that abortion is taking a life would yield immorality in hurting others and damaging their lives. Such a construction of the dilemma appears confused in terms of a priority of rights. But a perspective that considers concrete effects and includes relationship and care as primary values can yield the conclusion, "I still think abortion is wrong, and it will be unless the situation can justify what you are doing" (p. 85). Justification arises from a consideration of the real effects of a given decision on actual relationships and from an evaluation of the realities of care and response.

Responsibility for these women, then, signifies response; it involves doing what others are counting on them to do. The males Gilligan studied tended to define responsibility as *refraining* from doing what one wants; it involves obeying the rules that limit interference, thus making "life in community safe, protecting autonomy through reciprocity" (p. 37), defined as formal equality of rights. The mode of action is assumed—that is, not performing the desired act—and the question is whether or not to act (or rather, to refrain from action) on an individualist assessment of conflicting rights. Within the care conception, however, responsibility requires positive action rather than restraint, an "extension of action rather than a limitation of action" (p. 38). Taking connection as given, this mode assumes the need to respond—the need to act—and questions which actions would produce the most inclusive response.

Yet response must include responding to the self. In the abortion study, the women felt compelled to evaluate the effects of the decision on everyone else, sometimes even to the point of excluding themselves. This self-exclusion stemmed as much from a conventional conception of a feminine morality of self-sacrifice as from a fear of taking responsibility for choice. Adulthood is defined in terms of independence, which connotes violence for these women, career ambition, which means one "stomps on people" (p. 97), self-development, which requires disconnection from the incipient child, even "murdering the fetus" (p. 86), and accepting responsibility for that choice in a society that hierarchizes absolute rights and wrongs. This notion of adulthood as signifying violence and an aggressive concern for self conflicts with conventional notions of femininity as self-sacrifice, as not asserting one's own desires because they are by definition selfish, as caring for and protecting others even at the expense of taking care of oneself, and as being incompetent and too weak to take responsibility for one's choice (p. 79). In addition, the primacy of rights in the society at large reinforces a woman's conviction of her own incompetence as a moral agent, as she is continually told that her feelings about moral dilemmas are regressive or simply wrong, and she is alienated from herself in the context of making moral decisions.

The conflict between adulthood and feminity, then, becomes itself a moral problem. Moral goodness becomes entwined with the conventional values of a "good woman," which revolve around a capacity for caring. In the context of abortion, however, such values conflict with themselves because any decision made in this dilemma will express a lack of care for someone. Furthermore, the consequences for the woman are often so great as to bring into sharp relief the inadequacies and contradictions of a feminine ethic of self-sacrifice. The choice is ultimately hers, a fact that the concrete nature of the consequences of this particular dilemma—either disconnection through abortion or adoption, or a lifelong responsibility of care for another human being—makes it impossible to deny or hide. A realization of the need to take responsibility for that choice, and to include the self in any considerations of who requires care, presses in. "Responsibility now includes both self and other, viewed as different but connected rather than separate and opposed" (p. 147).

The Politics of Gender Psychology

The responsibility model or care conception of morality thus approaches and frames moral dilemmas differently from rights conception. It considers the problem in terms of concrete effect before abstract principle; it takes care and avoidance of harm to others as a primary goal; it sees the priority of relationship and locates the self in a network of relationships. But furthermore, by studying the two models from Gilligan's perspective—and indeed by adopting care as an interpretive framework for examining rights—we can see that the two represent different models of development and growth. It is not

true that one is absolutely superior, that one denotes growth and the
other stultification. Indeed, as Gilligan and Grant Wiggins argue, it is
precisely when theorists interpret from "the assumption of a single
moral standpoint, defined as *the* moral perspective," that such reductive evaluation occurs.[52] Indeed, from the perspective of rights, such
invidious comparison seems inescapable as a rigid hierarchy of evaluation is formed. But from the perspective of care, attention to the
voices of others is required. As Belenky et al. hold of "connected
knowing," a care perspective requires listening and attending to
others' perspectives.[53]

If we view these varying perspectives as products of two different
gender-related modes of development, they end up achieving some
similarity in the attainment of moral maturity. These "two disparate
modes of experience . . . are in the end connected" (p. 172). Both
perspectives come to recognize the links between identity and intimacy, integrity and care; both are marked by the move away from
absolutes in moral judgment (pp. 164–66). But these absolutes differ.
For the responsibility model, the absolute of care "becomes complicated through a recognition of the need for personal integrity." For
the rights model, "the absolutes of truth and fairness . . . are called
into question by experiences that demonstrate the existence of differences between other and self" (p. 166) as growth is indicated by considerations of care and relationship. It is vital to recognize, however,
that such a reading of the rights model is not possible from within the
conceptual outlines of that model.[54] Care as an epistemological framework offers a way of reading rights in which growth and development lie in new directions. Thus, by looking at the two perspectives
from the standpoint of care, we see their superficial dualism transformed into an overlapping relatedness, just as by examining them
from a perspective of individualism, we produce an artificial dichotomy.

But how are we to use this literature to deepen our understanding
of political theory? Indeed, the differences posited by Gilligan, Flax,
and Chodorow in many ways mirror claims made for centuries as the
precise justification for excluding women from public life. The historical insistence that women cannot follow the rigid discipline of logic
might seem to gain new force with this "scientific" reassurance that
women are oriented toward an inductive, intuitive, nonrationalistic

---

[52]Gilligan and Wiggins (1988), p. 113.
[53]Belenky et al. (1986).
[54]Again, the rights model itself conceives of growth as culminating only in rationalism and rules.

ideology and moral methodology. The public-private split would seem to be given a new lease on life.

This returns us once again to the interpretive-empiricist debate I introduced at the beginning of this chapter. It is important to keep in mind that we cannot—and I believe that these theorists do not—assume that these gendered differences hold true for every man and woman. Gilligan's work is, as she points out, a theory of interpretation, and "the different voice . . . is characterized not by gender but theme. Its association with women is an empirical observation . . . but it is not absolute" (p. 2). That is, her work is made possible by attention to the voices of women expressed in these studies but does not depend on those voices' belonging exclusively to women. Certainly she and her colleagues seek to understand a gender relationship, which is why Gilligan goes on to trace this voice through women's development and says that she thinks her work "will offer a representation of [women's] thought that enables them to see better its integrity and validity" (p. 3).

Historically the voice of concern, of feeling, induction, flexibility toward rules, connection, and relationship has always been associated with women and has justified the radical historical separation of public from private. Women have been said not to have the ability to reason or to use rational deductive thinking, and this failure has been cited to justify their exclusion from public decision-making processes. Their relationality has made them the appropriate caretakers of the private realm, where such values have been permitted, even required, to flourish.

Certainly in her own studies Gilligan found a gender relationship between the two voices. But the relationship is more subtle than a simplistic gender correlation. Nona Lyons found that the two modes of moral thinking identified by Gilligan's care and rights models correlated strongly with divergent perceptions of self as either connected to or separate from others.[55] Furthermore, she found that although there was no strict correlation to gender, there was a relationship to it: that is, whereas men and women both combine the perspectives of care and justice, or at least have both modes in their conceptual vocabulary, women tend "to rely *more* on considerations of care and response in defining and resolving moral problems and to describe themselves in the connected mode, while the men, as a group, relied *more* on considerations of justice and rights and tended to define themselves as separate in relation to others."[56] That priority is given to

[55]Lyons (1988), pp. 21–48.
[56]Gilligan (1986), p. 11; emphasis added. See esp. Lyons (1988), pp. 42–43.

one mode does not preclude other kinds of reasoning from being utilized by an individual moral decision maker.

Gilligan and Wiggins call this priority a "focus phenomenon." Two-
thirds of their male and female respondents mentioned both care and
justice, but the same proportion also took one or the other as their
primary focus in addressing a moral dilemma. The care focus was not
characteristic of all the females in their sample, but almost all of the
care focusers were female. Thus out of twenty-two women, ten took a
justice focus and twelve a care focus; of thirty-one males, thirty fo-
cused on justice.[57] Gilligan, Langdale, Lyons, and Murphy found that
whereas males and females use both conceptions, 75 percent of the
females studied used predominantly the response orientation and
only 25 percent used predominantly a rights orientation. Among
males, 79 percent relied mainly on a rights orientation, 14 percent
predominantly followed the response model, and 7 percent of the
males were divided in their usage between the two.[58] Sharry Langdale
found a similar gender relation with the two moral conceptions in her
study.[59]

The phenomena of focus, spontaneity, and choice are highlighted
by Donna Kay Johnstone, who related a tale to children about a porcupine who has kindly been allowed to take shelter from winter in a
cave occupied by a family of moles. When the moles find that the
porcupine's quills create too much of a difficulty for them, they ask
him to leave, but he refuses. The children are asked what the moles
should do. Three-quarters of the boys "spontaneously" chose the
rights solution, the issue for them being the interrelationship of
power and rules. The girls assumed relationship between the animals
and suggested solutions that led to inclusion, such as digging a bigger
cave so everyone would have room, or putting a towel over the porcupine so he would not poke them. In addition, when the children
were presented with an alternate model to the one they chose, almost
all the children agreed that the inclusive solution was better; even
those who had not spontaneously seen the possibilities of such a solution preferred it to the rights model. Johnstone holds that "gender
difference does not reflect knowing or understanding only one orientation, but rather choosing and/or preferring one over the other as a
solution to a moral dilemma."[60]

[57]Gilligan and Wiggins (1988), p. 118.
[58]Gilligan, Langdale, Lyons, and Murphy (1982), cited in Kohlberg (1984), pp. 340–
41.
[59]Langdale (1983), cited in Gilligan (1986), p. 14.
[60]Johnstone (1988), p. 65. Actually, in Johnstone's study "73.3% of males use[d] the
rights orientation for their initial solution. In contrast, 50% of the girls used the response orientation, 40% used rights, and 10% used both orientations in their initial
solution." See Johnstone (1988), pp. 56–58, 60.

But again the apparent empirical orientation of this work should not make us lose sight of its even more important interpretive dimensions. These are similarly highlighted by Belenky et al. in their concepts of "connected knowing" and "separate knowing." Although they explore the former in women's and girls' voices, and consider the latter a "masculine" mode, their work seeks to highlight different ways of learning and knowing that are not necessarily gender related. Separate knowing coheres with Gilligan's rights model. It operates from premises of separation between knower and the known; it incorporates a concept of knowledge that is rule governed and objective. The known is an object, an other in an opposed relation to the self, the knower. Separate knowing is an "adversarial form" of knowledge. It also displays a disjunction between knowing and feeling. Objectivity is equated with dispassion, a process that excludes all private concerns and feelings, both one's own and those of one's adversary.[61]

Connected knowing, in contrast, involves an orientation toward relationship rather than rules, intersubjectivity rather than objectivity. It involves treating the known as a subject rather than an object and treating others on their own terms, considering their selfhood directly. In short, the "connection" in connected knowing is not merely between the knower and other knowers but between the knower and the known; but in the process, intimate relations with other knowers —and with their knowledge—becomes a central enterprise of human social life: "Connected knowers develop procedures for gaining access to other people's knowledge. At the heart of these procedures is the capacity for empathy. Since knowledge comes from experience, the only way they can hope to understand another person's ideas is to try to share the experience that has led the person to form the idea." As a central feature of connected knowing, empathy—a characteristic similarly attributed more prominently to girls and women by object relations—is described as "feeling with," as merging the self *with* the other, rather than intrusively imposing the self *on* the other.[62]

This concept is similar to Gilligan and Wiggins's "co-feeling," which involves the "ability to *participate* in another's feelings (in their terms)."[63] They juxtapose co-feeling to sympathy, which they conceptualize as involving an evaluation of whether or not to feel concern rather than taking the need for concern as given and deciding what form that concern should take. The reason that co-feeling is more caring, they suggest, is that rather than thinking of how *I* would feel in your place (Kohlberg's "reciprocity"), I think of how *you* actually feel. In what they call sympathy, as in Kohlberg's reciprocity, the self is

[61]Belenky et al. (1986), pp. 106, 109.
[62]Ibid., pp. 113, 122.
[63]Gilligan and Wiggins (1988), p. 122.

the referent for assessing and measuring the other; the other is not directly considered as a self but is treated as an object. Co-feeling thus involves greater concreteness as well as greater contextuality, for any two people have different histories and other features that might cause them to feel quite differently in similar circumstances.

Connected knowing also establishes a link between emotion and epistemology; particularly in the location of empathy in knowledge, connected knowing and co-feeling highlight the epistemological implications of moral psychology. Rather than juxtaposing reason and emotion, connected knowing suggests that the two are intimately related, and that the dichotomization of the two, and the devaluation of the latter, produces the exaggerated emphasis on a "pure" objectivity, as well as the abstract universalizability of rights and justice characteristic of modernist epistemologies and political theories. It suggests not just different kinds of knowledge but different ways of acquiring and pursuing knowledge and different notions of what it means to know. Similarly, co-feeling suggests different methods of understanding others and different criteria for evaluation.

Yet this work also suggests that the interstices of connection and separation, care and justice, and gender are neither reductively absolute nor irrelevant. Gilligan and Wiggins thus maintain that "children know both stories" of justice and care, and "test them in a variety of ways." These tests must come out of social experience, which is culturally constructed for males and females. Thus by adolescence a male child's experience is reinforced by cultural images of masculine dominance, which can underscore the prominence of inequality and motivate violence and aggression in the attempt to gain and equalize power. Similarly, culturally constructed messages of feminine dependence and the apparent hopelessness of women's gaining respect and status equal to men's may cause girls to focus their attention and concern on attachment as a way of "attenuating inequality."[64] Thus—as with care and justice—although attachment and equality both play important roles in all children's conceptions of themselves and the world, equality becomes more of a concern for boys through the meaning that is gained by way of the social construction of masculinity, just as attachment becomes more important to girls by way of the social construction of femininity. As gender is learned through a child's acquisition of language and observation of social relations, the social construction of gender plays into and in turn further constructs these two "stories."

Just as socialization and psychology have an interactive and inter-

[64]Ibid., pp. 115, 116.

dependent influence on each other, object relations theory provides a theoretical framework that makes this relationship not merely an empirical observation for particular samples but a systematic basis for an interpretive theory of gender difference arising out of the socially constructed relations of child rearing. For the two different moral perspectives Gilligan articulates revolve around "two modes of describing the relationship between self and other" (p. 2), and, as we saw in the discussion of object relations theory, the difference between "masculine" and "feminine" revolves crucially around differences in this perception. These differences are central to the meaning of being a gendered person.

In sum, there would seem to be substantial evidence that validates the different voice as a *woman's* voice; yet to leave it at that would be a reductive misrepresentation of gender psychology. The concepts and language offered by psychology can be used effectively by political theory without its embracing an essential view of gender. Indeed, the aspects most useful in the study of political theory are not to be found by taking object relations or moral psychology at face value. Rather, it is far more useful and accurate to understand these as theories of *power*. For instance, in discussing a broader application of Gilligan's thesis, Rachel Hare-Mustin and Jeanne Marecek have pointed out that those in positions of power tend to express themselves in terms of rules and that the powerless tend to invoke considerations of care; thus a mother might refer to rules while her children appeal to understanding.[65]

Psychology and psychoanalytic theory, in spite of their misogynist history, provide a language and vocabulary of power that are very useful for political theory and can transcend gender. There have been, and indeed are, men who have expressed the voice of care and connection, and have been just as marginalized as women. For instance, Martin Luther King, Jr., writes of a "network of mutuality" that defines community and connects justice with love; he is importantly marginalized. Sandra Harding has discussed the "curious coincidence" of (white) western feminism and black (male) African world views; again, these latter views are marginalized as the West arrogantly dubs them "third world."[66]

It is not merely coincidental that such marginalized men are frequently also members of (especially racially) oppressed groups. The interconnections between gender and race are particularly significant here, precisely because gender psychology has been accused of race

[65]Hare-Mustin and Marecek (1986), pp. 205–12. See also Hare-Mustin and Marecek (1990), pp. 184–201.
[66]King (1969), pp. 73, 83; Harding (1986), chap. 7.

and class biases. Patricia Hill Collins develops an "ethic of care" from African-American experience, and she explicitly draws connections between this ethic and a (white) "feminist" ethic of care. But while she claims that this ethic characterizes the experience of African-Americans of both sexes,[67] she focuses predominantly on black women, and specifically on their style of mothering, which differs in significant ways from the model patriarchal nuclear family which underpins much of object relations theory. Collins holds that mothering in black communities is more communal, and that black women fill important roles as "community othermothers." This practice may defuse the intense exclusivity of the mothering relationship which object relations posits. Simultaneously, the necessity of black women's participation in the labor force, as well as their role as head of family, she argues, offers their daughters consistent models of strong, well-differentiated women.[68] Yet although she argues, citing bell hooks, that "this form of [shared] parenting is revolutionary,"[69] it is explicitly women who do this othermothering. At the heart of Collins's argument is the suggestion that the experiences of black (female) community othermothers provide not a challenge to but a better model for a theory of care: "Nurturing children in Black extended family networks stimulates a more generalized ethic of caring."[70] Indeed, far from rejecting an ethic of care, connected knowing, contextuality, and concreteness as merely reflective of white women's experiences, she implicitly questions the ability of white women, as well as African-American men, to embody such an ethic consistently because of their connections to privilege: white women to race privilege, black men to gender privilege.

> While white women may value the concrete, it is questionable whether white families—particularly middle-class nuclear ones—and white community institutions provide comparable types of support [to the black family and community]. Similarly, while Black men are supported by Afrocentric institutions, they cannot participate in Black women's sisterhood. In terms of Black women's relationships with one another, African-American women may find it easier than others to recognize con-

[67]Collins (1990). She also cites King's unification of love and justice (p. 197).
[68]Collins notes that "as much as 70 percent of low-income Black households are headed by women." Ibid., p. 64, and chaps. 3 and 6, passim.
[69]Ibid., p. 122, citing hooks (1984), p. 144.
[70]Collins (1990), p. 129. Collins also draws on Belenky et al. (pp. 160, 210, 212) and Gilligan (p. 219) to describe a (presumably white) feminist ethic of care which converges with an African-American ethic of caring. She says, "African American women . . . experience a convergence of values from Afrocentric and female institutions" (p. 219). See Tronto (1987) and Okin (1989) on the importance of creating a generalized theory of care such as Collins refers to.

nectedness as a primary way of knowing, simply because we are encouraged to do so by a Black women's tradition of sisterhood.[71]

Collins's work suggests that, although gender is not the sole source of an ethic of care, it is a significant one. Various cultural and ethnic contexts can deepen or diffuse this ethic and can even appear to transcend gender. But at the same time, gender provides a useful category for understanding the ways in which care can transcend cultural differences as well. Accordingly, when I refer to "the boy," "male," "feminine," "the girl," it will be helpful for the reader to view these as, in part, abstractions that idealize and represent relationships of power, as symbolizations of power relations. That these relations have one key source in gender is important but not exhaustive or exclusive. Thus, gender psychology can be seen as a heuristic device for uncovering the structural sexism and resulting epistemological bias of western thought. More particularly, by identifying individual development as in part the product of created institutions—that is, the social relations of child rearing—object relations can translate individual experience into cultural phenomena, or at least explain the institutional and cultural aspects of a supposedly individual experience. This offers great potential for challenging many ideals of liberal theory, such as the public-private dichotomy and the inviolability of the individual, for it suggests that what happens in the "private" relations of child rearing influences how we maintain and define "public." It further reminds us that individuals are personalities that are the products of a variety of factors, including, above all, relationships with others.

At the same time, Chodorow's warning against overly interpretive uses of gender psychology persists. We should not forget that women have historically given expression to the voice of care. That voice has a history, and so does obligation, and indeed these two histories help constitute each other. It is not just a coincidence that women have been for the most part powerless and have expressed the voice of care. Indeed, the activities of the private sphere to which they have been assigned—child care, nurturance, love—have required women to draw on and develop that voice. Thus we should not be surprised

---

[71]Collins (1990), p. 212. She points out that King and his Southern Christian Leadership Conference staff "laughed" at a request by the black activist Septima Clark for increased inclusion of black women: "You can work behind the scenes all you want. . . . But don't come forth and try to lead. That's not the kind of thing they [black men] want." Collins (1990), p. 157. In his "Letter from Birmingham City Jail," King vacillates between addressing "brothers and sisters" equally and specifically directing a patriarchal message to men, who are humiliated because "your wife and mother are never given the respected title 'Mrs.'" King (1969), p. 77.

if women's experience highlights this voice for us. The crucial distinction between this position and essentialism, however, is that the theory does not have to *depend* on women, and women alone, to express that voice. While rejecting the strict thesis that this is a woman's voice, I would argue that there is a loose gender relationship, one that derives from history, material experience, and socialization as well as psychology. This grounding in women's experience is the whole point of calling it feminist.

Furthermore, because of the historical relation of this voice with women, we can listen to women to understand the themes of that voice: care, response, connection. What Gilligan's empirical observation provides is a point of entry. We trace the voice through women's experience because there it is more obvious and apparent, precisely because it was required to flourish within the context of family and the private sphere to which women were bound exclusively. Indeed, the activities of affective life required of women in the private sphere depended on that voice's being allowed a limited and contained expression within that sphere; and those activities made the integrity and necessity of that voice more apparent to women, hence increasing its centrality in women's lives. Furthermore, its denigration is likely to have had its historical source in the fact that it *was* associated with women's activity and was hence considered a "woman's voice." Such a voice could not be tolerated in the public sphere, whether it came from a man or a woman, because it would threaten the barriers between public and private—barriers that were necessary to the resolution of male psychic dilemmas concerning the repression of primary femininity. These differing voices thus need to be examined from the perspective of a symbolic language of power and powerlessness as a heuristic device for understanding the power relations inherent in our political theories and their underlying epistemology.

The point of my use of gender psychology, then—that there is another equally compelling moral voice which moral psychology as well as moral philosophy has denied and denigrated—is made and articulated in our listening to women's voices, and yet it is not invested in that voice's belonging wholly and exclusively to women. As Susan Okin argues, although the empirical evidence Gilligan and her colleagues have accumulated is an unsatisfactory basis for conclusions about "women's morality," "the virtue of Gilligan's work is that, because of the richness of its detailed quotations from respondents, it helps us to understand, far better than do more quantitative but less detailed findings, what the difference is."[72] Thus Gilligan talks about

---

[72]Okin (1989), p. 157.

justice versus care, not male versus female. To say that the association of the care conception with women is empirical is, in my view, to say more than that a particular sample of women studied were found to express this voice (though Gilligan et al. may intend to convey that more limited meaning); it is also to consider history, the psychic ramifications of institutions, and the material activities of women's lives in their interactive, confluent, and reciprocal effects, one upon the other. The word *feminist* not only recognizes the origin of this voice in women's experience but takes upon itself the task of transforming this devalued and ignored conception of reality into a conception that is valued and powerful, one that needs to be integrated with the skewed but dominant rights conception that pervades our public life and our epistemology.

The existence of different referential frameworks, different perspectival starting points, means that the paths of development not only diverge from one another but also produce in that developmental process an entire mode of thought, a different language, a separate reality. Because of that the end points of development, though related or connected, are not the same. Hence, each mode's conception of reality and morality differs. Indeed, there are two ontologies and two epistemologies. Yet these two models are not as dichotomous as they might seem to be. Between absolute rigidity and isolation at one extreme and absolute identification and connection at the other lies a variety of positions that embody a combination of values. Men may be as capable of seeing the morality of love as women are of asserting rights; but one or the other perspective forms a context, a frame of reference, a medium through which moral decisions are made.

Thus the significance of Amy's and Jake's responses does not lie in the fact that Jake advocates theft whereas Amy does not—that is, in the decision itself—but rather in the framework that informs, evaluates, and translates the decision. Jake advocates theft because he reasons from a frame of reference that assumes the universality of deductive rationality and the primacy of individual rights: the "fact" that people are separate yields the inescapable view of the dilemma as a head-on conflict of rights, one of which (life) has primacy over the other (property) in a natural hierarchy. Amy disagrees because she reasons from a frame of reference that assumes the givenness of care and concern, the universality of relational rationality, the primacy of responsiveness. The "fact" that people are connected yields a view of the dilemma as encompassing all three characters in a web of relationships that is breaking apart because of a lack of concern. Relationship is not a condition to be factored into the decision but is rather a crucible for Amy's moral perspective: it is the core of her reasoning, her starting point for reality.

That is the key to understanding the meaning of this different voice. I am not talking merely about two ways of resolving conflicts, such as utilitarianism versus Rawls's justice as fairness. We are confronted with two different bodies of knowledge, two perceptual frameworks as foreign as two unrelated cultures, two different "language games,"[73] if you will. Yet these different language games use the same diction and share a conceptual vocabulary; these two frameworks share a cultural backdrop; these two bodies of knowledge share an empirical reality. But gender psychology further points out that shared forms of life are not necessarily neutral just because they are shared; it suggests that the cultural backdrop, the conceptual vocabulary, and even perhaps the empirical reality that are shared may themselves be gender biased to greater or lesser degrees. This bias gives an intrinsic added weight to the rights conception, which both justifies its institutionalization as public ideology and further perpetuates its development as such.

Thus, the problem that lies at the heart of liberal political theory is that concepts such as obligation are defined from the basic assumption of the primacy of individual rights and freedom. Such assumptions limit criticism that can be made within the structure because of definitional biases. Since these biases and definitions are viewed as natural and self-evident, a claim that brings the entire system into question can be easily dismissed. Yet the basic dissatisfaction with the language of rights expressed by Gilligan's female subjects is legitimate; their avoidance of that language is based on a different perspective that shows rights talk to be inadequate for the resolution of moral dilemmas.

The implications for political theory thus go well beyond the suggestions I made earlier in this chapter concerning moral theory. They begin with the conceptualization of two differing ontologies and accompanying epistemologies. Object relations theory and moral psychology suggest more than the idea that certain political theories might tend to be more "feminine" in the values they put forth and others more "masculine." They suggest implications for both the framework and the method of political theory in general. It is to the exploration of these implications that I now turn, as I consider the ways in which the epistemological and ontological implications of object relations and moral psychology afford a deeper understanding of what is so problematic about political obligation.

[73]Wittgenstein, *Philosophical Investigations*.

CHAPTER FOUR

Implications for
a Feminist Epistemology

GENDER PSYCHOLOGY suggests an alternative epistemology and moral methodology that have existed as long as the dominant masculine ideology but have been repressed and ignored except in the inner sanctum of women's "private world" experience and the "inessential" material activities and work that have defined and dominated women's lives, at least in the modern era. The theory highlights the notion that our understanding of the world as it is expressed through the ideology and institutions of the public realm is not the universal understanding it purports to be but may have a specifically gendered bias. As Gilligan notes: "Theories formerly considered to be sexually neutral in their scientific objectivity are found instead to reflect a consistent observational and evaluative bias. Then the presumed neutrality of science, like that of language itself, gives way to the recognition that categories of knowledge are human constructions . . . when we begin to notice how accustomed we have become to seeing life through men's eyes."[1]

This noticing can help us begin to understand the ways in which the problems of political obligation are generated by masculinist perspectives. But it can further help us understand that the problem goes much deeper than, for instance, translating "man" in Locke's theory as "men and women." We cannot simply add women to existing categories of thought, because such thought is premised on a distortion of women's "nature" which is described only as it is experienced by men or seen through men's eyes. As Sandra Harding says, "The prevailing

[1]Gilligan (1982), p. 6.

theories of the social and natural sciences draw on and legitimate a conceptual screen that systematically distorts our vision of women and their lives."[2] How can we "plug" women in to a political theory that systematically denigrates the activity in which they have historically engaged? That marks as periods of great progress times when women suffered severe setbacks in social recognition and their ability "to act as historical and rational agents"?[3] And even if we do gender neutralize liberal theory and declare that women's "natures" are identical to men's, then why, we may ask, have not women created theories and conducted wars like men? The obvious answer would seem to lead to a theory of "natural" inferiority. In such a world, of course, "woman" will appear inferior: the world as created by men is not hers, and the standards by which her achievements are judged are alien to the values on which her practices rely.

The epistemological dimensions of the arguments I have constructed in earlier chapters of this book, and particularly in the previous chapter, strike at the heart of the structural sexism of political theory. It is not merely the case that Locke or Rousseau created theories of political society that favored men and oppressed women. If this were the case, the remedy would be straightforwardly to alter the specific aspects of such theories that adversely affect women. The problems, as I have indicated, lie deeper within the theories. They reach down to the understanding of the world from which the theorists write to the definitional "bedrock"[4] concepts they employ, the conceptual framework that defines what they know and how they know it. The questions I have posed about obligations—what values and ideas these theories accommodate, what questions they do and do not allow—can thus be seen as epistemological questions.

The Ontological Dimensions of Epistemology

The claim that these questions are epistemological is, to put it mildly, controversial. Particularly in light of my use of object relations and psychology, is it not ontology, the nature of being, that is at issue? Certainly my theory is concerned with the concept of being: what it means to be male or female, for instance. In the rationalist and

[2]Harding (1984), p. 46.
[3]Ibid., p. 47.
[4]Wittgenstein, *Philosophical Investigations*, p. 85, para. 217. Wittgenstein uses the metaphorical phrasing "I have reached bedrock, and my spade is turned. Then I am inclined to say 'This is simply what I do'" to explain the fact that there are certain fundamentals to language and concepts, certain givens, that cannot be so much explained as accepted.

empiricist epistemologies of Descartes, Locke, Hume, Mill, and Kant, which dominate liberal theory and western thinking, ontology and epistemology are separate and distinct. If true knowledge must be objective, then it is vital that what is known be radically divorced from whoever the knower is; or at least, whoever the knower is should be irrelevant. Objective knowledge should be true for all.

Yet part of what gender psychology suggests is that epistemology is very closely related to ontology, that indeed it is at best difficult to separate them. If the processes of psychic development produce differences in views of the self as either fundamentally separate or connected, then these will inform one's view of the world, which in turn will shade one's perception and interpretation of "truth" or "reality." Perception, one might reply, is hardly the same as epistemology (although, one might argue, they were importantly related for the empiricists, particularly Hume). Nevertheless, gender psychology can provide a critical perspective on our understanding of epistemology and can offer some insights into the ways our dominant epistemology is biased.

A significant part of this bias is the dichotomy itself. From the perspective of object relations, in fact, we can see that the dichotomy between epistemology and ontology, which characterizes both rationalist and empiricist epistemologies, is specifically masculinist, for it follows from, or at least echoes, the mind-body duality: if the body is separate and distinct from the mind, then theories of knowledge and the ways we conceptualize knowing must be distinct from theories of existence and the ways we conceptualize being.

The major themes of these positivist epistemologies, revolving around the concepts of objectivity and interiority, support this notion. These concepts are particularly masculine in their replication of pre-oedipal themes of rejection and repression of the mother. The boy, in perceiving himself as radically separate from the world, turns inward to confirm reality rather than outward to the object world, which he must subjugate to his own existence and self. Or more precisely, he relies on the external—for instance rules and roles that form a positional identification—only insofar as he has been able to exert, or to convince himself that he exerts, control over it. Thus objectivity becomes a useful means of classifying and understanding the world; but it achieves its importance because it derives from the objectification of the woman/mother, a central task of masculine development that is undertaken as a means to escape the mother and solidify masculine identity.

The bias of modern epistemologies affects the kinds of questions that are asked, the modes of inquiry that are used and considered legitimate, and what is taken as evidence of particular knowledge claims; it ensures "that certain questions and ways of answering them become constitutive of philosophy."[5] In creating the split between epistemology and ontology, rationalist and empiricist epistemologies created a particular concept of knowing that revolves around objectivity. Once this category of objectivity was developed, the epistemologies could claim the status that they created. The assertion that epistemology and ontology are entirely separate is granted the status of objective truth, and epistemology comes to be further defined as excluding ontological considerations. In a sense, the split between ontology and epistemology is itself an epistemological claim: it is part of the rational and empiricist theories of knowledge that knowing is divorced from being. That is just what epistemology means. Thus, by "explicitly ignor[ing] gender while implicitly exploiting distinctively masculine meanings of knowledge seeking,"[6] these epistemologies were able to mask their own bias.

But the claim to objectivity must be recognized as circular. As Harding argues, "Once we stop thinking of modern Western epistemologies as a set of philosophical givens, we can begin to examine them instead as historical justificatory strategies—as culturally specific modes of constructing and exploiting cultural meanings in support of new kinds of knowledge claims."[7] I maintain that feminist theorists writing on questions of epistemology are in fact recasting epistemology in terms that allow for ontology, if not melding the two completely. Bordo, Flax, Harding, and Hartsock all work from the implicit or explicit claim that the way epistemology is defined and its false juxtaposition to ontology not only limit and (mis)direct the kinds of questions that philosophy and political theory ask but also thereby misrepresent the nature of social relations. As Flax most explicitly points out, "In philosophy, being (ontology) has been divorced from knowing (epistemology), and both have been separated from either ethics or politics." We need to recognize the overlap of all four if we are to avoid the "frozen postures" of patriarchal social relations and achieve more comprehensive and accurate ways of knowing.[8]

The conceptualization of these ways of knowing that is my primary focus has been expressed by Nancy Hartsock as "the feminist standpoint." This is a variation on the more general conceptualization of Marxian "standpoint epistemology," which was specifically formulated as "the standpoint of the proletariat."[9] Feminist standpoint epis-

[5]Flax (1983), p. 248.
[6]Harding (1986), p. 141.
[7]Ibid.
[8]Flax (1983), p. 245.
[9]Hartsock (1984), p 117.

temology rejects the idea that epistemology is objective or universal; it holds that epistemology is itself a product of particular social relations. Not just knowledge, or what we know, is shaped by particular experience and the relations we have to others, but *how* we know and how we conceive of knowledge are also similarly shaped. Unlike a Kantian or Cartesian epistemology, feminist standpoint epistemology rejects the concept of pure objectivity, or the "purity" of "true" knowledge.

But what do I mean by standpoint? A standpoint is the perspective from which one views the world, social relations—reality, if you will. It is composed of factors such as race, class, gender, and the kind of work one does; I would also add psychosexual development. The idea behind a standpoint is that different people will develop different knowledge frameworks depending on their experiences and circumstances. Out of these experiences is formed a crucible for perception, interpretation, and understanding, as many of the unconscious aspects of experience are moved into the realm of consciousness. To the degree that a particular group of people share socially and politically significant characteristics—for instance, women—they will share a standpoint. Since "epistemology grows in a complex and contradictory way from material life," the standpoint "structures epistemology in a particular way" that reflects experience.[10] If that experience differs among people—as I have suggested it does for men and women under mother-only child rearing—then, according to the concept of a standpoint, their epistemological orientations will be different.

The feminist standpoint, however, is not "natural" to all women; it is not a *feminine* standpoint but must be achieved or at least acknowledged. Hartsock calls it an "engaged" position; that is, it is not a mere unconscious bias but must be struggled for. This is where feminist theory enters. The role political theory can play is to help identify, articulate, and explain the standpoint through an analysis of women's experience. In particular, female feminist theorists can engage in the description of their own experience, as well as in the analysis that gives added meaning to experience. Political theory can help us translate experience into political meaning or can articulate the political significance of women's experience. The project of feminist theory is thus part of the political struggle in which, according to Hartsock at least, women need to engage in order to achieve a feminist standpoint.

This epistemological approach is obviously controversial. But its advantage from a methodological point of view is that it reveals that "there are some perspectives on society from which, however well-

---

[10]Ibid.

intentioned one may be, the real relations of humans with each other and the natural world are not visible."[11] The standpoint of an oppressed group, she asserts, provides a certain advantage in enabling members of the group to see, if not "objectively," at least more sides of a question. Just as the proletariat has a potentially superior vantage point from which to understand the relationship between worker and capitalist, so do women have the greater ability to understand more fully the relationship between men and women. That relationship is defined by male privilege or the system of male domination. This makes it difficult for males to see the problems of gender relations. As Harding points out, "Objectively, no individual man can succeed in renouncing sexist privilege any more than individual whites can succeed in renouncing racist privilege—the benefits of gender and race accrue regardless of the wishes of the individuals who bear them."[12] Thus, the myths that have developed to explain women's inequality cannot be seen as readily by men, even when men specifically look for them, because men do not *experience* them as myths, and do not directly suffer from this experience.

This analysis might suggest that a feminist standpoint is gender exclusive, but many theorists would disagree. Although a feminist standpoint derives from the particular experiences of women, Hartsock specifically uses the term *feminist* rather than *female* to point out both "the achieved character of a standpoint and that a standpoint by definition carries a liberatory potential."[13] It also suggests that a feminist standpoint is not limited to women; the process of feminist struggle welcomes male participants. Other theorists, such as Harding,[14] are much more ambivalent about this conclusion, not because they do not want men to be feminists but because they doubt whether the standpoint approach will allow them to participate in the "struggle."[15] Advocates of a feminist standpoint approach maintain that it can reveal, or help uncover, ways in which the current society and dominant ideology deny or ignore "real relations of humans" because of a masculinist bias. As Harding and Merrill B. Hintikka have put it, it can help us to "dis-cover" reality.[16] Object relations theory can pro-

---

[11]Ibid.

[12]Harding (1987a), p. 658. Georg Simmel made a similar point at the turn of the century.

[13]Hartsock (1983), p. 289.

[14]See Harding (1986), esp. chap. 6. But see Harding (1991) for arguments that men should strive to achieve feminist standpoints in spite of the difficulties.

[15]Hartsock in particular uses the language of feminist struggle. Within this imagery perhaps we could say that men can be soldiers but not generals, though this begs the question as to whether a true feminist struggle would involve military hierarchies.

[16]Harding and Hintikka (1983).

vide an important aspect of a feminist standpoint. By identifying individual development as in part the product of created institutions, it can translate individual experience into cultural phenomena, or at least explain the institutional and cultural aspects of a supposedly individual experience.

Furthermore, object relations can help us see the importance of a feminist standpoint for political obligation by highlighting questions of epistemology. If people experience and display differences in defining the self as either fundmentally separate or connected, and if this definition then serves as the framework for one's perceptions, understanding, and interpretation of the external world, then to a significant degree the processes of psychic development shape our concept of reality for us: they shape our knowledge and our framework of knowledge. To the degree that such self-conceptions—as isolated or connected—are at least historically gender related, the accompanying world view will differ by gender as well. Thus, I suggest that the dominant epistemology that defines political concepts such as obligation, as well as the method of our dominant political theoretical discourses, may themselves be an important locus of gender bias. So object relations can be a means to understanding how the problems of liberal democratic theory go beyond the empirical exclusion of women from politics to the fact that the epistemology from which these theories operate is premised on that exclusion. And in fact, by examining the epistemological implications of object relations theory, we may be able to tease out some ways in which the problems of consent are a result of this bias.

Let us begin this task by returning to the dichotomization of ontology and epistemology characteristic of rationalist and empiricist epistemologies. I have suggested that we need to consider these two entities as related. My earlier discussion of object relations and moral psychology highlighted the overlap between epistemology and ontology; that is, how individuals conceptualize themselves, how they view their being, influences the way they conceptualize and know the world. In object relations, the fact that boys and girls conceive their self-identities in particular ways gives rise to different frameworks for understanding the relations between self and other, subject and object, and hence of interpreting and giving voice to the objects of the world. In Gilligan's work it is the ontologically based assumptions underlying moral reasoning and not the content of moral judgments themselves that account for the crucial differences in rights and care responses. Amy's ontological perspective of connection yields her reconstruction of the question being asked, her understanding of the world and of the psychological inquiry of knowledge. Not merely what she knows but *how* she knows, the framework that guides her interpretation of the information provided by the interviewer, is influenced and shaped by her ontological perspective.

Object relations theory can help us see not only that modern positivist epistemologies are gender biased but also that this separation of epistemology from ontology is itself a masculinist ideology. Because masculinist ontology gives rise to dualism, it creates an epistemological orientation that conceives of the world in oppositional categories. We know things because we, as subjects, observe objects, which are entirely distinct from us, and this observation gives us an "objective" assessment of meaning. This constitutes the rationale for the rejection of so-called feminine ontology from the world of the public; the ontological assumption of connection creates an epistemology that rejects dualism. Indeed, it cannot even be granted the status of epistemology within modernist discourse, precisely *because* it rejects dualisms of mind and body, subject and object, fact and value, and ultimately of epistemology and ontology.

Theorists have been quite willing to allow that women have a different ontology. That women's being is defined by their bodies is essential to the justification of their exclusion from the public realm. But to allow that this ontology indicates a separate epistemology is threatening on several levels. Not only does it suggest that women may have ways of knowing just as valuable as men's, but also such an admission questions the very concept of knowledge as it is defined by (male-created) empiricist epistemologies. If knowledge is conceived of as pure, dependent only on true thought, achieved only by the rigorous exercise of the mind, if such a conceptualization of thought is a way to reject the body, if this rejection is necessary to achieve masculinity by rejecting the feminine, then the admission that knowing can come from being is a contradiction not only of this definition of knowledge and epistemology but of the (unconscious) purpose of defining and developing epistemology in this way in the first place. That is, the very concept of a "feminine" epistemology that invokes the interaction of ontology is fundamentally at odds with the values of western ideology and with the (unrecognized) values underlying its conceptualization and construction as well.

Having said that, however, I should immediately reformulate the concept of a feminine epistemology in favor of a concept of feminist epistemology, something quite distinct. To say that women have a different epistemology by virtue of their psychic development and other experiences does not in itself address the degree to which these experiences are the product of patriarchal social relations. Although I have outlined, and will continue to discuss, differences between masculine and feminine experiences and the ramifications of these differences, it is vital to remember that much of women's experience itself can be seen as a product of masculine action through patriarchy. After all, Chodorow, Flax, and Dinnerstein all point out that mother-only child rearing is itself an institution of patriarchy, a self-perpetuating practice that facilitates men's fulfillment of the very needs that it creates and inhibits women from resolving the very dilemmas it brings about.

So it is not the case that by looking at women's experience we can achieve some "pure" theory or analysis based on a nonmasculine world.[17] Perhaps part of women's historical, psychic, and epistemological opposition to dichotomy involves a recognition of the fact that even the practices within which women express and define themselves are not directly opposed to masculinity and masculinism but are themselves products of it. That women's reality differs from men's does not mean we can or should simply reject a masculine point of view: "Men's power to structure social relations in their own image means that women too must participate in social relations that manifest and express abstract masculinity."[18]

Problems and Challenges

This last point implicitly raises some questions about my use of gender psychology in the development of feminist standpoint epistemology. A variety of gender-related aspects of women's experience are explored by feminist theorists in the development of feminist theory; these range from being daughters of women, to pregnancy and childbirth, to housework, to sexual harassment in the workplace. I agree with the authors of these theories that attention needs to be paid to all aspects of women's experience in developing this epistemology: pregnancy may well provide a woman with a different historical consciousness;[19] the daily necessity confronting the housewife may be qualitatively different from the material necessity facing the factory worker, and will likely produce a different material consciousness;[20] women's "kinwork" structures their perspectives on familial

[17]French feminists such as Luce Irigaray and Hélène Cixous are obvious exceptions as they try to create "écriture féminine," which "writes from the body." But even this, I would argue, is deeply entrenched in the world of masculinism, particularly given its indebtedness to Lacanian psychoanalysis. See particulary Cixous (1980), Irigaray (1985), and Marks and de Courtivron (1980).
[18]Hartsock (1984), p. 245.
[19]O'Brien (1981).
[20]Hartsock (1983) and (1984).

and social relations;[21] and mothering as a practice most likely produces different perspectives on the world.[22]

The obvious reason for my limited focus in this essay on the psychological and psychoanalytic aspects already discussed is one of space; adequate treatment of all aspects would require several books. But there is also a reason of priority. Just as the psychic development of one's early years sets the stage for the rest of one's life, so does our institutionalized practice of mother-only child rearing set the stage for our collective social and political life. A psychoanalytic approach can help strengthen other kinds of analysis and provide a way for different approaches to work interactively. For instance, socialization is an important but not a sufficient explanation for the continued sexual division of labor into adult life and even after supposed feminist enlightenment. Socialization theories may lend themselves too readily to the standard criticism that women "merely" need to choose not to accept these roles any longer, thus denying the intricate complexity of gender's social construction. Psychoanalytic theory can supplement socialization theories with an account of the deep-seated psychic origins that socialization then reinforces.

Similarly, biological aspects of womanhood such as pregnancy are important but insufficient to explain women's status and place in society and may lend themselves to biodeterministic conclusions. Mary O'Brien's work, which offers an insightful analysis of what she calls "malestream thought" based on a concept of "reproductive consciousness," is a case in point. One may well ask of her theory whether women who cannot or choose not to bear children have access to this reproductive consciousness she postulates. O'Brien says that one need not be a mother because reproductive consciousness is a "universal consciousness, common to all women,"[23] and she implies that this derives from the *capacity* to bear children and the consciousness of continuity that this engenders. But she leaves unclear where this consciousness comes from if not from biology; and at any rate, many women are not biologically capable of bearing children. Furthermore, although most women are capable of raising children, this is a capacity that they share with men.

Gender psychology can provide a more complete and plausible way to connect this theory to a more widely applicable theory of women. As I noted earlier, gender identity is established in a child at a very early age, and this identity consists largely in social and cultural expectations and messages communicated by the mother both con-

---

[21]Di Leonardo (1984).
[22]Ruddick (1984a); see also Ruddick (1989).
[23]O'Brien (1981), p. 50.

sciously and unconsciously as well as by the society at large. In addition, at a very early stage the girl's intense primary identification with the mother gives way to a personal identification as her secondary, gendered identity; and this identity is more positive and secure than the abstract positional gender identification achieved by the boy.

The firmness of such gender identity in girls, and its nonbiological genesis, is documented in the literature: children who were mistakenly identified as girls at birth (children with unusual chromosomal configurations or with ambiguous genitalia) and subsequently raised as girls display equally strong gender identity as biological females. Subsequent discoveries of the lack of a vagina or reproductive organs or correct chromosomal makeup does not cast the gender identity into question. What is at issue for the individual is how to remedy the anatomical error (how to construct a vagina, whether in vitro fertilization would be successful and so on). Thus, gender identity is likely not to have a biological grounding. In fact, Robert J. Stoller argues that gender identity comes from parents' confident belief in the child's gender and their unambivalent treatment of the child according to that belief. Suzanne J. Kessler similarly cites evidence that "from the moment of birth the parent responds to the infant based on the infant's gender."[24]

When the subsequent preadolescent discovery of where babies come from occurs, however, this information is transposed back onto one's early found gender identity: I am like my mother (whether or not this is in fact biologically the case), therefore I too can have a child. Being a mother, in this additional biological sense, becomes a part of the girl because it is a part of her mother—indeed, it *defines* the mother in an important way for the girl—with whom she identifies intensely. (Note also that the awareness of pregnancy occurs at the same age that preoedipal issues tend to resurface for the girl.)[25] Thus psychoanalytic theory can shed light on theories oriented toward biology and make better sense of them. In this case it shows that the postulated existence of a reproductive consciousness has a high likelihood of truth, regardless of whether a woman has a child, wants to have one, or is even physically capable of bearing one.

So not only does psychoanalytic theory reveal a highly significant aspect of epistemology, but also it has great potential explanatory power. This still fails to account, however, for a final set of objections to my approach, which are perhaps more profound and sweeping. It might be argued that a feminist standpoint approach to gender psy-

[24]Stoller (1973); Kessler (1990), p. 9, n. 15. See also Rubin, Provenzano, and Luria (1974).
[25]Chodorow (1978), pp. 130–40.

chology is problematic in its assumption that there is a "feminine experience." Feminist standpoint's key strength lies in its ability to challenge the supposed neutrality of current epistemological frameworks and resulting substantive theories. It is also powerful in its call for the recognition and revaluation of women's experience and perspective. But critics contend that it fails to account for differences among women according to race, class, geographic location, nationality, and historical period. It may well assume that *women* means white women, just as *blacks* or *Africans* often implicitly means black or African men.[26] Such questions also pose the postmodernist challenge once again. As I indicated earlier, I consider the relationship between postmodernism and feminism in my afterword; but for some readers these questions press imminently on the present discussion. To discuss gender psychology is totalizing enough in its declaration of what women and men are. But then to raise these constructions to the level of epistemology is to carry the evil of totalization dangerously further, for it is to elevate to a more profound level of truth claim the particularity of individual experiences, which must necessarily differ from all other individual experiences.

A feminist standpoint approach also may seem to cast reality in terms of duality, even as it ostensibly rejects dualism. It may seem to embrace the "flip side" mentality that seeks to reject all that is supposedly masculine and replace it with all that is supposedly feminine. Standpoint theory claims that the standpoint of oppressed persons is superior to the dominant ideology because the oppressed have a superior ability to see the reality of social relations and thus are more able to speak out about the truth of those relations. Are women, then, the vanguard? Certainly Hartsock's approach in particular grants the possibility of males' achieving a feminist standpoint. But this ability must be limited, according to her theory, since men do not experience women's oppression. This potential dualism threatens gender psychology as well. Chodorow seems to indicate that men could become more like women if fathers took a larger role in early child care. The implication is that women would become more like men as well, but the theory is always cast in terms of men's needing to develop "feminine" traits and abilities. This is true of Gilligan's work as well. Although she is rightly critical of the rights model's rejection of issues of care, she advocates an increased incorporation of the care conception without adequately addressing its weaknesses. Does this view present a gynocentric theory that excludes masculinity altogether?

[26] See Hull, Scott, and Smith (1982), and Harding (1986), chap. 7, for this point. More generally, for criticisms of Chodorow and Gilligan along these lines, see Fraser and Nicholson (1990), Gottlieb (1984), and Young (1984).

And what about the particular construction of femininity that gender psychology posits? Is it not essentialist and reductive, similarly ignoring differences in race, class, and historical period? Might there not be other factors in child-rearing relations that could compensate for or override the effects of being raised by a woman? Furthermore, there has been disagreement over whether mother-only child rearing is in fact a socially universal practice, with some evidence that men partake in child rearing in some nonwestern cultures. Michelle Rosaldo cites the Ilongots of the Philippines as one society where "men spend long hours with their children" and seem to share more in domestic responsibilities.[27] Other objections attack the patriarchal-nuclear form of the family that object relations assumes. Chodorow's work, and object relations in general, has been criticized for ignoring the fact that many children today are raised in single-parent households.[28] Where do we place women (and men) who do not fit the mold? This is a particularly pertinent question for today's infants (and perhaps tomorrow's political theorists), who are being raised in shared[29] and single, heterosexual and homosexual parental relationships. Gilligan's work has been criticized on similar grounds, with critics contending the race and class bias of her sample yields a particularistic and even reified notion of feminine morality.

My first response to these objections is that it is still valid to explore the experiences of women past and present, even if those experiences are not universal, because of their significance for social reality as well as for political theory. Even though it is true that the ignorance of differences among women is potentially oppressive, that should not forestall the attempt to define a common ground on which women of various races, cultures, and historical periods can find multiple bases for shared experiences and standpoints. Object relations does suggest that the cultural phenomenon of mother-only child rearing can cut across a variety of family relations and structures; it can offer at least a "large historical narrative"[30] and thus has the potential for providing such a common ground. There are many variations within child-rearing practices, but whether people have similar or different relations

---

[27]Rosaldo (1974), p. 41.

[28]Bart (1984). Although I agree that object relations does not take a variety of variables into account, the single-mother model of parenthood is really not very different from the model object relations propounds; in fact the effects of the father's absence might be exaggerated, with boys' positional identification becoming even more abstract.

[29]This so-called objection in fact supports object relations; indeed, object relations applauds shared parenthood as the solution to the psychic ills produced by the sexual division of labor. Thus, according to the theory, people raised in this way should produce a more liberated society.

[30]Fraser and Nicholson (1990), p. 25.

with their primary caretakers, to deny that it is women, and women alone, who have primary responsibility for child rearing in almost all cultures is to reject a large body of historical and anthropological evidence. For instance, in Rosaldo's example, her finding that there is greater sexual equity among the Ilongots than in other cultures, leading to her conclusion that "an egalitarian ethos seems possible to the extent that men take on a domestic role,"[31] reinforces rather than contradicts Chodorow's thesis.

Furthermore, the present work is concerned with theories that have come out of societies in which child rearing is, on the whole, the responsibility of women—that is, the modern West—and Chodorow explicitly locates her theory in modern western capitalism.[32] It is possible that there may have existed cultures in which women were not the primary caretakers, and for such cultures it may be that object relations theory has diminished explanatory force. But this is certainly not the case in the modern West. Since my argument centers around a body of thought—liberalism—that at least characterizes western capitalism, the argument really only need concern itself with the social relations of child rearing in the West and since the late seventeenth and eighteenth centuries. At the very least, object relations certainly characterizes the family structures of the Enlightenment and post-Enlightenment West out of which social contract theory emerged. Indeed, one could argue that object relations might well explain "the" Enlightenment family more accurately than "the" family of the late twentieth century.[33] In this sense, to the degree that object relations *does* rely on a model of the family and child rearing that is sexist, racist, and classist, it becomes a useful vehicle for interpreting modern liberal theory as a sexist, racist, and classist ideology. In this light, it would contribute more effectively to a critique of social contract theory than to attempts to build a feminist theory of obligation in its place; but this issue will be addressed in my final chapters.

In other words, the claim for virtual universality must not be taken too grandly. Indeed, to do so is to fabricate a totality that is not being sought; but such are the strategies of modernists, not (supposedly) postmodernists. As Keller points out, "Although the patterns that give rise to" the gender differences posited by object relations theory "may be quasi-universal . . . the conditions that sustain them are not." Thus,

---

[31]Rosaldo (1974), p. 39. Rosaldo provides an overview of the anthropological literature that defends the claim that mother-only child rearing is virtually universal.
[32]Chodorow (1978), pp. 187–200, 212.
[33]See Di Stefano (1991).

in a culture that validates subsequent adult experiences that transcend the subject-object divide . . . these early identifications are counteracted—provided, that is, that such experiences are validated as essentially human rather than as "feminine" experience. However, in a culture such as ours, where primary validation is accorded to a science that has been premised on a radical dichotomy between subject and object, and where all other experiences are accorded secondary, "feminine" status, the early identifications can hardly fail to persist.[34]

Mother-only child rearing is a practice that is not coextensive with the western patriarchal nuclear family. Even though it is the model most object relations theorists tend to focus on, the theory is broadly applicable beyond this particular family structure to others where prominence of the mother and absence of the father are characteristic. Critics may point to the rise of single-parent families; people of color may experience communal parenting;[35] lesbian mothers may question the need for fathers at all. But the fact remains that in the vast majority of these structures it is still *women* who bear responsibility for child rearing, and do so within patriarchal contexts; indeed, in all three of these examples absence of the father plays an important role in the structuring of mothering practices.

Furthermore, the father's absence must also be understood in terms of its symbolic content, particularly since gender is a learned category. In a patriarchal culture it is likely to be the absence of a father in the context of male *cultural* dominance, rather than the absence of a particular male person per se, that is significant. There can certainly be an intertwining of these two factors; for most people the cultural meaning of the masculine is symbolized by our fathers. But for people whose fathers were material presences in the family even if they were not involved in child rearing, the father's absence is significant because of a myriad of relations with him: loving, angry, conflicted, and ambivalent. Here the symbolic absence appears to cohere with the at least passive but concrete rejection by a particular man with whom one's emotional life is intimately tied. For others, for whom the father's absence entails a physical absence from the family altogether— let us say one was raised in a lesbian household and never knew one's father, or perhaps one's father died or abandoned one at birth—this deep emotional effect remains at a more purely representational and abstract level. But in both cases the significance of "the father" is still largely cultural; it still derives in circular fashion from the fact that, within patriarchy, gender is not only treated as an es-

[34]Keller (1985), p. 87.
[35]Collins (1987).

sential aspect of self-identity but is also oppositionally structured. Object relations theory suggests that the absence of the father for any reason results in positional identification for boys because of the cultural significance of gender identity to self-identity, and because masculinity must be conceived as not-female. Given this dualistic opposition in defining gender, and its perhaps artificial but certainly socially constructed prominence in conceptions of the self, the father's absence exists and develops its meaning in a context of mother-only child rearing.

So these arguments suggest that to denigrate the importance of women's role as mother is a typically sexist reaction. Although the effects of mother-only child rearing are likely to be modified by certain variables, the effects are too powerful to be completely eliminated. Indeed, denying its impact can be seen as a reaction perfectly in line with the predictions of object relations theory, a central tenet of which is that boys attempt to deny the supposed power of the mother, and do so by denying relationality. As Flax argues:

> The repression, especially by men, of these primary relations and the relational aspects of our subjectivity is necessary for the replication of male-dominant cultures. A feminist theorist might well ask whether certain postmodernist deconstructors of the self are not merely the latest in a long line of philosophic strategies motivated by a need to evade, deny, or repress the importance of early childhood experiences, especially mother-child relationships, in the constitution of the self and the culture more generally. Perhaps it is less threatening to have no self than one pervaded by memories of, longing for, suppressed identification with, or terror of the powerful mother of infancy.[36]

This response tends to ring with psychoanalytic smugness, but it does suggest that postmodernism can be seen as allied with postfeminism in its rejection of feminine experience as valid. This rejection, however, must itself be questioned. A number of theorists have done so, and powerfully.[37] Their criticisms have not stilled debate, but they

[36]Flax (1990), p. 232.

[37]For challenges to postmodernism, see particularly Hartsock (1987), Brown (1987), and the special issue of *Differences* 1, no. 2 (1989) devoted to feminist critiques of poststructuralism. An additional response on this issue is offered by Flax (1983). She addresses the problem of circumstances that might affect the impact of mother-only child rearing by discussing philosophers who are what she calls "'pure case' examples, since they each lived in a historical period in which these mitigating factors were largely absent" (p. 245). Since three of the four philosophers she discusses—Plato, Descartes, Hobbes, and Rousseau—are also discussed in the present volume, I could rely on her argument to defend even more strongly my application of object relations to theories of obligation and epistemology. I am reluctant to do this, however, because I would not want to defend the "purity" of these cases. Rather, I suggest that although the effects of mother-only child rearing can be modified, they will not be eliminated completely.

highlight an important question: Why is it now, when women and racial minorities are finding their voices, when literary and political theory are providing ways for such voices to articulate their own theories and ways of seeing and constructing the world, that postmodernists—all of whom, at least originally, were white privileged males within the academy—suddenly tell us that voice is illegitimate? Is it precisely *because* the feminist claim to voice threatens masculinism's need to repress connection, a need that I have argued is a theme traceable at least as far back as Hobbes? Indeed, I would further question whether postmodernism is not sexist in its attempts to perpetuate the ontological-epistemological split. By insisting on the separation of being from knowing—specifically by denying the degree to which people share an experience of being—postmodernists revert to the isolation and subjectivity of Descartes's "cogito."

This criticism of postmodernism is not limited to its attacks on gender psychology, of course; postmodern criticism of standpoint theory is similarly problematic. Indeed, I find that such criticism founds itself on a "straw woman," as the essentialism it attributes to feminism is reductive, naturalistic, oversimplified. Perhaps ironically, this is particularly evident in the work of feminist postmodern theorists. Consider, for example, this criticism of essentialism by Denise Riley: "The tactical problem is in naming and specifying sexual difference where it has been ignored or misread; but without doing so in a way which guarantees it an eternal life of its own, a lonely trajectory across infinity which spreads out over the whole of being and the whole of society—as if the chance of one's gendered conception mercilessly guaranteed every subsequent facet of one's existence at all moments."[38]

There is little to disagree with in this passage; indeed, what feminist would want to? Perhaps some biodeterminists and political conservatives seek to create new images of women "in a way which guarantees it an eternal life of its own," but no feminist theorists that I have read engage in such a strategy, and certainly none drawn on in the present argument do so. Even Chodorow and Gilligan, who are often criticized along such lines, display, as I have argued, a materialism that necessitates a concept of gender that is not naturalistic or biological, neither timeless nor inevitable, but rather responds to historical and social contexts. If those contexts—such as mother-only child rearing—have continued through long periods of history, then it might appear as if such characteristics are natural or inevitable, as patriarchs have long claimed; and in this case it would also appear that the theory endorses a naturalistic view of gender. But, as feminists have long argued in their attacks on patriarchal naturalism, such

---

[38]Quoted in Alcoff (1988), p. 426.

appearances are superficial and misrepresentative, calling for deeper and more complex analysis. Why does this distinction between appearance and reality not apply to readings of feminist theory? Should feminists not be held accountable to these same standards when critiquing one of their own?

The feminist postmodernist Susan Hekman offers a similar defense of Gilligan against essentialist interpretations. She goes so far as to compare Gilligan to both Gadamer and Derrida, arguing that Gilligan is "deconstructing the rationalist model of morality."[39] Yet she fails to extend such a reading to standpoint arguments, claiming that Hartsock "has argued consistently that feminists must reject all epistemologies that are formulated by male theorists and adopt an epistemology that privileges the female standpoint."[40] As I noted earlier, Hartsock explicitly differentiates between female and feminist standpoints, partly because she wishes to acknowledge that there are male feminists in the world, partly because a standpoint does not come naturally or spontaneously to anyone but rather must be achieved through struggle, wherein lies its liberating potential. She further welcomes the efforts of male theorists to adopt feminist standpoints. The Derridean postmodernism Hekman endorses may seem feminist insofar as it treats women as symbolic, leading to a feminized epistemology that embodies multiplicity rather than unity. Yet such a theory is reductive and ignores the emphasis on concrete material experience so crucial to feminist standpoint methods. Although symbolism is vital to critical theory, and indeed to my own use of gender psychology, to treat woman as *only* a symbol, even as a symbol of multiplicity, is to deny a *real* concept of multiplicity among flesh-and-blood women, and to deny the real oppression that women face under patriarchy.

Flax's claim that standpoint epistemology presupposes "that people will act rationally on their 'interests'" is similarly misrepresentative. In the first place, it contradicts Hartsock's lengthy and exhaustive critique of rational choice approaches, as well as her analysis of the concept of interest itself. Flax's claim that the standpoint approach "assumes that the oppressed are not in some fundamental ways damaged by their social experience" is even more misrepresentative and confusing.[41] Hartsock explicitly acknowledges the ways in which

[39]Hekman (1990), p. 57.

[40]Ibid, p. 154.

[41]Flax (1990), p. 141. Furthermore, Flax cannot simultaneously critique the notion of a unified self and then talk about a "damaged" self (p. 141): damaged compared to what standard? My reading of Flax as a standpoint theorist thus becomes revised in light of her own condemnation of it. She seems to go beyond standpoint and even displays affinities with modernism.

patriarchy informs women's experiences. Thus a feminist goal is not to "act out" women's experiences but to theorize them critically and to learn about women's responses to oppression as much as about the oppression itself. This is certainly consistent with my own use of standpoint.

I therefore find the postmodern challenge to standpoint epistemology and gender psychology to be seriously problematic in its anti-feminist potential; but I have another response to the objections I have just summarized that is much more sympathetic. Indeed, it involves highlighting the ways in which my own application of feminist standpoint borrows from postmodern insights. This begins with the recognition that I am looking at only one aspect of political philosophy, namely gender bias, and within that I consider gender psychology as only one source of explanation. My approach presumes to be neither comprehensive nor exclusive in either its methodology or conclusions, and it would be misleading to interpret my argument as seeking to replace one hegemony with another. My critique of consent theory in Chapters 1 and 2 obviously coheres with a postmodern suspicion and rejection of universalizing theories of human nature because such theories make invisible the particularity of difference in the experiences of women and other excluded groups. If liberal epistemology and dominant western theoretical discourses are reflective of specifically white male practitioners, then we need to uncover that bias and explore what is excluded. Gender is one such category. It is certainly not the only category, but it is an extremely significant one. The impact of gender bias and my own use of gender theory have potentially far-reaching implications, and I wish neither to minimize the importance of this work nor to dodge the controversy it raises. But it is crucial to remember that this work does not seek to construct a new, totalizing grand theory or ideology.

Nor am I attempting to create *the* definitive feminist standpoint epistemology here. Rather, I hope to raise some previously unasked —and unseen—questions about liberal theory and epistemology. Through this process multiple feminist stand*points* should be revealed. Indeed, if I were to carry my argument to its logical conclusion, multiple standpoints of a variety of excluded groups would emerge. But by approaching standpoint epistemology through feminism and women's experiences, I am also attempting to explore some of the common and overlapping elements that feminist epistemologies share. In the process my argument develops new approaches to political theory that involve locality, contextuality, concreteness, and particularity. In this, as I will argue in my afterword, although I reject the idea of a feminist postmodernism, I believe I am utilizing an approach I would call postmodern feminism. For in combining the quasi-modernist characteristics of standpoint theory and gender psychology with some of the deconstructive and antiuniversal qualities of postmodernism, feminist theory can gain access to the deepest levels of the symbolic in cultural practices and institutions such as the patriarchal nuclear family, the liberal state, and the social contract.

As my method of standpoint epistemology borrows from postmodern insights, so are my reading and use of object relations and gender psychology similarly compatible with many aspects of postmodernism, the most prominent being the rejection of essentialized views of gender. In its locating personality development and accompanying epistemological frameworks in the context of institutionalized practices of child rearing and suggesting that changes in those practises will bring about changes in self-other conceptualizations and hence in gender, object relations theory can be seen as strongly compatible with postmodern aspects of fluid notions of selfhood and relationship. It is true that object relations speaks in terms of a "core self" that can be evaluated as "true" or "false." But, as Flax notes in her discussion of Winnicott,[42] a true core self is *precisely* one that is fluid, that is not artificially static and afraid of ambivalence and change. That is, the core self of object relations theory is not a magic entity that exists inside each of us, unaffected by the external events that pummel our surface selves; a core self is simply that confidence in and security about our existence that allows us to cope with the ever-changing context that is life. The modernist notion of selfhood attempts to control this fluidity by posing a falsely universalized notion of autonomy as separateness. Object relations recognizes the ways in which the self is shaped by relationships. The core is thus a self-in-relationship. A disconnected self must engage in the false structures that deny the fragmentation which such disconnection necessarily entails. In other words, the masculinist self under patriarchy is not false in the sense that another (more) unified identity would be true; rather, the falseness comes from precisely this unified and static quality.

Thus, on the one hand, I have argued that my work is allied with elements of postmodernism; and on the other, I have argued that postmoderism is itself problematic in many of the areas in which it critiques gender psychology and feminist theory. Yet a third, perhaps more political response to the postmodern challenge is suggested by Harding. She has attempted to reconcile the tensions between postmodernism and feminism by arguing that standpoint epistemology is

---

[42]Ibid., p. 110.

a necessary step in the development of feminist theory; it is crucial to develop the standpoint approach so that it can transcend itself. Methodologically, to engage in postmodernist dialogue without the standpoint is like giving feminists feathers to fight bayonets.[43] In other words, one cannot arrive at postfeminism without completing the feminist enterprise. This makes a great deal of sense philosophically and politically. And though it may appear antithetical to postmodern method, Derrida himself can be read to suggest precisely such a strategy in *Positions*: "To overlook this phase of overturning [oppressive dualisms] is to forget the conflictual and subordinating structure of opposition. Therefore one might proceed too quickly to a *neutralization* that *in practice* would leave the previous field untouched."[44]

So the present work should be seen as sympathetic to and compatible with postmodernism and yet suspicious and critical of it. None of these responses is final, of course, and my own intellectual ambivalence about postmodernism as well as standpoint epistemology and object relations theory remains. I highlight these responses not to argue that the objections are ill-founded; rather, I seek to clarify what my use of this controversial literature does—and does not—seek to achieve. But I also wish to convey to the reader that I do not think there are any easy, or even clear, answers to these issues at this point. That, I suppose, is what makes something controversial rather than absolute (or obsolete) and hence worthy of philosophical reflection. These issues need to be considered if the power of the symbolic implicit in the theories is to be realized. Accordingly, my analysis operates from a hypothetical acceptance of gender psychology; but it also operates from a reading of these works and of standpoint epistemology that carries them beyond what is articulated explicitly to their necessarily implicit symbolic quality. This needs to be done precisely because of the challenge these theories pose to our accepted notions of epistemology, ontology, and even substantive political concepts such as obligation. It also needs to be done because these theories have gained so much attention and are being adopted by feminist scholars in various disciplines, including political science. Amid all this attention, few have yet asked the question, If these theories are correct, what exactly are the implications for political theory? A consideration of epistemology in light of gender psychology can provide not only a better understanding of the ways in which liberal epistemology is inherently masculinist but also a basis for understanding how and why the substantive aspects of political theory—our under-

---

[43]Harding (1986), p. 150.
[44]Derrida (1972), p. 41. This point will be returned to in the afterword.

standing of rights, freedom, justice, and obligation—display a similar bias.

Epistemology and the Patriarchal Unconscious

Susan Bordo, in her analysis of Descartes, supports this proposition by tracing the roots of Descartes's rationalist epistemology to a cultural and scientific revolution that "defeminized" culture and, not so coincidentally, corresponds to the beginnings of modern western capitalism's form of mother-only child rearing. As Bordo points out, the location of truth solely in the mind, the rejection of bodily or sensory experience, reflects a specifically masculinist conception of knowing and knowledge. The interiority of mental life, which, according to her, begins in the Renaissance—"the notion that the experience of individuals is fundamentally opaque, even inaccessible to others"—is most starkly presented in Descartes. The emphasis on "clarity, dispassion, and detachment . . . the imagery of objectivity" play a central role in Descartes's epistemology, and serve as the basis of "the model of knowledge that Descartes bequeathed to modern science."[45]

But this model of knowledge, she says, with its conceptions of objectivity and interiority and pure knowledge, can be seen as a specifically masculine response to cultural changes that echo preoedipal dilemmas. She asks, after a brief discussion of object relations theory:

> May not such a process reverberate, too, on the cultural level? Perhaps some cultural eras compensate for the pain of individuation better than others through a mother imagery of the cosmos (such as was dominant, e.g., throughout the Chaucerian and Elizabethan eras) that assuages the anxiety of our actual separateness as individuals. On the other hand, during periods in which long-established images of symbiosis and cosmic unity break down (as they did during the period of the scientific revolution), may we not expect an increase in self-consciousness and anxiety over the distance between self and world—a constant concern, to paraphrase Mahler, over the whereabouts of the world? All these, as I have suggested, are central motifs in the *Meditations*.[46]

If social and cultural embodiments of "the feminine" broke down during the scientific revolution, then it is more than coincidence that the understanding of epistemology as separate from ontology devel-

[45]Bordo (1986), pp. 443, 440.
[46]Ibid., p. 445.

oped so fully in the seventeenth and eighteenth centuries. Indeed, there is a specific reason and purpose relating to gender and mother-only child rearing. In this light, Descartes's assertion that God is all that stands between the inner life and the object world takes on added significance. In social contract theories in particular, patriarchal figures such as God or the Sovereign serve useful purposes of pre-serving men from being lost in feminine "nature." According to object relations, when threatened with engulfment by the mother, the boy turns to the abstract father, or more precisely to the rule-governed roles he provides, as a means to solidify his identity. The patriarchal figure is the constant and sole mediator between the individual boy's interiority and the object world. But this "father" is an idealization; real fathers will likely display the same problems their sons are at-tempting to grapple with.

This last point is important to remember: as Bordo suggests, it is not merely the experiences of individual philosophers that have sig-nificance. In order to understand the gendered bias of epistemology and political theory, we must attend to the cultural dimensions of the supposedly individual experience of psychic development. If a culture contains certain practices, such as mother-only child rearing, that res-onate psychically on individual members, this resonance will be mir-rored in the culture those individuals in turn help create and trans-form. It is here that the greatest potential for the symbolic is situated. Cultural manifestations of psychic issues will likely represent ideal-ized or even simplified translations of the variety that individual ex-perience embodies; but this culture will in turn have its own effects on individual participants in a dynamic interaction. Thus Descartes's concept of knowledge is not "merely" a manifestation of individual experience or of culture but instead reflects the interaction between these two.

Even so, this discussion ignores a final point which I find implicit in Bordo's discussion. In spite of Descartes's duality of mind and body, and the separation of epistemology and ontology that follows from that, his concept of knowing and knowledge follows very specifically from his concept of being. "Cogito ergo sum" and the concept of pure knowledge divorced from the body (and from the knower) operate centrally from a particular ontology. The definiton of true being, of the true self, is conceptualized by Descartes as bodiless, but it is a concept of being nonetheless. And this concept influences his concept of knowledge. Perhaps, then, what is truly significant about Des-cartes's philosophy is not the fact that his ontology actually does in-form his epistemology but that Descartes—and the epistemologists who followed him—unconditionally denied this unity even as they implicitly operated from within it.

This same duplicity of the unconscious is explored by Flax. She even more explicitly likens Descartes's "cogito," with the insistence on pure, bodiless, rational thought, to the narcissistic phase of the preoedipal period, when the boy subjugates the mother's and the world's subjectivity to his self so that they are "seen purely as a creation of and an object for the self."[47] She compares this to Plato's separation of mind and body, reason and appetite, involving an attempt to transcend the body. This further corresponds to his exclusion of (at least childbearing) women from public life. The victory of reason enables man to leave the cave/unconscious/womb, to control the world and woman/mother, to deny and subjugate her subjectivity for the security of his own.

According to object relations, the male child needs to repress and deny the subjectivity of the mother in excising the mother from the self. The female is less able to do so, both because of her greater psychic dependence on the mother and because she herself is female and therefore like her mother. Male positional identification as not-female involves the disparagement of the mother and the distancing of the self from her and all females. Recognizing this, and the fact that institutional frameworks of patriarchy have arisen interactively with this developmental process, Flax says, "Both individual male development and patriarchy are partially rooted in a need to deny the power and autonomy of women."[48] The ability of boys to split off the "bad mother" is tied to patriarchy in an obvious way: if parents of both sexes shared early child rearing, then splitting off would not be an available defense maneuver, and with denial impossible, resolution would be required. As it is, the availability of this maneuver perpetuates male denigration of women, and hence perpetuates patriarchy and mother-only child rearing.

This masculine experience reverberates in political theory. Flax argues that in the rationalist theories of Descartes and Plato, the rejection of the body demonstrates a repressive solution to the oedipal dilemma and an inability to resolve satisfactorily the longings for symbiosis with the mother. Desire and the body must be split off from the self, which exists only in pure reason and knowledge, safely secured from passion and the darkness of nature. For both Plato and Descartes, "reason emerges only when nature (the female) is posited as the other with an 'inevitable' moment of domination." Through this process women "become the embodiments of the unconscious,

[47]Flax (1983), p. 260.
[48]Ibid., p. 245.

just as men become the embodiments of reason and law (the ego and the superego)."[49]

Application of object relations to social contract theories is particularly powerful, for this kind of epistemological orientation readily lends itself to hyperindividualism (or abstract individualism). Indeed, C. B. Macpherson's criticism of Hobbes[50] can be viewed from this perspective. The Hobbesian state of nature, marked by a high level of anxiety, particularly about wounds (which Flax specifically parallels to castration anxiety), death (destruction by the mother), deprivation of desired objects (mother's warmth or her milk-giving breast), or frustration of passions (mother's lack of response, punishment, repression of masturbatory impulses), is highly suggestive of the infant's transition from the preoedipal to the oedipal phase. A central feature of Hobbes's theory is the denial of any sort of primary human relatedness. Indeed his "mechanistic model of human nature . . . excludes the traits culturally attributed to females—sociability, nurturance, concern for dependent and helpless persons."[51]

The dominance of unleashed passion and desire, the prevalent fear of nongratification, of mutilation and death, as well as the inability to recognize others as autonomous and to create reciprocal relationships can be seen to parallel the infantile preoedipal dilemma. The Leviathan, represented by a single all-powerful male ruler whose word is law, provides an externalized superego with systems of rules to guide behavior. The key to Hobbes's theory of the social contract is the belief that men cannot be self-regulating; the dangers of nature are far too powerful for mere mortal resistance. The will must be reinforced by an external system of rules, laws, and authority, which serve as powerful barriers against the self-destructive return to the state of nature.

Similarly, the boy, by attaching himself to the rules and principles of masculine roles through positional identification, relies on an externalized superego, or a system of rules external to the self, to prevent the return to symbiosis with the mother. Reliance on this external barrier involves and indeed facilitates the boy's repression of the conflict between symbiosis and autonomy rather than its resolution. Similarly, the reliance on the Sovereign for protection from the state of nature does not resolve the conflict; this is why men "consent" to a monarchy rather than trying to govern themselves through a democ-

---

[49]Ibid., p. 269. It should be noted that Plato's view of women in the *Republic* differs from that found in the *Laws,* and this has generated some controversy over Plato's views on women. See Okin (1979).

[50]Macpherson (1962).

[51]Flax (1983), p. 263.

racy. The moral is that man can never survive in the so-called state of nature, where the mother has the power of choice to "either nourish, or expose" the infant.[52] Nor can he survive in a democratic world of reciprocity, trust, and mutuality, for in such a world the pull back toward nature and the state of war would be irresistible. Rather, men must turn to a Sovereign (the father) who creates a world of order out of perceived chaos, safety out of perceived peril, and effective freedom out of perceived absolute freedom and terror.

Although there are vast differences between Hobbes and Rousseau, Rousseau's theory also demonstrates this same psychic repression and denies any sort of primary relatedness as either natural or good. In his state of nature people are isolated from one another, contacts are fleeting, and even mothers and children separate and do not recognize each other after nursing is over. In *The Origin of Inequality* Rousseau argues that the ability to discern differences among people and recognize them produces an idea that cooperation is possible; but this cooperation yields mutual dependence and slavery. Love produces jealousy, inequality, violence, and finally a state of war. The solution is a social contract and a system of law.[53] Again, analogies to object relations theory present themselves: the unregulated state of nature represents the very early infantile experience, where the infant is unable to differentiate the mother from anyone else and is totally self-oriented. The development of love, however, turns to fear of loss of the love object, jealousy, and slavery. The answer once again is an externalized superego, the turn to the father, and the triumph of external rules over the id. This creates the ability to separate and remain free by radical autonomy and moral freedom.

In Rousseau's polity, however, as citizens make their own laws together in the Sovereign, the rules are self-referential while at the same time they provide an external superego. I am not completely satisfied with Flax's interpretation of Rousseau because his participatory element and the structure it requires involve a high degree of contextuality and substantive fairness, which are important elements of feminist obligation. Yet Flax's framework offers some helpful interpretive tools for explaining and understanding many of Rousseau's inconsistencies. For instance, although Rousseau emphasizes moral freedom through self-legislation, he simultaneously leaps back from the precipice of that freedom to draw in the Great Legislator, a benevolent paternal figure. The prospect of individual citizens' working out their differences face to face and reaching an agreement evidently seems

[52]Hobbes, *Leviathan*, p. 254.
[53]Flax (1983), pp. 264–68. See also Rousseau, *A Discourse on the Origin of Inequality*, in Cole, esp. pp. 58–62, 79–83.

either too impractical or too frightening to Rousseau. Once again we see the conviction that cooperation and love yield mutual dependence and slavery, that relationships are not in men's best interest. Connection is a dangerous thing to Rousseau and presents the risk of loss of one's ability to perceive the general will, and thus the loss of one's true self. Hence instead of having full access to one another, citizens should not be allowed to speak to one another prior to voting so as not to be swayed: otherwise factions and "partial associations are formed at the expense of the great association."[54] The self is not strong enough to withstand the will of others. External rules, as well as a patriarchal wise father, the Legislator, protect male citizens from sacrificing their true will.

Likewise, in *Emile*, Sophie is taught by patriarchal norms to repress her sexuality and autonomy so as to safeguard her husband's. Emile cannot achieve moral freedom through an act of his own will because he is too weak; rather, Sophie herself must be repressed and dominated. The restraint that frees man's will to obey itself comes from an object outside the self, and the superego is externalized once again. In turn, Rousseau's fear of women's powers results in his pointed exclusion of them from the social contract and the Assembly. Not only must women be repressed to preserve the moral freedom of men; and not only must women fulfill the role of slaves to enable democracy to continue. More significantly, women, or the mother, must be excluded from the Assembly because the Assembly makes the laws, which constitute the structure of the externalized superego. Admittance of the mother/woman to citizenship would thus destroy male autonomy: it would deny a sphere of existence totally separated and differentiated from the mother; it would undermine the rigid self-other distinction that the law is supposed to provide and on which male autonomy and moral freedom are predicated; it would destroy the barrier of safety that prevents men from being absorbed back into the darkness of nature and the no-man's-land of cooperation and (symbiotic) connection.

Indeed, the entire society—which is structured in such a way precisely to preserve men's liberty by the oppression of women—would fall apart. Only through women's oppression can men discover the general will, and only through the general will can the moral freedom that civil society affords be ensured. The exaggerated fear Rousseau expresses of women echoes the male model of gender psychology: just as the boy totally rejects the mother and turns to the father and a womanless world as a fortress of safety to solidify his identity and

[54]Rousseau, *Social Contract*, in Cole, p. 185.

prevent return to the mother, so do Rousseau's citizens forcibly keep women out of public life to protect their identity and autonomy.

The point of Bordo's and Flax's work, however, is not to psycho-analyze these political theorists as individuals but to develop a pro-vocative yet plausible response to the problem of bias. As Flax asks, "What forms of social relations exist such that certain questions and ways of answering them become constitutive of philosophy?"[55] In ap-plying object relations directly to particular political theories, Bordo and Flax explore the dimensions of political theory that are rooted in social-structural forms of relationship; and in the process, I maintain, they reveal the ontological dimensions of the theories' epistemolo-gies. They reveal that the dichotomy between epistemology and on-tology is not only false but a smokescreen that masks—even from the theorists themselves—their very intimate relationship.

The analysis afforded by this application of object relations theory is useful in providing a feminist methodological tool for a deeper un-derstanding not merely of why women are excluded from the social contract but of why the conceptual frameworks *require* women's ex-clusion. Indeed, this approach strikes at the heart of what a theory such as Macpherson's argues: that the reality described by the social contract theorists is based on incorrect premises. This feminist inter-pretation suggests that these premises are not so much incorrect (or not simply incorrect) as they are the accurate representation of a faulty attempt at inner conflict resolution. That is, the description is not itself false: the experience it depicts, however, is biased and faulty. It cannot be dismissed as simply false because the world—and a kind of truth—has been created in this very image.[56] The western world under capitalism has been to a large extent structured as a se-ries of market relations, with the result that freedom must logically refer to the absence of external restraints, and obligation must refer to consent. In our language and conceptual history, this is what these terms mean to us. But that does not mean such a structure reflects human nature or that it describes as much of our lives as it claims to.

Relational Rationality

Another avenue taken by feminist theorists in applying gender the-ory to political theory lies more within the tradition of analytical phi-losophy than the history of thought. Theorists such as Sandra Hard-ing and Evelyn Fox Keller focus on particular concepts that are central

---

[55]Flax (1983), p. 248.
[56]Hartsock (1984), p. 245. Flax (1986) makes a similar point.

to our understanding of liberal political theory in general. Harding in particular explores the concept of rationality, which is deeply operative in liberal theory. Writing from the perspective of the philosophy of science, Harding argues that the central issues and methods of modern science were (and are) specifically masculine efforts to overcome specifically feminine problems: that is, science and scientific method developed as the attempts of male scientists to master the problems posed by an unpredictable "feminine" nature.[57]

This enterprise ramifies on epistemology. If Descartes provided the model of knowledge for modern science, the empiricist epistemologies of Locke, Hume, and Mill resulted from the effort to make sense of the findings of modern science. Harding points out:

> Descartes, Locke, Hume, and Kant were trying to make sense of the kind of knowledge-seeking exemplified by Copernicus, Galileo, and Newton. The creators of modern epistemologies were meditating upon what they understood to be a science created by individual "craft-laborers." Their perceptions of the nature and activities of what they took to be the individual, "disembodied," but human mind, beholden to no social commitments but the willful search for clear and certain truth, remain the foundations from which the questions we recognize as epistemological arise.[58]

Yet we can push Harding even further here, extending her point to questions that are *not* normally recognized as epistemological; for her work, I contend, reveals that such questions are epistemological even though we may not commonly recognize them as such.

Arguing that science has a "social structure," and even that "a critical and self-reflective social science," rather than an idealized physics, "should be the model for all science," Harding challenges the conceptualization of "objectivity," found in modern science, which denies that the "social identity of the observer can be an important variable" in scientific research.[59] Harding suggests that the emphasis on objectivity and the belief that truth can be achieved only through value neutrality echo specifically masculine developmental issues. As Keller argues in a similar vein, "The cognitive claims of science . . . grow out of an emotional substructure" defined by mother-only child rearing.[60] As I discussed earlier, the male child cannot afford to recognize the mother's subjectivity; such recognition would threaten his fragile autonomy. In order to preserve this reactive autonomy, he must see only the self as subject; (m)others must be objects. Yet this very fact

[57]This is also particularly noted in Keller (1985).
[58]Harding (1986), pp. 140–41.
[59]Ibid., pp. 44, 26.
[60]Keller (1985), p. 96.

must itself be repressed: the male cannot recognize what he is doing, for that would equally allow the possibility of recognizing the mother's subjectivity. If the mother is truly object, there can be nothing to repress.

Epistemology develops from these social relations of infancy. A boy's need to distance himself from the mother and all others produces a perspective on the world, an ontology, and an epistemology that fulfill this intense need. In light of this interpretive framework, Harding and Keller both conclude that the concept of scientific objectivity developed as a gender-exclusive concept. Not only did it express the need of male practitioners to objectify and dominate the female (that is, nature), but furthermore, these practitioners could effectively deny "how women's daily activities have shaped men's very definitions of their worlds."[61] That is, the nature of their activities allowed men to deny the reality of what they were doing. This, Harding argues, is where feminist standpoint epistemologies perform a crucial function, in creating the possibility of revealing the reality of these distorted relationships.

Rationality, the central concept of this positivist science and intimately intertwined with objectivity, is generally considered gender neutral in its scientific approach, but Harding points out its gendered character on a variety of levels. Throughout history men have ridiculed women's thinking as irrational. But Harding insists that the concept of rationality as defined in western thought "is not only one-sided but also, in some respects, perverse."[62] The concept of rationality, viewed from the psychoanalytic perspective, can be seen as masculinist in its emphasis on rigid lines of argument and narrow channels of truth and in its appeal as independent of human construction. The very characterization of rational thought as objectivity in part reflects the male infant's need to objectify the mother and to experience the self-other relationship as a dichotomy. Rationality so defined can be interpreted as the search for rules and norms—or the externalized superego which lies outside the mother's domain—so characteristic of the boy's attempt to sieze masculine identity.[63]

Positivists will reply that rationality as a concept is something of a closed door. Like obligation, rationality has a very particular meaning in our language, which cannot be violated without our ceasing to use the word correctly. Objectivity, distance between self and other, pure deduction, and generalized, rule-governed experience constitute the definition of rationality, just as knowing divorced from being consti-

[61]Ibid., p. 31.
[62]Harding (1984), p. 44.
[63]See also Keller (1985), esp. chaps. 4–6.

tutes the dominant understanding of epistemology. Perhaps we need another word to express this feminist version. But my reading of Harding suggests that we must reject this response. In keeping with the standpoint assumption that "women's subjugated position provides the possibility of more complete and less perverse understandings,"[64] the dominant conception of rationality actively distorts both our thinking and the social relations that shape and are shaped by that thinking. The rigidity of the refusal to realize the man-made nature of the concept, the pointed exclusion of women from its exercise, its use as a tool to distance the self, and its exclusive valuation at the expense of other valuable, reasonable mental processes belie the supposed neutrality of rationality and call for a new understanding of the word.

In this light it is precisely the fact that masculine development, like feminine development, exhibits elements of pathology which influences the gender bias of institutions and theories. The elaborate creation of rules to establish "appropriate relations between mind and body, reason and the emotions, self and external world, will and desire" is so important precisely because these relationships were "painfully sundered for men in their infancy."[65] The girl's less severe separation from the mother, relative to the boy's experience—and hence her "inability" to objectify the mother[66]—is seen as a failure to develop. Female experience is viewed as regressive compared with the standards set by male theorists to reflect their own experience. The construction of the world, on this view, has been structured precisely to answer the psychic needs of its creators.

Not so coincidentally, the dominant conception of rationality as objectivity also echoes Kohlberg's sixth stage of moral development. By thinking rationally, anyone can scientifically apply the rules to arrive at a decision that is "just," or "correct," or "moral." Yet Gilligan's work suggests that rationality as procedure, with its emphasis on rules and process at the expense of substance and context, takes on a decidedly masculinist tint. The abstraction of rationality is not a universal good, nor even universal per se. Indeed, my earlier use of Gilligan's argument is echoed in Harding's assertion that a major goal of liberal theory is the adjudication of competing rights of "generalized

---

[64]Harding (1986), p. 26.

[65]Harding (1984), p. 56.

[66]In personal conversation Harding has taken issue with my choice of the words *ability* and *failure*, because she holds that girls' nonobjectifying qualities are strengths of the female model of development. I do not imply any derogation in my reference to females' "inability" to objectify the mother. I merely wish to emphasize that, whereas boys are psychically required to objectify the mother, it is exceedingly difficult for girls to do so even though they may wish to, because of their intense identification.

autonomous individuals." But the goal of "resolving conflicting responsibilities to particular and dependent others"—a question of greater concern historically and psychically to women—is not considered important.[67] Indeed, it is not even granted the validity of conceptualization and articulation in mainstream thought.

The positivist still might reply that all we need to do is reevaluate what we consider rational and irrational along nonsexist lines; all we need is to be more "objective" in our assessment of objectivity and rationality.[68] But this response fails to acknowledge the depth of the problems that rationality poses. For it is precisely the difference in conclusion—not the adherence to procedure—that has served as evidence of women's supposed irrationality. That is, the fact of different conclusions produces the assumption that the procedure has been misused. But this assumption implicitly requires very particular values as premises and conclusions, and these reflect particularly masculine experience. The gender bias of rationality, which exerts certain constraints on the *content* of thought and conclusions, belies rationality's status as a *procedural* tool for reaching conclusions based on particular premises. It highlights the fact that rationality is not in fact pure procedure but rather that procedure requires substantive values to serve as a framework for thought processes. After all, if rationality were truly only a procedure, then the fact of different conclusions historically reached by women—different values, priorities, and moral judgments—would be insufficient to establish the notion that women cannot think rationally. Such a claim betrays that rationality is not merely or purely procedure; and thus a myriad of values can be considered to fall within the framework of rationality.

The masculinist construction of rationality contradicts its own values. On this level the positivist's suggestion that we need to think nonsexistly about rationality is inadequate. On a deeper level, this construction of rationality also presupposes that procedure itself is singular and uniform and fails to recognize the ways in which substance informs and influences procedure. The assertion that rationality is pure procedure excludes women by the power of two. Not only is "pure" rationality not value free, contrary to its formal claims, but also the values that actually inform this concept of rationality work with and from the exclusion and objectification of women. Be-

---

[67]Harding (1984), p. 56.

[68]This is the "feminist empiricist" conclusion, which Harding (1986) describes as a belief that "sexism and androcentrism are biases correctable by stricter adherence to the existing methodological norms of scientific inquiry" (p. 24). Harding rejects this approach, although she also maintains that the "successor science" project of the feminist standpoint is also problematic, as I have briefly indicated. See also Lloyd (1984) and Di Stefano (1990) for a discussion of the feminist rationalist argument.

cause of the formal claim to value neutrality, however, the attempt to identify these values is difficult at best. The masculinist model of rationality as pure thought divorced from concrete experience, the implicit claim that this reasoning is value free, and the automatic rejection of "the female" as rational ensure that women's experience, values, and thought, grounded in connectedness and human relationship, will always appear irrational by definition.

Rationality defined as objective thought is not only exclusive of women but harmful to them, because it is premised on particular concrete values, specifically on a notion of woman as object as a means to disempower and distance the mother. In contrast, a feminist construction of rationality, Harding's "relational rationality"—akin to Keller's "dynamic objectivity" and Ernest Schactel's "allocentric," or other-centered, perspective[69]—embodies the values, experiences, and psychic needs of women's lives. Indeed, Keller defines dynamic objectivity as "a pursuit of knowledge that makes use of subjective experience . . . in the interests of a more effective objectivity." Likening the scientist's "attention to the natural world" to an "ideal attention to the human world," she calls it "a form of love." And she links both to dynamic autonomy: "The capacity for such attention, like the capacity for love and empathy, requires a sense of self secure enough to tolerate both difference and continuity; it presupposes the development of dynamic autonomy."[70]

Harding similarly argues that the concept of a rational person may represent (historically or otherwise) different values for women, such as the ability to empathize and connect with others. Like Gilligan and Chodorow in particular, she points to relationship, connection, and emotion as central values of this feminist model of rationality; thus a rational person "wants to learn more complex and satisfying ways to take the role of the particular other in relationships" as a means of understanding and solving problems resulting from relational life. On this model, "A rational person naturally has problems when there is too little connection with particular others and when she is expected only to take the role of the generalized other," a requirement of women under patriarchy and the masculinist definition of rationality.[71] Beginning from these different premises, the procedural aspects of rationality yield vastly different conclusions from those reached by "malestream" thought. But, more important, these premises also suggest alternate procedures.

---

[69]Keller (1985), chap. 6, borrows from Schactel's *Metamorphosis*.
[70]Keller (1985), pp. 117–18.
[71]Harding (1984), p. 53.

Of course, it would be incorrect to say that women cannot and do not think rationally along the masculinist model, and I do not intend this implication. Because this rationality is premised on the objectification of women, however, women's adaptation to this thought is not necessarily an unqualified good. Asserting that women can think rationally along the male model is not enough. It is insufficient to open the door and allow for a wider variety of underlying assumptions merely to change rationality's contingent connections with substantive beliefs and values that are of a masculinist character. As Helen Longino and Ruth Doell ask, is the problem of sexist science that it is "bad science," or "science as usual?"[72]

Perhaps it is a bit of both. The problem of a sexist conception of rationality is a problem of bad thinking or bad philosophy, but it is not *just* bad philosophy; it is also philosophy as usual. We need to recognize the sexist inconsistencies of our dominant conceptions of rationality—its contingent sexism. But this recognition further requires us to recognize its structural sexism, and thus to change the very definition of rationality and the methodology by which we achieve that definition. This is necessary to ensure that other modes of thought, and not just other thoughts, are recognized as valuable. Once we can do that, we may find that perhaps it is not justice formally defined that is the truly central concept in the political theory that is supposed to reflect our lives; perhaps it is what Harding calls "social welfare," and other values that Gilligan and Chodorow attribute to women. A feminist relational rationality would not only allow for women's entry into the public realm by providing recognition of their thought processes as valuable, and hence their access to knowledge as real; it could also thereby reconstitute the public and the political. It could redefine what is primary in our considerations of political and social life.

Power and Epistemology

These arguments extend to more traditional and substantive concepts in political theory such as obligation, authority, and justice. Hartsock undertakes an analysis of dominant conceptions of power as specifically masculinist. In particular, she holds that the conceptualization of power as domination reflects specifically masculine psychosexual development under patriarchy. Like those of Bordo, Flax, and Harding, Hartsock's arguments unite epistemology and ontology.

[72]Longino and Doell (1983), p. 207. See also Harding (1986), chap. 6, esp. p. 138.

The conception of power as domination has been a central force throughout history in shaping our political institutions and theories, such as obligation, as well as our conceptions of love, relationship, and community. It has arisen from and in turn strengthened and reinforced an epistemology centered on domination and a self-other dichotomy. But as Hartsock reveals, women's material experience as wives and mothers and their psychosexual development as daughters generate a perspective on knowledge and reality that is at odds with this masculinist perspective. She traces the roots and development of the conception of power as domination and examines its ramifications for our thought, our theories, and our politics; and she also demonstrates that a feminist theory of power, reflecting the values and experiences of women's lives, embodies notions of capacity, energy, and empowerment.

Of the theorists discussed in this chapter, Hartsock is the most overtly committed to standpoint epistemology. Indeed, her essay "The Feminist Standpoint" introduced the concept and method to feminist theory. Hartsock's argument involves more than psychology, however; for her, the standpoint is based on material activity. Her analysis of this experience is multifaceted, working from a marxist-feminist notion that material life shapes consciousness. Although Marx may not have had anything in mind other than the relations of production when he suggested this, attention to and recognition of the material conditions of women's lives and the processes of reproduction, housework, and family care lead us to understand how women's consciousness and world view is oriented toward a concept of a continuum rather than a dichotomy.

In housework, a woman has "contact with material necessity," something she shares with factory workers in distinction to capitalists, but her contact is different. First, she works longer hours (the double day) and is more involved in the production of use-values than of commodities. Second, the nature of repetition is different, for she produces for her family to consume: her meals are prepared to be eaten immediately, her laundry is cleaned so that it may be worn again and soiled. This contrasts qualitatively with the repetition of a factory worker; not only is it in his interest that people wish to replace products, for he is paid for his work (as the housewife is not), but also the futility is not nearly as apparent. An automobile transmission may break down after six years, a cog wear out after six months, but that is qualitatively different from the daily, even hourly replacement engaged in by women.[73] Third, the woman's work is centered directly

[73]Hartsock (1983), p. 292; idem (1984), p. 235.

on the production of people, most obviously in pregnancy and par-
turition, but also in daily nurturance, whether through being an
understanding listener, preparing a favorite food, or getting a child
ready for school. Women usually supply the emotional "glue" that
keeps families and relationships going. Such affective work is a key
aspect of women's labor which is generally ignored by male theorists.[74] The significance is that "if the institutionalized structure of human activity generates an ontology and epistemology, and if the activity of women differs systematically from that of men, we must ask
whether epistemology is structured by gender as well."[75] Epistemology arises from ontology, ways of knowing from ways of being.

This materialist theory may seem to have little to do with my consideration of object relations theory, for the results Chodorow details
might be seen to arise somewhat passively from mothering arrangements, and not necessarily from any particular or even consciously
performed activities engaged in by women. Object relations may even
seem inappropriately esoteric compared with a marxist materialism.
Yet such a response considers mother-only child rearing abstractly.
After all, the point of object relations' findings of gender differences
depends on the active engagement of the mother in such daily care-
taking activities as feeding, changing, cleaning, supervising, teaching,
playing, and communicating. Without these activities, the child
would not be able to develop normally, even to survive. My failure to
focus heavily on such activities by no means implies a belief that they
are unimportant. Thus, although I do not discuss in detail this aspect
of Hartsock's work in favor of, in my view, the more important arguments she makes concerning eros and sexuality, such activities stand
as an assumed background for my discussion of mother-only child
rearing as a practice. This same reasoning may be why Hartsock refers to object relations theory as "materialist psychology."[76] The analysis it provides, while focusing on the psychic development of the
infant, bases that development not on biology (the absence or presence of a penis) or nature, but on a socially constructed relationship
of affective production.

Central to Hartsock's argument is the notion that (masculine) sexuality and a particular concept of eros are at the root of the conceptualization of power as domination. It is this aspect of her work that
holds the most potential for clarifying the ontological dimensions of
epistemology. She only loosely connects this notion to liberal theory—she is far more concerned with ancient thought—but she does

---

[74]See also di Leonardo (1984) and Ferguson (1984) for similar arguments.
[75]Hartsock (1984), p. 9.
[76]Ibid., p. 238.

not discuss its full implication. Yet it is this aspect of her theory that is best able to explain the implications of power as domination, and masculinized eros, for obligation. Although she refers only relatively briefly to object relations (she focuses more on the psychology of sexuality, and particularly the work of Robert Stoller), it is my contention that a reading of her work from the perspective of object relations and moral psychology can reveal the ontological dimensions of her feminist standpoint epistemology.

Because men (as fathers) are divorced from reproduction and nurturance, and because of the sexual division of labor when men are raised by women, men's experience (as sons grown up) has tended to be less continuous, more fragmented, both psychically and materially, than women's. As feminist psychoanalytic theory allows us to see, the "key structuring experience" for men in mother-only child rearing is the "fear of ceasing to exist as a separate being . . . because of the threat posed by a woman."[77] Because of the son's need to repress the mother and excise the female, connection with the mother/woman is seen as dangerous. The only way in which connection is allowable is through domination.

As I have shown, because of positional identification with abstract roles, masculinity develops negatively, as not-female; the son thus feels compelled to excise his primary female identity and repress his mother in himself. But these female aspects of his original psychic identity are too deeply embedded to be truly excised. And because gender is considered exclusionary, the intense struggle that results is resolved in the only way available. That is, the son devalues and dehumanizes his mother, denying her existence, belittling the importance of his relation to her. He tries to dominate her and his feelings for her by controlling who and what she is. This applies by extension to all other women as well: "Intimacy with a woman is so dangerous that she must be reduced to a nonentity or made into a thing."[78]

Because of the repression of this central relationship, the son is compelled to belittle the significance of all relationships, for he must fear connection with others as posing the danger of merging and loss of self. This is particularly true when a man engages in a love relationship with a woman, for in such a relationship is expressed "the dynamic of undoing childhood traumas and frustrations."[79] In sexual relations, particularly through intercourse for a man, a return to the mother is attempted; for him, intercourse is the "return to the

[77]Ibid., p. 246.
[78]Ibid., p. 252.
[79]Ibid., p. 159.

womb," a "return to oneness."[80] Yet such interaction, while psychically gratifying, is dangerous, for it poses the risk of losing one's self and merging back into the (m)other. The solution is to repeat and perpetuate the same devaluation of the female love object as was done to the mother, and, most important, to dominate and control her.

Thus masculine eros reveals a central construction of relationship as domination. In masculine sexuality, Hartsock argues, domination is the prevalent characteristic, involving the subordination, objectification, and often the victimization and brutalization of women. Through sexual relations with a woman, the male tries to revisit his early frustrations experienced as an infant back onto his mother, as well as his "rage at giving up the early identification with the mother and concomitant ecstasies of fantasy, the fear of failing to differentiate oneself from the mother, and a need for revenge on her for putting one in this situation."[81] This has resulted in a plethora of perversions of the concept of eros: the phallocentrism of heterosexual relations[82] involving the denial and ignorance of female sexuality and sexual desire (or, even more effectively, its classification as perversion in itself); the far greater incidence, as Stoller notes, of "gross hostility or eroticized hatred" in masculine sexuality than feminine;[83] the association of sex with violence and brutality and the eroticization of female victimization as depicted in literature, film, television, and popular music; the pervasiveness of rape, which, although an age-old offense, has in modern times a particularly gruesome connection with dismemberment and serial killings, and is currently on the rise in the United States;[84] pornography, which bases itself on the victimization

---

[80]Chodorow (1978), p. 194, particularly drawing on Michael Balint, "Perversions and Genitality," in *Primary Love and Psycho-Analytic Technique* (New York: Liverwright Publishing, 1965).

[81]Hartsock (1984), p. 169.

[82]Ibid., p. 163.

[83]Ibid., p. 162. She documents this finding in the work of Stoller, Kinsey, Dworkin, Millet, and Maslow. See pp. 157–60 and her notes to chap. 7 for more specific references.

[84]According to the Uniform Crime Reports for the 1980s, rape has increased at a rate three times greater than the increase in overall violent crime. In 1980 there were 13,408,300 violent crimes and 82,990 rapes; in 1990 the overall violent crime rate rose to 14,393,915 for a 7.35 percent increase, while rape increased to 103,005, an increase of 21.12 percent (I thank the U.S. Senate Judiciary Committee for this information). Increases in rape are often attributed to increased reporting of rape. But the Bureau of Justice Statistics survey for 1986 suggests that the incidence of rape has also increased in real numbers. That is, whereas rape in 1986 increased by 10.9 percent over 1985 (compared with an overall 5.5 percent decrease in all violent crimes), the survey indicates that reporting of rape to the police may have declined by 20.4 percent since 1985. See *New York Times*, April 13, 1986, B–4. For more recent statistics, see the following *New York Times* articles on the increase in rape: April 21, 1987, C–2; January 1, 1988,

of women;[85] fetishism, which reduces a woman to a part of her body, to a thing, thus relieving the man of having to confront a woman as a person. These are all in part defensive maneuvers, Hartsock says, "to avoid intimacy and fusion with another," to deny the humanity of women and thus assist men in maintaining their gender identity and ego boundaries.

> *Eros* and power are deeply connected, and when *eros* takes negative, masculine forms that point toward death rather than life, the community as a whole will be structured by those dynamics. . . . Masculine experience, when replicated as epistemology, leads to a world conceived of (and in fact) inhabited by a number of fundamentally hostile others whom one comes to know by means of opposition (even death struggle) and yet with whom one must construct a social relation in order to survive.[86]

Masculine ontology gives rise to a way of looking at the world—an epistemology—which requires a conceptualization of power as domination. As Hartsock points out, male writers from Plato to Bataille and Mailer have defined human nature in such a way that death is life, birth is death; eros is destructive rather than liberating; the body is irrelevant to the self; what is true is not subject to natural change; relations exist by choice; love is power, domination, and hateful destruction; mistrust and hostility spur the only true creation; "political community as community exists only on the battlefield"; and glory and honor—immortality—are preeminent over life.[87] These inversions run contrary to women's experience and perspective, in which birth is life, love creates, nature constantly changes what is real, and social

---

A-43; March 6, 1988, D-26; January 1, 1989, A-1; May 16, 1989, A-23; May 29, 1989, A-25; May 30, 1989, A-1; August 27, 1989, L-1; August 29, 1989, C-1; November 5, 1989, A-59; October 12, 1990, A-14; May 16, 1989, B-3.

[85]There is controversy among feminists about the issue of victimization. But even if there are many voluntary female participants in pornography, the prevalence of runaway teenagers' being coerced into the industry is an undeniable social problem. Furthermore, many would argue that women's "voluntary" participation demonstrates the success of the male pornography industry at masking the reality of victimization. See Griffin (1978, 1981), Dworkin (1981), Colker (1983), Lederer (1980), DeCew (1984).

[86]Hartsock (1984), pp. 170, 202, 242.

[87]Hartsock (1984), p. 188; see her chaps. 7 and 8 for more detailed discussion. One might point out that certain female writers also follow this norm; Hannah Arendt is famous for her scorn of the private sphere, claiming that the only truly human realm of action is the public. But Hartsock also points out that Arendt's concept of power—like that of other female theorists who have written on the subject—rejects the masculinist conceptualization of domination in favor of the concept of empowerment. Here would be a case for the standpoint's being specifically gender linked and not entirely self-conscious. See Hartsock (1984), chap. 9.

relations often exist not by choice though nonetheless desirably. A theory of power from a feminist standpoint would stress "aspects related to energy, capacity, and potential"[88] rather than domination. Thus, a feminist standpoint, and theories deriving from it, reflect an "opposition to dualism, a sense of a variety of interconnectedness and continuity both with other persons and with the natural world." It embodies an ontology that hearkens more to Gilligan's "web of relationships" than to a linear series of dyadic oppositions. It embodies a multilevel and interactive complex of connections and relations. A feminist standpoint allows us to see the fundamental misconstruction of social relations in terms of hostility. It does this by recognizing that women cannot escape or repress the fact, because they live it, that "we are born helpless and begin life with a relation that can only with great difficulty be described as an exchange relation—that between mother and infant."[89] Because of the sexual division of labor, men not only can repress and escape this fact but feel compelled to do so, and indeed have created theories and practices precisely to aid them in the effort to escape.

According to Hartsock, the masculinist concept of power and the "inversions" it entails are particularly realized in the literature of ancient Greece. The oedipal fears of intimacy, fusion, and loss of self are "memorialized in the construction of the agonal political world of the warrior-hero (and later the citizen) as a world of hostile and threatening others to whom one relates by means of rivalry and competition for dominance." But what about the implications for modern thought? Parallel to her discussion of eros and ancient Greece, Hartsock presents a marxist analysis of the market society of modern thought and liberal democratic society. She traces the development of "communities of exchange," market societies where the rules of exchange serve as the tenuous and abstract links between otherwise wholly discrete individuals. This community is "arbitrary and fragile, structured fundamentally by competition and dominance."[90]

Yet Hartsock strongly differentiates between the community of exchange and the community of eros both as they affect women and as they have structured institutions, social relations, and epistemology. Although there are obvious parallels and synchronicities between the class domination produced by the market and the gender domination

---

[88]Ibid., p. 210. Once again Hartsock's materialist approach takes a slightly different direction than does my interpretation. She would argue that this concept of power more accurately reflects women's material experience of labor as people very much involved in empowering other people, especially their children, in helping them grow and develop their capacities and potential.

[89]Ibid., pp. 242, 41.

[90]Ibid., pp. 252, 38.

of community formed by masculine eros, the latter is far more pernicious and repressive to women than the former, she maintains. In
market societies, even though the relation between buyer and seller is
exploitive, at least "each left the market (even after the purchase or
sale of labor power) with something they did not possess before the
transaction (money or commodity)." In contrast, the ancient Greek
"opposition of victory to death or dishonor does not present a situation in which one can argue that both sides gain, even if they do not
gain equally."[91]

Nevertheless, her analysis of the community of masculine eros
deepens our understanding of the domination found in market relations, and this is crucial to any comprehension of the structural sexism of its key concepts such as contract and obligation. Hartsock's
analysis of eros is particularly useful in showing how we can view
market society and ideology as specifically masculinist constructs, as
products of gender even more than class. Indeed, I think much of her
analysis of eros can be applied to the market far more directly than
she indicates. Even though the community of masculine eros apparent in ancient Greece may have overtly expressed the hostility of
domination, I would offer the thesis that the community of exchange,
or market society, represses the overt hostility and sublimates it into
forms of action that express the same hostility, but in subtler—and
perhaps more insidious—form.

The first point to note is that repression and sublimation do not
equal resolution.[92] That is, the market may present less ostensible violence against women, but the fact that the same fears are repressed
and sublimated through the market, and not resolved by mutual recognition and equal respect, merely means that they will be expressed
differently. Hartsock is correct that women of the eighteenth century
were better off than women of ancient Greece. The principle of equality that the social contract theorists espoused logically required them
to grant limited equality to women in the state of nature or even in

[91]Ibid., p. 202.
[92]In the final chapter of *Fortune Is a Woman*—an excellent example of the interpretive
power to be found in the application of feminist psychoanalytic theory to individual
political philosophers in the history of thought—Hanna Pitkin (1984) argues that although repression produces bad results, sublimation results in good things such as
"artistic, scientific or cultural endeavor." She says, "Without sublimation, without the
rechanneling of libidinal energy into acculturation, we could not become human persons at all" (p. 317). It is correct to note, however, that sublimation can produce both
good and bad effects and take positive and negative forms. After all, many "accepted"
channels into which libidinal energy can be sublimated express the cultural repression
of the fear of women: misogyny is "accepted." Sublimation into a channel that culturally expresses a collective neurosis will not provide a release from that neurosis. Accordingly, resolution must be distinguished from sublimation.

the family. But they all, including Locke (theoretically for reasons of efficiency in having the family speak with one voice, but also because of the Old Testament), assert the primacy of men as fathers, husbands, and citizens, which justifies robbing women of control over themselves, a political voice, and any form of power (masculinistly defined). As Rousseau most obviously demonstrated, men's fear of the power of the mother/woman and the attempt to restrain her in self-defense results in her total exclusion from public life, her disempowerment.

There are many subtle ways in which the market is based on a deep hostility toward women comparable to that expressed in community based on eros. Indeed, the first and most basic form of sublimated violence found in the market can be seen to be the isolation of market man's abstract individualism. Gilligan postulated that for men, violence is found in connection. In her studies men associated danger with images of connection and responded to pictures and narratives portraying intimacy and relationship by offering stories with violent resolutions that severed relationship and connection. Isolation is considered safe, so how can it be a sublimation for violence? In the first place, we should remember that the women in her study perceived violence in isolation; they constructed stories of brutality and death (usually happening *to* the woman in the story rather than being caused by her) resulting from isolation, whether it was isolation at the top of a hierarchy, on the edge of a circle, or in a dark alley. Safety and truth were seen in connection. Thus, from a rather simplistic perspective that considers only women's point of view, we could say that isolation stimulates violence.

But the analysis goes much deeper than this. To say that isolation breeds violence just because women think so would be to replicate the masculinist methodology critiqued here. For if men see safety in isolation, and structure their social contacts to preserve that isolation, then why are men, as the literature on the subject documents,[93] so much more violent than women? One possible response is that life cannot be constructed on the market model. Because of the centrality of human relationships to human life, men who view danger in relationship must nevertheless engage in relationships; hence, they are repeatedly forced to react violently. That is, we could take men's greater violence as evidence that abstract individualism is indeed a myth, that it is a sublimation of men's fear of connection, an attempt to repress that fear by denying it. The fear of connection—of re-merging with the mother—can be conquered only through domination of

[93]See Stoller (1973) and references in Hartsock (1984), chap. 7.

the other and by the false and exaggerated assertion of independence. This is the necessary implication of abstract individualism: an ideology that asserts one's isolation and total independence serves as a barrier to the return to the mother. The isolation of abstract individualism can be seen in this way as an expression of hostility toward the mother, a further attempt to gain recognition through domination.

Abstract individualism results in a society that is hostile and harmful to the mother/woman in other ways. By extension, it creates and promotes as necessary and good competition between discrete individuals for the realization of their interests. Each individual tries to promote his or her interests and gain as much as she or he can while giving up as little as possible; that is, one tries to gain recognition through realization of one's interests. Such recognition, as Hegel noted, requires granting the other some minimal recognition in turn to make one's own recognition have value: what Jessica Benjamin dubs "the master's dilemma."[94] Hence the self must give something— but just enough to make sure the other can grant worthy recognition, and not enough to lose the struggle for that recognition. On the market model, one seeks to gain dominance through commodities. The definition of a "good deal" (as opposed to a "fair price") is one that allows us to gain more than we give. The standards for goodness in the market are measured by gain—and, by necessary extension, owing to the concept of limited resources, by the other's loss. As Hartsock points out, the duality of the market ensures "reciprocal exclusion of ownership." The epistemology created by the market model, Hartsock argues, is one of dualism: exchange/use, quantity/quality, society/nature, mind/body, and the "reciprocal exclusion of ownership concerning two sets of commodities" that is involved in wage labor. These dualisms define the very being of such communities, ordering the definition of community and humanity. Within Hartsock's standpoint framework, this ontology of opposition and hostility create and work with a specific epistemology that reflects dualism as well: the "world conceived of (and in fact) inhabited by a number of fundamentally hostile others whom one comes to know by means of opposition (even death struggle) and yet with whom one must construct a social relation in order to survive" describes market society as well as ancient Greece.[95] Indeed, in the best of deals, one "makes a killing" or "wipes out" the competition; one gains all at the expense of the other's loss.

The social contract provides a system of rules, laws, and limitations

[94]Benjamin (1980).
[95]Hartsock (1984), pp. 98, 242.

on this interaction: it acts as an externalized superego. The social contract enables the (male) citizen to engage in the struggle for domination and recognition relatively safely. It preserves men from the return to seductive nature, which lures them to gain more and more by going to greater and more violent lengths to gain what they want (thus reverting to the state of war), an echo of the notion that the boy's positional identification with abstract roles and rules helps preserve him against the return to the tempting state of symbiosis. Furthermore, through the institutionalized division of private and public in the sexual division of labor, even men who fare less well or even fail in the market have in the private sphere a permanent other, a minimally recognized recognizer. Thus the market is also able to play off the dualisms it serves to perpetuate and which in turn perpetuate the market. The view of the home as a "haven in a heartless world"[96] is just that for market man. It provides a replenishment of ensured recognition by an already securely dominated other, which enables man to reaffirm his identity in order to go forth the next day to compete with perhaps worthier but also more formidable opponents.[97]

Indeed, this situation would seem to solve the "master's dilemma." By controlling the degree and forms of recognition of the other, by creating a separate sphere of real activity within which the other can work to provide real necessities and conveniences while at the same time maintaining a mythology that devalues this realm and eschews necessity as inhuman, the (masculine) self can sustain a controlled recognition of the (feminine) other: that is, just enough to make the other's uncontrolled and complete recognition of men worthwhile but not so much as to make the female other equal to the self, not enough to let the slave stop being a slave.

The attempt to gain dominance through commodities is an important link to the violence against women expressed in the market. Al-

---

[96]Lasch (1977).

[97]This "replenishing" can be seen to mirror the "emotional refueling" that occurs in the practicing stage of preoedipal development. As we saw earlier (see especially Flax [1978]), the child explores her or his motor skills and independence but must return to the mother for the reassurance that she is still there and still part of the child. If we apply this observation to market society, however, this minimal recognition would seem to go only so far in granting men a secure base. For instance, many men committed suicide immediately after the stock market crash of 1929; "wiped out" in the market, they seemed to view this loss as worse than physical death. Their wives were equally affected in the economic sense yet did not commit suicide. Were these men overcome by their frailty and sense of loss against the monster of the market? Did being poor make them feel like a nobody, an unrecognized other? Was total loss considered total defeat, total domination? Did women not commit suicide because of their different moral orientation toward responsibility—that is, "having to live for the sake of the children," and so on—or because, as other already, they did not feel the effects of this ultimate loss? Or are both answers true?

though women are not sacrificed for battle or crops in market societies, they are commodified. As Gayle Rubin notes, women have been and still are viewed by much of the world as commodities, as objects to be bartered, traded, and offered as gifts of political reconciliation or alliance.[98] This held true in modified form in seventeenth- and eighteenth-century Europe and colonial America with the endurance of the dowry and the fact that women could not marry without paternal consent.[99] For example, in the seventeenth and eighteenth centuries, when social contract theory was developing and exerting its influence on political thinking, the concept of women as property was evident in the legal provision that "no man shall be deprived of his wife and children, no man's goods or estate shall be taken away from him . . . unless it be by . . . some express law of the country."[100] Married women who were raped or were otherwise victims of assault could not bring suit for damages under tort law; only husbands could do so, and if the husband was missing, the woman was usually out of luck except for the possibility of a special bill granting her the right to bring suit in a particular instance.[101] Furthermore, only the claims of white husbands were recognized.[102]

In turn, husbands were sued for their wives' tortious acts, but their liability extended only to financial compensation. Corporal punishment was meted out to women, thus extending a nonreciprocal and inconsistent position on the recognition of women as responsible agents under the law;[103] that is, although denied equal rights, they were required to shoulder equal responsibility.[104] The point here, however, is not just that women were denied rights but that they were controlled as objects, disempowered and made subject to men,

[98]Rubin (1975).

[99]Smith (1961), p. 209. Although it can also be argued that dowries granted women a degree of independence and status, the characterization of marriage as a market, so wittily depicted in the novels of Jane Austen, holds true to the theme of women as barter. Of course, women of wealth have always had more status and power than women of the lower classes.

[100]*The Charters and General Laws of the Colony and Province of Massachusetts Bay* (Boston, 1814), chap. 4, sec. 1, p. 44. I do not mean to imply that the social contract theories created these laws; the laws preexisted the theories. Rather, I wish to highlight that this political milieu cannot be isolated from the theories that developed in them.

[101]Morris (1959) p. 186.

[102]Smith (1961), p. 236.

[103]Morris (1959), p. 185.

[104]Indeed, in the case of rape the burden of responsibility lay squarely on the woman not to be raped. This is certainly not an uncommon notion, but it is highlighted by a remarkable case in seventeenth-century western Massachusetts. When one John Bennet was sued by John Stiles for defaming the latter's wife, "saying that she was a light woman and that he could have a leape on her when he pleased," the court gave the defendant nine days to prove his allegation! He could (or did) not and was forced to pay John Stiles forty shillings. Smith (1961), p. 236.

were made victims of violence without recourse, and were dominated as the commodified other.

In more obvious fashion, prostitution, and in more contemporary times pornography, are key aspects of the market involving the commodification of women. The essential nature of prostitution is that a man sells a woman to other men; he controls her, controls access to her, and controls the money her body brings. Whereas in prostitution it can be argued that some women have some control—not *all* prostitutes necessarily have pimps, and some procurers are women[105]— pornography is a different matter. Pornography is a predominantly, if not totally, male-controlled industry and is based largely on the victimization of women and children, as Susan Griffin so compellingly argues.[106] In pornography, not only are women's bodies commodified, but their identity and subjectivity are also considered commodities. Their degradation—women being forced to eat excrement, women enjoying being beaten and raped—is the package to be sold. Indeed, so-called snuff films, in which the actress is apparently killed on screen, are the ultimate expression of the violence of such commodification of women. Here woman's life is the commodity that a man takes by trickery in the course of market transactions. Here is the ultimate in market man's "making a killing."

These remarks are obviously meant to be suggestive rather than to provide an exhaustive defense; but they support the notion that the market is another form of the violent struggle for selfhood and identity. When we combine the supposedly gender-neutral struggle for identity with an understanding of object relations theory, we can see that this conception of recognition through struggle and dominance is a specifically masculinist vision. And when we see the ways it comports with women's inferior status in the market as well as the active harm they receive at its hands, then the connection can be more clearly drawn between the exchange of the market and the violence of eros.

The significance of this connection goes beyond the substantive arguments of any of the theorists discussed in this chapter and leads to an understanding of how the epistemologies of obligation theories

---

[105]I would not want to overstate the power of women in prostitution, however. The vast majority of procurers are male, and indeed prostitution is often virtually inseparable from procurement. Furthermore, the fact that female procurers are generally former prostitutes is significant in attesting to the patriarchal character of prostitution. See Barry (1979).

[106]Griffin (1981). I say "predominantly" rather than "entirely," even though I refer to Griffin's work, because of the controversy within feminism over pornography (see note 85). I distinguish here between erotica and pornography in assuming the latter involves the victimization of women.

contain gender biases. If the theories' epistemological frameworks are an important source of the problem of political obligation, and if these frameworks are themselves masculinist responses to the need to dominate the female, then the sexism of these theories cannot be eliminated without a profound and fundamental alteration of the theories. This problem also suggests that the central concept of these theories—consent—may itself, like rationality, be epistemologically masculinist and may require a total reconstruction if it is to accommodate women as equals.

The feminist theories discussed here do not merely pick apart various elements of social contract theory and reveal them as sexist; they implicitly question the entire epistemological foundation of those theories. They reveal that the ideas from which social contract theory works—the intellectual device of the state of nature and, by extension, the ethical values of equality and particularly freedom that stem from it—are products of specific social relations (for example, child rearing) of a particular kind (that is, mother-only and patriarchal). It shows, furthermore, that these ideas are not just casual by-products of a "natural" relationship, or of "pure" knowledge, but are rather specifically and purposively created products, whether that purpose is conscious or not.

These feminist theories at least implicitly demand the reunion of epistemology and ontology and urge us to base the former on the latter. They are all—Harding's criticisms notwithstanding—standpoint theories.[107] They hold that men and women have differing ontologies, in part because of different psychic development. These experiences create different epistemological frameworks from which politics and ethics are derived. This feminist perspective allows us to see that "precisely because knowing and being cannot be separated, we must know how to be. To do so requires a transformation of knowledge adequate to our being and which points us beyond its present distorted forms."[108] By seeing the faults of our being—the gendered selves we develop out of socially constructed relations of

---

[107]Harding is not the only theorist to appear ambivalent in adopting a standpoint approach. Flax (1986, 1990), in contrast to her 1983 essay, also seems to reject standpoint epistemology in favor of postmodernism. She says: "Any feminist standpoint will necessarily be partial. Each person who tries to think from the standpoint of women may illuminate some aspects of the social totality which have been previously suppressed with the dominant view. But none of us can speak for 'woman' because no such person exists except within a specific set of (already gendered) relations—to 'man' and to many concrete and different women." Flax (1986), p. 37. But, as Harding points out in both the 1983 and 1986 essays Flax really links postmodernism with standpoint epistemology. Harding (1986), pp. 151–55. Furthermore, in her 1991 book Harding allies herself more explicitly with standpoint epistemology once again.

[108]Flax (1983), p. 271. In keeping with the standpoint's Hegelian and Marxian legacy, Flax suggests that dialectics is a way to begin the development of a "more adequate"

reproduction—we can more easily see what the faults of the dominant epistemology are and why those faults exist.

As I have argued, a central fault of modernist epistemologies is the contention that knowing, if not knowledge, is the same for everyone, though humans may feel and desire quite differently from one another. This assertion creates an image of a uniform public world that is knowable to all in the same way, and a private world that is not only unpredictable but inaccessible to all but the self. Since women solely occupy the private realm, they become the literal embodiment of such unpredictability and the locus of irrationality. This further justifies their exclusion from the public realm as it is defined to exclude the characteristics that it is designed to produce in women. Consent, as a central aspect of this epistemological framework, is thus similarly based on the exclusion of women. As Jean Bethke Elshtain points out, what makes contract possible, and makes it further an essentially public act, is that *"the same knowledge is shared by all* and that the public sphere is the *only* sphere in which this holds."* Contract, as the quintessential public act, is thus also the quintessential expression of this exclusion. "The 'voice' of woman . . . of privatized, irrational desire" and "cloying sentiment," is absolutely incapable of speaking the language of contract, and hence of *making* contracts.[109]

This is certainly true for Locke, for whom language is a "system of external signs" and symbols rather than a complex social activity that links inner and outer."[110] If women have a different voice, their lack of facility with the language of contract inhibits their ability to partake in the practice. In *An Essay concerning Human Understanding* Locke holds that, because of the weakness of our senses, on which we are dependent for knowledge, we cannot know the "real essence" of things and of man. We can know only the "nominal essence"; that is, we can

---

epistemology. She holds that if we treat knowing as an activity, as Hegel does (although, she points out, Hegel does this "abstractly"), we will be able to see that "this activity constitutes being in and through social relations which themselves have a history, just as individuals do." This recognition would bring about a "self-reflective society in which social relations (and relations with nature) are not organized on a principle of domination" (p. 271).

[109]Elshtain (1981), p. 118. Certainly there are private components to consent, as in promising; but the contract is explicitly public. Some might point to marriage as a private contract, but this would deny the degree to which the state regulates the institution, from licenses to the legal status of women in marriage to divorce law. In some ways this is not a bad thing; for, given women's political and social inferiority, marriage is in fact a public and very political relationship. My point here is that rather than simply remove the protections the state provides along with its intrusions, we must change the institution of marriage itself fundamentally if it is to become a truly "private" relationship.

[110]Elshtain (1981), p. 116.

know only a thing's nature as it is determined by the way in which we classify it. This classification is manifested in language, which is to a degree arbitrary; that is, words have no necessary relation to the things they represent. Language is a system of contingent or accidental regularities for Locke; it is not the product of rules or conventions. Although it enables us to communicate, this regularity cannot overcome the basic atomism of humans. A word or a name does not give us information to form ideas; one must develop thoughts or ideas directly from the phenomenon. This, of course, means that communication between humans is severely limited in its effectiveness. We will never be able to communicate our perceptions satisfactorily.

Yet simultaneous with this extremely individualistic view of knowledge and language, Locke wishes to situate individuals within a social context, namely, civil society. How can individuals with such severely limited abilities to communicate ever come to agreement on a social contract?[111] The conflict between atomism and sociability gives rise to the conceptualization of man as "naturally" free, to the problem of inalienable rights, and especially to the problem of tacit consent.

It also at least contributes to the central but problematic role God plays in Locke's theory. Locke admittedly limits the effect of empiricism on his epistemology by inconsistently bringing in rationalist assumptions; he talks about the relations of ideas. He also allows for certainty of knowledge by intuition (which produces knowledge of ourselves) and by demonstration (which reveals God to us). "Sensitive" knowledge, he asserts, is the only imperfect knowledge. This could explain the central role of God and his law of nature to the success of the social contract, for if men can be certain only of themselves and of God, one of these must provide the key to forming the social contract. And since men's knowledge of themselves is part of what creates the problem of the state of war, God is the only answer to that problem. But this resolution suggests that the tensions between individual freedom and governmental authority demonstrate, at least in part, a tension between Locke's epistemological atomism and his political values.

A feminist perspective on epistemological frameworks can also deepen our readings of social contract theories in other ways. In the earlier discussion of Flax, for instance, I identified ways in which Hobbes and Rousseau demonstrate the return of the repressed. But what about Locke? From the perspective of gender psychology, and particularly feminist psychoanalytic theory, we can identify the genesis and forms of gender bias in his theory. For instance, in a Macpher-

---

[111]Pateman (1979) also makes this point.

sonian reading of Locke, the state of nature is marked by largely isolated individuals whose community consists in self-created relationships of exchange. Nonvoluntary relationships are viewed as coercive in the context of male citizens in the market because they violate the priority of liberty which defines humanity. Although Locke's state of nature, governed by reason, is different from Rousseau's and Hobbes's, his emphasis on property and the need for the father/state to protect possessions is analogous to the infant's focus on desired objects.

From the interpretation that Dunn gives, by contrast, individuals may not be quite so isolated, but this is because of the centrality of a patriarchal God. In Dunn's reading of Locke, community does not consist in relations of exchange as much as in relations imposed on men by the laws of God the father.[112] This would allow for some nonvoluntary relationships, as long as they are consistent with the laws of nature, because such laws are in men's true interests. These laws define choice and freedom rather than inhibiting them. In psychoanalytic terms, one could say that the picture Dunn presents fits the oedipal stage of the turn to the father and his rules which serve as externalized superego. The state of nature is a state in which rational individuals adhere to the laws God gives them. The social contract is a further solidification of those laws and men's ability to obey them. Although all men are rational, the dark forces of nature are still powerful enough to make conflict inevitable. In such cases the lack of an independent judge makes resolution impossible. As do Hobbes and Rousseau, though in a qualitatively different way, Locke views face-to-face confrontation and communication pessimistically at best. It is safer and more effective, according to all three theorists, to depersonalize such engagements.

The role of God in Locke's theory is important beyond Dunn's interpretation. We cannot consent to slavery because we are God's property, and only he has the right to bind us in such a manner. Locke's inconsistency on consensual slavery probably best highlights the issues raised by gender psychology. Locke wants man to be absolutely independent and self-creative; hence the centrality of consent. Yet he recognizes that man cannot be the absolute arbiter because there are things that violate humanity, our ability to be rationally autonomous. But what can the criterion be for humanity in Locke's framework if it is not self-creation and the ability to choose? If God provides the answer, what is to ensure accurate interpretation of his will without recourse to individual self-determination?

---

[112]Dunn (1980).

Gender psychology allows us to interpret Locke as saying that there are certain things that violate adulthood—defined as independent, rational autonomy—particularly the desire to return to the symbiosis of early infancy. The aversion to consensual slavery within a theoretical context that gives primacy to individual choice strongly suggests, in the context of the psychoanalytic framework, an attempt to build in a structural, rule-governed safeguard against the strong desire to return to the state of symbiosis with the mother. Locke's solution—a turn to the all-powerful father, the patriarchal God—is a genuine expression of the oedipal drama. Rationality, scientific thought, and individual self-creation are necessary for independence. But when a serious contradiction is revealed, and the danger of the return to the mother (that is, dependence) presents itself to the unconscious, a turn to the father and the externalized rules he provides will yield our safe passage away from nature. This exclusive definition of obligation denies the obligations contained in women's privatized experience.

The centrality of property to Locke's theory is another significant factor for gender psychology. The institution of inheritance is important for Locke because of the centrality of property. But one could also argue that property is important because of the institution of inheritance. As I suggested in Chapter 1, property becomes a tool for creating an institutionalized rationale for developing ways for a man to be sure a child is his. It is not insignificant for Locke's theory that for the most part women cannot hold property; nor is it insignificant that women were themselves considered property, if not explicitly by Locke then implicitly, by virtue of his unwillingness to challenge the status quo of women's political position. Property, as the central political value, excludes women, much as contract does; yet it requires women to play a central though devalued and even subordinate role, and it defines that role very particularly.

Perhaps even more significant is Locke's insistence on reason and objective rationality in presocial man. His arguments that both reason and rights are natural and that we can be bound only by our own voluntary acts can be compared to the oedipal boy's efforts to assert his independence by constructing the world as he wants it to be and not as it is, thus giving him the illusion of control over his surroundings. The concept of obligation as only self-assumed ensures (and assumes) that the individual will be able to exert control over all connections with discrete others. It denies the son's relationship to the mother, which is not voluntary, and any possible connection with any possible other that is not under the son's control. The notion of natural rights and the need for government to carry them out ensures the institutionalization of the externalized superego; that is, the self's separation and independence are guaranteed by external structure. Under natural rights, one reasons not from one's innate sense of connection to others but from "laws" that "naturally" exist independent of all men.

Natural rights within the context of scarce resources embodies notions of competition, separation, and alienation, as Macpherson notes. The market society is one of unrelated, competing beings. Rights are the means by which these abstract individuals intersect by making claims against one another; rights thus serve to articulate and solidify our separateness. As Charles Taylor argues, atomism is, and must logically be, the ontology underlying primacy-of-rights theories.[113] Furthermore, by creating a world defined and controlled by natural laws and rationality, Locke creates a situation in which the individual is subject and all else is object. Abstract individualism is the ultimate expression of the subject-object or self-other dichotomy characteristic of the repressed oedipal dilemma.[114]

Thus gender psychology demonstrates different ways in which the "problem of women" goes much deeper than contingently sexist values. It is a structural, ontological, and epistemological problem that permeates our very conception of political theory. The feminist reconceptualization of epistemology, its methodologies, and the models it builds for new feminist critical analyses and theories can help point the way to an analysis of exactly how political obligation is structured and why it is so.

For instance, Flax's and Bordo's theories suggest that one way to understand women's problematic relation to political obligation is to examine the culturally symbolic psychic roots of political obligation as consent. Their arguments can be taken to suggest that perhaps the concept of consent, and the need to base obligations on consent, may be rooted at least in part in men's need to escape and dominate the female. Their theories also implicitly suggest that these psychic issues can be considered epistemological issues, systematically structured and fundamental to dominant conceptions of obligation. Harding reinforces this last claim particularly, indicating the broader-ranging im-

---

[113]Taylor (1979a).

[114]According to some theorists (Eisenstein [1981], Elshtain [1981]), Locke also denies that women are capable of rational thought; thus, the emphasis on rationality and its priority in the social contract is another way of distancing the self from the mother. Others, however (Smith [1984]), deny this, saying that Locke allows for women's rationality. I agree that Locke does not explicitly state that women cannot think rationally; but his refusal to challenge existing norms concerning property ownership, equality in marriage, and "women's lot" create a heavier burden on such challengers than the simple assertion that he never actually said it. It is part of the character of political theory that it often says what it never explicitly states.

plications of masculinist conceptions of ontology, epistemology, and methodology for theory in general. Her work suggests that the method in which we approach theory may itself contribute to the substantive conclusions that are reached. The theoretical divorce of process from substance is a particular value claim that is built into the structure of our inquiries and the activity of theorizing.

Similarly, Hartsock's analysis of power—both in its portrayal of how social relations and institutions are structured by the masculine psyche and in its analysis of the epistemological ramifications of such structure—suggests that the meaning of obligation may take on a very different significance once we comprehend the masculinist nature of the structure within which it is conceptualized. If we can understand the violence and misogyny underlying the market model of political theory, then we can better grasp the basis of market concepts, such as self-assumed obligation, as expressions of that violence.

Thus, a realization of the epistemological dimensions and ramifications of gender psychology is extremely valuable for a feminist analysis of the gender-biased structure of modern obligation theory, if not modern liberal theory in general. Instead of merely providing fuel for a basic disagreement (I reject your theory because it is premised on individualism) and hence a moral argument that breaks down, gender psychology can be used to cut through the dead end of liberal discourse and provide new insights as to why a theory takes a certain shape. An understanding of this "why" can provide stronger foundations for making judgments about theories. This would bring about the unity—or, more precisely, it would enable us to *recognize* the unity—of being and knowing with ethics and politics. Furthermore, these feminist theories point the way toward a feminist reconstruction of epistemology and obligation based on women's experience; for the public ideology of consent not only denies women the opportunities to participate in the political and hence to assume political obligations—its contingent sexism—but it also makes invisible the kinds of obligations that women in fact have historically had in the private sphere. More precisely, while tacitly asserting through the public-private split that such obligations—caring for husbands and children, reproduction and nurturance—exist, liberal obligation theory obscures the fact that these obligations have an entirely separate genesis and character. Through the mythologizing dimensions of the social contract story, the theories deny the fact that the obligations historically imposed on women are not contractual within the terms set by consent theory. And by segregating women and their activities in the private sphere, and then devaluing that sphere, the theories ignore the fact that the concepts and language of consent are not capable of accounting for the activities and relationships that such obligations have historically entailed. It is through this double obfuscation that liberal obligation theory has been able to exert its intellectual and epistemological hegemony. And because women's disempowerment and silencing are so central to this obfuscation, it is in a feminist understanding of the masculinist structure of dominant epistemologies that the most powerful challenge to liberal obligation theory lies.

CHAPTER FIVE

Feminist Epistemology
and Political Obligation

THE PREVIOUS chapters may seem to have taken us away from my main line of argument; for how can these feminist epistemological theories enhance our understanding of obligation? I maintain that application of these theories will not only help us understand the fundamental masculinism of consent theory but will also point to a feminist reconstruction of obligation. It is to that task that I turn in the present chapter. I explore ways in which gender psychology provides a powerful heuristic device for understanding liberal obligation theory as a language of power and exclusion, and how women's experiences provide ideas about how obligation needs to be fundamentally reconceptualized and restructured.

It is important, however, not to overstate the case: the concept of consent and contract is appropriate, even vital, to at least some (perhaps many) aspects of human existence. But when it is used to characterize all of social reality, including most significantly reproductive and other affective relationships—or, conversely, when it denigrates as nonhuman any relationship that cannot be viewed as a contract—and when it systematically depends on women's status of inferiority as it simultaneously espouses the principle of equality, then it reveals the pathology of the construct on which it is based: specifically, how the male fear of connection with a woman serves as a basis for establishing how and why obligation is always, and can only be, self-assumed.

Freedom, Recognition, and Masculinity

The central issue in the relationship between this fear, the masculine model of development, and self-assumed obligation is that of freedom, which is also a central issue of liberalism. Hobbes, Locke, and Rousseau all base their theories of obligation on the initial premise of natural freedom. This freedom—as well as, for Locke and Hobbes at least, the civil freedom that follows from it—uniformly coheres with what Isaiah Berlin has called "negative liberty," which holds that freedom consists in an absence of external constraints.[1] The individual is free to the extent that she is not restrained by external forces, primarily viewed as law, physical force, and other overt coercion. As anyone familiar with the debate between positive and negative liberty can attest, a central difficulty with the concept of negative liberty consists in determining what exactly constitutes a restraint.[2] Yet Berlin's general concept that restraints come from outside the self is a basic tenet of negative liberty; specifically, other humans' direct or indirect participation "in frustrating my wishes" is the relevant criterion in determining restraint. "By being free in this sense I mean not being interfered with by others. The wider the area of non-interference, the wider my freedom."[3]

This conception of freedom can be seen in several ways to arise from masculine experience under mother-only child rearing; indeed, Berlin's choice of words significantly echoes the boy's infantile dilemma. According to object relations, the primary goal of the emerging oedipal boy is to achieve freedom from the constraint of his mother: to excise his femaleness, detach thoroughly from the mother and be free of the female,[4] and thereby "escape from the body."[5] The mother is viewed in the boy's unconscious as a controlling force that seeks to keep the son imprisoned, that is, merged with her. Her presence thus presents a barrier to his self-realization of masculinity (or nonfemininity), a limitation and restriction on his ability to become male, to become himself. And this restraint, furthermore, is seen by the boy as coming from completely outside the self, in spite of the fact

[1]Isaiah Berlin, "Two Concepts of Liberty," in Berlin (1971), pp. 118– 72. Rousseau is certainly considered a positive libertarian when it comes to his concept of moral freedom in civil society, but here I am specifically focusing on natural freedom, which for Rousseau is much like Hobbes's concept. And just as natural freedom provides the rationale for constructing a state on consent, it is natural freedom that causes Rousseau to attempt to reconcile the general will with voluntarism, as I argued in Chapter 1.

[2]See Presston (1984).

[3]Berlin (1971), p. 123.

[4]Chodorow (1978).

[5]Flax (1983), p. 258. Gilligan (1982) also asserts that males attempt to escape or keep free of connection and an entangling, strangling web of relationships.

that his psychically female identity—that is, his primary self—is what he is trying to escape.

According to object relations theory, the girl, perceiving sameness between herself and her mother, incorporates that sameness into her self-definition and view of the world. She sees her relationship with the world as continuous: self *is* other. For the boy, perceptions of difference cause him to view self and other as totally separate, and these perceptions feed on themselves as the boy actively engages in the conceptualization of the mother as completely outside the self. By projecting his psychic femaleness onto the mother and viewing the mother as completely separate—as well as by viewing her as "bad"—the boy can dissociate himself from his primary femininity. Furthermore, in the dissociation of the masculine mind/self from the female body/other, restraint for the boy is embodied in the very presence (the body) of the mother as the reminder of his primary femaleness and how that is at odds with his masculine gender identity. This restraint evident in the mother's presence is viewed as coming from totally outside the self; its genesis is totally other. In reaction the boy cuts loose from the (m)other; he detaches, tries to escape her influence and control. In short, he seeks absolute freedom from her and from all "others."

But freedom, defined by this masculine psyche, further entails domination and contest. Because the mother is viewed as a controlling force, inhibiting self-realization by virtue of her very presence, the search for freedom becomes a struggle in the boy's mind for control. Gender psychology challenges the liberal-positivist self-other duality by showing that others—and one other in particular—are intrinsically part of the self. Yet it also reveals that the boy cannot accept this fact without a fundamental challenge to his identity. The mother appears an omnipresent force, precisely because she represents the boy's primary identity. Furthermore, in spite of his efforts, the deep nature of the boy's psychic femaleness makes it impossible to truly excise. The boy thus perceives his mother, as the embodiment of this aspect of himself, as the obstacle to be overcome. If he can dominate his mother, who represents his primary identity, then he can master that identity and rid himself of it. Thus, the boy devalues the mother and his relation to her, belittling all relationship in the process. He seeks to dehumanize her (and by extension all women as embodiments of the female). He denies her existence by denying her humanity, her presence, her subjectivity and selfhood, and particularly her sexuality. Thus this freedom is viewed as the product of a struggle: the boy achieves freedom only by virtue of the woman's subordination.

In reality, however, this freedom is a false abstraction; for contra-
dictorily, in the effort to escape the restraints created by the mother,
the boy must erect all sorts of other artificial barriers, in the form of
rigid rules of masculine behavior, limiting social labels, categories,
and sex roles, which are equally restricting if not more so. In order to
prevent loss of self to the mother, the boy erects these barriers to
keep her "out" and him "in" his self-identity and gender identity.
These barriers range from socially approved institutions and practices
of female-exclusive masculinity (from all-boy sports to all-male professions) to more pernicious aspects such as widespread belief systems
about women's natural inferiority. "The normal male contempt for
women" has been documented by analysts in boys by age five.[6] These
belief systems are, of course, partly produced by empirical observation and teaching. The boy can see that women are socially devalued
even by observing relations between his mother and father; he experiences privileges over his sisters or his friends' sisters; he observes the
restraints placed on women by virtue of their sex. But other beliefs
develop by extension of these observations because they fill a deep
need in the boy to believe that women are inferior, for if they are,
then his mother's power is perhaps not so threatening after all.[7]

These beliefs serve as an externalized superego. The boy's turn to
the father is a turn to an abstract role, as male gender identity comes
to consist in principles, ideas, and norms rather than a direct affective
relationship. Since the goal in being male is to be not-female, the boy
seeks out principles and rules to help prevent the return to the
mother and primary femininity and to guide his behavior and identity. That is, the boy's positional identification ensures an identity and
a superego that vitally depend on abstract principles that are articulated by others and rules that are defined by an absent father role.
The boy's superego thus comes not from within but from without.
And these belief systems, rules, and practices serve as barriers—restraints—to prevent the boy's return to the mother, to the supposed
end of self-identity, self-realization, and self-creation. Like Locke's
"natural law" which prevents men from consenting to slavery, these
belief systems and rules serve as restraints on self-creative action to
the supposed end of preserving freedom.

Thus, although this concept of freedom may ostensibly be defined
as an absence of restraint, perhaps it is better defined as an absence of
the female. Indeed, the notion that negative freedom is the hallmark

---

[6] Chodorow (1978), p. 182, quoting Ruth Mack Brunswick.

[7] Keller (1983). An example she offers from personal experience is a favorite of mine:
" 'Science,' my five-year-old son declared [after his first few days at kindergarten], con-
fidently bypassing the fact that his mother was a scientist, 'is for men!' " (p. 189).

of humanity provides another means of asserting women's nonhuman status. If women were human, they would have a right to freedom. To enact this freedom they would have to seek dominance, and such a search would destroy men, not to mention the fact that it would subvert the very purpose of defining freedom this way in the first place. As long as women are not considered human, then freedom is not relevant to their existence. They are dominatable, like all things in nature, and thus dominated. Yet this domination is what creates the conditions for and defines women's inhumanity in the first place. Although it may be true in one sense that freedom defined negatively is not appropriate to women's historical self-conception and experience, the simultaneous denial of other conceptions of freedom and of the priority of other values (such as relationship) ensures that women's subordination will provide a self-referential justification.

But of course the concept goes even deeper than this; for if female is other, then freedom entails the absence of the other, which, as de Beauvoir and Hegel both brought into our collective intellectual consciousness, constitutes the problem of recognition. Indeed, many readers may already have perceived the parallels between the boy's struggle for freedom and identity and the struggle between Hegel's master and slave for recognition. Recognition is a key issue to this negative conception of freedom in the masculine psyche, and it is a key to the conception of freedom found in the market and liberal voluntarist theories of obligation. Viewing the object relations "story" through the issue of recognition can yield a powerful means of understanding the epistemological gender bias of political theory.

Recall that at about the age of three months the infant begins to perceive itself as a separate being from the mother. For the next few years the processes of differentiation and individuation proceed and regress as the infant explores its independence and motor skills and yet seeks to return to the mother and symbiosis. If differentiation is successful, the child is able to resolve its ambivalence by understanding itself as a self in relationship, by accepting both connection and separation. The sense of agency and an "internal continuity of being" can then develop fully; and these are "fundamental to an unproblematic sense of self, and provide the basis of both autonomy and spontaneity."[8] So it is through differentiation that the infant develops autonomy and agency.

Differentiation thus begins with the child's conceptualization of the mother as not-me and of the self as not-you. But this negative ele-

---

[8]Chodorow (1979a), p. 60.

ment is not enough to create a successful differentiation: "True differentiation, true separateness, cannot be simply a perception and experience of self-other, of presence-absence. It must involve two selves, two presences, two subjects. Recognizing the other as subject is possible only to the extent that one is not dominated by felt need and one's own exclusive subjectivity."[9] That is, differentiation is a product of the mother-infant relationship. It happens in relation to the mother and, moreover, to a mother who is her own subject, not, in spite of the phrase *object relations*, an object that exists only in the infant subject's perception. Nor can the infant be used by the caretaker as a symbolic object for working out her or his own unresolved problems. As Jeffrey Blustein argues, "The achievement of autonomy is a developmental process."[10] That is, the achievement of this full, complete agency can arise only through relationship with a caretaker, and specifically (in object relations parlance) a "good enough" caretaker who does not project her or his own experiences or feelings onto the infant and at the same time does not let the outside environment impinge on the infant indiscriminately. The development of an infant's autonomy and agency cannot occur without "empathic caretakers who understand and validate the infant's experience as that of a real self."[11] Agency can thus develop only through a relationship with a mother as subject. It is for this reason that Chodorow says, "*Differentiation is not distinctness and separateness, but a particular way of being connected to others.*"[12]

Yet differentiation is usually not completely successful for either gender: girls experience too little separation and an overly strong identification with the mother, and boys experience far too much separation in trying to distance themselves completely from the mother. One reason for this situation is linked to the issue of recognition. It is only through recognition that true separation, and hence full agency and autonomy, can be achieved; for the self depends on relationship, and relationship is impossible without recognition of the subjectivity

---

[9]Ibid., p. 58.

[10]Blustein (1982), p. 10. Of course, the originators of object relations theory—Klein, Mahler, Winnicott—did in fact choose the name *object relations* to refer to the notion that the mother *is* an object to the child. My point, however, is to highlight the faultiness of such a conception of the mother by the child, and to assert that autonomy requires individuals to transcend such a vision of the mother as object.

[11]Chodorow (1979a), p. 59.

[12]Ibid., p. 59. The need for the caretaker to be empathic might suggest that bringing men into the practice of child care is not itself sufficient. If men, because of their child-rearing experiences, have had to repress their capacity for empathy, then simply giving them the responsibility of child care will not likely be sufficient to draw it out again. Conversely, however, it could also be argued that participation in this responsibility will in fact require men to draw on their repressed capabilities.

of the other. This is where the masculine model displays serious shortcomings, and it is to this that one central cause of the gender bias of political theory can be traced; recognition of the mother would entail the boy's recognizing and accepting his own primary femininity. To forestall this, the boy resorts to the defensive reaction of assimilating difference to differentiation, taking difference—specifically masculinity as not-female—as ostensible validation of his separation. This, however, is an artificial solution with mixed results: it "involves an arbitrary boundary creation and an assertion of hyperseparateness to reinforce a lack of security in a person's sense of their self as a separate person."[13] It also leads to images of the mother as nonhuman, both powerful monster and helpless animal. This defensive conceptualization of the mother does not produce true relational autonomy, an understanding of the self that draws strength from connection and relationship, but rather creates reactive autonomy, a separateness and independence that is fragile and unstable, and entails great psychic and emotional cost. It produces a conception of agency that abstracts individual will, the ability to make choices and act on them, out of the context of the social relationships within which it develops and within which it is exercised.[14]

Freedom, Recognition, and Liberal Theory

In political theory these themes are displayed most obviously in Hegel's writings. Although Hegel is not a social contract philosopher, his theory is relevant to this discussion because his dualism of conflict and domination is in many ways the paradigm for western ontology.[15] His theory offers a particularly stark presentation of the problem of domination in recognition. In *The Phenomenology of Spirit*, particularly in the chapter titled "Self-Consciousness," Hegel argues that the self seeks affirmation by declaring a radical independence. In this, of course, it requires recognition by another being, and hence must have some sort of relationship with an other. Self-consciousness seeks to reconcile this contradiction by gaining recognition from an other without making a simultaneous recognition. Self-consciousness seeks to be perpetually the self, keeping the other perpetually the other. As Mitchell Aboulafia says: "If this subject were to speak it would declare: 'I am above the things of nature, for they have not the power to

---

[13]Ibid., p. 58.
[14]Bakan (1966); Chodorow (1974), pp. 55–56; Keller (1985), chaps. 5 and 6.
[15]See, for instance, Whitbeck (1984), p. 69.

resist me. I deny them any independent status; as a subject, a self, I am the only self-conscious, independent being.' "[16] Self-consciousness is prepared to die for this recognition. And even though it realizes that death would bring a dubious if not a Pyrrhic victory, this readiness, in Hegel's theory, is what creates masters. Those not so prepared become the slaves, the perpetual objects: "Locked into thinghood for not being prepared to die for an ideal [the slave] remains part of the merely natural world, and as a living 'thing' it is 'the dependent consciousness whose essential nature is simply to live or to be for another.' "[17]

This description presents an obvious parallel to the infant boy's development. In the effort to grow up and separate from the mother, the boy asserts a total independence, denying the subjectivity of the mother. Because of the difficulty of repressing his primary identification and excising the female, the boy finds that the need to deny the mother becomes intense, and the struggle for recognition becomes a life-and-death struggle for dominance. The mother obviously does not experience this intense need her son feels. In the first place, she is not emerging as a person. But moreover, girls, being tied to their mothers in acceptable and fundamental ways, do not need to separate from them by denying their existence, and so this need is not (usually) part of the mother's psyche or personality. Indeed, because the girl's identity is so closely entwined with the mother's existence, she cannot even fathom such a denial. Finally, such a struggle is antipathetic to the practice of mothering. As Whitbeck notes, "If a mother saw the emerging person who is her child in the way that Hegel describes, human beings would not exist."[18] As a result, not prepared to die for the ideal—one that is contrary to her very being in the first place—the mother (woman) becomes the slave. She is a thing, the perpetual object.

Because of her perspective—which values the concrete and real over the abstract and ideal, and which takes relationship as primary— the mother/woman does not readily perceive this as oppression: she cannot conceive of wishing to die for recognition, which seems to her an inherent contradiction. Her realism and her orientation toward relationship, however, ensure her "enslavement"—her objectification, dehumanization, oppression. She, like Hegel's slave, is doomed to

---

[16]Aboulafia (1984), p. 176. He also compares the male-female relationship to the master-slave relationship but focuses on relations between adult men and women. This is quite different from my analysis in which the relations between men and women are influenced by the relations between parents and children.

[17]Ibid., p. 177. See also Hegel, *The Phenomenology of Spirit*, p. 115.

[18]Whitbeck (1984), p. 69.

live for another. Yet the reason she does so is not the natural outcome of the dialectic but the result of masculine perspectives and action. Because of the male's intense need for unidirectional recognition, he creates institutions that solidify woman's role as other. And because of the female's assumption that there will be mutuality in recognition and trust, she has no reason to reject such institutions, for their oppressiveness is not immediately apparent to her.

This one-sided recognition is far from being the full recognition required by trust, mutuality, and reciprocity, or indeed by agency and autonomy. "Mutual recognition entails a basic respect for the other, which is impossible in a master-slave, independence-dependence, relationship."[19] Rather, there are relationships of domination. But these "fail to promote mutual recognition because they prevent individuals from seeing others as anything but totally other; and they accomplish this false othering by promoting differences meant to keep individuals on one level of a hierarchy from being able to recognize individuals on different levels."[20]

While this part of the master-slave dialectic is most reflective of the son's emerging struggle against the mother, Hegel's account of the struggle does not end here. The struggle moves on to the slave's transcendence of his[21] dependence on the master and to his achievement of an independent self-consciousness. The master, as a recognized being, merely consumes the fruits of the slave's labor, who produces solely for the master. But this situation provides the slave with the potential for a kind of recognition not available to the master. That is, because the slave works on objects in the world, he gains an affirmation of his own existence. "Through work . . . the bondsman becomes conscious of what he truly is. . . . Consciousness, *qua* worker, comes to see in the independent being (of the object) its *own* independence."[22] This recognition which is achieved through objectification provides the slave with the ability to emerge, to achieve a superior position over the master, to become more human. Once the slave has achieved this position, he will no longer tolerate his status as slave; and this will transform the struggle itself into new modes of interaction.

[19]Aboulafia (1984), p. 178.
[20]Ibid., pp. 182–83.
[21]I return to the use of *he* because this is Hegel's usage, and because I believe that the very structure of the master-slave dialectic, the structuring of human relations in oppositional ways, is itself androcentric. I should also note that I realize that the Hegelian dimensions of the present work are sorely underexplored, but because of the enormity of that task it must be reserved for future work. Balbus (1982) and I undertake very different projects, but his *Marxism and Domination* provides one neo-Hegelian reading of object relations theory that the reader might find helpful.
[22]Hegel, *Phenomenology*, p. 118.

In mother-only child rearing, however, the mother does not come to this realization; or at least, perhaps, she has not been able to until recently. That is, although this part of the dialectic would not seem directly applicable to the mother-son relationship as I have described it, it does point out the Hegelian origins of standpoint epistemology as well as the usefulness of gender psychology in developing a feminist standpoint. Hartsock's version of the feminist standpoint in particular bases itself on the material activity of women: women's labor on objects in the world in the process of creating use values provides the grounds for a feminist consciousness in which women recognize their own subjectivity. On this reading, and from the perspective of my focus here, women's recognition of the quality of labor involved in raising children might enable mothers to achieve their own self-consciousness.

The feminist standpoint goes beyond Hegel's dialectic in important ways, however. In the first place, this parallel cannot be carried to the conclusion that the mother achieves a superior or more human position than the son, for it would be part of the mothering relationship to use this self-consciousness to help the son, as well as the daughter, become more human. Second, the feminist standpoint allows women to achieve a *collective* self-consciousness, to develop relations with other women, and to overcome the institutionalized bondage of privatization.[23] Hegel, by contrast, does not truly provide for relations among (former) slaves.

Hegel does discuss a new concept of human relationships, however. By the end of the *Phenomenology*, he argues for a conception of reciprocity or unity that forms the basis for the truest and highest self-consciousness. As Isaac Balbus notes, for Hegel, "labor is only one mode of the struggle for recognition; it by no means exhausts the forms through which human beings strive to achieve integration with nature and among themselves." Objectification gives way to a "higher form of recognition that entails a purer or more perfect unification between humans and the world in which they live."[24] By the eventual assimilation of the master-slave relationship into *Geist*, human relationships of the highest form can be achieved. Indeed, on Balbus's reading, Hegel goes beyond the standpoint because he goes beyond objectifying material labor to a universal telos.

But Hegel's concept of human relations is qualitatively different,

---

[23]This point echoes Marx's criticism of Hegel that the concept of self-consciousness did not allow for relations among slaves. But see Balbus (1982), esp. chap. 8, for an argument that Hegel in fact had a more complete and human picture of human relations than did Marx.

[24]Balbus (1982), p. 13.

and perhaps even less human, than the feminist standpoint conception, because Hegel seeks to achieve specifically *self*-consciousness, and this raises questions about the possibility of individual self-consciousnesses forming real relations of mutuality. Furthermore, the feminist standpoint is not limited to objectification. One aspect of women's material experience is that in their labor women must work "with" nature rather than against it, for instance in childbirth and nursing. In this light nature is not "devoid of any subjectivity,"[25] but rather its subjectivity is recognized. On this reading, the feminist standpoint could take us further toward liberation and recognition than mere objectifying labor.

So the feminist standpoint both can and cannot be interpreted as one stage in the Hegelian struggle for recognition. Hegel's transformation of human relations has a different genesis and foundation. Nevertheless, a reading of Hegel from the perspective of the feminist standpoint argument[26] can yield a more complete picture of the relationship between master and slave (or men and women). That is, one could argue that the standpoint achieved through material labor ultimately enables the slave to see that it is the struggle for dominance itself, and not just his or her role within it, that creates the inability to achieve true self-consciousness. The slave would be permitted to see that although relationship with the master per se must end, relationship with the *person* in the master's role must continue on a new basis of equality. Equality, on this reading, would provide the only potential for reciprocal and noninstrumental recognition.

In the same vein, a feminist standpoint creates the potential for men and women to achieve fully human relationships of reciprocity and mutuality. In the context of my discussion of the mother-son relationship, it would enable the mother to appreciate fully the quality and significance of her activity, and it would enable the son to recognize the mother as her own subject. It would thus allow parents and children of both sexes to achieve unity and mutuality of recognition. This is not achievable through a nonfeminist understanding of Hegel, for he rejected the parent-child relationship as the model for human relationships of recognition and instead chose the brother-sister relationship. It would take us too far afield to pursue this matter, but his choice of the brother-sister relationship (rather than sister-sister, for instance), his account of that relationship, and his rejection of the

---

[25]Ibid., p. 279.
[26]I say this rather than a Hegelian reading of the feminist standpoint because the latter is much more problematic, owing in part to Hegel's sexism. Both projects should be carried out but must be reserved for future work, as they would be far too involved to undertake here.

parent-child (that is, mother-child) relationship, rather than recasting that relationship in terms of mutuality, further suggest the sexist limitations of Hegel's argument.[27]

These thoughts have taken us away from my main line of argument, but they help provide a deeper understanding of the theoretical possibilities of gender psychology. The discussion of Hegel has made it possible to examine the issue of recognition in a deeper way than liberal theory would at first glance suggest. But in reality, while less obvious and direct, these themes, and the desire for dominance and nonreciprocal recognition, have evident parallels in liberal theories, and particularly in theories of obligation. They are represented more subtly; but now that they have been identified and defined, their place in liberal theory will be easier to see.

To begin with, agency is one of the most central concepts of individualism and consent theory; the individual has the capacity to make choices and thus can assume obligations. Moreover, this capacity also carries a moral imperative that obligations can be assumed *only* through the exercise of this agency. Agency is the hallmark of independence, autonomy, and adulthood. To be able to make one's own decisions indicates an end to dependence on the will and abilities of another; hence, agency is what justifes the rejection of divine right and the adoption of the social contract. This is a vital historical move. But because it is a reactive rather than relational autonomy that this agency embodies, it is also what justifies—indeed, creates and perpetuates—the radical and abstract individualism of liberal democratic theory, the market model of society, substantive theories that require the dehumanization, oppression, and nonrecognition of women, a theory that obligation can exist only by virtue of voluntary assumption.

That is the primary significance of gender psychology as far as political theory is concerned. The boy—because he must become masculine in a world where mother-only child rearing ensures that he is psychically female, where gender is an exclusionary category, and where the female is devalued while the male is elevated—cannot afford to grant recognition to the mother, and hence to all women and indeed to all "others." This inability to grant such recognition is the vital seed from which the self-other dichotomy grows, as well as all other dualisms which are variations on that theme: subject-object, mind-body, public-private, fact-value, exchange-use. Not coincidentally, these dualisms involve identification of men with the first member of each pair—the public world of fact, the subject, and the ego—

---

[27]Hegel, *Phenomenology*, esp. pp. 274–78.

and women with the second—nature, the id, privatized objects—thus taking as a primary value the denial of women's subjectivity and personhood. But as a way to secure independence, autonomy, and selfhood, this strategy is hopelessly self-contradictory. The need to dominate "arises not so much out of empowerment as out of anxiety about impotence."[28]

Numerous feminist theorists have identified this dualism as a central element of liberal theory and as a key to liberalism's difficulties.[29] The need to deny recognition is what gives rise to the need for artificial constructions that present such inaccurate and skewed visions of "man," "nature," and social relations, and for theories that insist on the individual's complete control over "his" connections to the political community. Hartsock's description of the market model of society and masculinist conceptions of power are a particularly important case in point. In her theory masculinist ontology gives rise to a market model of community that is, like the boy's reactive autonomy, "fragile and arbitrary, structured fundamentally by competition and domination."[30] The notions that the individual is fundamentally isolated from all others and that contact must thus be based at least initially on opposing interests and established through formal agreements and contracts are part of the problem of recognition, or the failure thereof. Just as the boy's severed relation with the mother will ensure the repression of femaleness and relationship because they are confusing and threatening to the masculine psyche, so will relationship based on competition rather than cooperation ensure that "the very *social* character of activity can appear as something alien and puzzling."[31] In such a situation it is certain that relationships of domination will become apparent; that is, it is certain that "exchange" is a power relationship rather than one of association, reciprocity, or mutuality.

Recognition will be sought through this form of interaction, but only the unidirectional recognition that Hegel outlined: to be acknowledged not as equal but as superior and privileged. Thus men compete in the market to establish their preeminence by establishing the preeminence of their interests over others', by accruing wealth and property. The "fetishism of commodities" that this ethic makes apparent means that things, not people, become the objects of pri-

---

[28]Keller (1984), p. 124.

[29]Indeed, this is such a basic building block of most feminist theory that it may not need citation; but in addition to the theorists discussed in the previous chapter, see Eisenstein (1981), Elshtain (1981), Okin (1979), Pateman (1988), Sargent (1981).

[30]Hartsock (1984), p. 38.

[31]Ibid., p. 45.

mary attachment and mediate human thought and activity. In this world, "attainment of complex and deep-going series of relations with others is indeed difficult."[32] The extent to which men enter into contracts that promote the interests of another is determined by the good to themselves. As Mancur Olson argues, the only reason man gives up anything is to gain more for himself; the only reason man participates in a group action is to benefit his individual life by a manifold factor over and above his contribution to the group.[33]

This one-sided individualistic concern with one's interests as an extension of the self, the identification (or sublimation) of interests with passions,[34] the focus on desired objects and the self-absorption apparent in market man's striving to fulfill his interests echo the preoedipal concern with objects, the self, and escape from the body/mother. The liberal market, in providing a means of expression for the repressed passions of infancy, contributes to this concept of interests as misogynist, as expressive of the desire to dominate women. That does not mean other desires are not expressed in the concept of interests, of course; but it is in this particular aspect that the problem of recognition lies. For in the market model that Hartsock and Macpherson analyze, the relevant point is not just that individuals are atomistic, nor is it just that atomism creates duality. What makes individuals atomistic is the fear of and refusal to recognize the subjectivity of others because to so recognize would be to lose the self; that is, to give in to others without the struggle of competition is to relinquish one's interests and hence to lose one's self. But this in reality only perverts the self and makes genuine individuality, agency, and autonomy unattainable, for without mutuality in recognition, domination persists and relationship fails.

Obligation and Recognition

The implications for political obligation are powerful and manifold. On the most obvious level, the institutionalization of unidirectional recognition and sexual inequality ensures an absence of genuine choice for women, a condition often decried by liberal theorists as coercive when applied to the male citizenry. In the theories and practices of the seventeenth and eighteenth centuries, women were denied the means of consenting, such as the vote and other forms of political expression, but political obligations of obedience to law ex-

[32]Ibid., p. 103, pp. 101–4.
[33]Olson (1971).
[34]Hirschman (1977).

tended to them equally as to men. And even with the granting of women's suffrage, the pervasiveness of sexual inequality in laws and opportunities to this day, it can easily be argued, seriously undermines women's ability to consent and participate fully in the public realm.

The question of unequal starting points or de facto inequality raises a serious problem for consent theory. As Rousseau argued, the liberal contract, rather than securing freedom, presents in institutionalized form the same relations of dominance and servitude found in the state of nature.[35] Whereas liberal consent theory works from stated premises of formal equality, gross substantive inequality ensures political inequality not only in political voice in determining the laws but also in the ways the laws apply to people: the laws apply unequally to those who are unequal. But because equality is defined in the liberal democratic contract solely in formal terms, this deeper inequality can never be redressed; and so the inequality becomes not merely de facto or contingent but structural. The prior political group in power has already been able to structure social institutions, as well as conceptual definitions, to benefit itself, and it will always be ahead as long as freedom, equality, and obligation are defined abstractly and negatively because such conceptions leave it to the worse-off individual to pull herself up by her own bootstraps.

In contemporary theory, often working off the principles of the early social contract theorists, the problem persists, though in perhaps subtler ways. Joseph Tussman's characterization of the non–fully participating citizens of both sexes (the modern counterpart to Locke's "tacit consenters") as "political child-brides" supports the notion that women are considered by modern theorists to be incapable of true participation in the social contract, and that such inability is nothing to be alarmed about.[36] The point is not just that Tussman chose such an image (and hence was contingently sexist), but that such an image *made sense* and was acceptable to theorists in a way that, say, a racist image would not (consider the difference in our reading of his theory if Tussman had chosen an equally offensive racist image such as "Uncle Tom"). While racism is just as pernicious as sexism, I am suggesting among other things that the reluctance to see sexism in such terms reveals the "deep structure" of masculinity, to invoke Di Stefano once again, that pervades obligation theory.[37]

The notion that inequality and dominance serve as a basis for obligation suggests important things about its theoretical, ontological,

---

[35]See Rousseau, *The Origin of Inequality*, in Cole, esp. p. 89.
[36]Tussman (1960).
[37]Di Stefano (1983), p. 634.

and even epistemological grounding and characterization. If the conception of freedom central to consent theory, namely negative liberty, is premised on the struggle for recognition, and particularly on the ability to be recognized without reciprocation, and if nonrecognition is, as it is for the oedipal boy and Hegel's master, a form of power and violence, then freedom too must be at least in part an expression of that same power and violence. Other concepts based on the premises of that freedom will then likewise express power and violence.

Thus, equality, in referring to abstract opportunity and rights, sets the stage for competition and dominance. Opportunity is equal until someone wins the contest, and even then only for those who start off equal in the relevant respects. The idea of rights embodies the concept of claims against others, again suggesting competition; and a right further provides a boundary line between various individuals' needs, desires, and wants and hence serves to divide individuals. The concept of equal rights says we must respect one another not because we are connected but because of rights which highlight the lines of demarcation between us. The old adage that your right to swing your fist ends where my nose begins is illuminating as much for its articulation of separate and discrete individual spheres of action as it is for its image of violence; that is, the potential for violence lies at the precise point where discrete individuals have contact. Freedom, defined negatively, is to a certain degree zero sum: my greater freedom by definition consists in the existence of fewer laws, lower taxes, and so on, but this will yield unfreedom for those who are not as well off, who depend on redistribution of income and state regulation of potentially exploitive relationships, such as between a capitalist and a child laborer. So freedom becomes a competitive relationship among beings, some of whom seek to win out over others, establishing their freedom at the expense of others'.

Obligation as self-assumed is a particularly significant product of this conception of freedom, because far more than equality, justice, or rights, obligation centrally involves connection, relationship, and bondedness. The absolute natural freedom of the state of nature outlined by the social contract theorists entails a total absence of restraint: people must fight against the restraints imposed by competing and alienated others. The absolute freedom of the state of nature—particularly in Hobbes and Rousseau, and to a less obvious degree in Locke—is marked by a mean existence and lack of control; fear of ceasing to exist, fear of losing one's possessions, hostility, and suspicion are dominant characteristics. The state of nature, like the boy's relationship with his mother, is a kind of prison, for within it man cannot realize himself, he cannot create and control. He is constantly reminded of his fleshliness and mortality. "Natural man"[38] seeks to escape this chaotic prison by turning to the social contract, thereby trading absolute freedom, which produces absolute terror, for effective freedom, or the freedom to act effectively, with the assurance that one's actions will produce the desired results. Civil society exists to protect possessions and property. By having control over his possessions, the individual has control over his identity; for Locke in particular, for example, who you are is determined largely by what you have.

But civil society also exists to ensure that the individual can act rationally. Rules and laws provide predictability; they provide assurance that the individual can act with certainty and hence control "himself." By protecting property and preserving (or making possible) rationality, the social contract not only preserves the citizen from nature but also assists in the individual's preservation of autonomy, defined reactively as self-control and self-mastery. And this reactive autonomy is intrinsically tied up with the notion that obligations are always and only created by voluntary actions. The conception of people as absolutely separate, which the boy develops both from his perception of difference from his mother and from his exaggeration of that difference to bolster his differentiation from her, results in a structure in which those separate individuals can resolve conflicts only at discrete and controlled points of contact. From this perspective, obligation necessarily exists only by an act of free will: if I am free above all else, I can be bound—that is, I can have connections and relationships—only by an act of my own free agency.

The concept of obligation as self-assumed depends on a conception of people as inherently separate and fragmented, and this resonates strongly with the conception the boy develops as a result of mother-only child rearing. The significant aspect of self-assumed obligation is that one has complete control over one's bonds or connections to others because one creates those bonds. Creation is a form of power in the sense of control and mastery. The act of consent preserves my right to autonomy as self-determination. It thus asserts my separateness and self-control even as I give up some of that control by creating an obligation. By establishing bonds through an act of free will, I maintain control over myself, self-determination, and freedom.

Indeed, obligation within the social contract can be seen as a rela-

---

[38]In this section I again use masculine terminology to indicate not males per se as much as a masculinized conception of the individual. Again, although consent theorists may assert that this model applies to women, and their exclusion is merely contingent, my point is that "the individual" is specifically masculine, and women are structurally excluded from the world of politics constructed by these theories.

tionship of exchange. Citizens exchange or trade absolute freedom for security according to Hobbes, for effective and economic freedom according to Locke, and for the moral freedom of self-mastery according to Rousseau. Man gives up some liberty to the government and agrees to obey it, and in return he receives the goods of a "well-ordered society," to borrow from Rawls.

But within this exchange relationship also lies a relationship of power and domination. One potentially puts oneself in another's power when one places oneself under an obligation by giving up part of one's freedom—one's essence—for something else. In a relationship of obligation, the obliged person must recognize the obliger in performing the obligation, while the obliger need only accept whatever deed is performed in fulfillment and need not recognize the actor. The dangers inherent in this kind of relationship—in this formalized connection—are what require the centrality of voluntarism as the legitimator of such a relationship. If obligation is viewed as a power relationship, then being placed in such a relationship without active control over one's placement would seem to make such a relationship doubly coercive. Voluntarism would seem to save the individual from nonreciprocated recognition—from connection itself—by giving the individual the power of control over that relationship. Furthermore, since it is an exchange relationship, each self recognizes the other only to the extent that he chooses, that is, to the extent that it is in his interest. Ostensibly this would seem to pose another solution to the "master's dilemma," for both parties, through the expression of their interests, control the degree and form of recognition of the other.

Yet the apparent reciprocity of this exchange is belied by the strict adherence to consent and voluntarism in the face of the fact that such consent is nonexistent for all but a select few. In social contract theories political obligation is not in fact self-assumed in the full sense by very many people, as critics since Hume have pointed out. Yet those who have not consented are nonetheless considered obligated to obey the law and government. It is rather widely accepted among modern theorists of obligation—even those who put forth variations on the consent theme—that the conditions for true consent are often absent from political society; that a large number of people are not given the opportunity to consent, or else "consent" by performing acts about which they have little choice; that even acts of dissent are interpreted as acts of consent; that unfair bargaining positions belie the freedom implicit in free choice. These "tacit consenters"—usually, as in Locke's theory, the nonlanded workers, the poor, not to mention white women and men and women of color—are subject to the political decisions of the "express consenters," the landed and wealthy white men who have historically been the voters and holders of political office. The class of masters is thus recognized in every sense—political, social, economic—while the slaves are not only denied their political voice but are told that their enforced silence constitutes voluntary expression, and they are obligated thereby.

The Feminist Standpoint and Feminist Obligation

On the most obvious level, the definition of obligation as determined exclusively and unavoidably by consent conveniently denies the fact that women have historically been, and indeed in many ways still are, obligated to the state without consent. In this denial, however, lies a more significant factor, which is that women are and have historically been bound to an entire series of other obligations—child care most obviously—to which consent is not only unavailable but of questionable relevance. And it is in these obligations that we may find the beginnings of a feminist theory of obligation.

I earlier suggested a hypothetical case in which a woman is raped and becomes pregnant to highlight how women's lives challenge the clear standard of consent in determining obligation. But less extreme examples provide similar challenges. Consider, for example, a married woman who conscientiously practices birth control but becomes pregnant anyway, and fears that having an abortion will drive her husband not only to beat her but perhaps even to abandon her and their three existing children. Are not her choices sufficiently unfairly limited to problematize any notion of obligation to care for this child within the standards of consent theory? Or even consider a couple who decide to have a child. Suppose the child is born with a severe mental or physical disability that will require full-time care well into adulthood. Do people "consent" to all contingencies when they decide to have a child? Indeed, most couples who decide to have a child often do not really know what they are consenting to.[39] Do women, and in more recent years men, who become the caretakers of such children really consent to such situations, or do they recognize obligations of care that are not explicitly chosen? These examples may appear to lie on a continuum of sorts—most people would probably concede that rape is by definition nonconsensual, while there would be substantial disagreement about whether a couple's ignorance of the risks in childbearing excuses them from consent—but each of

[39]The idea for these alternatives was originally suggested to me by Christine Di Stefano.

these cases problematizes a liberal individualist notion of choice and consent.

And the fact that it *is* largely women who are subject to the obligations of care is significant to the claim that women's options are generally restricted in comparison to men's. Not only have men historically escaped responsibility for the actual raising of children, but socially tolerated (if not officially condoned) practices of paternal abandonment and spouse abuse locate such practices within a sexually oppressive context. Yet we cannot say that women have been enslaved against their will. Throughout history, women have participated to some extent voluntarily in many of the practices and activities socially required of them. Does love, for instance, negate the absence of choice and free will in any of these examples? Does it justify the fact that women's participation in such sexually oppressive practices perpetuates their own political and social powerlessness? Do these factors negate the obligatory force of care? From gender psychology I derived the notion that women's moral reasoning begins from premises of connection, responsibility, and response. In terms of a feminist standpoint approach, we can take these values as important premises for a feminist conception of obligation. This conception is very different from that of consent theory; for if relationship is the overriding feature of women's lives, as these theories suggest, if it is the core of their being, the source of their vision, then connection is given and obligation is a presumption of fact.

This is particularly evident in Gilligan's analysis of the Heinz dilemma. Amy assumes an obligation to do *something* for Heinz's wife. The question for her is which action will be the most responsible, which action will best respond to the needs of everyone in the story. The girls in Johnstone's porcupine dilemma do not entertain the notion that the porcupine can be forced out of the burrow; they assume that a relationship exists and try to find a solution that literally leaves nobody out in the cold. Women contemplating abortions in Gilligan's study speak in terms not of freedom or rights but of responsibility and care. Obligation is assumed—to the father, one's family, the potential child whether or not the pregnancy was intended, and finally oneself—and the dilemma becomes how to reconcile the conflicting obligations stemming from this complex web of relationships.

In these examples, women's conceptualization of the substantive principle operates from their ontological framework, the givenness of connection and responsibility, just as obligation determined solely by consent derives from a masculinist ontology of individualism. The ontological perspective of enmeshment in a web of relationships leads to the moral conclusion that freedom, while central to the concept of a person, is not the only or even the primary value. Indeed, it also suggests a different definition of freedom from that found in liberal obligation theory. A prior and perhaps more central concept would be obligation itself; and the examples I have given suggest that obligation, from a feminist standpoint, needs to be considered from a perspective that takes obligation as given.

Such a perspective requires a different conceptual and epistemological framework for understanding obligation and not just another definition within the existing framework. This understanding can be achieved only by developing a different approach to the question, and indeed perhaps different questions altogether. In consent theory, working from an assumption of separateness and freedom theorists seek to understand how isolated individuals can develop and sustain connections and still be separate, how they can engage in relationships and still remain free. Thus, the central approach involves asking how obligations arise, how they come into being. But if obligation is given, then it does not really make sense to ask how it can arise; from a feminist standpoint, obligation is the standard against which other things, such as the freedom to act as one wishes, are measured. Beginning with the self as separate, the rights model seeks to find areas and modes of connection that are safe, that can provide for needs without risking the loss of self. The responsibility model, beginning with connection, tries to determine how to provide space for the self without violating the moral imperative of care. This perspective would indicate that although freedom is certainly achievable in the context of human relationships, it must be achieved; it is not a given. Freedom is an entity that must be created, as an individual carves out space for herself. And since freedom is created by a stepping away from or out of obligations, freedom must also be justified. Relations cannot be severed by a "mere" desire or act of will. There must be, in a sense, "good reasons" for the desire *not* to fulfill obligations.

This does not mean such justification is not possible or even likely for a wide variety of cases. In a century that has seen Stalin, Hitler, and Jim Jones, the concept of a given obligation may make some uneasy about the "totalitarian menace." A second source of unease comes specifically from women's experience: nonconsensual obligations have been imposed on women all their lives. Isn't it time the yoke was shaken off? Why fall back into the mire of *Kinder, Kuche, und Kirche*? Should not women be able to choose their obligations, just as men have?

I certainly share these concerns. But at the same time, these objections miss the significance of the reformulation I am suggesting and the depth of the reorientation it requires. The purpose of a feminist theory of obligation is not to bind us more tightly to the state or to relations but to enable us to see the reality that women's lives reveal: that men and women alike are often in fact nonconsensually bound more tightly than our public discourse admits. The ideology of consent allows us to believe that all obligations are created. We can thus deny the obligatory force of any relations that we do not create or do not wish to maintain. This "we," however, is largely masculine, for this belief exists, operates, and flourishes in a public realm separate from the private. In the private realm, by contrast, obligations are often not consensual at all for those who occupy it, that is, women. This creates a dichotomy; but more than that, it creates a dichotomy that is doubly oppressive for women, particularly in the modern era. The modern world ostensibly rejects the notion of natural inferiority. It ostensibly grants women equal rights, such as the vote, and takes the provision of these rights as evidence of equality. Women, it is claimed, can now choose all of their obligations, just as men do. Therefore, it is concluded with Hobbesian logic, women must in fact have chosen the situation they are now in. If they are in the private realm still, if they are responsible for child care, it is because they have chosen these roles.

Yet the reality is that such choice is systematically denied. The denial of political rights is often a de facto phenomenon, ignorance of which is made possible by the continued political ghettoization of women.[40] And the continued assertion that women do in fact have equal rights in the face of the fact that these rights cannot be realized begs, rather than answers, the question of obligation. Rather than trying to create a situation in which women meet the criteria for obligation defined by consent, what theorists need to do is redefine obligation to articulate and accommodate women's experience as well as men's.

In using gender psychology to articulate differences between men's and women's experience, however, and in arguing for the basing of political theory on concrete experience, I do not wish simply (or simplistically) to model obligation on women's experience, or on child care in particular; nor am I arguing that political theory should model political obligations on the relationship between mother and child. Rather, the point is that women's experience, which is systematically eliminated from public ideologies such as political theory, can tell us important things about *human* life. Consent theory tells only part of the story of human experience; it presents, therefore, a biased and

[40]Nelson's (1984) work on the feminization of poverty is one of the more powerful illustrations of this ghettoization.

distorted picture of obligation. The answer is not to reject this part and adopt another (feminist) part but rather to fit together the various pieces: gender, class, race, history, geography, age, and so forth. And in order to do that, we have to be able to adopt a different framework. We cannot merely add on women's experience to the dominant discourse because the two operate from different starting points and within different frameworks.

This is why grafting the feminine model onto the masculine distorts the feminine. The reverse strategy, grafting the masculine onto the feminine, may distort the masculine as well; but because of the dominance of the masculine model, because of the deep entrenchment of rights and consent in our consciousness, ideologies, and institutions, this is much less likely, and is even, perhaps, a necessary methodological stage. Much as an unbalanced scale dips out of alignment in the opposite direction when an equal weight is placed on the lighter side, feminism may appear to overemphasize the advantages of the care model in the attempt to achieve equality. As Hartsock says about the "bodily aspect" of the sexual division of labor, we may need to "grasp it overfirmly in an effort to keep it from evaporating altogether."[41] Yet considering my analysis in the context of patriarchy reveals how very carefully that equal weight is being placed on the scales by feminist theorists, precisely because of their sensitivity to the problems of hegemony. Because of this self-conscious, self-critical approach to theorizing, a feminist theoretical perspective is likely to afford a clearer vantage point from which the two models can be mixed together, if perhaps not in unbiased fashion, at least in a less biased one.

As standpoint epistemologists argue, a feminist standpoint can provide a perspective on social relations that is more "real" than the dominant ideology. Oppression does not provide the oppressed with pure objectivity by any means. But in oppression there lies the potential to see more objectively, as Harding puts it, to come closer to the truth by being able to see more sides of the question, and hence to get beyond the causes of oppression. As Joan Ringelheim's work on the women of the Holocaust suggests, the experience of oppression can produce, in dialectical fashion, what one might call growth in both our relations with others and our understanding of ourselves. Part of my own previous argument has been that powerlessness and oppression have contributed to the development and articulation of the voice of care. Yet Ringelheim also points out that few people, herself included, would argue that oppression is desirable or good. I agree,

[41]Hartsock (1984), p. 233.

and would further argue that it would be incorrect to presuppose from these arguments that oppression is inevitable or necessary to human development. Rather, given that oppression does exist, it may tell us something about human capacities that we are able to learn and derive good things from oppressive experiences and conditions. It is not oppression per se that produces the good but human responses to it. We cannot say that these responses, and the valuable things humans have extracted from oppression, could not have been learned from other, nonoppressive experiences.[42]

Thus the purpose of reorienting our inquiry to the consideration of obligation as given is not merely to redefine it but to articulate a different perspective from which to view social and political relations. A difference in perspective changes the terms of the discourse. The questions we ask ourselves and others shift into another framework altogether. The problem of women's obligation exists within the context of social institutions and thought that creates two different sets of values for men and women: men are naturally free, women are naturally obligated. Within this context, of course, feminists do not wish to maintain the givenness of obligation for women, for that would perpetuate their inferiority. The context needs to be changed. But it is not merely the case that feminists want men to be nonconsensually obligated as well, for that *would* give way to totalitarianism if it occurred within the current ideological and epistemological context (and if such a situation developed from the current state of affairs, it would be run by men; it would not be a "feminist" totalitarianism).

Rather, the point is to call attention to the fact that men already *are* nonconsensually obligated in many ways, but that our public "male-stream" ideology refuses to recognize this fact. Again, some would say that men themselves refuse to accept this fact, as opposed to blaming it on a generalized ideology; and one could cite the incidence of paternal abandonment and failure to pay child support to defend such a claim. But that would be a gross overgeneralization. I believe it is much more accurate to argue that our public ideology of consensual obligation creates a framework that men find easier to adopt and use. It is also more desirable to men than to women owing to circumstances they have not entirely chosen or consented to, given the gender differences in self-other orientation I outlined previously. So although it is true that individual men make the decision to abandon their families or refuse to pay child support, it is the context within which that decision is not only made but socially and politically upheld and approved that is of greater significance; for it is this context

---

[42]Ringelheim (1985).

that must be changed if gender equality is to be achieved. Without a change in the context, individual change is possible but perpetually crippled.

In denying men's nonconsensual obligations—or even the nonconsensual dimensions of their supposedly voluntary obligations—such a context obliterates the hope of a human theory of obligation that recognizes choice and givenness. Simultaneously, women should and do have the capacity to create many of their obligations but are often effectively denied the opportunity to do so. This denial similarly obliterates the hope of a human theory of obligation. We need to get beyond the current framework of the dominant discourse in order to begin to make sense of the claim that obligations should be considered as given. Within the existing framework such a construction not only does not make sense but is indeed nightmarish.

This different conceptualization of obligation can be achieved only if we ask different questions. Rather than asking, How does an obligation arise? a feminist concept of obligation might need to ask, Is there a legitimate justification for not fulfilling this obligation? In the rights conception, the assumption of freedom demands an explanation of any curtailment of that freedom such as obligations impose. In the care conception, such a demand does not make sense because it violates the imperative of responsibility; the assumption of obligation demands an explanation for nonfulfillment. This different orientation requires inquiry into the contextual conditions surrounding an obligation and an obligated person so we might understand the content of an obligation as well as possible justifications for not fulfilling it. Such an inquiry would articulate not a justification for restraint of action but the conflicting pressures that lead to a particular action as the fulfillment of an obligation or that provide a possible reason for not fulfilling it. This approach can in many ways be seen as interested more in what particular obligations consist of rather than in how they came to be. It also requires an entirely different approach to theory in redefining what the goals of a theory should be, how a theorist should attempt to reach those goals, and what the criteria are for judging success in reaching those goals. The issues of structural sexism indicate that a fundamental rethinking of obligation is in order. A feminist conception of obligation thus entails not just a new definition or formulation but an entire reorientation of what is meant by a theory of obligation.

The foregoing analysis reveals liberal obligation theory to contain many elements that link it epistemologically and structurally to a masculinist conception and representation of the world. I have attempted to show that the problem of political obligation really constitutes a set of problems that result from gender bias. This bias exists not only in the values that theories of political obligation endorse and promote but also in the frameworks within which the theories are created. I have argued that the tension between individualism and community found in original social contract theory and its modern revisions originates in part in an ontology and an epistemology that reflect specifically masculinist concerns and perspectives. The analysis reveals that women's exclusion from the public realm of politics, and indeed from political theory in general, is not just the historical, temporal, and contingent result of gender-biased views of individual theorists. It is not merely the case that women were absentmindedly forgotten, that theorists simply did not think of them when picturing the public. It is not merely the case that theorists failed to carry through to its logical end the Enlightenment attack on the historical legacy of patriarchy, that they simply did not see far enough. It is not merely the case that theorists were confused by an ideology of nature that seemed to support but actually contradicted the principles of freedom they sought to expound. It is not merely the case that certain theorists were overtly sexist and sought actively to disempower women for their own personal reasons. All of these things are true, but they do not go far enough to give an adequate account of the treatment, ignorance, and exclusion of women from political theory. They take for granted and fail to question the very genesis of the key concepts employed by this genre of theory. The ways in which consent, freedom, choice, individual, society, authority, and obligation are defined, applied, and utilized in liberal obligation theory are themselves important loci of the structural and epistemological gender bias of liberal political theory. This exclusion extends well beyond either the choices or limitations of any individual theorist to the epistemological structure within which these theories of obligation, and their construction of the political, were created and are maintained.

The negative dimension of feminist theorizing utilized in the present chapter—critique, analysis, deconstruction—is thus exceedingly powerful in unmasking the gendered dimensions of constructs and concepts that have long been accepted as completely devoid of gender content. Feminist methods can thus help political theory understand itself more profoundly and can help theorists conduct the theoretical enterprise in a more self-conscious and self-critical, and hence intellectually responsible and productive, manner. It contributes to the development of theories that are more consistent with the principles (we think) we wish to espouse, and in particular for modern theory, which takes democratic ends and means as constitutive underpinnings of almost all of its conceptual and intellectual categories, it can create theories and epistemological frameworks that are more egalitarian, inclusive, democratic.

This leads to the constructive side of feminist theory. A feminist epistemology is vital not only to the feminist analysis of dominant "malestream" theories but to the creation of feminist alternatives as well. I have argued that a feminist standpoint suggests that obligation should be considered the starting point for understanding political institutions and social relations. The analysis so far indicates that a feminist theory of obligation will require some thoroughgoing recon- ceptualizations of the standard categories of analysis. It suggests that feminist theory must engage in the articulation of a new epistemology and ideological framework, that it will not succeed as long as it con- tinues to operate solely within the dominant discourse. In order to develop feminist understandings of substantive political concepts such as justice, freedom, and obligation, theorists must redesign the existing framework itself.

In particular, I have suggested that a feminist theory of obligation would have to begin by considering obligation as a given. But in or- der to make sense of this idea, we must understand it from the per- spective of feminist standpoints. It will not make sense to consider this theoretical construction from the standpoint of existing ideology any more than it is possible to understand women's experience fully from the dominant masculinist perspective. The problem of cross- translation means that we must engage in a certain degree of philo- sophical schizophrenia, moving back and forth between two ostensi- bly opposed worlds. I have shown here, however, that, although they are very different—and even fundamentally so—in fact they are not opposed; each model has something to offer a human theory of obligation which incorporates the values of connection and separa- tion, which enables us to theorize self-in-relationship to the level of political community.

This enterprise has its dangers. At the very least, the problem of cross-translation can create difficulties in communicating the depth of the reorientation that feminist theory requires. This in turn can result in the continued marginalization of feminist theory because of its sup- posed incomprehensibility in terms of the dominant discourse. The foregoing analysis, however, by making clear the character of this dif- ficulty, can help tackle the problem of how to approach and develop feminist theories of concepts such as obligation. It points the way to the articulation of this alternative epistemological framework through the existing one. It thus does more than straddle these two worlds of political theory and feminist theory; it begins the process of bringing them together.

Yet the problem of cross-translation once again invokes postmodern challenges, which threaten to undermine from the start the fundamental project of positive feminist theory building. Indeed, postmodernists hold that feminism should be devoted to ending this kind of positive theorizing altogether. Particularly through the invocation of Foucault, feminist postmodernism decries the attempt to replace an old sexist hegemony with a new hegemony that may well still be racist, ageist, speciesist, or even sexist in a different way. As Julia Kristeva claims, the only task that feminism can face with a clear conscience that it is not buying into the mind set of the ruling intellectual class, gender, race, and so forth is the negative method of deconstruction. "If women have a role to play . . . it is only in assuming a *negative* function: reject everything finite, definite, structural, loaded with meaning, in the existing state of society." In keeping with the deconstructionist's imagery Kristeva argues, "A feminist practice can only be . . . at odds with what already exists so that we may say 'that's not it' and 'that's still not it.'"[43] It can only be the intellectual watchdog, so to speak, of theory.

Yet politically, if not theoretically, this view is in many ways antifeminist; for postmodern strategies cannot *in themselves* give rise to any alternate vision of politics that empowers the heretofore excluded, such as women, people of color, the poor, the very young and old, animals. Although there are methodological advantages to be gained from a post-structuralist approach to theory, I am also somewhat suspicious of its claims from a feminist point of view. As Hartsock asks:

> Why is it that just at the moment when so many of us who have been silenced begin to name ourselves, to act as subjects rather than objects of history, just then the concept of subjecthood becomes problematic? Just when we are forming our own theories about the world, uncertainty emerges about whether the world can be theorized. Just when we are talking about the changes we want, ideas of progress and the possibility of systematically and rationally organizing human society become dubious and suspect. And why is it only now that critiques are made of the will to power inherent in the effort to create theory?[44]

On the one hand, the attempt to build theory based on feminist analyses such as the foregoing *is* to run the risk of creating new hegemonies, new power structures through the creation of new forms of knowledge, as Foucault held. On the other hand, it is a risk that must be taken. I realize that this is a controversial and problematic

---

[43]Kristeva (1980a), p. 166; Kristeva (1980b), Hartsock (1990), pp. 163–64.
[44]Hartsock (1990), pp. 163–164.

view. Why should feminists accept the standard of what political theory is supposed to be and do if that theory has been premised on
women's epistemological exclusion? This question may best be addressed by analogy. After women's claims of the 1970s to equal rights
and opportunities to succeed at traditionally male professions, many
women found that the standard (classist and racist) definitions of success—say, working a seventy-hour week to become a partner in a law
firm—are also sexist. That is, they put a double burden on women
because such definitions are premised on an economic and social
model of the family in which one member is responsible for precisely
those areas of life that the business world by definition excludes.
What has made the seventy-hour professional work week possible is
that such workers have generally had wives, people who did not
work outside the home, who made that home possible by raising children, cooking, cleaning, hostessing (particularly for the partners),
and providing for affective life in general.

So on the contingent level, we find that women are still burdened
unequally because they are held responsible for domestic obligations.
Thus, if men shared more equally in child rearing and household
work, women would not suffer from the "double day." On the structural level, however, such sharing is still not enough. Much as John
Stuart Mill suggested the "exceptional woman" had to do if she was
to combine the career of wife and mother with work outside the
home,[45] these white, middle-class working parents must rely on a
new "ghetto" of workers in child care and housekeeping, often third
world immigrant women who are not paid for their work nearly as
well as the working parent. By refusing to recognize child rearing and
housework as socially valuable, by continuing to demand the seventy-hour work week, the social structure of success makes the
achievement of affective life either exploitive or impossible. Furthermore, existing definitions have denied the ways in which professions
were effectively closed off to large segments of the population—particularly women of color—whose family life did not necessarily conform to the white, middle-class model. The subject of success thus
retains its privileged gender, race, and class. On this view, the problems of gender inequality lie not with women per se but with the
socioeconomic model within which they seek both to work and to
maintain their personal lives. The structural barriers to gender equality are built into the system. The difficulty of introducing into the
workplace such innovations as on-site child care, job sharing, and
flextime, the pervasiveness of pay and promotion differentials, and

[45]Mill, *On the Subjection of Women.*

the speed with which the "mommy track" mentality was embraced by the business community[46] all suggest that the problem is not how to get women to achieve success by the old standards but how to change the meaning of success itself.

Perhaps political theorists need to take a lesson from these experiences. Just as feminists are saying not that women should stay out of the workplace but rather should change it, so I maintain that feminist theorists need to engage in positive theory building, but in the process they must change the enterprise to allow for new kinds of theory and new approaches to it. Postmodernists effectively claim that positive theory building is inherently corrupting and should be avoided altogether. I contend rather that through feminists' participation in these structures and practices of political theory, the structures and practices themselves are being not merely *reformed* but profoundly *transformed*. Their political concerns lead feminists to analyze and deconstruct differently from nonfeminists. Certainly feminists are more eager to deconstruct in the first place than are liberal theorists. But more than that, they need to be more concerned with building new structures out of deconstructed material than postmodernism allows. This does not mean that feminism provides the final word on obligation, that its theory is airtight, perfect, comprehensive, exclusive, or even "true." Rather, it provides a step toward a new theoretical future, one in which women, with all the subdivisions that postmodernism insists on, can tell their stories.

I largely defer my disagreements with postmodernism until my afterword, but I make these comments here to foreshadow my concerns about both theory building *and* postmodernism, and simultaneously because the theory that I develop in the next chapter demonstrates some affinity with postmodern methods and ideas, even as it seems to keep one foot planted, if somewhat ambivalently, in post-Enlightenment modernism. This "principled ambivalence,"[47] or position in between modernism and postmodernism, I argue, is an important strategy for feminism; but, as will become apparent, it also has its costs. Thus, aware of the dangers of the enterprise I undertake, with repeated self-conscious and self-critical warnings that I am not claiming to have a true, full-blown feminist theory of obligation, that I doubt that "one" even exists, I shall plunge headlong into the dangerous abyss of answering the, as Di Stefano points out,[48] often hostile question, Can you do any better? Can feminist theory offer us something in place of what it has just torn down?

---

[46]Schwartz (1989).
[47]Harding (1991) uses this phrase.
[48]Di Stefano (1991).

Feminist Obligation and Feminist Theory: A Method for Political Theory

AN ANSWER to the question that closed the previous chapter begins with a repetition of the warning that gender psychology as it is used here provides not an essentialist definition of man or woman but rather a heuristic device that offers a model and a language for understanding some of the specifically gendered dimensions of power and powerlessness in liberal obligation theory. In this context, gender psychology allows us not only to critique the masculinist bias of liberal obligation theory but also to formulate new visions more consistent with a feminist standpoint of care, responsibility, and responsiveness. By utilizing a feminist epistemological framework, we can sketch an outline of a feminist notion of obligation; and this is achieved by theorizing women's experience from the perspective of that experience.

The focus of a feminist theory of obligation is not directly on the obligation itself but rather on the (political) context within which it is located. If, as I have argued, a feminist concept of obligation operates from an understanding of context and concrete social relations, then a feminist political theory needs to attend to those contexts, to drawing out certain general characteristics that ensure a contextual approach to moral and political dilemmas, one that allows for the working out of the content of obligations within the context of connection. Through the construction of a feminist politics—a feminist practice—a feminist theory of obligation is deepened and enriched.

As I indicated in the conclusion to the previous chapter, however, in calling this a theory of obligation, we must recognize that the concept of theory is itself transformed. Given the demonstrated masculinism of mainstream political theory, an approach that begins from women's experiences suggests that standard methods of theory will prove inadequate to the task at hand. Feminist political theory must be able to utilize other strategies to articulate its political vision, particularly those demonstrating some affinity with more literary traditions (which have been much more accessible and responsive than political science and philosophy to feminist enterprises) including narrative, confession, interpretation, and story building, thereby bringing into theoretical method women's historical experience as contextual and local rather than formal and abstract. Just as Gilligan found the narrative to be central to unearthing and defining women's different voice, so must feminist theorists engage in their own political narratives. This story may help to elucidate—in ways that analytical philosophy, which has figured prominently in my discussion, cannot yet reveal because of its indebtedness to the dominant positivist epistemologies—the feminist epistemological perspective of obligation as given.[1]

Thus, rather than the linear progression of liberal theory, the theory of feminist obligation that I develop here is itself, like the central image that it incorporates, an elaborate web. Indeed, at its heart is a challenge to the liberal positivist idea that theory should proceed in a direct line and provide clear-cut, well-defined answers to the questions it poses, implicitly valuing the answers—even answers that reduce, simplify, and misrepresent—more than the questions. It requires a reevaluation of how theory should proceed and progress, what its goals and intentions should be, what sorts of methods and approaches can or should be implemented. The supposed theoretical advantage of liberal consent theory is that it is clear-cut: obligations arise from promising, political obligation from consent. Hence, although "the liberal vertical conception of obligation may be sadly empty of moral and political content . . . it does give a clear answer to the question of what counts as political obligation."[2] Any argument or ambiguity centers on whether or not I have consented, and hence am obligated; but this does not shake the fundamental understanding of what an obligation is and how it comes to exist.

In contrast, feminist theory does shake that understanding, but it may not be able to provide prima facie rules and procedures to govern the creation of obligations. In this sense there is no way to predefine a feminist theory of obligation, because as we attend to substance and context, all obligations will seem somewhat "*ad hoc*, contextual,

---

[1]For arguments about narrative as feminist method, see Bulker (1987), Abrams (1991), Estrich (1987), Belenky et al. (1986), Bumiller (1988), Ginsburg (1989).

[2]Pateman (1979), p. 97.

local, plural, and limited,"[3] a product of a collective understanding, negotiation, and working through of the concrete factors surrounding particular relationships, conflicts, and dilemmas. What it must articulate is more complex and layered than the straightforward liberal rule that obligations arise only from consent, and consent always creates obligation. Rather than defining feminist obligation in the standard fashion of analytic philosophy, feminist theory must attend to the context of relationships within which obligations are created, articulated, enacted, and sustained.

The Importance of Talk

The previous chapters most obviously suggest that the context for feminist obligation must begin with a process of communication and dialogue. In the care model, communication is vital as a means of establishing connections and maintaining relationships. The issue of voice, so central to Gilligan's and other feminist work discussed here, suggests that a feminist theory of politics would need to incorporate the issue of voice into its construction of politics; and voice is most commonly and readily expressed by talking, by communicating through language. In other words, a feminist theory does not make the liberal individualist appeal to rules and the umpire government. Instead it holds that participants to relationship (for example, a society) need to talk about how their obligations are determined. So although I have argued that feminist obligation is concerned with content rather than process, we must attend to (a certain concept of) process at least sufficiently to see how the content of obligations is determined. After all, the care model does not necessarily lead to the conclusion that obligations spring "naturally" from a relationship; or to the extent that they appear natural to the parties involved, there at least needs to be communication between parties to acknowledge that they are in fact in agreement.[4] Yet this is not as contradictory as it may seem. To the extent that we must focus on a process of talk, a

---

[3]Hartsock (1990), p. 159.

[4]On natural obligation, see Shapiro (1988). I admire but disagree substantially with his argument. The concept of naturalism he utilizes embraces, I believe, many aspects of existence that are culturally determined. The process of collective negotiation I invoke here operates from a concept of given obligation because it recognizes that relationships require obligations, but also that the kinds of relationships that exist and can be created are rarely natural to humans. Object relations shows that even a mother-child relationship is a socially constructed one, which can be replaced with other sorts of caretaker-infant relationships to the benefit of infants as well as adult women and men.

different notion of process is engaged, for the process itself is one of substantive meaning and concrete connection rather than of the rules and abstraction of liberal obligation theory. In the context of connection, participants to a relationship need to talk through the elements of a dilemma to determine how to act, what to do, how best to fulfill obligations established by that relationship.

The web of obligation thus locates at its center the (re)assertion that recognition is a key to feminist political theory and practice. Indeed, if there is anything even remotely approaching a prima facie first principle here it is recognition. I have argued that the problems of liberal obligation theory derive in important ways from an epistemological framework that defines the individual as a being who seeks recognition for the self while denying it to others. Those beings who do not engage in such a life-or-death struggle for dominance, who grant recognition to others, become slaves, less-than-individuals, less-than-human. I have argued that this masculinist representation of reality must be abandoned in favor of a model of interaction, an ontology and an epistemology that revolve around mutuality of recognition, relationships between selves and multiple others, and that take as central a concept of the individual as intimately involved in, created by, and understood in the context of relations with others, not as a separate entity defined in opposition to others.

Recognition in a feminist sense does not follow the Hegelian notion that we all desire others to recognize us as superior, for such a conception automatically defines all relationships in terms of dominance. In direct contrast, feminist recognition involves not a subject and object, a self and other, but two subjects, two selves, with the object and the other absorbed into the dynamics of the relationship between subjects and selves. Just as in human relationships the mother's own subjectivity must be recognized, so in political theory do nonrecognizing, unidirectional dualities need to be dispelled. Operating from the centrality of recognition, a feminist conception of obligation begins from premises of human connection and relationality and hence recognizes the legitimacy of obligations that exist prior to abstract consent. Such a conception emphasizes individual consideration and context over abstract general rules and outcome over procedure. It considers related concepts, such as equality and fairness, in substantive, not formal, terms and takes as its cornerstone the concrete conditions of people's lives, not a sublimated abstraction such as the state of nature.

Such a notion of recognition also obviously requires substantive values of inclusiveness as well as an inclusive political methodology. It should be clear from my earlier arguments that exclusion is a form of domination. Women's exclusion from political power and participation has been instrumental not only to their immediate political powerlessness—being denied a vote or the right to property drastically curtails their ability to affect policy outcomes—but to their epistemological disempowerment as well. Women's voices and their understanding of reality have been considered by definition not political, a definition that ensures their silence and powerlessness. I have argued that in order to end such domination of women by men—or, more precisely, of women and men by patriarchy—women and others whose voices are excluded must be brought in. But I have also indicated that such inclusion cannot be merely a liberal tolerance that lets women and others have their say and then continues to shape the world in the same old way. The stand*points* epistemological approach requires that excluded voices be brought in in the more active sense indicated by mutual recognition; this would not just allow voices to express themselves but would help them realize their expression, and would attempt to see and understand the world from these other perspectives. Inclusion and recognition, therefore, are intimately intertwined and conceptually interdependent, lying at the heart of a feminist theory of obligation.

Immediately, however, the idea of a first principle invokes my own earlier arguments about the problems of hegemony faced by liberalism as well as by a feminist theory (such as standpoint epistemology) that attempts to order and predefine the world according to either abstract principles or the supposed experiences of some abstract category of people (such as "women"). Furthermore, it may subscribe to the very same kind of abstraction for which I have criticized liberal theory. Is not the priority of recognition itself an abstract principle? Is it not a value judgment that is imposed on a given group of people who are engaged in the process of making a moral decision? I will keep coming back to the importance of recognition for human development and social relations, but I am trying to forge an understanding of it as a new kind of primacy, qualitatively different from the privileged place of freedom in liberalism. I say this because by the nature of the concept itself, recognition does not have a unitary meaning; rather, the inclusiveness it requires means that recognition is and will be negotiated in an ongoing way by the very process of conversation that it establishes. Parallel to my earlier reading of Rousseau's general will, the concept of recognition offered here provides the genesis for a participatory politics of mutual trust, and yet it is a subject of continual renegotiation by that politics and its participants.

One way to begin describing this model is to examine how it differs from the liberal dialogue. What I am proposing would better be called conversation.[5] Part of the critical argument I have made is that the liberal dialogue of political theory is an interaction of two totally separate individuals each of whom has a particular point of view and tries to "win" by convincing the other person. It again replicates the struggle for recognition, the struggle to have one's views recognized without recognizing the other. Dialogue presupposes and operates from individuals who are predefined, as is the dialogic method. In granting the identical weight to all points of view, dialogue becomes a procedural battle with the outcome dependent on who is the most persuasive, who puts forth the better argument. Yet the standards for defining the better argument are not only predetermined but biased. To the degree that liberal political theory is methodologically masculinist, so is this masculinism embodied in the liberal dialogue. It is an adversarial form, working from the modernist disjunction between knowing and feeling. Objectivity is equated with dispassion, a process that excludes all private concerns and feelings, both one's own and those of one's adversary.

By contrast, conversation operates from the principle that people can really listen to what others say, can attempt to incorporate those views into their own and indeed become somewhat transformed by that incorporation. If epistemology is ontologically influenced and generated, and if experience is not uniform for all people, then intersubjectivity must take priority over objectivity as talking and listening play central roles in achieving knowledge. Conversation also entails recognizing the ways in which this very process of knowledge seeking is itself transformative of being. The imagery of the web is once again useful: I have a place in the web, I am a self, and yet I am also related to myself and to what I know through my relationships with others. Hence the processes of interaction with those others will likely bring about continuous changes in my socially influenced self. These

[5]The idea of conversation is of course adopted by (among others) Michael Oakeshott in *Rationalism in Politics*. Although there are certain superficial similarities, the differences between feminist conversation and Oakeshott's conception will become apparent, only the first of which is his juxtaposition of philosophy and politics with conversation. Jürgen Habermas's "communicative ethics" is also obviously relevant, and many feminist theorists writing on democracy highlight his arguments. See Habermas (1979); for feminist theories of democracy drawing on Habermas, see Fraser (1991), Love (1989), Young (1987, 1990). See also Rorty (1979, 1990) for interesting remarks on conversation.

In her discussion of black feminist thought, Patricia Hill Collins makes a similar distinction but uses the term "dialogue" in the way that I use "conversation," and "debate" for what I term "dialogue." Collins (1990), p. 212. Regardless of the terminology, I believe we are making similar points.

changes can in turn generate new kinds of knowledge and knowledge frameworks for problem resolution and policy decisions.

This conversational mode of knowledge seeking draws in part from the idea of "connected knowing" in Belenky et al. (1986). As we saw in Chapter 3, they argue that separate knowing entails a dichotomy between the knower and the known. It shares with the positivist epistemologies of liberalism the concept of objectivity as completely value free, impartial, unbiased, and true. Along with liberalism, it embraces a quality of rule-governedness and an emphasis on the idea of mastery over the known. The relation between knower and known becomes a dualistic hierarchy parallel to subject-object, self-other, master-slave. Thus, separate knowers conceive of themselves as dissociated from the objects of knowledge and, in the process, from other knowers, who are treated instrumentally as means to knowledge and evaluation. In contrast, connected knowers treat other knowers as integrative parts of their own knowledge process. Objects of knowledge must be reformulated as subjects. Connected knowing and knowledge seeking involve relationships and intersubjectivity. As I discussed in Chapter 3, the notion that experience generates knowledge coheres with the relation between being and knowing, ontology and epistemology. Connected knowing involves sharing in others' experiences to fathom their knowledge.

Thus the epistemological implications of object relations theory are realized in connected knowing, as such knowers "learn through empathy," and as knowledge stems in part from "a joining of minds."[6] Knowledge is a collective enterprise, and so individual knowers must necessarily seek one another. Knowers are not instrumental to the self's search for knowledge; rather, knowledge, as an enterprise central to human social life, becomes a conduit for relationship. As a result, trust is central to connected knowing. In order for relations between knowers, and hence between knowers and known, to be genuinely intimate, trust must exist. This trust requires a shift of emphasis from *judgment*—which is central to separate knowing, to the attempt to sift out truth from falsehood by objective standards—to understanding, in which knowers seek to attain a complete picture of another's context and situation, to comprehend that person's subjective reality and hence to reach an intersubjective agreement as to what is known.[7] This process is extremely social, requiring the complex relationships of group interaction; and through this process of

[6]Belenky et al. (1986), p. 115.
[7]Ibid., p. 116.

"mutual stretching and sharing the group achieves a vision richer than any individual could achieve alone."[8]

Belenky et al. may exaggerate the fluidity of knowledge in their study, and they appear to underrepresent the degree to which disagreements about knowledge are disempowering, with the result that their emphasis on consensus building is counterproductive. But their account of connected knowing offers insights into the varied, nonunified ways in which knowledge can be developed. Although there may be certain facts in the world, facticity and certainty have often been granted an unearned, undeserved status, and have been misused. It is not the case that everything is relative; yet perspective must be accounted for before something can be declared a fact.

Furthermore, although I find that their argument tends too much toward overgeneralization, and perhaps even displays essentialist tendencies,[9] the idea of connected knowing can make obvious contributions to a feminist concept of conversation. Indeed, Belenky et al. identify something they call "real talk" as an important dimension of connected knowing. Trust, empathy, connection, contextuality, and relationship are all central to a feminist model of obligation. And of course the whole point in giving priority to recognition is that it is necessary to make conversation work; it is a principle that refuses to allow oppressive dialogue. Conversation becomes the means to express and explore human sociality, to understand our connections. We recall that in Rousseau's Assembly, for instance, citizens could not interact in such a manner. The procedure Rousseau prescribed involved citizens' expressing their views concisely in the Assembly, with no interpersonal association and no opportunities for the development of ideas through interactive or mutual discussion. Relying on virtuous home life to help male citizens realize the truth of the general will individually, Rousseau feared that interaction and talking would sway citizens away from the general will to the antisocial inter-

---

[8]Ibid., p. 119.

[9]One must remember that Belenky et al. are exploring these different ways of knowing particularly toward the end of understanding women's relation to education and the classroom, and thus developing a feminist pedagogy. Academics have long noted women's reticence in the classroom, and it is therefore important to examine the gender dimensions of this different voice. But doing so does not require us to embrace an essentialist conclusion that all females—and only females—are connected knowers. Given that women's silence creates a particular problem for political science—including their reluctance to participate in classroom discussion and to choose the field as a major—it is especially important that political theorists not bristle too readily at gender-related claims for these two kinds of knowledge; theorists must acknowledge the degree to which women—feminists included—have been forced to adopt a separate knowing approach in order to learn and succeed in the profession. See Department of Government, Harvard (1989), particularly remarks on classroom dynamics, pp. 18–24.

ests of more particular wills.[10] Conversation, in contrast, presupposes no such absolute truth that can be conceived separately from social interaction. Working from the potential for empathy, it presumes that communication through social relationships, in revealing to participants as much information as possible, is a more effective way to achieve any sort of general will, which would embody a dynamic of community action that allows individuals to see both their individuality and their commonality through their connections to others. This ideal of connection embodied in conversation can make better sense of the Rousseauian notion of a collective good that transcends narrow individualist interests even as it operates from individual assessments of the best course of action for the self and society.

Conversation is thus much more interactive than dialogue. My participation in the conversation is mutual; I seek to help others articulate their views in a positive sense, as they help me. If I perceive my own views as different from others', I do not automatically define them as opposed. Rather, I come to define myself partly in terms of others and my relationship with them, and the working out of those differences—defining what they are, seeking common ground, and attempting to forge a solution—becomes a means for me to gain greater clarity about what is in fact in my interest. This is not to say that because individuals are social beings, they must be mistaken about their preferences if those differ from what some monolithic, abstract entity called society decrees it needs. Rather, sociality and society are created and defined through the communication and mutual understanding of members' preferences and needs, for these are in turn shaped and influenced by their location in the social context and by individuals' recognition of this location through the communicative process. In this sense, borrowing again from Belenky et al., what I call conversation turns talking into a form of therapy for the community: just as "therapists learn to use their reactions to a client to help them understand the client,"[11] citizens would be able to engage in self-reflection about their desires, preferences, feelings, and empathetic responses in order to learn more about what both their society and they as individuals need and want by observing and experiencing the mutual interaction between individual and society that conversation inspires.

[10]For a different reading of Rousseau's views on talk among citizens, see Mostov (forthcoming) and Cohen (1986). My own earlier reading of Rousseau similarly allowed for an interpretation of the general will as pragmatic and flexible, reflecting changing conditions articulated through democratic discussion; but I maintain that this reading reveals what democratic theorists can pull out of Rousseau rather than what Rousseau put in.

[11]Belenky et al. (1986), p. 123.

Conversation is also more inclusive than dialogue. On the most obvious level, of course, women could not be segregated in the private sphere as moral guardians of male power. The inclusiveness of conversation requires that women and other excluded groups be involved in democratic assemblies. But more than this, conversation embraces an inclusive methodology. With its attention to winning arguments, to listening to others solely for the purpose of discovering the chinks in an opponent's armor, dialogue is exclusive, establishing a circular method for the dominant discourse and value system to maintain its hegemony. By refusing to enter the framework employed by an alternate perspective, the dominant perspective can always demand that dialogue be conducted in its own language, utilizing its own conceptual vocabulary, its own categories of meaning. Here we see the problem of developing a feminist epistemology within the confines of a hostile dominant epistemology; for by conceiving of intellectual exchange as dialogue rather than conversation, the dominant liberal discourse can assert its own epistemological primacy and demand that all challenges to it be launched on its own terms. This is an inherently exclusive and dominating intellectual stance. In contrast, by incorporating active listening into conversation, a feminist model invites and is concerned to include all views. By virtue of its concern for and sensitivity to the disempowered, the silenced, the marginalized, a feminist conversation must give priority to such inclusion. Thus Gilligan maintains that the care conception conceives of morality "as a problem of inclusion rather than one of balancing claims."[12]

Yet the notions of inclusion and the absence of timelessly true answers that adhere to independent moral principles such as natural rights suggest the problem of relativism. If recognition and inclusion are central, then what safeguards are provided against views such as Nazism or white supremacism? Is not a feminist conversation obligated to accord such views full recognition and equal consideration? Although it makes me uneasy, this feminist approach must allow for the expression of views that are largely accepted as abhorrent if it is to avoid the hegemony of modernism. And it must even allow for the possibility that the process of conversation in certain contexts may even *produce* such conclusions. Given the other elements of conversation I outline later in this chapter, I find it extremely difficult to imagine a context of mutual recognition that would actually foster something like Nazism, but this possibility must be allowed. To take a

---

[12]Gilligan (1982), p. 160.

more ambiguous and perhaps complex example, it is not uncommon for feminists and others, both male and female, to defend practices such as purdah, which as a feminist I find offensive; but the approach outlined here requires me to attend to these defenses and consider the possibility that my views on purdah are hegemonic, oppressive, exclusive. A true commitment to this method prohibits me from pre-judging the conclusions reached, for example, by other cultures and limits me to questioning the methods used to reach those conclusions: Was the process inclusive, or was it an exclusive one, like patriarchal tradition, in which men imposed the practice on women? Have women accepted and engaged in this practice self-consciously, self-critically, recognizing themselves and their own well-being as well as men's? Or is it premised on the power of one group—men—to deny recognition to another group—women—and then create and repre-sent that group's desires and subjectivity?

The centrality of recognition provides criteria that do not predeter-mine any outcomes but guide conversational attempts to determine outcome. There is admittedly an element of Lockean circularity here: just as Locke argued that we must tolerate all beliefs except intol-erance, so must a feminist politics recognize all beliefs except the non-recognizing. But there is a significant difference between Locke's doc-trine and what I have offered as its parallel. Rather than simply exclude the Nazi from the conversation because she or he is "wrong," or even nonrecognizing, we find that including him or her in conver-sation is the only way to end (or at least disarm) exclusive ideologies such as Nazism. In this way we act like Gilligan's subject Amy, who insists that if Heinz, his wife, and the pharmacist talk their problem out long enough, they can reach a decision that meets everyone's needs. But here there is the added notion that the conversation helps its members redefine their needs, both individually and as a group. Now, critics may well scoff at the idea that conducting conversation through mutual recognition will convince those advocating excluding ideologies to reject their beliefs because they are wrong. But if *wrong* is used in the sense of exclusive rather than in the sense that there is only one true story, a different meaning emerges, for it creates pa-rameters for the conversation that, on the one hand, restrict what can count as a legitimate view while, on the other, allowing for an ongo-ing negotiation of those restrictions. The logic of recognition makes it extremely difficult, if not impossible, to sustain exclusive and non-recognizing views.

This may indicate on my part a certain theoretical ambivalence about the role and justification for first principles to order all discussions and moral decisions. Yet I emphatically consider such ambivalence a source of strength, not weakness. Willingness to be ambivalent is part of the model I have outlined. If I am truly committed to mutual recognition, then ambivalence is the beginning of allowing myself to see others' viewpoints; in a sense, there is no place for absolute moral certainty in this model. There can only be agreement about what is the best decision in the limited context at hand. Indeed, if I am to be truly commmitted to a feminist morality that operates contextually, then the enterprise of deciding beforehand how one would achieve a moral decision is impossible, or at least not possible in the customary ways of political theory. I have argued that that is one of the primary reasons why the focus of my argument is on epistemology and method rather than on developing a new hegemonic feminist theory of obligation. The point is to highlight the fact that the evaluative criteria of liberal models cannot be used to judge and assess the methods of a feminist model.

It is also why I have argued that any development of a feminist theory of obligation must attend to the *context* for obligations and the working through of their content. My point in giving priority to recognition is that it is necessary to make conversation work; it is a principle that disallows oppressive dialogue. Obviously this method of problem solving will not eliminate the "gray area" in morality. But this sort of theorizing prefers to err on the side on inclusiveness— even at the cost of what liberalism would consider moral inconclusiveness—than on the side of allowing the privileged to determine "truth" and then impose it on all others. It prefers to do so because it questions whether "truth" exists in the ways we have heretofore conceived it. Through such an approach the web begins to be constructed. Already, threads have been cast out from the central concept of recognition to other concepts—mutuality, inclusion, conversation, community—all of which are indeed part of the concept of recognition and not merely separate concepts that must also be considered. Yet they have somewhat separate meanings as well, which require further articulation, a task to which I now turn. In the attempt to organize these various threads in the most cogent fashion, I have constructed the discussions that follow around two elements that I believe occupy the most important place in the web next to recognition. These are vital to recognition and conversation and to the feminist context for obligation. They are trust and participatory democracy. In my discussion of these elements other terms, such as mutuality, reciprocity, inclusion, and conversation, will be developed in their specific meanings within this feminist theoretical context.

Trust

Trust is the first such element to be pursued—or the next ring of threads to be woven—because it in turn is a major context for participatory democracy. A theory that begins from premises of connection and relationship must operate from a further premise that trust exists between connected beings and within relationships. Rather than a series of fleeting contacts at discrete points, interaction in this model is by necessity more comprehensive. And without the externalized superego of the market to regulate interactions among discrete individuals, trust must be the operative belief of truly interactive, interdependent beings.

Trust is an element sorely missing from liberal theory's market model. From Hobbes to Rawls, individuals act in ways that presume a lack of trust. Descartes reverts to pure thought and the isolated self, dependent on no other person, because the only thing that can be known for certain, that can be trusted, is the self. In Hobbes's state of nature, the Prisoner's Dilemma is the model for action; the only way to be safe is to strike first. Hence the state of war is inevitable because every person thinks everyone else is out to get him. In Rawls's theory, individuals must go behind a veil of ignorance in an original position where they know very little of substance about themselves. The realities of life must be removed to ensure impartiality. If one knew one's position, the assumption is that one could not be trusted to desire true justice over narrow self-interest. And indeed, in the original position justice arises only because people act defensively against the possibility that they will be the worst off when the veil is lifted. Even in Rousseau's Assembly, citizens are not to have access to one another for private discussion for fear that men will be swayed against the general will in favor of narrow interests. And of course there is no trust between men and women in Rousseau's theory; women will destroy men if given the chance, so they must be harnessed and repressed to ensure men's freedom.

Dunn has argued that trust is an important element in Locke's theory; he argues that, for Locke, trust is "the bond (*vinculum*) of society."[13] Certainly my argument in Chapter 1 suggested that there may be a very particular kind of trust in Locke's civil society based on property ownership; those with political power belong to the class of privileged male property owners who share an interest in preserving that property. This self-interested and limited trust obviously fails to

---

[13]Dunn (1984), esp. p. 52. See also Dunn (1985).

extend to the general population of tacit consenters. But there is a broader meaning ostensibly intended by Locke, as Dunn points out, in which trust is founded on faith in God, the patriarchal overseer of the natural laws of promising and contract; under God's watchful eye, trust is "a duty under the law of nature." Without God, we are in mortal danger of anarchy and the destruction of community: "Bereft of a concerned Creator and left on their own, men could have no good reason to trust one another and hence no capacity to live in society together."[14] Without God, men would be thrown back on individual interests as the sole basis for society, a basis, Dunn says, about which Locke was not optimistic. It is this reliance on God, however, that—while perhaps saving Locke from the sins of possessive individualism—makes the concept of trust an odd one. In the first place, a concept of trust based on obedience to a patriarchal deity is inappropriate to a modern rationalist epistemology, and hence Locke's concept of trust is not truly available for modern theory.

From a feminist perspective it is positively harmful, for it works hand in hand with women's exclusion from the public sphere as well as their devaluation in the private. As I argued earlier, Locke's reliance on God is a major theoretical difficulty, because it represents a turn to the patriarchal father to ensure safe passage away from nature rather than requiring resolution of the conflicting wishes for autonomy and symbiosis. Pitkin further points out in her study of Machiavelli, although the point holds for Locke as well, that this absolute trust in the "father" corresponds to a total mistrust of the mother/woman as a product of the male child's differentiation, turn to the father, and positional identification.[15] Thus the source of trust for Locke can be seen as the source of women's oppression; this "trust" is a further way to distance the mother and claim (reactive) independence. It is not the trust of mutually recognizing individuals.

Yet, as Annette Baier points out, trust *is* oddly at the center of liberal obligation. Promises "not merely create obligations apparently at the will of the obligated, but they create trust at the will of the truster."[16] In most cases, the fact that A has promised to do X gives me more reason to trust that she will in fact do X than if she had not promised. Yet, as with consent and promising as the model for obligation, it is precisely this overemphasis on the self-creative dimensions of trust, and the repression of the nonvoluntary aspects, that makes the liberal notion of trust problematic. For the promise provides *more* reason only if I have *other* reasons to believe A's promise, such as a history of trustworthy relations with her or a social context that will produce censure (Hume's "love of reputation") if she breaks her promise. Otherwise—and often this is the case—trust is simply a function of powerlessness. Most of us would not trust a terrorist, for instance, simply because she had promised to release us if we do X. In this case trust, if given at all, would derive either from powerlessnesss (we have no choice about doing X anyway) or from some other evaluation we have made of the terrorist (for example, she has kept every other promise she has made to us so far, or she has revealed information about herself that makes us feel compassion and sympathy for her, or we have undergone the psychological twists of identifying with our captor). Parallel to my earlier arguments, Baier points out that promising is often an elite right: it creates the ability to trust for those in power, but for the less powerful it merely creates dependency, as Rousseau argued in *The Origin of Inequality* about the liberal social contract. Yet, as daily experience reminds us, not everyone is equally free to bargain or equally powerful to see a promise enforced. For instance, although a labor contract defines the terms of the relationship between illegal alien workers and Texas fruit growers, some growers can fail to pay pickers for their time secure in the knowledge that the workers will not seek redress through the law. Thus, while acknowledging conscious and chosen trust relationships as a part of human life, Baier points out that we also live in relationships of "unconscious trust . . . [and] conscious but unchosen trust."[17]

How would the infusion of trust alter these theories? And what is its significance? Furthermore, what does trust mean in feminist terms? A feminist conception of trust, operating from the assumption of connection and relationship, is based on mutuality and reciprocity, the key to which is mutual recognition. Only through recognition of women's/the mother's subjectivity can the self-other dichotomy be transformed into relations among selves and others, or even multiple selves, multiple subjects. Trust can come only from a secure sense of oneself as an agent fully capable of truly independent action, as opposed to reaction. It can flourish only in a self not dependent on the negation of and dominance over the other. Agency and (relational) autonomy cannot evolve from actions taken to deny and repress the mother, for such behavior locks people into ways of thinking and

[17]Ibid., p. 244.

acting that not only contradict their humanity but are highly restrictive of liberty. Rather than promoting self-creation, they promote self-destruction. Gender psychology offers the insight that in order for people of either sex to develop a genuine sense of themselves as individuals and agents, they must accept self-in-relationship. In the feminine model, the sense of self must emerge from an overly strong identification with the mother and the world; a sense of individuality must be realized. In the masculine model, the sense of self must be able to merge gender conceptions with primary identification; the self-other dichotomy must be seen as self-*others* relationships.

Similarly, in political theory dualisms that oppose self to other and subject to object must be reconstructed as relationships between beings and factors. Rather than a self-other opposition, we must see self (or selves) and others in relationship. Dichotomy must be reformulated as continuum. But we should not go to the extreme of total identification; we must not forget the individual in favor of some group or community, replicating the pathology of mother and daughter, and presenting as abstract an entity as is found in liberal ideology. After all, the goal is to theorize feminine experience critically and not merely to "act out" women's historically contingent values and experiences under patriarchy. That is one reason why there is such a difference between "the standpoint of women" and a feminist standpoint or even feminist theory. Just as we must understand and accept a notion of self-in-relationship, so must we realize a conception of individuality-in-community. Recognition would thus end the dualities that have been identified as a source of liberalism's problems; but it would preserve us from the merging found in more extreme theories (or extreme elements of otherwise useful theories, such as Rousseau's) that insist on a complete identification of individual and community interests.

Reciprocity in recognition does involve some elements found in the liberal contract, namely elements of exchange, of explicit agreement and shared understandings. These are important elements I do not wish to eliminate, though I do want to alter them as against their masculinist articulation. But reciprocity goes beyond the character of the liberal contract, and requires elements of equivalence and substantive equality. What is exchanged, what is agreed on, must be based on a true equivalence between agents, a full self-knowledge and understanding of one's needs and wants. There can be no unequal bargaining positions, and agents must recognize and respect the agency and subjectivity of other agents. "Reciprocity thus presupposes equality . . . [but also] goes beyond equality in that it involves the recognition by each agent of the differences of the other."[18] Reciprocity precludes the self-focused pursuit of interest that disregards the needs and existence of others. It does not rely on the market as an impersonal arbiter of conflicting wants. Instead it requires each individual to be responsible for mediating his or her own wants within the context of a community in which others have desires equally worthy of being fulfilled. Reciprocity in this sense thus transforms relations of competition into relations of cooperation.

But reciprocity is an insufficient condition to ensure trust and recognition in relationship. Mutuality must also be a primary characteristic of social interaction. Mutuality is, according to Carol Gould, "the most highly developed form of such reciprocal relations."[19] It goes beyond equivalence to the full and complete recognition of other agents. In mutuality, "each agent consciously endeavors to act in such a way as to enhance the agency of the other."[20] Although reciprocity recognizes others' agency, it leaves the responsibility for the agents' actions with the agent. This is appropriate to much of human life, but it is inadequate to account for all of human experience. Mutuality, then, involves a fuller notion of recognition in finally transcending the individualism of liberal theories of obligation and describing relationships of people who are "for" each other; who assist one another to be, to realize themselves and their potential; who work cooperatively with one another, on one another, and for one another. Reciprocity requires individuals to be responsible for modifying their own wants within the context of a community of differing individuals; mutuality further requires each individual to be responsible in the additional sense of being responsive to those others and their needs. People must engage in connected knowing in their interpersonal relationships; they must come to know one another in connected ways.

This concept of mutuality may be extremely difficult to grasp for a variety of reasons. The dominance of liberal individualism may make many uneasy about and hence unresponsive to such a conception. Indeed, my own training as a political theorist in the fundamental assumptions of liberal individualism may inhibit my ability to articulate them in a clear and honest fashion. The process of its presentation thus can become muddled at both the theorist's and the reader's end by an ideology and a framework hostile to the idea being presented.

[18]Gould (1984a), p. 6.
[19]Ibid., p. 5.
[20]Ibid., p. 6.

This possibility for "bad faith" in attempting to articulate a feminist theory within existing linguistic and theoretical frameworks is the fundamental notion underlying the work of several French feminist theorists who have tried to develop theory in a different vein by the use of nontraditional approaches. These writers of "l'écriture feminine" (they eschew the idea of theory as in itself antithetical to the emergence of any meaningful expression of women's experience) combine psychoanalysis (primarily Lacanian), literary theory (particularly a Derridean deconstructionist approach), poetry, and fiction to develop new ways of telling women's story. They have also taken more radical approaches that include writing "from the body," in considering the body as the one truly feminine entity that has not been altered and created by patriarchy (or at least as the entity least influenced).[21] Although I have substantial disagreements with this body of theory, particularly the last-mentioned strategy, these theorists have made valuable contributions to feminist writing which may prove useful here.

In particular, Luce Irigaray's "And the One Doesn't Stir without the Other" (1981) bears discussion. Irigaray writes about the relationship between mother and daughter, arguing that it is the model for the development of an "ethic of nurturance," which must be the basis for a feminist construal of social relations and ethics.[22] Irigaray's conception of recognition begins from this most complex of relationships in which recognition is extremely complicated and interactive. This is not a relationship of innate competition and hostility wherein each individual tries to establish ascendency, to establish her subjectivity at the loss of others' and by their objectification. Irigaray describes the relationship between mother and daughter as defined by mutual self-sacrifice, a giving up of the self for the sake of the other. The pathology of this relationship is also mutually destructive and is not to be perpetuated; but it provides a perspective from which the mother and daughter can emerge as truly connected individuals and avoid the

[21]Jones (1981), p. 252. See also Marks and de Courtivron (1980), Marks (1978).

[22]This phrase is from Kuykendall (1984). My own reading of Irigaray, inspired as it is by an object relations perspective, is largely in agreement with Kuykendall's essay. And I should note that there are other theorists—particularly feminist postmoderns—who would disagree, and have done so, with such an interpretation, holding that the only correct way to read these texts is through a strict Lacanian framework. See Mac-Dermott (1987). Given the sexism of Lacanian theory, however (see Flax [1990], esp. pp. 89–107), and particularly given the profound resonance between object relations' narrative and the story Irigaray relates, I must challenge this position. Indeed, the pro-Lacanian position contradicts the postmoderns' own notion that texts have meanings beyond authorial intent, and indeed have multiple (even infinitely so) meanings. I discuss the relationship between feminism and postmodernism in the afterword to this book.

frozen death of patriarchal isolation, the relation with a father "who leaves me empty of him, mouth gaping on his truth."[23] From their perspective, the mother and daughter can strive for mutual recognition, for staying alive while giving each other life: "What I wanted from you, Mother, was this: that in giving me life, you still remain alive."[24] For Irigaray, as Eleanor Kuykendall notes, the relationship between the nurturer and nurtured must be "not merely symmetrical, but at least potentially mutual and reciprocal."[25] That is, these relationships must involve a recognition of subjectivity, and the relators must have as a primary interest the development and maintenance of the other's selfhood and subjectivity.

Irigaray particularly focuses on the mother-daughter relationship because of the need (in her view) for women to stand together as sisters, an event that will not occur if the central woman-to-woman relationship is not healed and transformed from the perversion that patriarchy has created. But the principles she articulates can and should apply to all other relationships as well. The concept of mutuality found in the mother's remaining alive while giving the daughter life explicitly rejects the self-other dichotomy presented by traditional psychoanalysis and demanded by patriarchy and focuses on a notion of one's empowerment to develop and become a self without destroying the subjectivity of the other. Such development of the self, in fact, can help create and further develop the subjectivity of the other; thus, such a feminist ethic recognizes and develops a sustenance in mutual growth rather than the destruction found in the competitive struggle for dominance. In order to bring this empowerment about, we must "mourn an all-powerful maternal presence." We must put an end to the yearning of the unconscious for the mother of our infancy, who appeared as all-powerful grantor and frustrator of our desires. As a culture and a society, we must move beyond what Dorothy Dinnerstein calls our "murderous infantilism," the belief we harbor in our unconscious that our mothers could have given us all that we wanted but chose not to, and recognize the limitations in our mothers that make them human subjects.[26]

It is significant that Irigaray chooses the mother-daughter relationship for discussion, not only because it is the central woman-to-woman relationship but also because of the dynamics of the mother-child relationship and the activities of mothering, or what Sara

---

[23]Irigaray (1981), p. 62.
[24]Ibid., p. 67.
[25]Kuykendall (1984), p. 264.
[26]Dinnerstein (1976), p. 109.

Ruddick has called "maternal practice."[27] Trust is a central value in maternal practice in many ways. In the first place, mothers have historically had to trust their mates in their dependence for subsistence through the sexual division of labor. But trust is even more intrinsic in other ways. A core goal of mothering involves promoting the child's ability to trust, to form lasting relationships, to love. Love cannot survive without trust. Furthermore, the mother-child relationship itself is one of trust. It is not even remotely described by the liberal market model of relations, in which connection is fleeting and exists only for the purpose of mutual gain. Nor does it fit the market's conception of trust, for a mother does not carry out the activities of mothering because she has promised or contracted to do so or because the child relies on her in any conscious way; the infant has yet to learn the concepts of promising, obligation, and responsibility. The trust that characterizes this relationship is much deeper, and involves a way of viewing life, relationships, and reality that takes relationship as given, that begins from premises of connection.

Baier has developed a similar concept in her notion of "infantile trust," a phrase she uses not only to indicate the necessary innateness of some degree of trust in surviving infants but also to suggest the ways in which the general trust of human social life differs from the very special, particularized trust of promising. Trust is not necessarily something that one is suddenly able to give when one reaches the age of reason. Rather, although some facility and tendency for trust may be inborn, it is something that grows out of social relationships. As a child achieves adulthood, nonvoluntary or unself-conscious trust may grow into more self-conscious forms, but that does not negate trust's genesis: "No such contractual or quasi-contractual agreement can convert the young child's trust and the parent's trustworthiness retrospectively into part of a contractual mutual exchange."[28] In this sense perhaps Baier would argue that liberal contract theory represents a certain arrest in human development. Indeed, linking the primacy of promising as the universal model for trust to a specifically masculine perspective, Baier argues that "the psychology of adolescents, not infants, then gets glorified as the moral ideal. Such a reaction against a

[27]Ruddick (1984a); see also Ruddick (1989).

[28]Baier (1986), p. 243. Although she does not develop the source of this masculinist definition of trust very fully, her primary focus seems to be relatively straightforward: she argues that staunch liberal theorists such as Hobbes, Locke, and Bentham had little contact with women in their adult professional lives, whereas more complex and socially oriented theorists such as Hegel, Hume, and Mill were extensively exposed to the contradictions that women's daily experience poses to the ideas of liberalism. She postulates this contrast as an important source of the basic differences between the two kinds of theory.

religious vision of the ethics of trust is as healthy, understandable, and, it is hoped, as *passing* a phenomenon as is adolescent self-assertive individualism in the life of a normal person."[29] Like Irigaray, Baier can be read as suggesting not that we create a society where everyone trusts like infants in their parents, but rather that such relationships, such human experiences, can provide us with clues about ourselves that can lead to understandings of social relationships which a liberal voluntarist ideology subverts and represses. To the degree that such relationships are destructive, deceitful, and damaging, the ability and motive to trust will be hindered;[30] to the degree that they are nurturing and supportive, the ability and motive to engage successfully in trust relations, both voluntary (such as promising) and nonvoluntary (such as falling in love), will be developed.

Baier goes beyond Irigaray in offering more concrete guidelines for trust which may allow easier communication with liberal theory, for the questions that plague the liberal—What justification can there be for trust? How do I know when I can trust someone?—are not addressed by Irigaray. Baier begins her answer with a "test for the moral decency of a trust relationship," namely that the *motive* for the other person's trust can be revealed to one without hurting the trust relationship. Baier here attends not only to trust as a context but to the context of trust as well. She asks, "What is a trust-tied community without justice but a group of mutual blackmailers and exploiters?"[31] Trust requires an open community, one where it is possible to excercise Baier's moral test; and that requires a context of conversation such as I have described. Participants' ongoing discussion of mutual recognition requires certain assumptions of trust; but it also provides the means for an assessment of whether that trust continues to exist, and whether it continues to be sincere. For instance, Baier suggests, if I discover that you trust me to behave in a certain way because you love me, that will strengthen the trust relationship; if, however, I discover that you are relying on my fear of you, that will weaken the trust relationship.

If such a concept of trust is to be applied and utilized on a larger social scale—for Baier admits the weaknesses of the two-person model she adopts, suggesting that trust relationships really involve a "network,"[32] as we are once again drawn back to Gilligan's image of

---

[29]Ibid., p. 242; emphasis added. The turn from divine right to the social contract could be described in this way.

[30]Although not explicitly adopting this thesis, Di Stefano's (1991) account of Hobbes's early life provides a very interesting interpretation of why Hobbes believes trust is impossible between "natural men."

[31]Baier (1986), p. 253.

[32]Ibid., p. 258.

the web—openness and honesty require a context such as the one I have described. In this, Baier—like Irigaray though perhaps less ambivalently—highlights the centrality of love to trust: "The best reason for confidence in another's good care of what one cares about is that it is a common good, and the best reason for thinking that one's own good is also a common good is being loved."[33] Gilligan argues that love is an important dimension of moral reasoning in the care conception, that it is not peripheral to morality but central to it. This broader notion of trust embodied in a feminist analysis works from that very same dynamic: love becomes part of morality in creating the context for the development and expression of trust.

In this sense, the affective abilities developed and sustained through the relational models of Irigaray and Baier, as well as Ruddick's "maternal practice," provide important models for feminist trust and obligation. As Ruddick argues, regardless of the success or even desire of any given practitioner (that is, the maternal caretaker), the practice of mothering involves the development of mutuality and trust as elements necessary to the realization of the goals of the practice. Certainly I do not want to overstate the theoretical potential of mothering; in light of the problem of child abuse, it might be asked whether this "trust" is really a reciprocal or reciprocated relationship. To what extent do mothers have to trust their children, especially their infants? Many would argue that the child's dependence on the mother and the mother's power over it preclude the mother-child relationship from being a model for any political relationship between adults.

But this view also oversimplifies; for women, too, are dependent within the same framework as their children. We must ask what this shared dependence signifies. Furthermore, women become dependent on their children; as Chodorow and Flax assert, mothers are dependent on their daughters for resolving their own preoedipal issues. This provides potential for an abusive relationship, but it also creates the possibility for deep, empathic interaction. Children are, in most senses of the word, helpless; yet any mother who has felt guilty when her child cries or who has felt inadequate as a mother can assert that this helplessness is not merely one way.[34] As Baier notes, "The parents' enormous power to harm the child and disappoint the child's trust is the power of ones also vulnerable to the child's at first insignificant but ever-increasing power, including power as one trusted by the parent," thus creating a relationship of "mutual, if unequal vul-

---

[33]Ibid., p. 243.
[34]See especially Rich (1976).

nerability."[35] Perhaps, as I am suggesting about obligation, and as Hartsock suggests about power, we need to expand this understanding of dependence beyond its traditional meaning in order to grasp a fuller conception of trust. What such maternal thinking suggests is the possibility of theorizing this aspect of women's experience, along with other aspects, to the end of developing a concept of trust that would articulate more clearly our social relations.

It must be remembered that the theory I am attempting to develop involves relationships between beings old enough and conscious enough to understand the responsibilities inherent in relationships. Similarly, it should be kept in mind that Irigaray writes about the relationship between a mother and an *adult* daughter through the latter's reflection on her own psychic childhood. The problem of that relationship is for the daughter to be able to accept from a mother who is, but has difficulty seeing herself as, a subject. For Irigaray, both mother and daughter are caught in the problem of overconnectedness. But for either of them to resolve the problem, each must help the other; the connection needs to be loosened, but it cannot be severed. To offer this relationship of two distinct but interwoven adult women as a model for trust perhaps better expresses the element of mutuality than does Baier's concept of infantile trust, though both writers allow us to see that the origins of adult trust in infancy contradict contractual images of trust. Such a model can help establish the idea that trust in the feminist sense of full and mutual recognition is vital to any understanding of the concept of obligation from the perspective of a given. With mutuality and reciprocity as cornerstones of relationship, with recognition being mutual, trust transcends the contractarian notion of the market as independent arbiter and works from a concept of subject relating to subject, working together for each other, developing their agency with and through each other.

In such a situation, agency and (relational) autonomy can emerge more readily than in the reactive dynamics of liberal epistemology. An agent will be able to act on an honest assessment of her situation rather than merely reacting to aspects of that situation. This, of course, will strengthen the sense of individuality—not as a doctrine of individualism, an ideology that establishes external principles to keep people separate, but as a recognition of the uniqueness and difference of all individuals and a simultaneous recognition of the ways in which culture, institutions, relations, and other beings influence that uniqueness. This sense of individuality is strong because it comes from within and includes concrete relations with others who are part

[35]Baier (1986), p. 242.

of yet separate from the self, rather than arising from abstract and artificial roles, principles, and rules. Liberal theory gives us some important values and concepts, such as a recognition of the individual as a social and political entity, yet it also distorts those concepts. A feminist theory of obligation based on trust will not only clear our lenses of these distortions but will also redirect our vision to other values, social characteristics, and institutional constructions that liberal theory has ignored and denied, or been unable to see.

Participatory Democracy

Thus, trust is a necessary context for a feminist conversation devoted to determining the limits, meaning, and content of obligations. If recognition is to work as an operative ideal, it must be reciprocal and mutual, and participants must be able to trust that others will recognize their subjectivity and listen to them as they express themselves.

Yet, although trust among connected knowers is a more reasonable and realistic possibility than it is among Hobbesian egoists, we also, as Baier suggested, may wish to rein in our reliance on trust with some caution. If humans are not Hobbesian atomists, there still may be a bit of Hobbes (or at least Locke) in us, perhaps rightly so, at least under certain conditions; and Rousseau's idyllic image of citizens sitting under an oak tree is perhaps a bit too pastoral for a (post)modern world. So how can we be *sure* that trust will inform people's interactions? How can we, so to speak, trust in trust? On the one hand, we cannot. It is part of the concept of trust that it is invoked precisely when such certainty of knowledge is absent. But on the other hand, just as feminist theory does not seek truth as much as it seeks less falseness, perhaps certainty is not the goal here so much as increasing probabilities. Perhaps the whole point of invoking trust in a feminist approach to obligation is to highlight the profound transformation required not only in creating a new theory but also in reassessing what the goals and ends of political theory are and what they should be.

Nevertheless, our modernist sensibilities nag: If trust is central to a feminist theory of obligation, how can it be implemented? This question brings us to the dimensions of feminist practice that have to do with the form of government a feminist theory of obligation would require. This is so not because a feminist politics requires that trust be reinforced by authoritative sources; indeed, that would contradict its basic tenets. Rather, the role and character of government—the realm of the more explicitly and traditionally political—is a key aspect of the theoretical attempt to concretize the context for feminist obligation. Feminist politics is the core of such praxis. Although Benjamin Barber's assertion that "the 'Other' is a construct that becomes real to an individual only when he encounters it directly in the political arena"[36] may overstate the case (I have shown that "the other" becomes extremely concrete in the daily operations of child rearing and personality development), there is nonetheless something to be said for the special place the political arena that we call government holds for the concept of recognition. And certainly, government harbors a valuable potential for the gender equalization of power relations. Furthermore, if conversation is to have social and political meaning, it must be linked to the policy-making and common decision-making processes of a society. Less formal and even unorganized opportunities for conversation can encourage and amplify the voices of otherwise powerless people; but the relation of such individuals to the power structures of policy making, and their participation in them, must also be considered if conversation's potential to transform such structures is to have any plausibility. Finally, we must remember that *political* obligation, which is the major focus of liberal theory and of this book, is about the obligations of citizens to governments. Although I have argued that there are important connections between political obligation and the nonconsensual obligations of the traditional private sphere, and I have challenged the liberal dichotomy between public and private as a partial cause of the pathology of social contract theory, it is at the same time necessary to understand the kind of government and politics a feminist theory of obligation requires, for it is a central dimension of the context within which the content of obligations is to be determined.

The feminist concept of obligation constructed thus far would most obviously point to a participatory form of government. Participatory democracy best provides for both the individuality and the community necessary for reciprocal and mutual political and social relations. The most fundamental and remarkable quality that distinguishes political obligation in participatory democracy from that in liberal democracy is, as Walzer puts it, its "horizontal" character.[37] In the liberal social contract, each individual citizen supposedly has a direct contract with the government. This contract entails an obligation of obedience to the government, which in turn has an obligation to represent each citizen's interests. Citizens' relation to one another is at best indirect, passing through the filter of government. Even when citi-

[36]Barber (1984), p. 152.
[37]Walzer (1970), p. 207.

zens contract with one another, the relationship is defined by laws created by the government. Thus, private contracting occurs and operates only in the context of government as creator, overseer, and referee.

In participatory democracy citizens are related to their government through their relations to one another; indeed, these relations are what (at least to a large part) constitutes the government. Participatory democracy must therefore reject the traditional liberal view of politics as belonging to the realm of government only, separate from the private sphere of action among contracting individuals. Similarly, a feminist political society would involve itself in the merging of public and private realms, a notion as consistent with participatory democracy as it is opposed to its liberal counterpart. Individuality and community have traditionally been seen as gender exclusive: men have been seen as concerned solely with the former, women with the latter. But the previous chapters suggest that this exclusivity has resulted in the perversion of these concerns; for it is their dichotomous counterposition—the duality of public and private, individual and community, male and female—that creates the need to exaggerate their differences. It is thus that individuality turns into abstract individualism, community into the fearful or self-defensive nurturing of an isolated family. Theorists such as Gould, Okin, and others[38] argue that the values of each realm must be introduced into the other. I have further argued that such interweaving will also bring about the modification of these values so that they conform and work more easily together, at least reducing both the extremism and the dualism that characterize their liberal translations.

Although the public and private should be highly interactive and overlapping in a feminist democracy, however, the aim of feminist theory is not to make them synonymous. Personal and individual privacy must be preserved, as liberal theory is correct to point out. Public and private are not absolutely separate, but neither should they be subsumed one in the other: "In any society, there will remain a *level of individual desire that can never be totally reconciled with social need*, without destroying the individual personalities whose self-realization . . . is the ultimate object of social life."[39] For instance, should a woman be required to have a child if her society needs it? In one sense, a merging of public and private would suggest an affirmative response; yet most feminists would be opposed to such an idea. After all, women have for centuries been required to bear children for the supposed

[38]Gould (1984a), Okin (1989); also see Gilligan (1982), Hartsock (1984), Ruddick (1989).
[39]Petchesky (1980), p. 685.

good of society, usually to provide soldiers but also workers. The most famous case in political theory, of course, lies in ancient Greek sources, in Pericles' funeral oration; but more recent and vicious examples abound. In the antebellum United States slaves were bred to produce more workers. The Ceausescu regime's natal policy in Romania produced workers as well as soldiers. Former Greek President Christos Sartzetakis chastised Greek women for the country's low birth rate, exhorting them to produce more babies to help confront a possible future military threat from Turkey.[40] This enforced social control of women's bodies is one of the practices that the current women's movement and feminist theory seek to end.

Thus feminists may want to hold on to the concept of individual integrity which an extreme communitarianism would seem to deny. As Barbara Love and Elizabeth Shanklin argue, socialist constructions of society, in which public and private are supposedly merged, can be as opposed to feminist values of care and responsibility as are liberal-capitalist constructions, although in different ways.[41] Yet the fact that women in nonsocialist societies have historically been required de facto to bear children, thereby suffering from this requirement while at the same time suffering as well from the public-private dichotomy and denial of political voice, would suggest that it is in fact *not* the merging of public and private per se that would lead to social control of child bearing and child rearing in a socialist society. Rather, such control would relate to some other element that socialist societies share with liberal-capitalist, medieval, and classical societies, namely patriarchy, or male control of the family and public decision-making processes. To the degree that men do not dominate in any given society, women would have that much more control over their bodies; and at least within a socialist society, that control might well result in a collective effort to repopulate the society. Such a "choice" might smack of a Rousseauist "forcer d'être libre," but such a decision in the context of women's true participation must be qualitatively different from such a decision made solely by men and imposed on women. Because liberal theorists tend to see public and private as dichotomized, they often couch such dilemmas in dichotomous terms; they

[40]*New Haven Register*, December 1, 1985, A32; Eisenstein (1990). Along less militaristic and more culturally motivated lines, in Quebec, Premier Robert Bourassa's "baby-bonus" program guarantees parents $500 for a first child, $1000 for a second, and $4500 for each additional child in addition to generous work leaves, tax credits, and interest-free housing loans. *New York Times*, November 5, 1989, 6. Even *Roe* v. *Wade* (410 U.S. at 163–64, p. 478 n.11) says that "a State may have legitimate demographic concerns about its rate of population growth" as a justification for denying or prohibiting third-trimester abortions. See also *Maher* v. *Roe*, 432 U.S. 464 (1977), and Scales (1989), p. 36.
[41]Love and Shanklin (1984). See also Scott (1974).

seem to fear that without a total split, there will be total merging, and the individual will be lost. Such a formulation obscures the fact that the individual is, in many ways, already lost because of the dichotomy. In many respects women are just as socialized in liberal democracy as they are in socialist states, while men are kept from realizing relational autonomy by the fearful need to keep dichotomies rigidly in place.

How would a participatory form of government alter this situation? Participatory democracy would provide for the mingling of public and private by allowing for equality through mutual recognition. The refusal to recognize the other's subjectivity, I have noted, is a source of the dichotomy between public and private. By fostering the recognition of others' subjectivity, a participatory form of government allows for the full engagement of all citizens in political conversation. It further ensures that all citizens have the ability not only to make contributions but to have their contributions accepted and valued as well: they can speak, but they can also be heard. In this sense, participatory democracy is the political counterpart to what Irigaray describes: reciprocal and mutual relations among individuals who are "for" one another, who not only recognize one another's agency but also have as a core goal and concern the development of others' agency. Participation, by allowing for the existence of a self-conscious community of equals—in all senses of that term—can transcend the abstract individualism of liberal democratic society; it can identify a mutality of interests and allow citizens to focus on common goods and exercise collective wills.

Yet because recognition is mutual and reciprocal, individuality remains a vital, even absolutely necessary foundation for this society. Recognition is made of individuals with subjectivity, a subjectivity that consists in varying desires, wants, goals, and visions. Thus, in this feminist construction, the concept of mutual recognition ensures against the subsuming of public into private and vice versa; but at the same time, it also ensures an interactive overlapping and mingling among all aspects of human life. Indeed, the discussion in terms of public and private spheres itself needs to be recast, for it implicitly accepts and works from a concept of duality, finitude, and predetermination. Feminist theory seeks not to mix two separate and predefined entities but to recast human social life in terms of a variety of dynamically interdependent aspects, some of which—the most personal—will be connected to others—the most open and community oriented—only very indirectly. Again, the imagery of a web is appropriate: although some threads are connected directly to some others, and each thread is connected indirectly to all the others, some segments are quite far from others, and a complicated path must often be traced to get from one thread to another. There is no definitive, wall-like division of these aspects from one another, yet there is distance and distinction.

In important ways, if somewhat ironically, Rousseau's concept of participatory democracy hearkens to these elements. I earlier demonstrated that Rousseau's vision of politics depends structurally on the exclusion of women. Yet any consideration of participatory democracy will most readily and obviously bring us back to Rousseauist ideals, though perhaps not to his actual theory. In a society that utilized a feminist conception of obligation, the givenness of obligation would imply that all citizens would not only feel bound to participate politically but perhaps would also want to do so. Rousseau's conception of the political nature of men would find a similar counterpart in the feminist idea that individuals, seeing themselves as selves-in-relationships, will understand that the growth of society is important to their growth as individuals. If recognition of others' subjectivity is a key to individual autonomy and development, this recognition is most readily and effectively made through individuals' political interaction as members of a community. And if the givenness of obligation stems from a recognition of the basic sociability of humans, of the fact that we come to be who we are through relationships, then it is plausible to reason that individuals will come to see social and political interaction as positive, self-fulfilling aspects of their lives.

Rousseau's suggestions concerning economic equality are also relevant to a feminist conception of obligation. A significant source of political inequality can be and has been traced to problems of economic inequality. Rousseau pointed out that laws affect unequals unequally, thus revealing the insufficiency of the tenet of liberalism that people are equal under the law. This issue is an especially appropriate one for a feminist theory of political obligation and society, for women's economic inequality is a particularly important source of their political disenfranchisement. If a woman is the sole supporter of one or more children, makes sixty-four cents to a man's dollar, and therefore can ill afford domestic help or child care, she not only works a long double day but must deal with all the other problems usually associated with poverty as well. Such a woman is hardly likely to have time for politics. So although her participation is not legally proscribed, her exclusion from the public realm is ensured de facto.

Yet since such proscription would fit well with Rousseau's actual theory—in contradiction to his basic theoretical ideals—perhaps a turn to more contemporary models of participatory democracy that are not specifically feminist, particularly those of Benjamin Barber and

Jane Mansbridge, can help develop the role of recognition, trust, and conversation in feminist obligation. Utilizing these models in a feminist theoretical context once again emphasizes the degree to which feminism gives way to a new humanism, a transgendered account of human relations. At the same time, a feminist reading of these works can deepen them to provide an awareness of the degree to which specifically gendered concerns, such as attention to gender inequality, reveals certain limitations of consistency and application, as in my earlier discussion of Rousseau. In contrast to my previous analyses, however, the present discussion seeks not to conclude that participatory democracy, like liberal democracy, is inherently based on women's exclusion but rather to demonstrate how their contingent sexism might be remedied to produce a nonbiased theory of inclusion.[42]

In *Beyond Adversary Democracy*, Mansbridge theorizes two kinds of democracy: adversary and unitary. Adversary democracy is closely allied to what I have been calling liberal democracy. Premised on the notion of individualism and inherent conflict of interest, it holds that society can operate only through the competition of those interests, which must be resolved through majority rule. Linking adversary democracy to the rise of capitalism and the nation-state, phenomena also linked to the rise of liberalism, she argues that although this model is useful to the reconciliation of competing interests, its flaw lies in the exaggeration of the degree to which interests do in fact conflict. In this overemphasis it dehumanizes citizens by denying community, unity, sharing, and common interests.

It is this idea of common interest, of course, that is central to participatory democracies such as Rousseau's and yet is the prime reason for liberalism's objection to such theories. What Mansbridge calls unitary democracy exhibits precisely such common interests, and she attempts to identify them in the democracies she has studied; but in the process she transforms the notion of interest from Hobbes's narrow

---

[42]I admit this may be a somewhat problematic task, for Barber's frequent reference to citizens as "men" and the different roles for women and men in Mansbridge's study of the town meeting in Selby both suggest that there may be as much structural sexism here as in Rousseau's civil society. For instance, in Selby, women participated less than men in the meeting because they were preparing for and cleaning up after the luncheon, or because they had responsibility for child care. See Mansbridge (1980), chap. 5. Although feminists may well point out that these activities are also important forms of participation, in the context of Selby, it is the kind of participation relegated to Sophie and defined as nonpolitical. Yet these are elements of structure that could be changed without any alteration in the mode and meaning of politics, except perhaps to strengthen the participatory structure. In contrast, women's inclusion in Rousseau's Assembly would challenge its very meaning and existence. Barber is a bit more problematic because the sexism of his theory stems largely from unspoken assumptions; yet he also strives on a conscious level to include women along with men, and his theory could be fine-tuned to eliminate its potential for sexism.

egoism to one consistent with "ideal preference"[43] not to replace but to rest side by side with the conventional liberal sense of individual interest. Suggesting, via Aristotle, that friendship is the basis for unitary democracy, Mansbridge argues that we must open up our conceptions of what humans are like, what humans need and want, if we are to achieve political structures that meet those needs and desires. Adversary democracy, she holds, can meet some of them but not all; and indeed, by its "perverse" representation of personhood, adversary democracy ends up promoting the very qualities—manipulation of power, coercion, conformity—that its advocates fear are the inevitable result of unitary democracy.

Unitary democracy creates the conditions most conducive to allowing common interests to present themselves. According to Mansbridge, the "three distinguishing features of a unitary democracy—equal respect, consensus, and face-to-face meetings of the whole—encourage members to identify with one another and with the group as a whole. This process of identification in turn helps develop common interests" (p. 5). Through fostering "emotional identification," participants' "empathy" is developed and enlarged (p. 272); empathy in turn aids citizens in seeing the ways in which their interests are similar, as well as in seeing that differences are not necessarily threatening. Unitary democracies can thus bring forth recognition and trust by "deliberately foster[ing] emotional identification by stressing a shared past. They can consciously create a perception of mutual likeness by harnessing the known effects of experiences like working together under stress, a common 'transcendant' experience, or self-revelation in consciousness-raising sessions and encounter groups. . . . Small size allows an intense interaction that soon becomes a meaningful common history" (p. 243).

In unitary democracy, membership—connection—is something of a given, and hence the obligation is to enact what the group decides. Again, as with Amy's approach to the Heinz dilemma, the need for deliberation and decision is given, but *how* to act is the matter for consideration, not *whether* to act; or at the least, the latter becomes a collective decision and is a function of how (that is, the answer to "how" may well be "do nothing") rather than a separate question that the individual asks of herself when the mode of action is already given by impersonal law or authoritative structures existing above the individual. The focus of unitary democracy is thus the working out, through a process of equal respect—or what I have called mutual recognition—of what the group wants and needs to do. In its method

[43]Mansbridge (1980), p. xii. Subsequent references to this source will be cited in the text.

unitary democracy strives to achieve consensus in face-to-face conversations as a way to work out the content of obligations.

In this process, somewhat reminiscent of Rousseau's general will, Mansbridge asserts that in unitary democracy there often is a "right" answer which can be achieved through the unitary democratic process. But in contrast to "forcer d'être libre," individual participants in the unitary democracies she discusses do not subvert their particular wills or interests to "the group," conceptualizing these two entities as inevitable opposites. Rather, taking the connection of membership as their epistemological starting point, members come to an agreement about the best plan of action through the process of consensus building. The effort to achieve consensus in unitary democracy does not produce "weak compromise" between equally subjective individual interests but rather "the very best plan," which addresses the concerns of the group as a whole through its individual members. But just as it is difficult for theorists trained in the liberal tradition to comprehend fully the importance of mutual trust and recognition, so do "observers in the adversary tradition . . . find it hard to interpret consensus in a positive light" (p. 257–58). Focusing on a "soulless aggregation of interests," liberal adversary democracy can see only the dangers of unitary democracy—conformity, stagnation, manipulation, "too many evenings"—and none of the advantages. Just as liberal theory sees only the positive elements of traditional "masculine" experience (individuality, agency, choice) and the failings of traditional "feminine" experience (emotionality, overidentification, disempowerment), thereby perverting those qualities into things they are not, the adversary democrat, by decrying conformity and lauding individualism, entirely misses the respect and recognition that unitary democracy provides, and the dehumanization and elitism that adversary democracy produces. But human experience needs to encompass both visions.

Mansbridge's description of unitary democracy thus invokes many of the concepts and images embodied in the feminist account of obligation I have discussed. The prominence in her account of mutuality, emotion and feeling, shared felt experience and perception, recognition and equal respect echo the themes in my discussion of obligation. The foundation of unitary democracy in the equal respect of friendship provides a powerful model for the mutual recognition of feminist obligation. And just as the masculine model is not simply wrong but partial and perverse, so must we also recognize the positive dimensions of adversary democracy, as Mansbridge does. There is no necessarily right answer or general will in all cases, after all, which is why Mansbridge urges a combination of the two kinds of democracy, just as I have argued not for the abolition of consent but for its decentralization to allow for other kinds and concepts of obligation.[44] By magnifying certain aspects of human social life and universalizing them to account for the whole of human relations, the truth (though I use that term self-consciously and self-critically) contained in the model becomes distorted, perverted. By taking the masculine model in concert with the feminine model—adversary with unitary— we can reclaim what the former has to say about human beings that is more true, or at least less false.

Similarly, the importance of equality—as opposed to (negative) liberty—as the core political and personal value resonates with a feminist conception of participatory politics. Although both liberal adversary democracy and unitary democracy are concerned with equality, the relative priority and meaning of that term differ. In contrast to liberal democracy's formal de jure equality, unitary democracy is concerned with equal respect, and thus strives to achieve an equality of voice that has substantive weight. This difference, Mansbridge suggests, may ironically be due to unitary democracy's decentralization of equality. It is not an aim so much as a by-product of a more important goal, which she somewhat unfortunately terms "'fraternity'—or, as they [members of the unitary democracies she studied] preferred to call it, 'solidarity,' 'community,' or 'sisterhood.' It was from this concern that their commitment to equality, face-to-face assembly, and consensus primarily derived" (p. viii). Similarly, a feminist politics, in placing connection at its core, would give rise to a concern for equality in interpersonal negotiation and agreement, but again more in the sense of the equal respect inherent in mutual recognition than of a formal, legalistic equality. By conceiving of the world as a network or web of relationships, by placing care and empathy at the core of their moral framework, such citizens would embrace a conception of politics—of conflict resolution, policy making, and common decisions— that gives priority to egalitarian values as a means of promoting relationship, or communitarian values. In this respect Mansbridge's notion of friendship is very useful for a feminist model of caring and empathy, for it provides a "qualitative" equality, "the feeling of equal respect that prevails among friends" (p. 5), rather than the "quantitative" equality attained by weighing competing interests (p. 4).

---

[44]Indeed, it was Mansbridge, in personal conversation, who pointed out to me that my theory calls for a pluralist notion of obligation. By "pluralist," however, I interpreted her to mean not that all grounds—consent, tradition, care—are equally valid, so that we cannot make value discriminations among these sources, but rather that all obligations have elements of more than one source, that there are consensual and nonconsensual elements in at least most obligations. I believe this meaning is most consistent with the reading I have given of Mansbridge's work.

Mansbridge also gives weight to context, substance, and outcome in her remarks about the place of power in the two models of democracy. Arguing that equal power is important only when interests conflict, and that common interests can sometimes be achieved through unequal power, she argues for a concept of equality that is contextual and practical, acknowledging specificity and diversity:

> Thus equal power is a conditional value, not an absolute one. Rather than opposing "democracy" to "elitism" as if equal power were an end in itself, members of a group should spend their scarce resources on making power more equal only when equal power is most needed—when interests most conflict, when equal respect cannot be generated from other sources, and when citizens are atrophying from not having enough power and responsibility. Understanding that even a radical democrat need not press for more equal power in every instance but only when these three ends cannot be achieved by other means is, in my view, the most important practical lesson in this book. (p. ix)

Yet there certainly is a danger of circularity here: unequal power can produce situations in which those in power declare certain interests to be common, thus glossing over and suppressing conflict. Similarly, while Mansbridge holds that unitary democracy "appeals to humanity's most exalted sentiments—the deep joy of spontaneous communion, unselfishness, and commitment to a larger good" (p. 293), she also recognizes its dangerous potential for pressured conformity in the desire to avoid conflict and promote harmony. Adherence to a feminist model of recognition could help provide mechanisms to forestall such dangers. An ongoing conversation that provides for mutual recognition would allow those with less power in enacting a certain policy to retain the equal power of claiming the necessity of being heard. This would ensure that the inequality of power is allowed only *after* it has been determined that the common interest has been declared through consensus, and *after* it has been democratically decided that a temporary unequal distribution of power is the most efficient and desirable way to achieve that common goal. Like Rousseau's distribution of administrative powers—what he calls "government"—a feminist framework would ensure that Mansbridge's unequal power would be created in a limited and conditional manner for a specific end. It would not be the open-ended unequal distribution of power to representatives found in adversary democracy. Hence, whereas Mansbridge holds that unitary democracy is not the same as direct or participatory democracy (p. xi), a feminist concept of obligation would most likely need to embody a generous and inclusive notion of participation to set the terms of and oversee power distribution.

As Barber argues, this would require ongoing popular assembly. Indeed, Barber's own model of "strong democracy" adds much to the foregoing application and can deepen the image of a feminist participatory context within which the content of obligations is worked out. Like Mansbridge, Barber advocates a vision of democracy that incorporates elements of ancient classical republicanism (unitary democracy) with the "thin" democracy of liberal individualism (adversary democracy).[45] What Barber calls "political talk"—similar to feminist conversation—is the chief element of his strong democracy, and certainly the key to drawing out the usefulness of his theory for a feminist concept of obligation. In a way reminiscent of Pitkin, Barber holds that "language is ineluctably communal and its evolution determines the evolution of self and other" (p. 193). Political talk also invokes a concept of "weaving—the interlacing of strands in a cable . . . rather than the forging of links in a chain" (p. 32). The web image once again provides not only a model for substantive value—where priority is given to connection, relationship, affection—but a method, a way to order social relations, to communicate, to arrive at decisions. Thus talk is the key social (inter)activity in strong democracy, stemming from but in turn enhancing and extending human connection; but it is also essential for individual agency as, in an echo of feminist obligation, "Freedom is what comes out of this process, not what goes into it" (p. 152).

Language is thus the key not just to community but to our communal selves, to the dimensions of humanity that need social relationships for their realization. Thus talk produces two primary effects in terms of feminist theory: empathy and recognition. Talk does not

---

[45]Barber (1984). Subsequent references to this source will be cited in the text. Whereas I have paralleled classical republicanism to unitary democracy, Barber might not; but I should also note that I believe Barber mischaracterizes unitary democracy. To the extent that he does so, his theory may indicate a structural gender bias. He characterizes unitary democracy as a Hegelian or Rousseauian nightmare of totalitarianism, forcing individuals to be free rather than providing the means for individuals to free themselves together. He focuses on what Mansbridge identifies as the problems of unitary democracy, such as fear of dissension and pressure to conform. But I believe he goes too far. He describes the problem of democracy as "how to contrive institutions that facilitate democracy without supplanting it and that enhance participation without making it unnecessary. The danger is that the nurturing of affective ties will impede genuine cognitive debate and that the enhancement of empathetic imagination will corrupt the capacity for moral autonomy" (p. 233). Barber could be seen here as echoing my warnings about the dangers of overconnection found in the "feminine" or "care model," but he also expresses a specifically masculinist problematic, where empathy and autonomy, affection and cognition, are opposed as dualistic pairs. The problem of democracy then becomes the reconciliation of these pairs, the maintenance of the tension, rather than a full reconceptualization of them as defining each other. This notion is curious, since Barber's thesis is otherwise in agreement with that put forth in the early chapters of this book: that the liberal tension between freedom and community stems from the way the two are conceptualized.

equal "speech," because it includes an empathic "listening," which Barber describes as a striving for mutuality: "Listening is a mutualistic art that by its very practice enhances equality. The empathetic listener becomes more like his interlocutor as the two bridge the differences between them by conversation and mutual understanding" (p. 175). Through listening, what I have called recognition is brought into play: "Consciousness is a socially conditioned intelligence that takes into account the reality of other consciousnesses operating in a shared world" (p. 223). The recognition and awareness of others' subjectivity must logically be a requirement of political talk, because it is attention to others' words that yields the potential for transformation by listening. The collectivity of the effort to achieve a common understanding and agreement requires the recognition of others. Otherwise individuals are trapped in liberal dialogue where competing claims create a cacophony that disempowers them by requiring conflicting parties to give over the decision-making power to a third party, a "representative" government, as the sole way to reconcile these claims. It is only through the mutual recognition found in conversation that people in strong democracy are able to retain the decision-making power for and over themselves as individuals and common members.

Through the process of talking and listening—through this recognition—talk fosters empathy and identity, or "the imaginative reconstruction of self as other" (p. 259). Empathy can help citizens reach consensus by its "power to enlarge perspectives and expand consciousness" (p. 189), by the "commonality and affection" it engenders, by "friendship" (p. 188) forged by the shared political perspective that talk can achieve. Here Barber would appear to diverge from Mansbridge in his analysis of unitary democracy. He criticizes the unitary conception of citizens as brothers as much as he derides the liberal idea of citizens as parties to contracts. In contrast, strong democracy conceives of citizens as "neighbors bound together . . . by their common concerns and common participation in the search for common solutions to common conflicts" (p. 219). For instance, if a group of homeowners on a busy street seeks to put up a stop sign to deter heavy truck traffic or midnight drag racing, it is not merely the interest of each individual, separate from every other, that motivates participation in the effort. I cannot separate my property values from yours; they are intimately interdependent. I am concerned not merely with my own children but with the safety of all children, including— particularly but not exclusively—my own. But this does not make my fellow homeowners and me a family any more than we are just a conglomeration of atoms. We are united by something more than contract, something less than blood and love. It is this sense of common concern, I believe, that Barber seeks to elucidate.

But of course talk does not always produce such understanding. Mansbridge's more overt recognition of this fact creates a perhaps more realistic reconciliation of adversarial and unitary democracy. Yet like Mansbridge, Barber does not argue that strong democracy requires a transformation of human nature. Rather, he operates from the notion that humans already have these potentials, but that our skewed (theoretical) understanding of humanity makes it easy to forget or ignore precisely the social dimensions of humanity that participatory democracy calls on. Liberalism has exaggerated certain human characteristics (those pertaining to separation and individualism) at the expense of others (those pertaining to connection and sociability), distorting the former and repressing the latter. Like Mansbridge (as well as Gilligan, Chodorow, Hartsock, and Belenky et al.), Barber advocates restoring the balance, and in the process transcending liberalism; he seeks "to develop a form of political consciousness [that is, mutual recognition] that will *enlarge* the understanding and sympathies of interest-motivated individuals" (p. 173; emphasis added).

As gender psychology reveals, empathy is not a Humean "artificial virtue." It is a human potentiality that is more predominant in some people's understanding of the world than in others'. That there is a gender relationship associated with greater and lesser empathy is highly significant but not determining; and in the notion of its potential in all people lies the hope for the success of a participatory politics. Like Hume, Barber posits empathy as a product of the imagination. Exercise of the imagination is part of the activity that is required of citizens engaged in strong talk: seeing identity between self and others, trying to see the situation from others' points of view even when in severe disagreement, imagining satisfactory solutions to objections others have raised even when they are in the minority. Indeed, the power of talk is "to stretch the human imagination so that the *I* of private self-interest can be reconceptualized and reconstituted as a *we* that makes possible civility and common political action" (p. 190). Whereas Hume argued that sense perception (for instance, seeing someone in pain) stirs the imagination, Barber holds that talk stimulates the imagination; but though Hume doubted that the imagination itself leads to action, Barber holds that the imagination further stimulates talk, decision, and action. As in feminist conversation, talk in strong democracy is not adversarial; one listens not to discover the weaknesses of other arguments but rather to help put oneself in others' place (p. 175). Talk in strong democracy is "affective" as well as "cognitive" (p. 176). But it is also pragmatic, concerned with concrete realities rather than abstract principles and rules. Thus Barber holds that "political talk is not talk *about* the world" as some predetermined and unified reality; rather, "it is talk that makes and remakes the world" (p. 177). Thus real talk involves setting agendas, defining the terms and subjects of political discourse and even citizenship itself. It is not merely limited to discussion of an agenda predetermined by an entity smaller than the group but involves an ongoing process of renegotiation.

It is in this potential for empathy that the hope for the success of a participatory politics lies. Empathy and recognition give rise to inclusion, an element as obvious and necessary to strong democracy as it is to feminist obligation. For both, inclusion is sought even at the possible cost of error. Participation in conversation must be universal; the burden of proof must be on those who wish to exclude. Participatory politics is "served by many voices rather than by one" (p. 185). Yet the process of talk "respects the *initial* legitimacy of every human perspective" (p. 185; emphasis added). There are no prima facie first principles for strong democracy, but neither does it become mired in an absolute relativism. Thus, a nonracist majority would be required to listen to and talk with a white supremacist but not to accommodate her views in policy, for she would in turn have to listen to the majority. If she refused, then she would no longer be maintaining the lines of communication, thus justifying a temporary end to the conversation. But Barber's provision that the white supremacist be allowed to reexpress herself periodically is the key to at least minimizing the danger of suppressing minority voices.[46] In this Barber seeks to combine the majority rule–minority rights approach of liberal democracy with the consensual collectivism of unitary democracy, as the centrality of difference is rescued from a paralyzing emotivism and the primacy of inclusion is saved from coerced homogeneity.

This example again indicates a theoretical and political priority of *how* to act over *whether* to act. The question for the strong democrat is, "What shall we do *when something has to be done* that affects us all, we wish to be reasonable, yet we disagree on means and ends and are without independent grouds for making the choice?" (pp. 120–121; emphasis added). If inclusion is a given, the issue is not *whether* the white supremacist needs to be included but *how* she can be included without her views dominating de facto, that is, without her initial premise—that nonwhites do not deserve recognition—being accepted. Although a theory of mutual recognition does not exclude such philosophies outright, it does create a structure in which such

[46]Even criminals, who Barber says may be temporarily excluded because the criminal act involves a voluntary breaking of communication with the community, may reclaim membership by reentering the dialogue; presumably jailed criminals would be allowed to vote (contrary to contemporary U.S. law) and participate in Barber's video town meetings.

views would have a difficult time surviving. Strong democracy does this as well. It puts the burden of problems raised by a view on its advocates: those advocating abortion on demand are asked to determine how the rights of children, even of fetuses, are to be safeguarded; those opposed to public funding for abortion are asked to determine how to address the inequities produced by unequal wealth (p. 289). In both, the assumptions of inclusion and recognition pass over the issue of *whether* these problems need to be addressed and proceeds to *how* they can be solved. So a white supremacist would be asked to determine how nonwhites can be granted mutual recognition: how to provide for the genuine and full inclusion that nonwhites are entitled to by virtue of their biological humanity, how to ensure that they are heard and listened to. Through this strategy, as Mansbridge also suggested, the notion of a "right answer" suggests itself, because white supremacists cannot answer those questions without violating the very premise of their philosophy. Indeed, that initial premise is automatically disqualified. As in feminist conversation, the requirement of recognition as a basic foundation ensures that the only way to solve political disagreements is through the exercise of empathy, listening, and mutual respect. This solution at once provides for the protection of minorities that liberalism provides while also promoting the development of empathy and inclusive community in precisely those who seek to exclude. The process of conversation thus maintains the quality of working differences through to agreement, without conformity.

The context of participatory democracy helps make more sense of a feminist concept of obligation and its enterprise of determining the content of specific obligations, especially political obligations. Participatory democracy helps locate the concepts of mutuality, recognition, and trust in concrete ways. In particular, the models offered by Barber and Mansbridge suggest how a feminist theory of obligation that works from the priority of inclusion and recognition provides a model or guide for a form of political life that can transcend gender even as it attends to and redresses the problems and concerns that gender inequality raises.

More broadly, however, this discussion of the context of political obligation shows how participatory democracy can in turn be deepened by a feminist theoretical framework. For the model of participatory democracy pursued here turns on the notion that empowerment engenders responsibility. Including all in a full citizenship, one that is engaged in decision making, agenda setting, discussion, and action, will encourage the development of humans' ability to think of concrete factors, of ends and outcomes, and not just of abstractions and processes. In other words, inclusion provides the grounds and context for people to adopt a responsibility approach to moral and political issues. Acting responsibly involves a two-way relationship of trust: I may (have to) trust you to act responsibly, but in turn your acting responsibly can make you vulnerable, as Hobbes most brilliantly argued. The first to fulfill her end of the contract risks giving without getting; the first to put down her weapon risks being killed. Indeed, in the ontology of social contract theory, responsibility can be seen as *too* risky. We fall back on rights to protect ourselves from hostile others. But that itself suggests a certain arrest in human development, as in reactive autonomy. Participatory democracy, by contrast, suggests the development of a relational autonomy. Through empowerment, responsibility becomes more possible and safe; hence, in synergistic fashion, trust can flourish more readily and easily, and recognition of mutually respecting subjects can become a new epistemological framework to support a democratically empowering model of political action. As rights dialogue provides a language of distrust and competition, a responsibility model offers a language of trust and relationship. Only through the mutuality of talk, inclusion, and participation can trust flourish and hence can responsibility be the primary focus of political actors, with rights taking a secondary (albeit perhaps still important) role.

This model also of necessity places difference, or human heterogeneity, at its core. Liberal theory generally assumes that any participatory politics, working as it does by way of discussion, negotiation, and ultimately agreement, must work from assumptions of sameness, unity, and conformity. Yet Barber has argued that the opposite is the case, that difference and individuality are better preserved through the empowerment that liberal democracy denies and that strong democracy affords. And although Mansbridge allows for a "right answer" to be discovered through unitary democratic means and forms, her argument demonstrates even more richly than Barber's the ways in which difference can operate to strengthen community rather than necessarily pulling it apart. She redefines difference so that it is just that: different, not opposed. A feminist concept of difference draws in part on the liberal claim that humans have their own interests and preferences, personalities with particular strengths and weaknesses, often in unique combinations; but unlike liberalism it denies that this makes humans fundamentally incompatible and opposed.

In this sense a feminist concept of diversity highlights the poverty of what liberalism calls difference. Liberal obligation theory ostensibly claims the primacy of individual freedom, but in fact individuals have little freedom at all in their political obligations; authoritarian community is the true value underwriting disingenuous claims to liberty. Similarly, while liberalism makes loud claims about the irreconcilability of conflicting human interests, it actually denies heterogeneity by locating differences among people within a context of sameness, and it does so in at least two ways. First, it assumes that humans' *motivation* in their various interests is all the same, that different interests all have a similar genesis, that there is a unified human nature that creates these "inevitable" conflicts. Second, it also assumes a univeral agreement on the *means* of reconciling difference, that is, the social contract. By claiming that consent to the social contract is in fact universal—by claiming that it is tacit, implied, inferred, hypothetical, and so forth—liberalism maintains that there is a fundamental identity among humans that supercedes and overrides, theoretically *and* practically, the ostensible centrality of differences among people. In so doing, liberalism privileges some perspectives and desires over others; just as some are "more equal" than others, so are some "more different" than others. By overtly equating difference with opposition, and then placing it in a hidden context of unity, liberalism cheapens and corrupts difference. In casting a dualistic typology of difference and sameness, it fails to recognize nuances and multiplicity of difference. It imposes a false one-to-one correlation between similar interests and an exaggerated or false opposition on different views.

We have seen the structural gender bias of such a conceptualization. Just as the boy's apparently stronger identity is revealed to be fragile and artificial because it depends on a dualistic conception of being not-female or not-other, so does this artificial and exaggerated concept of difference belie the complexity of individual differences and thus trade an apparent heterogeneity for an actual homogeneity. In contrast, feminist obligation operates from a more complex notion of difference by recognizing the ways in which qualities of overlapping, of sharedness, of nuance all play important parts in an understanding of diversity. It further acknowledges that feelings, emotions, beliefs, and reasons can generate different preferences and also different ways in which those preferences are developed and satisfied. A feminist notion of human heterogeneity thus embraces a concept of difference that is more complete—at least in the sense of being more inclusive, of including a vaster array of genuine differences—that recognizes that differences among people do not constitute a linear duality. Again, the image of a web comes into play: each thread represents a distinct view or experience which is not identical to any other but which shares certain common points of intersection; or, to invoke Wittgenstein, each perspective has a family resemblance to other perspectives but rarely exhibits a one-to-one correlation or identity with any other.

Yet here it may become more apparent than anywhere else in my argument that the metaphors of continuum and web are still somehow inadequate to the feminist vision I have articulated. Because both employ images of center and periphery, the notion of privileging some perspectives over others—some differences over others—seems unavoidable. But if the concept of difference I am suggesting is successfully employed, then there can be no periphery or end points—and hence no fixed center, if any center at all—because new perspectives, experiences, views—new differences—are constantly being introduced and must be included. The edges of the web continually grow, change, shift, decentering what may previously have been at the center. Thus, even when at any given time it may appear that a specific participatory democracy has considered and included all the possible differences its current members can conceive, a self-critical and self-conscious attention to diversity prevents any one position from occupying a center in the hegemonic way in which that term is used in the modern era. An implicit recognition of the temporality and nonabsoluteness of any collective decision creates a world where new centers are always possible and likely; new factors may be added on to the periphery, thus creating a temporary new center. Or at least, if there is a relatively consistent center to this web, it lies not in any substantive viewpoint of any given group or individual but rather in the priority of difference and recognition themselves.

The centrality of human heterogeneity to feminist politics obviously requires a participatory framework for its realization. If difference is to be not only respected, in the sense of tolerated, which often suggests the liberal passivity of "equal opportunity," but also encouraged, developed, even centered, then all differences must have equally powerful means of expression. The conversation provides this means, for it ensures recognition of all perspectives, as well as the working out of ways of resolving colliding differences, which do not merely accommodate all differences in a liberal relativism but allow for a common and collective evaluation of difference that can strive for agreement without uniformity, that can maintain the priority of recognition *both* procedurally (allowing all views to be expressed and heard) *and* substantively (not allowing inherently exclusive views such as white supremacy or Nazism to dominate). This "both-and" approach of feminist inquiry contrasts with the either-or approach of liberalism, in which substance is always sacrificed to procedure because the two are seen as inherently contradictory; for once again this supposed contradiction masks the degree to which liberal procedure in fact privileges a very particular substantive position.

Iris Young, in "Impartiality and the Civic Public," has argued for something similar to the model of participatory politics I have presented here. She places "discourse" at the center of a feminist conception of the political. Arguing that the unity found in "malestream" democratic theory (the common good, the general will) has been preserved by modern theory only through the exclusion of certain groups of people, particularly women and some racial groups, she supports the notion that racism and sexism are structural biases of modern theory.[47] Only by rejecting a false concept of universality and unity, only by embracing particularity, partiality, need, and emotion, can a feminist politics be realized; and these qualities can be embraced only if interactive, mutually respectful discussion is part of what we call public activity. She draws partially (and critically) on Habermas's concept of reason, which is closer to Barber's "reasonableness" and Flathman's "good reasons" than to liberal positivist rationality (p. 68). She also works from Habermas's ideal of a "communicative ethics" in which conversation provides

> a conception of rationality with a pragmatic starting-point in the experience of discussion that aims to reach an understanding. Reason in such a model does not mean universal principles dominating particulars, but more concretely means giving reasons, the practical stance of being reasonable, willing to talk and listen. Truth and rightness are not something known by intuition or through tests of consistency, but only achieved from a process of discussion.   (p. 68)

Communicative ethics invokes a notion of "reason as contextualized, where answers are the outcome of a plurality of perspectives that cannot be reduced to unity" (p. 69).

Young also draws on the French feminist Julia Kristeva to argue that "communication is not only motivated by the aim to reach consensus, a shared understanding of the world, but also and even more basically by a desire to love and be loved" (p. 72), describing a community in which morality and emotion are linked. Again Gilligan's assertion that morality and love are intertwined is invoked; love is an entity so central to humanity that it must be included in public conversation and particularly in our interpreting what others say—their needs, desires, preferences, beliefs in all their particularity—if public heterogeneity is to be realized, as it must be if recognition is to be genuine. A feminist communicative ethics involves the intermingling of interpersonal relationships and multiple dimensions of every person involved in the conversation with the traditional activities and

---

[47]Young (1987), p. 63. Subsequent references to this source will be cited in the text.

aims of politics. Individuals are not sequestered in a private sphere. Instead their political features are drawn on and highlighted to the end of liberating participants from the "discipline" of the public-private dichotomy of liberalism. Young particularly draws on the politics of the "rainbow coalition," which does more than merely respect differences and particularity. She argues that it "institutionalizes in its form of organizational discussion the heterogenous groups that make it up" (p. 76).

Young is not the only theorist to call for a rainbow coalition as a model of feminist politics. Nancie Carraway, Teresa de Lauretis, and Linda Alcoff all see identity politics as a way to reconcile the need to recognize and incorporate difference and particularity with the need for theory.[48] In identity politics, "one's identity is taken (and defined) as a political point of departure, as a motivation for action, and as a delineation of one's politics."[49] Identity politics starts from an understanding of how certain of our features and characteristics (such as skin color and body parts) become social constructions (called race and gender) over which we have little choice or control, but which nevertheless have tremendous political significance in determining the power relationships that affect our lives. But identity politics also involves a choice of identity, an explicit naming of who one is, and hence reflects our abilities to create ourselves. Thus, my having a vagina and breasts may mean that society labels me "woman," but I choose a political identity as "feminist" as a stance to empower me to analyze and name the ways in which my identity as woman is created for me and in which it holds both potential and actual power for me to create myself. Certain Americans of color may be called Negroid but may choose a political identity of African-American to acknowledge and announce explicitly to the world their history as both an oppressed and a self-empowered people. These political identities reflect and help to deconstruct the oppressive social constructions that victimize and discipline individuals, but they also contain great liberatory potential; and in this, identity politics once again demonstrates the affinity between postmodern feminism and standpoint epistemology. For the liberating potential in identity politics comes from the achieved position of feminist or African-American; and the achievement stems partly from the oppressive social construction, partly from the human responses to that oppression that lead in liberatory

[48]See Alcoff (1988), Carraway (1989), de Lauretis (1989). Nor is Young the only one to invoke Habermas; Love (1989), Fraser (1991), and (perhaps to a lesser extent) Benhabib (1987), adopt a Habermasian concept of communicative ethics to construct a feminist democratic politics.

[49]Alcoff (1988), pp. 431–32.

directions, and partly from the conscious recognition of the political potential lying dormant in the identity.

Identity politics can thus provide a political epistemology for a conversational participatory democracy. Indeed, it suggests what I call caucus democracy, an idea that might helpfully supplement Mansbridge's and Barber's participatory democratic models. In caucus democracy the multiplicity of individuals' identities is realized and enacted through the existence of political groups that embrace these identities in their most basic, even crude form—feminists, African-Americans, senior citizens, parents of adolescents, and so forth—cohering with different aspects of various people's experiences. Countless groups could exist (though by the standards of inclusion and recognition that I discussed earlier, groups that advocated nonrecognizing beliefs would not be likely to exist for long). And since any individual has multiple identities, individuals could belong to as many groups as they wished, though they would not *have* to belong to any group with a claim on their identity. For instance, I might be the parent of an adolescent, but I might consider that a less important aspect of my identity than, say, my race or the kind of work I do. Caucuses could help facilitate participatory democracy by providing a kind of representation to individuals (if individuals desired it) and by helping to articulate the meanings and agendas for these identities. They could thus provide an extra source of empowerment, perhaps as a means to help in the transition from adversary to unitary, from liberal to strong, from masculinist to feminist democracy.

The rainbow coalition that Young in particular links to identity politics coheres with the idea of caucus democracy and provides an extremely useful image for the feminist theory I have been building here. The inclusive character of the rainbow coalition—Jesse Jackson's image of the patchwork quilt in his 1988 Democratic convention speech comes most eloquently to mind[50]—is a particularly powerful embodiment of feminist notions of recognition and diversity. As Young says, a "heterogenous public asserts that the only way to ensure that public life will not exclude persons and groups which it has excluded in the past is to give specific recognition to the disadvantage of those groups and bring their specific histories into the public."[51] This is particularly important to the attempt to develop a feminist concept of politics in a world that perpetrates and allows so many gross inequities and disadvantages. A society that embraced feminist values of connection would give priority to the problems faced by

[50]Jackson (1989).
[51]Young (1987), p. 76.

those previously excluded and disadvantaged. In this, the political claims of various feminist groups are in accordance with the theoretical principles outlined here. Federally funded day care or supplemental compensation for child rearing, stricter controls over child support and more equitable divorce laws, the recognition of abortion as an issue of responsibility and concern and not just a right, stronger affirmative action programs, equitable credit legislation for women: all of these would provide women increased access to political participation, to involvement in the stream of political life, and to an effective voice in the decisions of their society. As such they would be compatible with and instrumental in the realization of a feminist theory of obligation, for only with such political voice can women achieve the full expression of their connectedness to others in community.

Such a construction of the political would also address a more deep-seated aspect of women's exclusion; for not only is women's isolation from political community in the public-private split a factor to be considered, but their isolation from one another through the patriarchal nuclear family is also a source of political disenfranchisement. Such isolation keeps women from realizing their connectedness, which sits at the heart of a feminist understanding of political life while promoting the abstract individualist forces of liberal theory and institutions. Ruddick points out how many positive aspects of maternal practice can degenerate into narrow-mindedness and selfishness through the incorporation or imposition of patriarchal values.[52] Extension of relationships, which would enable a mother to perceive the connections between her maternal concerns and the welfare of children not her own, becomes difficult; concern with relationship degenerates into selfish concern for the good of one's immediate family. These perversions actively contribute to perpetuating the competition of the market, which, as we have seen, is harmful to women. Ann Ferguson has argued that Victorian culture not only created moral values that oppressed women but also ensured their success by making women the moral guardians of their own enslavement.[53] This same argument can be made about the market and the family as well, for in such a perversion of maternal practice as can happen in a competitive market society, by being "good mothers" women can and do swiftly become the unwitting but fierce protectors of their own political muteness and economic powerlessness.

Certainly, community among women is not the sole requirement for political participation, for such community has existed throughout history in a variety of cultures and at a number of historical moments

[52]Ruddick (1984a).
[53]Ferguson (1984).

without substantially changing women's political status. But the absence and prevention of such community is even more common, particularly in modern liberal societies, and contributes considerably to women's exclusion from politics. The existence of such community would enable women's historical experiences, and the feminist epistemology these give rise to, to enter into our understanding of obligation and thus to foster new ways of looking at and conceptualizing the questions of determination that obligation raises. The realization of community would thus bring to light the political and collective aspects of responsibilities commonly ascribed to individuals. For instance, a woman's decision about how best to meet obligations of child care would no longer be considered merely her problem; it would exist and be made within a context of community care for children and the active engagement of other adults (the father, an extended family, and so on). As the privatization of women is ended, their political responsibility would be increased in two ways. With that responsibility divided among various participants, women would be freer to engage in traditional political activities and responsibilities; but also the political nature of their conventional responsibilities, such as child care, would be not only recognized but recognizable.

The feminist construction of the political offered here reflects the idea that a feminist theory of obligation must derive from women's material experiences and practices. Women's material work, both for wages and in the home, their affective production, reproduction, maternal thinking, and sexual relations all concretely reveal how a feminist perspective can yield a concept of obligation as given and a concept of morality and political theory deriving from that. A feminist understanding of obligation requires a fundamental rethinking and restructuring of the way politics is conceived and implemented. And this restructuring brought about through a feminist politics in turn contributes to the attempt of feminist theory to refocus our thinking about political obligation. It urges us not to concern ourselves with the genesis of obligations but to attend to their content. A feminist conception of obligation shifts attention from the questions Should I act? Do I have an obligation? to How should I (or we) act? How should I (or we) fulfill my (our) obligations? Such a shift of focus does not eliminate the existence of a gray area in morality, of course; a feminist ethic will certainly not make all questions of obligation and morality cut and dried. But neither can one say that this shift, by not eliminating all gray areas, gets us no further than consent theory. Certainly, by paying attention to the context of concrete circumstances and relationships we can narrow the range of answers to a stricter scope than a vague location somewhere between minimal altruism and the cut-off for heroism. But even without such narrowing, focusing our attention on the question of *how* to meet the obligation is a far cry from saying that the relevant question is *whether* to act. Surely the question of *how* does not always have a determined and definitive answer; but consent theory in particular points to that fact as a sufficient reason to conclude that we must leave the question of *whether* completely to the individual.

Consent theory involves an all-or-nothing approach to morality and obligation which denies at the outset the reality and necessity of the nonconsensual obligations with which women are historically familiar. Yet it is precisely the desire for the all-or-nothing approach, which is part of the problem of masculinist ideology, that has given consent theory its hold, for it provides the (masculinized) individual with the illusion of total control over his life: obligations exist only if one creates them; (political) connection can exist only by virtue of (social) contract. But, as I have shown, many unplanned aspects of life exist beyond our control to create connection and obligation without our consent, a fact that reproduction makes most apparent but is demonstrated by other examples as well. These examples, taken not solely but in important ways from women's lives and history, compel our attention, as the contemporary demand for gender equality makes more and more apparent the fundamental ways in which the worlds of both politics and philosophy have been structured to exclude women.

Women's experience also provides the basis for the more constructive project of envisioning a feminist alternative to liberal obligation theory. Critically theorizing women's historical experiences—particularly their experiences as mothers and daughters, as well as their experiences of moral dilemmas from the perspective of relative powerlessness—produces an epistemological framework for an understanding of liberal obligation theory and its representation of social relations, politics, and the state. Deconstructing these experiences to learn how what we call feminine or female is in part shaped by patriarchy simultaneously reveals that patriarchy does not determine all aspects of women's experience, but rather that women's capacity for choice and action means that their responses to the strictures of patriarchy in turn shape the (patriarchal) world. In this capacity and its results we find the grounds for a feminist conception of obligation that can make sense of the notion of obligation as given, that can begin theoretical reasoning and political argumentation from starting points of connection and relationship. This approach eliminates many of the structurally sexist problems of liberal obligation theory from the start by re-envisioning what and who human beings are. Through a reconceptualization of who citizens are and what sorts of characteristics they are likely to display, their desires and preferences as political actors and subjects, their relation to the state and fellow citizens, even the possible lines of thought that citizens may engage in and hence the possible conclusions that they may reach are all radically reformulated through the adoption of different starting points and epistemological assumptions.

As I earlier (dis)claimed, a feminist theory of obligation could not define obligation in the same ways that we are used to in post-Enlightenment political theory, because there is no way both to attend to context and predefine obligation. Nevertheless, I have sought to provide guidance as to how a community engaged in the struggle to define and act out obligations might (have to) proceed. It may not be as fully developed a picture as it could be (I will make the standard though legitimate plea that such a project requires another book), but perhaps that reflects the difficulty of an honest attempt to struggle with the immense problem of concretizing the general principles drawn from feminist standpoint epistemology and gender psychology.

There is, for my purposes, only one step remaining in the present project, and that is to critique the very enterprise in which I have just engaged. The challenges of feminist postmodernism have presented themselves throughout the book, requiring immediate if brief responses accompanied by promissory notes to explore such issues more fully. It is time to claim payment on those notes, for an exploration of feminist postmodernism is necessary on two counts. On the one hand, a consideration of postmodernism may help me anticipate certain readers' objections to the dangers latent in the foregoing account of replacing one totalizing fiction—the social contract and consent—with another—participatory democracy and recognition. On the other hand, postmodern insights can also help explain and strengthen the foregoing argument (and hence forestall the potential objections of an entirely different set of readers) by providing a sophisticated theoretical framework on which a feminist democracy can hang its hat. Although these two goals may seem to travel in conflicting if not opposite directions, they illustrate the carefully crafted ambiguity of postmodern theory. Feminist postmodernism probably presents the most serious challenge to feminist standpoint theory (though it also provides one to gender psychology) and therefore must be addressed if the feminist theory of obligation that I have crafted is to stand.

Afterword: Democracy, Difference, and Deconstruction

A THEORY OF feminist obligation requires us to attend to the political context for obligations, and that context requires participation, communication, and interpersonal relationship as the model for political community. I admit that this "conclusion" may seem somewhat inconclusive to many readers, not all of them traditional or mainstream. Describing the context for obligation may be interesting and useful, but it is still not the same as developing a theory of obligation such as consent theory. If obligation is given, what are those obligations *to*? What are my *exact* political obligations in any given situation? In any given relationship? In any given society? The short answer is that citizens are obligated to connections and relationship with their fellow citizens. Their obligation is one of participation, involvement, the conversation itself. But if that is the case, then feminism would seem to get us no further than consent theory, because it seems to beg rather than answer the questions of obligation and leaves wide open the idea of content. There is no formula for describing what any given community, regardless of its context, can require of its members when it engages obligation.

Individualism and consent theory have the advantage of being clear-cut; by focusing on procedure, liberal democratic theorists can point precisely to what one is obligated to do in a particular case and to how one became obligated. A possible problem with feminist theory is that it often seems unable to reach the kind of crisp, incisive conclusions that liberal theory does seem to achieve and which have set the standards for philosophy and political theory. In one sense, of course, this problem is a false construction of patriarchal epistemology and a sexist academy. In other words, it can be argued that the valuation of incisiveness and the control it affords are part of the same pathology that produces the masculinism of liberalism. As Flax suggests, "Perhaps 'reality' can have 'a' structure only from the falsely universalizing perspective of the master. That is, only to the extent that one person or group can dominate the whole, will 'reality' appear to be governed by one set of rules or be constituted by one privileged set of social relations."[1] Within such an epistemological structure the goals and conclusions of feminist theory become misunderstood not only by "malestream" theorists but also by feminists themselves trained in the disciplinary standards and expectations of their professions: "The complexity of our questions and the variety of the approaches to them are taken as signs of weakness or failure to meet the structures of preexisting theories rather than as symptoms of the permeability and pervasiveness of gender relations and the need for new sorts of theorizing."[2]

But in another sense the problem is genuine and stems from the current state of feminist theory. Apparent inconclusiveness may be an unfortunate price that feminists must pay for attempting to argue for a new theory within the epistemological and conceptual framework of the old. Feminist theory often finds itself at the stage of laying groundwork; being beholden to their predecessors, feminists may feel intellectually uncomfortable about assuming a vision of people so vastly different from the dominant view. More significant, however, that dominant view exerts limits on the kinds of alternatives that *can* be conceived. Feminists work, after all, in a tradition with a language and must work within that language if they are to be understood. In this light, feminist theory, as much as women's experience, is in part shaped and defined by the dominant masculinist discourse. That may seem to slow down the process. Yet this method of analysis within existing frameworks seems an important tactic for feminist theory, even if it means that the theory appears to fail to measure up to standards established by the discourses it seeks to deconstruct.

This last term will lead many readers to question whether an exploration of postmodernism can help explain the apparent inconclusiveness that may seem to some to mar the previous chapter. As Harding argues, feminist theory is and should be opposed to complete and completed universal theories of explanation: "Feminist analytical categories *should* be unstable at this moment in history. We need to learn how to see our goal for the present moment as a kind of illuminating

[1]Flax (1986), p. 205.
[2]Flax (1990), p. 179.

'riffing' between and over the beats of the various patriarchal theories and our own transformations of them."[3] She points out that "coherent theories in an obviously incoherent world are either silly and uninteresting or oppressive and problematic, depending upon the degree of hegemony they manage to achieve. Coherent theories in an *apparently* coherent world are even more dangerous, for the world is always more complex than such unfortunately hegemonous theories can grasp."[4]

It is in this embrace of complexity that feminist postmodernism has so much to offer. The attention to particularity and difference required by my earlier account of participatory democracy certainly requires that attention be paid to the body of theory most notably concerned with *différance*,[5] namely postmodern theory. Such consideration is important for a more immediate reason as well: the postmodernist challenge, which asserts the dangers of positive (that unfortunate word) theory building, challenges the very legitimacy of the foregoing chapter, specifically the attempt to articulate a new, feminist concept of obligation to replace—or at least displace—the old patriarchal one. My repeated disclaimers throughout the book that I am not creating a new essentialism, that I do not seek a new hegemony to replace the old, that the story I create does not constitute a new totalizing fiction, the qualifications continually introduced into the theory about truth and centers and values, the conditions that are carefully crafted around this feminist theory to make it concrete and particular all fall on cynical postmodern ears as the rejoinder is formed: What you say belies what you do, and what you do is racist, classist, and as a result even sexist.

Elizabeth Spelman, for instance, would most likely maintain that my entire argument is illegitimate on these grounds. In talking about women, she holds, feminist scholars make race and class invisible by not explicitly recognizing and attending to it, and they pervert gender as a result. "Unless I know something more about two women than the fact that they are women, I can't say anything about what they might have in common."[6] Feminists have argued that rape (or the fear thereof), menstruation, pregnancy, abortion as a personal issue (that is, one that potentially affects one's person directly in ways that male persons and bodies are not affected) are all things that any two women may have in common without our knowing anything else about them. Yet, Spelman might reply, either or both of them may be

---

[3]Harding (1986), p. 244.
[4]Ibid., p. 164.
[5]The term is from Derrida (1982), esp. pp. 1–27.
[6]Spelman (1988), p. 136.

unable to conceive—one may lack ovaries and thus not menstruate, one may have been born without a vagina—and these are particularities that would make the two women different from each other. Or if one is poor and Chicana, the other white and wealthy, certain matters such as abortion have very different meanings for the two because of likelihood, availability, necessity, and so forth.

Even the claim that the kind of positive feminist theory building that I attempt in Chapter 6 is necessary to transform political obligation theory—that it is a means to a larger end of gender equality and the transformation of patriarchy which all feminists, postmodern or not, share—falls short for many feminist postmodernists, who respond that their method of deconstruction and analysis already does in fact transform theory, that by decentering the subject of liberalism, by deconstructing its categories of analysis and conceptual vocabulary, it exerts a profound impact not only on actual bodies of theory but also on the way theory is thought about and written.

This last point is compelling. One intention of the present project has been precisely to deconstruct liberalism, to analyze the ways in which patriarchy pervades, informs, and creates liberalism's epistemological foundations, to reveal consent theory's structural sexism. It is my intellectual indebtedness to this enterprise, and to methods that may be seen by some as sympathetic to postmodernism, that leads to the present chapter, for I believe that postmodernism has much to offer feminist theorists. Postmodernism's attention to complexity, its rejection of "one true story" and its recognition of the ways in which exclusion, power, and knowledge interact are important strategies for feminists engaged in the effort to identify and empower their devalued and marginalized differences. Postmodernists' recognition of the dangers of reductively coherent theories that communicate one truth and their complementary sanctioning of a new method of theorizing that is partial, suggestive, and perhaps even tentative in its representation of complexity and particularity provide a model for feminist theory, and it is a method that has been adopted in at least the previous chapter, if it is not evident in other sections of the book.

Indeed, the importance of a postmodern understanding of political life to feminist theory is in a sense precisely the point of the previous chapter. If we are to take seriously the role of context, of concrete relationships and material conditions, if we are to recognize subjectivity and the ongoing particularity of individuals in community, then we can have no formula for obligation. It is here that the postmodern approach can provide a vital theoretical framework for a feminist politics, for it allows—even requires—that there can be no predetermined or even predeterminable answer to the question, What am I obligated to do? In spite of the givenness of obligation, its mode of determina-tion must be pragmatic, "*ad hoc*, contextual, and local."[7]

But then is it legitmate still to call this a *theory*? Is this really political theory anymore, which concerns itself with foundations and struc-tures of states and of the ideals that states embody, or with princi-ples, ideas, and values that guide and shape what we consider to be political? Or is this simply critical analysis, a contribution to the ni-hilistic tendencies of postmodernism to tear down and criticize with-out offering anything better? We are brought face to face with the dilemma that confronts the debate between modernism and post-modernism: What is theory? What is its role, its structure, form, and content? Or, even more provocatively (and perhaps disturbingly), as Glen Tinder asks, "What *should* political theory be now?"[8]

I believe that any answer to that question today will have to include some reference to both feminism and postmodernism; but the precise character of their relationship to each other is a subject for debate that has potentially wide-ranging implications for contemporary political theory. I believe that a growing number of feminist theorists agree with me that postmodernism has a great deal to offer feminists. And almost all also agree that there are some serious problems with the relationship between the two.[9] Thus the debate is not really between feminism and postmodernism as I see it, for such a formulation is itself totalizing, assuming from the start that the two approaches are opposed and contradictory as well as assuming a unity and totality within each school. Rather, the debate is between feminist post-moderns and postmodern feminists. It is my position that there can be a postmodern feminism; that is, in order to realize its goals of deconstructing patriarchy and bringing women's excluded voices in to be heard, feminist theory can and in fact must borrow from certain strategies, insights, and methods that postmodern theories have made accessible and available. But by the same token there cannot be

[7]Fraser and Nicholson (1990), p. 21.

[8]Tinder (1983), p. 153; emphasis added.

[9]Any number of anthologies support this claim. See Nicholson (1990), Bordo and Jaggar (1989), Diamond and Quinby (1988), Benhabib and Cornell (1987), Rhode (1990). See also Alcoff (1988), Flax (1990). Even those who claim to be opposed to postmodern-ism, or at least resolve the dilemma in favor of feminism, obviously draw from post-modern insights: see esp. de Lauretis (1989), Fuss (1989), Schor (1989), Hawksworth (1989), Balbus (1987). Nancy Hartsock is probably among the most strongly opposed, saying that "postmodernism represents a dangerous approach for any marginalized group to adopt." Hartsock (1990), p. 16. Hartsock, however, would not disagree with the interpretation I give to her original feminist standpoint formulation; I have argued that I see that not as a postmodern idea per se but as one that definitely borrows from postmodern insights. Similarly, strong feminist postmoderns such as Susan Hekman (1990) recognize the sexism of Gadamer, Derrida, and others.

a feminist postmodernism. The tenets of postmodern theory make the concept of woman, and hence feminism, impossible. Certainly there are significant differences among postmodern theories; for instance, the postmodernism of Jean Baudrillard offers helpful criticisms of a Foucauldian post-structuralism. But I use the term *postmodernism* in such a way as to link all kinds of postmodernism with post-structuralism because I believe that the perils of post-structuralism in a sense take over all postmodern projects, making a feminist postmodernism impossible. The order of the terms is not a quibble but is very important to this point, for the noun's relation to its modifier indicates the relative priority and, more important, the limits of the terms. With *feminism* as the substantive and *postmodern* as the modifier, the strategies of the latter shape and influence the former but can never come to redefine it out of its own parameters. Thus a postmodern feminism will always have something to do with revaluing *women*, even when that term does not have an essential, natural, unified, or timeless meaning.

The crucial issue between postmodern feminism and feminist postmodernism focuses on different methodological approaches to the question of how to create new theories that recognize difference, particularity, and individuality in genuine ways that neither totalize nor slip over into relativist oblivion. Thus the debate is not between two opposed entities but between—or among—those who slide toward (but not necessarily all the way *to*) different orientations on a continuum. This image may still appear to utilize a dualistic typology, in that every continuum has two opposed extremes, but that may justly be due to the caricatured forms in which feminism and postmodernism have been articulated and constructed and which form the cultural-intellectual context for understanding and defining them. It is to be hoped that reconceptualizing the debate in this new way will lead to a further reformulation of both feminism and postmodernism as existing in a web—a web that comprises many co-identities and strong similarities as well as very weak or distant connections and distinct differences.

Notes toward a Postmodern Feminism

Postmodern theory certainly demonstrates considerable resonance with the political model I have described. A claim that context, concreteness, and particularity are crucial to a feminist understanding of politics locates feminism in postmodern methods. Although postmodern theories demonstrate many variances, all the different strains of postmodern theory are "deconstructive; they seek to distance us from and make us skeptical about the ideas concerning truth, knowledge, power, history, self, and language that are often taken for granted within and serve as legitimations for contemporary Western culture."[10] This is obviously important to a variety of feminist enterprises dedicated to displaying the ways in which mainstream political theory is really "malestream." The chief effects of such deconstruction for the present work include the decentering of the liberal subject, the revelation that the universal "man" of liberal theory is a historically located subject with a particular race and class as well as gender. Postmodernism can help reveal that what has been claimed to be universal, timeless, and true is actually particular and temporal, if not downright false. It helps uncover the ways in which the timeless and universal images of modern political theory, particularly the social contract and political obligation, in fact describe particular people of a particular race, gender, class, historical period, and culture. Indeed, it seeks to "replace the search for and enunciation of truth . . . with the art of conversation or persuasive speech,"[11] a redirection of theory and politics similar to what I have already suggested.

Along these lines, the recognition of gender as a social construction is another element common to postmodern theories which a feminist methodology finds valuable. The problem of attributing certain "natural" qualities to women—whether unrestrainable animal sexuality or modesty and shame, helpless weakness or maternal omnipotence, hopeless emotional irrationality or manipulative cunning, whether being guardians of virtue or the devil's temptress—is something for which feminists criticize modern political theory. The argument that gender is socially constructed—whether through socialization and role learning, through the psychosexual effects of a socially created institution of mother-only child rearing, or through attitudes toward and treatment of pregnancy and sexuality—is a powerful feminist tool for establishing and understanding the ways in which women's identities have been made for them by men. But postmodern theory goes beyond this sociological notion of construction to a more deeply theoretical level concerning the ways in which language determines knowledge and creates power to the extent that it is virtually impossible to see all the ways we are constructed. As Linda Alcoff describes it, "We are constructs—that is, our experience of our very subjectivity is a construct mediated by and/or grounded on a social discourse beyond (way beyond) individual control. As Foucault puts it, we are

[10]Flax (1990), p. 29.
[11]Ibid., p. 32.

bodies 'totally imprinted by history.' "[12] Postmodernism thus uncovers the ways in which women's experiences and identities—including the standpoints of connection, context, and care—are shaped and defined not just by patriarchal practices and institutions but by patriarchal discourses as well.

Like the standpoint epistemology utilized in earlier chapters, postmodernism is also concerned with the problem of duality; it seeks to reveal how the world is structured in terms of opposed pairs (or "binary oppositions," to borrow from Derrida) and to recognize how these dualities are not only artificial but perverting. They create realities that discipline people into certain identities which are not only not of their own making but are oppressive as well. Thus Susan Hekman writes: "The strongest argument for a postmodern feminism is still that, unlike any other contemporary philosophical position, postmodernism attacks and seeks to overturn the polarities of western thought that have resulted in the inferior status of women. The postmodern position offers the only truly radical critique of that dichotomy. Instead of attempting to reverse it . . . the postmoderns attempt to transcend it."[13]

I believe Hekman is in fact a feminist postmodern rather than a postmodern feminist, because she is dedicated to the goals and not just the methods of postmodernist enterprises. Her embrace of Derrida in particular supports my belief, although Derrida himself offers methodological insights that are vital to a postmodern feminism. As Hekman argues, Derrida "supplies a reconceptualization of epistemology that is uniquely suited to the demands of contemporary feminism."[14] Most obviously, he provides the method of deconstruction, the negative approach utilized throughout this book. Particularly important is his attention to the deconstruction of the binary oppositions male-female, subject-object, self-other, in which the former is not only opposed but superior to the latter. Parallel to my own argument in Chapter 5, Derrida challenges not merely dominant epistemologies themselves but western conceptualizations of what can count as epistemology. For instance, my earlier argument that epistemology and ontology are linked in important ways can be seen as somewhat Derridean. Indeed, that discussion, in which I argued that epistemology and ontology may be viewed as neither opposed nor coextensive but as overlapping and occupying shared space, invokes Derrida's notion of "the in-between," which Mary Poovey points out comes from Derrida's concern with the deconstruction of binary op-

[12]Alcoff (1988), p. 416.
[13]Hekman (1989), p. 25.
[14]Ibid., p. 4. See also Hekman (1990), chaps. 1 and 2.

positions. She argues that the notion of "the in-between" suggests that it is the opposition itself, and not merely the things that are opposed, that are social constructions.[15] But I read this as further suggesting that the space *between* subject and object, self and other, male and female—between all the signifiers of paired oppositions—constitutes a separate meaning; and that meaning adheres not just to the words themselves but to the relationships the terms have to one another. Although this notion certainly coheres with the idea that the opposition of, say, male and female is itself a social construction, such a conception of meaning also challenges the ways in which we have previously looked for—and found—meaning, and thus radically alters not just how we think of what is represented by the term *woman* or *man* but how we think about our thinking about those terms.

Derrida's approach to theory creates a "politics of resistance"[16] that is useful to feminism. He has in mind particularly resistance to the totalizing fiction of a single, unified, and unitary truth that explains all peoples and cultures. As he writes in *Spurs*, "There is no such thing as a truth in itself. But only a surfeit of it. Even if it should be for me, about me, truth is plural."[17] "Hence the heterogeneity of the text."[18] The absence of unified truth means that texts, such as political theories, have multiple meanings; they contain complex layerings of representation, and narrate multiple and multifaceted stories. But Derrida also seeks to resist a Hegelian dialectical approach wherein the opposed pairs create a synthesis through what he calls "undecidables, that is, unities of simulacrum, 'false' verbal properties (nominal or semantic) that can no longer be included within philosophical (binary) opposition, but which, however, inhabit philosophical opposition, resisting and disorganizng it, *without ever* constituting a third term, without ever leaving room for a solution in the form of speculative dialectics."[19]

Derrida's resistance to the restrictive categorization of gender follows from this directly. In challenging the "will to truth," Derrida is particularly concerned with issues of "the female." Derrida introduces the notion of *différance* (spelled with an *a*) to indicate how in binary oppositions the two members of the pair, such as male-female, involve not just "difference" but also "deference," that the dualism involves a hierarchy of superiority and inferiority, power and subjugation. "Neither simply active nor simply passive," *différance* attempts to

[15]Poovey (1988), p. 58.
[16]Hekman (1989), p. 21
[17]Derrida (1978), p. 103.
[18]Ibid., p. 95.
[19]Derrida (1972), p. 43.

communicate the ways in which such differences between nature and culture, subject and object, and particularly men and women are social constructions which we daily perpetuate and participate in and yet have little control over.[20] In viewing women's historical social construction as "ambiguous" in western "logocentric" epistemologies and ontologies, Derrida highlights the ways in which "phallocentric" culture projects certain aspects of all humans, male and female, onto women alone. By then deconstructing "woman," we learn not only what men and women are not but what we are as well. So for instance, in the quoted passage from *Positions* in which Derrida rejects dialectics, he discusses by way of illustration what Gayatri Spivak calls his "hymeneal fable": "The *hymen* is neither confusion nor distinction, neither identity nor difference, neither consummation nor virginity, neither the veil nor the unveiling, neither the inside nor the outside."[21] Linking problems of "representing the female" to truth, Derrida maintains: "There is no such thing as the truth of woman, but it is because of that abyssal divergence of the truth, because that untruth is 'truth.' Woman is but one name for that untruth of truth."[22]

Immediately it sounds as if Derrida echoes Freud in his equation of women with ambiguity. Women are so vague, so ambiguous, that men find it impossible to figure them out. Women are dehumanized through the idealization and abstraction of desire and experience. But Hekman, Poovey, and others maintain that Derrida adopts metaphors of the feminine not to perpetuate the dehumanized, ethereal, and idealized conceptions of women that have pervaded philosophy and political theory, but to highlight the ways in which what we have come to accept as reality or as natural is in fact not only artificial but the product of power. I find this argument persuasive.

Derrida goes on to explain: "The credulous and dogmatic philosopher who *believes* in the truth that is woman, who believes in truth just as he believes in woman, this philosopher has understood nothing. . . . Because, indeed, if woman *is* truth, *she* at least knows that there is no truth."[23] Ironically, this passage invokes notions utilized by a feminist standpoint approach. Hartsock argues that women, by virtue of their oppressed status, are in a "superior" position to men because they have available to them not only their own vision as oppressed but also—because they are forced to engage in it—the vision of reality that the dominant ideology creates and promotes. For Derrida it would seem that because women are the victims, so to speak,

[20]Derrida (1982), p. 9.
[21]Derrida (1972), p. 43; see Gayatri Spivak, "Introduction," in Derrida (1976), p. lxvi.
[22]Derrida (1978), p. 51.
[23]Ibid., p. 53.

of being forced to represent and embody a falsely universalizing set of
characteristics or principles which have been labeled true—victims of
"essentializing fetishes"[24]—they are in a superior position to understand that such truth does not exist, that what they are told they
represent is not the reality that they live: "It rather is the 'man' who
has decided to believe that his discourse on woman or truth might
possibly be of any *concern* to her."[25]

Indeed, according to Hekman's reading, Derrida in fact embraces a
strategy that sounds quite similar to one proposed by Harding, which
I discussed in Chapter 4, that feminists should confront the "meta-
physical presuppositions" of patriarchal political thought in a two-
stage process: first to reverse them, to elevate previously neglected
and denigrated aspects of women's lived experiences while pointing
out the weaknesses and pathologies of the "male model"; and then
second to explode them, so that we no longer have duality at all but
multiplicity. As Derrida says in *Positions*:

> In a classical philosophical opposition we are not dealing with a peaceful
> coexistence of a *vis-à-vis*, but rather with a violent hierarchy. One of the
> two terms governs the other (axiologically, logically, etc.), or has the up-
> per hand. To deconstruct the opposition, first of all, is to overturn the
> hierarchy at a given moment. To overlook this phase of overturning is to
> forget the conflictual and subordinating structure of opposition. There-
> fore one might proceed too quickly to a *neutraliziation* that *in practice*
> would leave the previous field untouched, leaving one no hold on the
> previous opposition, thereby preventing any means of *intervening* in the
> field effectively. We know what always have been the *practical* (partic-
> ularly *political*) effects of *immediately* jumping *beyond* oppositions, and of
> protests in the simple form of *neither* this *nor* that.[26]

This passage resonates considerably with my reading and use of a
feminist standpoint approach. The goal of feminist obligation as I
have developed it is not to replace a male-model rights orienation, or
consent, with a female, care-centered notion of obligation *simpliciter*.
Rather, it seeks to move beyond such oppositions. Where it perhaps
falls short of Derrida's prescription is that my approach may in fact
seek third terms from the socially constructed yet dialectical opposition of male and female, rights and care, freedom and obligation. It is
true that I seek not a *single* third term but rather several; yet I believe
that Derrida and postmodernism in general would reject this enter-

[24]Ibid., p. 55.
[25]Ibid., p. 63.
[26]Derrida (1972), p. 41.

prise. (I discuss these disagreements with postmodernism in the following section.)

The rejection of overdetermined dualities as definitive of reality is a core concept for Foucault as well, who offers feminism valuable insights on the intersection of knowledge, discourse, and power, the social construction of sex as part of the construction of gender, the importance of recognizing and not repressing "difference," and the necessity to deal in "local" rather than "global" knowledge. In all this, "Foucault opens space for feminist questions that have been obscured" by Enlightenment liberalism and other mainstream discourses.[27] Indeed, the notion of discourse, a term used broadly in feminist political theory and throughout this book, comes from Foucault's concept of how "the production of truth" stems from the "manifold relations of power which . . . constitute the social body. . . . We cannot exercise power except through the production of truth."[28] Power in this sense is not conceived of as one person or institution acting on another, unidirectionally—this Foucault calls "violence"—but rather is much more pervasive, diffuse, all-encompassing. It is not *just* the physical power of a master over a slave (although that is part of it) but the way in which the master creates reality for the slave, provides her not only with an identity but with language—discourses—that limits the terms the slave can use to define herself, limits which ensure that such definition will not only fall within the parameters of the discourse and hence the relationship of power but will advance and enlarge them. The relationship of power and knowledge is thus a totalizing one, for it creates reality itself (indeed, modern discourse has allowed or required me to conceptualize reality as an itself, a tangible and hence perhaps definable thing).

Although Foucault's emphasis on the social construction of truths and the rejection of the idea of one final truth has opened him to criticism for extreme relativism—a charge I pursue in the next section[29]—Foucault dissociates himself from such a view. He holds that the "struggle" of the critical theorist—the archaeologist of knowledge, the genealogist—is not "a skeptical or relativistic refusal of all verified truth. What is questioned is the way in which knowledge circulates and functions, its relations to power. In short, the *régime du savoir.*"[30] Foucault is interested not in examining *which* truth claims are "in fact false" but rather in understanding how and why certain beliefs get to

[27]Martin (1988), p. 7.
[28]Foucault (1980), p. 93.
[29]But see Taylor (1984), pp. 152–83, and (1985), pp. 377–85; see also Hawksworth (1989).
[30]Foucault (1982), p. 212.

be considered "truth" in the first place; what social relations and structures have existed in history and exist today that create conditions susceptible to particular constructions of human beings as individuals.

In this, Foucault's most important insight for feminism is the methodological reforms, or perhaps revolution, he urges on theory. His approach engages in both archaeology—which is an analysis of "subjugated knowledge," knowledge that is subverted and perverted by the claims and expressions of the dominant discourse(s)—and genealogy, which involves using the (formerly) subjugated knowledge to know in new ways. Archaeology is thus akin to what I have called the negative dimensions of feminist critique, whereas genealogy is like the positive. But its particular aptness for feminism is that it engages us in a different kind of positive theory building altogether, one that avoids (insofar as possible) the trap I have identified of trying to construct new theories within the framework of old and structurally biased epistemologies. In fact, Foucault's method is not to build or construct per se but rather to facilitate the unfolding of new understandings. It is not theory as we normally understand the term so much as an "ongoing conceptualization . . . [which] implies critical thought—a constant checking."[31] Indeed, Foucault claims to create "neither a theory nor a methodology" but rather "a history of the different modes by which, in our culture, human beings are made subjects."[32] The focus on specificity—cultural, historical, geographical—is central to Foucault's approach. Viewed as "a kind of attempt to emancipate historical knowledges," genealogy is "based on a reactivation of local knowledge."[33] So, for instance, a marxist interpretation of madness would provide a universalized concept of man's dehumanization through the alienating labor relations of capitalism and a set of relations that subverts all to production and hence must deactivate nonproductive people. But Foucault says such broad theories dehumanize and disempower those who are mad. What is needed to understand madness is to examine the family, the local and particular institutions, relations, and how "mechanisms of power . . . become economically advantageous and socially useful."[34] But more than this, the contemporary institutions and conditions that create power must also be understood historically: "We need a *historical* awareness of our *present* circumstances."[35]

[31]Ibid., p. 209.
[32]Ibid., p. 208.
[33]Foucault (1980), p. 85.
[34]Ibid., p. 101.
[35]Foucault (1982), p. 209; emphasis added.

Foucault seeks to alter radically the ways we think about, analyze, and create theory. His goal is to have us rethink the questions that we ask rather than the answers we come up with to the old questions. In his critique of the social science approach to the study of social and political institutions and practices, he asks, "What types of knowledge do you want to disqualify in the very instant of your demand: 'Is it a science?'"[36] If we substitute the question, Is it gender and race neutral? we see that feminism is of course ostensibly not neutral. But we can also see (and indeed have seen in the preceding chapters) that the very method of disqualifying certain knowledges that "fail" the test of gender neutrality will then systematically obscure the fact that science, or liberal theory, or the other dominant discourses of the existing disciplines are not themselves gender or race neutral at all but reflect particular biases. Foucault does not critique existing discourses for their failure to realize the goal of neutrality or objectivity; he criticizes the goal itself, saying that the point is simply to recognize the ways in which theories are informed by their particularities, and to be aware of what effects follow.

The attention Foucault pays to sex has located him prominently in feminist critical theory; and applying his methodological insights to issues of sex and the body yield important loci for questions of gender. As Biddy Martin notes, for Foucault "the body does not give knowledge that is then merely transmitted by an essentially neutral language . . . discourse makes the body an object of knowledge and invests it with power. Our task, then, is not to search for the truth about sex, but to ask what is at stake in the historical question."[37] This question of what is at stake parallels Foucault's comments about science in the passage just quoted. Earlier I argued that the turn to objectivity, central to the scientific turn in social and political analysis, is a historical phenomenon that is specifically gendered. Thus there is no surprise if Foucault's remarks about science reverberate directly with the feminist analysis engaged in this book.

The implications for politics and political theory are manifold, as the observations Foucault makes about the body cohere with those he makes about political structures. As Flax notes, Foucault offers us the insight that "the modern state . . . depends on the creation and widespread acceptance of a fictive but persuasive account of 'human nature' and on the emergence of a group of 'experts' whose story about [the relation between human nature and political order] . . . will be considered authoritative and final,"[38] an insight certainly pursued in

[36]Foucault (1980), p. 85.
[37]Martin (1988), p. 7.
[38]Flax (1990), p. 40.

the foregoing chapters. Thus Foucault locates the concept of right, which allegedly underlies western legal and moral systems—the legitimacy of which is supposedly based in contemporary theory on its democratic nature—in the history of royal power; it derives from disciplinary systems (that is, law) that were erected for the "profit" of royal power and "to serve as its instrument or justification."[39] "When it comes to the general organization of the legal system in the West, it is essentially with the King, his rights, his power and its eventual limitations that one is dealing. . . . The essential role of the theory of right, from medieval times onward, was to fix the legitimacy of power."[40] This observation is certainly not at odds with Hobbes, at the least, and is also consistent with the reading of Locke offered in Chapter 1. As I have argued about consent, such an elitist, or structurally biased—in terms of class and gender obviously (though Foucault talks only of kings, not queens) but possibly race as well—foundation for rights calls into question not only the *legitimacy* of using rights as a basis for inclusive, participatory democratic vision of politics but its very *possibility* as well. Indeed, democracy itself is a potentially problematic idea if we pursue Foucault's suspicions. This analysis fits well with my earlier claims that rights are power claims, that a rights-based conceptual framework for obligation and freedom involve not autonomy in some abstract sense of freedom from external impediments but power as domination. Obligation, as defined by and within the social contract, is itself a relationship of power, a conclusion that challenges the very foundations of consent in the "natural freedom and equality" of all "men."

Yet Foucault's primary concern is not with power per se but rather with the subject. Power is considered an essential means to understanding the subject in the modern era. There are four notions of subject that Foucault at least tacitly incorporates into his various writings. The first is the sense in which I have used the term throughout this book: the subject as a self, as an entity with desires, needs, ideas, and expressions. The second involves the idea of subjects as citizens, political obedients who are the "loyal subjects" of a monarch or government. The third is a related notion of *social* subjection, which involves the power of the "normal" over "deviants," particularly sexual deviants (including sexual "perverts" and prostitutes). The fourth sense lies in the modern notion of the object of study: the subjects in a psychology or medical experiment, the focus of analysis or discussion in a philosophical work (the subject of my book is political obli-

[39]Foucault (1980), p. 94.
[40]Ibid., p. 95.

gation). Although the third sense could perhaps most comfortably encompass the patriarchal subjection of women to men, I believe that all four meanings are not only intertwined for Foucault but interdependent in their meanings. In "The Subject and Power" Foucault does not make this argument explicitly; indeed, he holds that "there are two meanings of the word *subject*: subject to someone else by control and dependence, and tied to his own identity by a conscience or self-knowledge." The subject of a sovereign and of study would be encompassed by the former, the subject as self constitutes the latter. Foucault also says that "both meanings suggest a form of power which subjugates and makes subject to."[41] Thus the ways in which I am a subject of my queen informs my subjectivity, my self-identity; and the ways in which social scientists and philosophers analyze and interpret my self-definition and my relation to my ruler—treat me as the subject of their inquiry—in turn affects those relations themselves as well as my self.

This notion of how the different senses of *subject* intersect reveals the interconnections of knowledge, power, and identity. The modern state—that is, "since the eighteenth century," thus already involving considerable overlap with the sovereign power discussed earlier—embodies "a new form of pastoral power," a power that "implies a knowledge of the conscience and an ability to direct it." The pastoral power of the modern state is a "totalizing" power structure which determines not only how we may live—what we may and may not do with impunity, the limits to freedom, the obligations of obedience—but also who and what we are. It is a "sophisticated structure" which *creates* the individual, who is "shaped in a new form, and submitted to a set of very specific patterns." Thus the liberal state, for all its emphasis on the negative liberty of individualism, in fact requires one very specific meaning of individualism, one particular kind of individual, and one kind alone; so we have not "government of and for the people"—of and for individuals—but rather the "government of individualization," a totalizing structure that constructs the "objectivizing of the subject." Thus the pastoral power of the modern state "is coextensive and continuous with life; it is linked with a production of truth—the truth of the individual himself."[42]

For feminist political theorists interested in examining the questions of power and subjectivity Foucault raises, this means that rather than ask how philosophy is "able to fix limits to the rights of power," we must ask instead, "what rules of right are implemented by the rela-

[41]Foucault (1982), p. 212.
[42]Ibid., pp. 212–14.

tions of power in the production of discourses of truth?"[43] Not only does his approach help theorists understand power in new ways—and hence affect the answers to the questions of power we have been asking all along—but it can help us redefine the questions themselves, to think of and about power in new and different ways, to see it located in contexts and situations where before it was invisible (at least to theorists), to reconceptualize the entire political theoretical enterprise. Thus philosophy, according to Foucault, must engage in modes of resistance and refusal. Its task is "not to discover what we are, but to refuse what we are . . . to imagine and to build up what we could be to get rid of . . . the simultaneous individualization and totalization of modern power structures. . . . We have to promote new forms of subjectivity through the refusal of this kind of individuality which has been imposed on us for several centuries."[44] It is precisely such resistance that lies at the heart of feminist politics, and precisely the quest for such new subjectivity that informs the feminist attempt to construct political theory from the feminine model of relational autonomy.

Consistent with my version of feminist standpoint theory, Foucault conceptualizes social relations, and particularly power, as a network or web: power "circulates"; it is "exercised through a net-like organization"; and individuals "are not *only* its inert or consenting target; they are always *also* the elements of its articulation . . . the vehicles of power, not its points of application."[45] I have emphasized *only* and *also* to illustrate the methodological intersection of standpoint epistemology with postmodernism. I have argued that the web imagery revealed by attention to women's and other marginalized voices describes many different (if not all) aspects of life, but the dominant discourses prevent us from seeing the interconnections and relationships among people, institutions, practices, and so forth. When we define the world in terms of a false model of linearity, power is hidden, obscured, and in the process made even more dangerous and oppressive. It is the refusal to recognize the web—a refusal achieved in part through the silencing of women—that has produced the problems of obligation, of liberalism, of "malestream" theory.

Yet, just as I have argued that feminist theory seeks not merely to embrace a care model, to act out women's experiences, but rather to theorize that experience critically in order to explore how care can shift the dynamics of understanding dominant discourses such as liberal obligation, so Foucault holds that seeing the webbed character of

---

[43]Foucault (1980), p. 93.
[44]Foucault (1982), p. 216.
[45]Foucault (1980), p. 98; emphasis added.

power is not itself a solution, because the imposition of the "false" linear model of unidirectional power in turn structures the web. Its falseness creates its own "truth." Like feminist standpoint epistemologists, Foucault does not advocate the simplistic idea that conceiving power as a web in itself means that power is "democratically distributed." Power has a mode of exercise, and some people do more exercising than others. Furthermore, some are able consistently to exercise it over certain others. But this power is not *only* unidirectional: "The individual which power has constituted is at the same time its vehicle."[46] The slave has some power vis-à-vis the master, as does the worker vis-à-vis the capitalist and women vis-à-vis men. But although the masters, capitalists, and men have more opportunity and ability to exercise power over the slaves, workers, and women, and do so in far more obvious ways that define discourses that encode reality— indeed, that *construct* slaves, workers, and women—to ignore the power of the marginalized, to view them completely as victim, is not only to rob them of the essential Enlightenment feature of humanity—that is, agency—but also to misrepresent the dynamics of human relations between the (relatively) powerful and (relatively) powerless as static, unitary, and monolithic. It is their position on the margins of the web that creates the potential for their empowerment, just as standpoint epistemology holds that the oppressed are able to see less falsely than the oppressor.

Yet the comparison between marginality and oppression does not sit entirely comfortably, a point that may be made if we turn to another postmodern theorist. Ironically, in spite of his exhortations to "forget Foucault," Jean Baudrillard provides a similar understanding of power. Reminding us of the "reversibility" of power,[47] he creates a useful picture of power not as zero sum at all but rather, in an interesting variation on Hartsock's argument, as constitutive of exchange. "Power *seduces*, but not in the vulgar sense of a complicit form of desire on the part of those who are dominated . . . [but] by that reversibility which haunts it, and upon which a minimal symbolic cycle is set up."[48] Viewing power in this way helps feminists become more aware of, and hence to be more critical of, the ways in which women's apparent powerlessness and victimization are partly historical products of their own actions, and how their oppression and marginalization work together with their agency and power. Unfortunately, an example that borrows from modernist social mythology

[46]Ibid., pp. 98–99.
[47]Baudrillard (1987), p. 44.
[48]Ibid., pp. 43–44.

best illustrates this point: if a poor black man rapes a wealthy white woman, the duality of victim/victimizer is not clear or simple, nor should it be.[49] The woman is not *simply* victim (of patriarchy, of misogyny), because the power structure within which she participates (as wealthy and white) contributes to the context that allows, causes, invites, and/or permits men to rape. But neither does she determine or control that context; as a woman, she *is* a victim of male domination. She thus participates in a power structure (of race and class) that seems to privilege her but also disempowers her as a woman. Nor is the poor black man merely victim (of racism, of classism, of poverty); the rape, while in part an act of patriarchal power, itself contributes to the context that disempowers the rapist as poor and black. It allows the rapist as male to participate structurally in his own (dis)empowering. So, even as we avoid blaming the victim, such a conception of power allows us to recognize the complex, multiple layers of power: power is not unitary or unidirectional. Such a conceptualization also allows feminists and others to be aware, and hence self-critical, of the ways in which women and other apparently disempowered groups participate in perpetuating their own apparent powerlessness by failing to see their location within networks of power.

Although Baudrillard's version of postmodernism seems in some ways to back off from the extreme nihilistic possibilities of post-structuralism, his approach also requires the development of new methods of theory, methods that have applicability to feminism. Arguing that sexual discourse is invented through repression rather than repression being an effect of discourse, Baudrillard's work sets forth a notion of theory very useful to feminism. "It is a good thing that terms lose their meaning at the limits of the text," he writes. "This is what a theory should be at best, rather than a statement of some truth."[50] The role of marginalization with respect to truth—or to the ability to see false truth claims more fully—is one that feminism can draw on. Indeed, part (though not the totality) of standpoint logic suggests that feminists *must* be on the margins, or in the position of the oppressed, to be able to continue to see clearly the dynamics of relations between men and women, powerful and powerless. Postmodernism, by highlighting the liberation to be gained through marginalization, empowers women and other oppressed groups to excercise Kristeva's nega-

---

[49]Although rape most commonly occurs between men and women of the same race and class, it would be considerably more complex to illustrate my point through such examples, for they would ostensibly reduce questions of power to gender alone. The contrasting implications of the reverse scenario—say, a wealthy white man raping a poor woman of color—is presented in the next section.

[50]Baudrillard (1987), p. 38.

tive function of critique, dissemination, and deconstruction. These activities cannot be adequately carried out from the center because then the critic or theorist is part of the very structure that she seeks to decompose; and her location within that structure will therefore prevent her from achieving her (erstwhile) goal.

Jean-François Lyotard goes even further than Baudrillard—and perhaps even Foucault and Derrida—in his emphasis on marginality and the reluctance to construct new theories which may produce new truths. Indeed, Lyotard posits the relationship between modernism and postmodernism as another Enlightenment duality between "two kinds of knowledge . . . the positivist kind . . . [and] the critical, reflexive, or hermeneutic kind."[51] He holds that much postmodern theory is merely reactive, and hence overly determined by the modernist methods and epistemology it seeks to critique. As a result, "this partition . . . attempts to resolve, but only reproduces" (p. 14) the duality of modernism. Thus theorists must continually work to operate from the margins, to resist the temptation to claim "a viewpoint that is in principle immune from [the] allure" of totality, answers, "truth" (p. 12).

Lyotard attempts to conduct new methods of theorizing that faithfully embody postmodern principles of resistance. Of particular note is his emphasis on the narrative as a mode of theory. As Fredric Jameson points out in his introduction, in Lyotard's work the "narrative is affirmed, not merely as a significant new field of research, but well beyond that as a central instance of the human mind and a mode of thinking fully as legitimate as that of abstract logic" (p. xi). Lyotard goes so far as to say, "Lamenting the 'loss of meaning' in postmodernity boils down to mourning the fact that knowledge is no longer principally narrative" (p. 26). It is not just the historical overemphasis on rationality but the focus on thinking and knowledge defined in very particular ways without any recognition of the fact that these ways *are* particular and not timeless or universal that is the danger of modernity. For humans become cut off from vital dimensions of their self-understanding; indeed, they come to understand themselves as selves *without* narration, without stories, and hence without histories. Lyotard thus seeks to restore narrative techniques to the status of legitmacy. Like the feminist literature drawn on in this book, narrative knowledge involves "speech acts . . . performed not only by the speaker, but also by the listener, as well as by the third party referred to" (p. 21). This communicative strategy seems to invoke feminist ideals of mutuality and intersubjectivity, wherein through the process of

---

[51]Lyotard (1979), p. 14. Subsequent references to this source will be cited in the text.

conversation others come to understand and develop themselves further as subjects. Lyotard argues that a community that practices narrative "finds the raw material for its social bond not only in the meaning of the narratives it recounts, but also in the act of reciting them" (p. 22).

Like Foucault, Lyotard invokes images of a web or network of social relations; according to Nancy Fraser and Linda Nicholson, for Lyotard "the social bond is a weave of crisscrossing threads of discursive practices, no single one of which runs continuously throughout the whole. Individuals are the nodes or posts where such practices intersect, and so they participate in many practices simultaneously. It follows that social identities are complex and heterogeneous."[52] Indeed, it would be difficult to find another ready-made description of society any closer to the feminist political vision articulated in the previous chapter than that offered by Lyotard:

> A *self* does not amount to much, but no self is an island; each exists in a fabric of relations that is now more complex and mobile than ever before. Young or old, man or woman, rich or poor, a person is always located at "nodal points" of specific communication circuits, however tiny these may be. Or better: one is always located at a post through which various kinds of messages pass. No one, not even the least privileged among us, is ever entirely powerless over the messages that traverse and position him at the post of sender, addressee, or referent.   (p. 15)

The approaches, methods, and ideas of Derrida, Foucault, Baudrillard, and Lyotard are all helpful to the effort to give meaning to a feminist concept of obligation and to the notion of recognition through feminist conversation which lies at the heart of feminist participatory politics. I argued that one of the tasks of a feminist theory of obligation was to ask new questions; that the question, How does an obligation arise?—the central question of social contract theory—falls out of the picture, or at least to a secondary role, for this question is one of legitimation. Indeed, if all people are naturally free and equal, the central problem of modern political theory becomes precisely one of legitimation: Under what conditions can restrictions on my liberty be legitimate? The goal of consent theory is to answer that question, to develop a single unifying and universal principle that constitutes the legitimacy of limiting freedom through the expression of freedom. The legitimating metanarrative of the social contract creates a metadiscourse of human nature, natural rights, and the only possible political structure that can consistently represent those prem-

[52]Fraser and Nicholson (1990), p. 24.

ises. And this justificatory representation is self-referential; that is, the dominant discourse's credibility comes from its power. As Lyotard observes, "It has the means to become a reality, and that is all the proof it needs" (p. 12).

In contrast, as I argued in the previous chapter feminist obligation looks to the content of obligations and works out the problem of legitimacy—what obligations are to be met in what ways, what reasons for nonfulfillment are acceptable—through a mutualistic enterprise of communication and interaction. The idea that the process of conversation itself serves as legitimator hearkens to postmodern visions: "In the postmodern era legitimation becomes plural, local and immanent. In this era, there will necessarily be many discourses of legitimation dispersed among the plurality of first-order discursive practices. . . . Legitimation descends to the level of practice and becomes immanent in it."[53] An emphasis on practice, particularity, concreteness, and context is a central element that postmodernism and feminism share.

They also share the criticism of totality, homogeneity and unity. As Iris Young has pointed out, the idea of the civic public from ancient Greece through modern liberalism has given priority to concepts of unity as a precondition for political stability and hence political success. But this unity has always been a lie; it has relied on the "expulsion of persons from the civic public in order to maintain its unity."[54] So people of color, women, foreign nationals, laborers, the poor, the uneducated have all been excluded from political participation in the name of order and stability. The concept of a general will, even in its Lockean liberal formulation of a public good, "itself results in exclusion."[55] In particular, as I have argued throughout this book, women must be excluded from political participation, for their particularism, their irrationality (that is, their supposed inability to take a general point of view), and their sexuality threaten to "undermine public deliberation by fragmenting its unity."[56] "The distinction between public and private as it appears in modern political theory expresses a will for homogeneity that necessitates the exclusion of many persons and groups, particularly women and racialized groups culturally identified with the body, wildness and irrationality."[57] I have argued throughout that liberalism rests on a false unity that is derived from sexism as well as from classism and racism, that the exclusion of women, peo-

[53]Ibid., p. 23.
[54]Young (1987), p. 63.
[55]Ibid., p. 66.
[56]Ibid.
[57]Ibid., p. 73.

ple of color, workers and the poor are necessary foundations for the success of its logic as a political model.

Thus a postmodern feminism is a powerful strategy for understanding the structural sexism of liberal theory. It can reveal that what appears by modernist standards as "fragmentation, lack of organization, absence of a coherent and encompassing theory, and the inability to mount a frontal attack may very well represent fundamentally more radical and effective responses to the deployment of power in our society than the centralization and abstraction"[58] of "malestream" theory, including particularly liberal-democratic theories of political obligation. But postmodern feminism can also provide the tools for articulating a new vision of political life like the participatory democracy I have begun to outline. The replacement of discourse with conversation; the recognition of difference and multiplicity without a predetermined hierarchy of value; the ongoing awareness of the dangers of hegemony, totality, and unity and the complementary move toward being more self-critical, self-conscious, and self-reflexive in our theorizing; the recognition of the importance and power of marginality and the parallel requirement to listen to marginalized voices: all of these radically change the enterprise of theory itself, which I have argued feminism seeks to accomplish. Postmodern feminism can help feminist political theorists further develop their arguments on sexual difference and the need to attend to context and particularity; it can help articulate and bring about the theoretical turn to conversation I and others have advocated. Finally, postmodern feminism reveals (as Flax originally saw but later recanted)[59] that feminist standpoint epistemology is itself a postmodern strategy, or at least a strategy that coheres with certain ideas crucial to postmodernism, suggesting even that object relations and gender psychology *can*, if used in ways that avoid reductive claims to universal truth, be effective tools of both deconstructive and reconstructive strategies.

The Impossibility of a Feminist Postmodernism

These last claims will be the most problematic ones for postmodernists. Admittedly, these positive elements of postmodern feminism are

[58]Martin (1988), p. 10.

[59]Flax (1986), p. 194. Flax says this not specifically about standpoint approaches, of which, as I have indicated, she is suspicious, but about feminist theory in general. Her description of what feminist theory is, however, prominently includes standpoint approaches, and particularly Hartsock's (see pp. 194–95, n. 1). This inconsistency is never acknowledged by Flax, who then goes on in *Thinking Fragments* apparently to repudiate standpoint theory altogether, as well as to misrepresent it unfairly.

really extrapolations from postmodernism; they are not themselves postmodern principles per se. The rendition of postmodern theory offered here may, by some accounts, be a misrepresentation. In the act of using *postmodern* to modify *feminism*, the meaning of postmodernism itself is changed. For instance, I noted in Chapter 4 that although postmodern feminism considers itself intensely political, postmodernism itself may be postpolitical. Does this mean that postmodernist ideas cannot be taken beyond their authorial intent and applied to feminist political purposes? To be consistent with postmodernism, they must: deconstruction does not allow certain sets of meanings to be prima facie excluded or limited by an author's supposed intent. In this, the strategy is very useful to my own project of deconstructing liberal obligation theory, rooting out the structural elements of gender bias that have founded politics on women's exclusion, and attempting to salvage—and simultaneously redefine—certain dimensions of liberalism, such as agency and choice, that are important legacies of the historical turn away from divine right.

Yet obviously at the same time postmodernism cannot be used in this way. The project of empowering women that lies at the heart of feminist politics is antithetical to the entire post-structuralist enterprise. My account of postmodern insights has been pursued from the specific perspective of one who adopts a feminist standpoint epistemological approach. I read this theory "like a feminist"[60] and look to the dimensions and elements of postmodern theory that can help feminist theory. But a strict postmodern theorist might argue that the four theorists I have just discussed would strongly object to my drawing connections between their theories and a feminist standpoint approach, arguing that the fact that I can draw such connections in and of itself suggests that I have misread their theories. Do these theories in fact make themselves inaccessible to feminist concerns? In the process of developing a postmodern feminism, a feminism that borrows from postmodern insights, is the "postmodern" part of the label distorted, turned into something else? And furthermore, can we reverse the order and have a feminist postmodernism, an approach that asks what feminism can contribute to the postmodern enterprise?

Lyotard is a particularly appropriate theorist of whom to ask these questions, because of all the postmodern theorists I have discussed, he seems the most willing to carry postmodern theory to its logical extreme. For even narratives, as Lyotard points out in *The Postmodern Condition*, have an inherent tendency toward power insofar as they "determine criteria of competence and/or illustrate how they are to be

[60]See Fuss (1989).

applied" (p. 23). Since we cannot "judge the existence or validity of narrative knowledge on the basis of scientific knowledge" because "the relevant criteria are different" (p. 26), narratives "are legitimated by the simple fact that they do what they do" (p. 26). Thus Lyotard exposes a two-pronged dilemma. On the one hand, as in modernism, the concern of narratives with legitimacy is a question of power, and one that threatens to totalize: "It has the means to become a reality, and that is all the proof it needs" (p. 12). On the other hand, the theorist committed to postmodern principles cannot even compare narratives, or cultures, or language games, without drowning in a sea of relativism. As Charles Taylor argues (about Foucault, though the point applies to Lyotard and Derrida as well), "For all the connection, transitions are between incommensurables."[61] Hence Derrida holds that "dissemination," which Flax describes as "a constant and open-ended disruption and displacement of a text's authority through interventions that create an infinite stream of interpretations and meanings for it,"[62] is the preferred task of theory, for it allows for the many contradictory readings that a text can give rise to and prevents any authoritative claim to the "correct" interpretation. Lyotard, perhaps going even further, concludes that "all we can do is gaze in wonderment at the diversity of discursive species" (p. 26).

Lyotard himself may not like my claim that such a critic is "drowning." He champions postmodernism's dedication to marginality and uncertainty. But from a feminist perspective in particular, "gazing in wonderment" does little to address the very real, concrete political realities of women's lives. As Flax notes, "It is questionable whether any of the spaces opened up by postmodernism would be comfortable to or inhabitable by those concerned with issues of gender and gender justice."[63] Indeed, she holds that "the absence or disappearance of concrete women and gender relations [from postmodern theory] suggests the possibility that postmodernism is not only or simply opposed to phallocentrism but may also be 'its latest ruse.'"[64] Indeed, from the perspective of object relations theory, where there is no self more threatening than a female self, Flax points out that postmodernism can be seen as another attempt "to evade, deny or repress the importance of early childhood experiences, especially mother-child relationships, in the constitution of the self and the culture more generally."[65]

[61]Taylor (1985), p. 382.
[62]Flax (1990), p. 39.
[63]Ibid., p. 210.
[64]Ibid., p. 216, quoting Schor (1987), p. 109.
[65]Ibid., p. 232.

The problem with a feminist postmodernism is that postmodernism deconstructs itself because there is nothing for it to hold on to. In its efforts to decenter the subject, to recognize the ways in which no one—as woman, man, black, lesbian, white—creates his or her own identity but all are disciplined to be certain things and to live in certain ways, postmodernism, and post-structuralism in particular, "reject the possibility of defining women as such at all."[66] They also reject the possibility of feminist theory, which also makes feminist postmodernism such a problematic concept. As Lyotard's theory most obviously demonstrates, postmodern approaches rule out "the sort of larger-scale, normative political theorizing" inherent in, say, a theory of participatory democracy such as the one articulated in the previous chapter.[67] In "true" postmodern fashion, "there is no place in Lyotard's universe . . . for critique of broad-based relations of dominance and subordination along lines like gender, race and class."[68] The conversational participatory democracy outlined in the preceding chapter, then, in spite of the lengths to which I have gone to demonstrate how it depends on postmodern insights, might well be considered by Lyotard and other postmoderns as a leftover project of the Enlightenment.

Yet as Taylor and others observe, this strictly negative function of postmodernism—its deconstruction without a parallel reconstruction—threatens nihilism. Hekman, who offers some of the strongest resistance to this charge, admits that "the newness and radicalness of [Derrida's] approach entails that exactly what this new way of talking . . . will be is as yet unclear. It also entails that the politics implicit in this approach are unspecified."[69] Feminist projects certainly are—and should be—largely sympathetic to the problems and challenges of constructing new political and social meanings to replace the old. For decades feminism has involved itself primarily in the deconstruction of patriarchy, of institutions that are sexist in their very structure, in the gender bias of our dominant epistemologies and ontologies. Yet, as the question with which I closed Chapter 5 indicates, we continually want to know what will come in place of what is torn down. This nature-abhors-a-(theoretical)-vacuum approach may well be a legacy

---

[66]Alcoff (1988), 407.

[67]Fraser and Nicholson (1990), p. 23. In this it is significant—particularly given the debt that many postmodern feminist theorists writing on democracy owe to Habermas in their development of a feminist democratic politics (Love [1989], Fraser [1991], Young [1987, 1990])—that a large portion of *The Postmodern Condition* is dedicated to Lyotard's rejection of Habermas's communicative ethics as the foundation for a new kind of communitarian, democratic politics.

[68]Fraser and Nicholson (1990), p. 23.

[69]Hekman (1989), p. 25.

of the Enlightenment, a continued testimony to our misguided and self-destructive tendencies to create new hegemonies to replace the old; but from a feminist perspective, it is a vital move.

Fraser and Nicholson would seem to concur. While agreeing with the postmodern rejection of metadiscourse and critiquing much of feminist theory, including Chodorow and Gilligan, for falling prey to the sins of "quasi-metanarratives," they also hold out hope for "large narratives." I read their argument as being more consistent with the standpoints approach to theory I articulated earlier—that shared experiences and commonalities can provide the basis for shared stories that simultaneously preserve the differences contained in the commonality, and hence do not essentially reduce themselves to the common elements—than with postmodernism per se (hence they may be postmodern feminists). They point out that Lyotard "goes too quickly from the premise that Philosophy cannot ground social criticism to the conclusion that criticism itself must be local, *ad hoc*, and non-theoretical," that is, that we could have no "feminist" theory—or any other kind, for that matter. Lyotard "throws out the baby of large historical narrative with the bathwater of philosophical metanarrative and the baby of social-theoretical analysis of large-scale inequalities with the bathwater of reductive Marxian class theory. Moreover, these allegedly illegitimate babies do not in fact remain excluded. They return like the repressed within the very genres of postmodern social criticism with which Lyotard intends to replace them."[70]

Even more significantly, however, Lyotard also slips in a very particularized and masculinist construction of reality when he places "agonistics" at the heart of social relations as they are defined and constituted in and through language games (p. 16). The "accepted language" is the "adversary" to the critical theorist (p. 10). As my earlier chapters made clear, such a construal of language and epistemology betrays at least in part a gendered orientation. This in itself does not necessarily trouble the postmodern, as we are all socially constructed into genders by our totalizing societies. But Lyotard presents this as if agonistics is inevitable, even natural. At the very least, Lyotard's failure to be self-conscious and self-critical of the gendered dimensions of his position and argument means that he fails to respond to his own theoretical exhortations.

Derrida similarly slips over into sexism. He certainly is antifeminist: "They too are men, those women feminists so derided by Nietzsche. Feminism is nothing but the operation of a woman who aspires to be like a man. And in order to resemble the masculine dogmatic philos-

---

[70]Fraser and Nicholson (1990), pp. 27, 26, 25.

opher this woman lays claim—just as much claim as he—to truth, science and objectivity in all their castrated delusions of virility. Feminism too seeks to castrate. It wants a castrated woman."[71] Derrida sees feminism reductively as the effort to replace an androcentric hegemony with a gynocentric one.

In his defense Hekman points out that Derrida "is attacking a particular form of feminism," namely one "that attempts to replace the unitary masculinist epistemology with an equally unitary feminist epistemology." Such a feminism will find itself locked into the very dualities that ensure women's inferiority. In stopping at the step of inverting dualities, and not moving on to their transcendence, this kind of feminism finds itself trapped in the same "logocentric closure" it seeks to end.[72] Yet Hekman also seems to include most kinds of feminism in this category, indeed, any feminism that is not postmodern. Although she argues that there is a strong convergence between postmodernism and feminism, thus suggesting an equal and reciprocal relationship between the two, in fact the structure of her argument ensures that the former sets boundaries to her discourse while the latter merely influences that discourse. In adhering to a strict reading of postmodernism, she regards most feminists as resisting postmodernism, a move she sees as misguided and self-defeating. At the base of most feminist theory, she argues, is a desire to retain the Cartesian subject and other elements of modernist philosophy which have at their own base the subjection of women. She criticizes feminist standpoint theory in particular because, she says, it seeks to reverse dualities such as male-female rather than eliminate them. Reversing dualities, she points out, is impossible; it merely ensures the continued existence of the duality without truly challenging the foundational hierarchy. So, for instance, in asserting the importance of care, she would say, feminists perpetuate essentialist arguments about women's nature without at all disempowering the oppressive force of rights and rules.

But the circularity of such an argument is apparent. Hekman holds that feminist methods that do not start from postmodernism—that do not adopt the parameters set by postmodernism and bring feminism in only as a modifier—will inevitably revert to the phallocratic notions of subject and self of masculinist modernism that are premised on the inferiority of women. Such so-called feminism is automatically defined as self-defeating and hence antifeminist. Not only is this feminist postmodernism antithetical to the ideal of multiplicity and pluri-

---

[71]Derrida (1978), p. 65. See also Derrida (1985).
[72]Hekman (1990), p. 170.

vocality which postmodernism seeks to further but it is blind to the ways in which postmodern theory is itself premised on women's inferiority. It presents a double bind for feminists, because postmodernism requires that we deconstruct woman; but because women are an oppressed class of people, the danger of invisibility is precisely the problem that feminism needs to address.

Indeed, Derrida *proscribes* a feminist postmodernism (as well as a postmodern feminism) by prohibiting women's self-definition and self-identity. Even further, he implicitly assumes the task, even as he denies it, of defining women himself. Derrida may use feminine pronouns and metaphors "in order to break the binary oppositions of phallocratic thought,"[73] but in the process he slips in a gender-biased picture of social relations, power, and text. For instance, his "hymeneal fable" can be seen as very much a masculinist account, not a feminist account certainly, and not even a multiple one. Derrida holds that the hymen as a location of ambiguity is "neither the inside nor the outside";[74] but this can make sense only from the perspective of the phallus. The hymen may be and has been constructed as a barrier—an "outside"—to the phallus's penetration of the "inside," that is, the female body. But to a woman the hymen is very much inside, *not* outside, as the example of rape makes clear. Viewing the hymen as Derrida suggests is thus exceedingly phallocentric, to use Derrida's own terms; it can be seen once again as an attempt by a masculinist discourse to use women's fragmented body parts—vagina, hymen, labia—as abstract metaphors to construct its own representation of reality. Certainly such a construction of the hymen *also* may challenge the "linear, unitary, phallocratic 'will to truth'" with "a sign of fusion [that] . . . abolishes opposition and difference";[75] but it is a masculinist representation of such an endeavor.

Perhaps women represent, or even *can* represent, ambiguity for Derrida only because Derrida is male; for after all, if the ambiguity stems from social constructions of gender, are men really any less ambiguous? If the hymen is as much "outside" as "inside," the phallus is as much "inside"—connected to and constitutive of the most intimate of self-conceptions—as "outside." The alignment of women with ambiguity echoes Freud's confusion about women, the patriarchal view of woman as mystery. Certainly, Derrida's explicit recognition of this mysteriousness as social construction is an advance over Freud's naturalistic puzzlement. Derrida is saying that what has historically been attributed to women embodies certain aspects of

[73]Ibid., p. 165.
[74]Derrida (1972), p. 43.
[75]Hekman (1990), pp. 165–66.

both men and women, making relevant the question why this has happened. If "truth, like woman, is plural," then "what 'woman' represents . . . [is] consistent with [Derrida's] effort to deconstruct the will to truth."[76] Yet the problem remains. For in order to empower women, or to enable women to realize the power that they already have to end their disciplining, feminists need to construct the category of woman and to search for identity, and this Derrida will not allow, except possibly, as I noted earlier, as a short-term political stage in reversing the male-female duality before then exploding it. But the problem with this short-term strategy is that it contradicts Derrida's warnings about essentialism. Even a temporary claim to such a definition feeds the will to truth, for we may easily forget that this definition was intended to be a temporary strategy. Indeed, according to postmodern tenets, we will be compelled to forget by the logic of the discourse. Indeed, that is the whole point of feminist postmodernism's rejection of standpoint approaches. At the same time, from a feminist perspective this two-part strategy would end up at a different point from that which Derrida asserts; that is, the "explosion" would mean not necessarily the end of the subject but rather a world in which subjects can see and define themselves in and through relationships.

Similarly, in *Forget Foucault*, the logic of Baudrillard's argument may compel him to go too far for feminism when he says that the reversibility of power leads to the conclusion that "dominators and dominated exist no more than victims and executioners. (While exploiters and exploited do in fact exist, they are on different sides because there is no reversibility in production, which is precisely the point: nothing essential happens at that level.)"[77] This notion would in fact trivialize the rape of the wealthy white woman by the poor black man. Furthermore, if a disabled Hispanic woman were raped or otherwise sexually harassed by her white male employer, or if a third world woman were killed in a snuff film produced by white men, it would be hard to see such power relationships as reversible. They appear one-sided after all, or at least lopsided enough to make talk about the woman's "power" rather disingenuous. Furthermore, Baudrillard's problematic views of female sexuality and pornography also force feminists to question the usefulness and applicability of his theory.[78] So the danger of reduction, and the possibilities for structural sexism that this allows, pervades Baudrillard's work as it does postmodern theory in general.

[76]Ibid., p. 168.
[77]Baudrillard (1987), p. 43.
[78]See esp. ibid., pp. 56–57.

The most problematic postmodern, in my view, because potentially the most helpful as well, is Foucault. I would not go so far as to agree with Balbus that a "Foucauldian feminism is a contradiction in terms,"[79] primarily because I do not think that Balbus gives sufficient credit to the ways in which Foucault highlights gender as a social construction. But Balbus's point that Foucault rejects psychoanalysis as a totalizing discourse presents obvious problems for my earlier attempt to claim Foucauldian insights for my postmodern feminism. Like other postmodern theorists, in his challenge to the modern subject Foucault may go too far to sustain feminism. "Foucault 'dispenses' . . . with individual identity *tout court*"[80] and indeed requires us to struggle against identity: "An attachment to an identity that one *recognizes and is recognized by others* is . . . the result of the form of interactions peculiar to the technologies of the self that proliferate in the contemporary disciplinary society. . . . 'Nothing in man—not even his body—is sufficiently stable to serve as the basis for self-recognition or for understanding other men.' "[81] The problem that Balbus identifies is that Foucault makes patriarchy an impossible target for feminism: "His ban on 'continuous history' would make it impossible for women even to speak of the historically universal misogyny from which they have suffered and against which they have struggled."[82]

In short, for Foucault identity equals unfreedom, or totalizing discipline. Yet the challenge of claiming identity, I have argued, is part of the enterprise of feminism. The tension between Foucault and feminism, I believe, lies in the fact that the identity that Foucault rejects is object relations theory's male model of identity. By constituting autonomy as opposed to community and by defining the community as inevitably disciplining and totalizing, Foucault buys into the not-other conception of identity. Foucault produces an abstraction that replicates "the androcentric and fundamentally humanist universalizing 'I,' this time in the apparent form of the 'Not-I.' "[83] He does not even consider a female model of identity, in which "community and autonomy are not only not inconsistent, but are, in fact, mutually constitutive."[84]

Although this argument may display some psychoanalytic circularity and threatens a breakdown in communication between the kind of feminism developed in this book and Foucault's postmodernism, it

[79]Balbus (1987), p. 110.
[80]Ibid., p. 117.
[81]Ibid., pp. 117–18, quoting Foucault, *Language, Countermemory, and Practice;* emphasis added.
[82]Ibid., p. 120.
[83]Martin (1988), p. 17.
[84]Balbus (1987), p. 126.

also points to the same kinds of objections to other theorists that I identified earlier. Foucault operates from a highly gendered point of view even as he denies such a possibility. For instance, in his *History of Sexuality* he seeks to understand sexuality as constructed and disciplined by law and social institutions, and he advocates alteration of this situation to remove sexuality from the domain of law. Rape, then, would be punished not as a sex crime but as a crime of assault. Yet in taking the sex out of rape, Foucault denies the ways in which men and women are treated differently by society as having different sexual identities; and he thus denies the reality that such social constructions create. For even though rape is an assault (that is, an act of violence), it is also an act of sex, and women are raped by men far more commonly than men are raped by either men or women. Would changing the prosecution of rape lower its incidence? Make it more "democratic" among its victims and perpetrators? Foucault's goal in desexualizing rape is to break down the power/knowledge monopoly of state authority, but such an abstraction of power ignores the concrete realities of rape.

In a similar vein, Linda Alcoff points out that Foucault's deconstruction of the subject with an authentic core means that "there is no repression in the humanist sense."[85] Although "subjective experiences are determined in some sense by macro forces,"[86] and even though Foucault's concept of power, like Baudrillard's, entails a notion of reversibility, for Foucault we basically cannot and do not choose who we are. "As Derrida and Foucault like to remind us, individual motivation and intentions count for nil or almost nil in the scheme of social reality."[87] The idea that humans are constructs of discourses beyond their control is a powerful insight to help feminists and other critical theorists understand and cut through the mythologizing claims to truth of liberalism and other schools of modern political theory; yet the parallel recognition that we also do choose must be made. As Taylor puts it, "There not only can be but *must* be something between total subjectivism on one hand . . . and the strange Schopenhauerianism-without-the-will in which Foucault leaves us."[88] An important contribution of feminism has been to reveal the ways in which women have been denied opportunities to choose, to consent, even though it also urges us to redefine and reconceptualize such terms. That has involved the revelation of consent ideology as a totalizing fiction which mischaracterizes obligation and the nature of hu-

---

[85]Alcoff (1988), p. 415.
[86]Ibid., p. 416.
[87]Ibid.
[88]Taylor (1984), p. 171.

man relations. Worse, that mischaracterization in turn depends on the active as well as the larger-scale institutional, societal, discursive oppression and disciplining of women. To then deny women the tools of choice and means of consent by declaring them to be part of a discourse that oppresses us all, to claim that there is no "self" to do this choosing anyhow, goes beyond disingenuous to dangerous. The demand that women be provided more opportunities to make choices cannot be dismissed so easily without raising questions of whether masculinist hegemony is merely being perpetuated in a new guise.

These particular examples of postmodern sexism, however, stem not from individual theorists' failure to implement postmodern principles successfully but from the logic of postmodernism itself. The overriding problem with postmodernism, in my view, is that when we focus on difference and particularity to the exclusion of commonality and sharing, the concept of theory itself implodes. Because no two experiences are ever *exactly* alike, there can never be any sort of common ground for the development of theory; or rather, there are so many narratives that they can never form social wholes but only "social holes." As I argued earlier, the beauty of adopting feminist stand*points* is that while recognizing difference, particularity, and context, we can also set certain limits on what can count as a *feminist* standpoint. This approach does not mean that there is some universal and timeless conception of feminism or femaleness, any more than it means there is "Truth." But it is immanently pragmatic in that it does provide certain grounds for a particular group of people—say, members of a participatory democracy—to make decisions and judgments about the kinds of views that it will allow to guide common action, that it will allow to (at least temporarily) occupy the center of the web called politics (inherently nonrecognizing views are antifeminist, for instance). Alcoff's and de Lauretis's parallel arguments that the notion of women constitutes positions rather than a unitary collection of attributes echo this notion of standpoints. Feminism constitutes certain perspectives and positions which are influenced not by timeless and universal characteristics but by temporal, material dynamics, which shape individuals' own assessments and understandings of their positions.[89]

The postmodern notion that "the category 'woman' is a fiction and that feminist efforts must be directed toward dismantling this fiction"[90] is as problematic as it is helpful, suggesting the dangers of relativism that loom large for any kind of postmodernism, feminist or otherwise. As I noted earlier, writers such as Elizabeth Spelman chal-

[89]Alcoff (1988), de Lauretis (1989).
[90]Alcoff (1988), p. 417.

lenge the idea that theorists can draw any conclusions about women without knowing a variety of details about the particular individuals involved; and in her article with Maria Lugones the challenge arises as to whether any theorist of a particular race, class, sexual orientation, cultural specificity, condition of physical ability, and so forth can ever actually know these other details without engaging in a dangerous imperialism.[91]

But is it accurate to say that women are entirely different from one another? Does not the wealthy white woman suffer emotionally from abortion as well as the poor Chicana? The fact that abortion is more difficult for the latter because wealth affords more protection, or that Hispanic religious and traditional culture present more social and perhaps psychological restrictions than, say, some sects of Protestantism and certainly than agnosticism: these factors create differences that feminists want to recognize. And perhaps such recognition will lead to the conclusion that the Chicana deserves more of society's collective resources. But does that allow feminists to deny the pain felt by the former or to deny the shared qualities of the women's experiences? And what about the woman without ovaries or a vagina, who will never even need an abortion; what is it that makes her call herself woman and allows others to do likewise? She at least shares a certain cultural treatment as woman; and although she may suffer psychological pain, fear, deprivation, ostracism, and doubt from such treatment ("I can't conceive; am I a real woman?") even as she may not be directly affected by abortion policy, there is also much to be shared. The fact that such differences exist within cultures that treat all women the same, that ignores those differences, does create a certain commonality of experience.

In other words, although recognition and conversation must—not merely morally but in the logic of the process—address, recognize, and include differences, it is just as faulty to overemphasize difference and forget the sharedness and similarity that is often a part of difference. Works like Spelman's reduce the problems of sameness by holding it to be essentialist in the most extreme form. What she calls "plethoraphobia [is] a series of related questions: Is there *a* oneness in all this manyness? Is there some*thing* all women have in common despite (or maybe even because of) their differences? *A* thread running through all our accounts of our lives? *An* underlying identity as women? . . . *A* shared viewpoint?"[92] I agree with her that "we'd have to have more than superficial knowledge about one another to answer these questions," but we can also in some measure answer it right off

[91]Lugones and Spelman (1983).
[92]Spelman (1988), p. 160; emphasis added.

the bat: no, we do not have *a* oneness or *an* identity. Criticisms of *the* feminist standpoint reduce and misread the argument by claiming it holds that there is one single standpoint for all feminists, if not for all women; understanding it as allowing, even demanding, multiple feminist standpoints yields a reading of the theory that is not only more accurate but also much more useful to feminism than either a reductive essentialism or a totally decentered deconstruction. Like the notion of family resemblances which I argued is found in identity politics, the "thing called woman" embraces a multiplicity of experiences and yet is nevertheless identifiable. Not every woman—indeed, hardly any woman—demonstrates a one-to-one correlation with any other; but there are shared characteristics and experiences that link each woman directly to *some* other women, and through implementation of a web imagery indirectly to all. I may share the experience of being a poor black woman with other women, some of whom are also poor and black women, some of whom are poor and white, some of whom are black and middle class. The black middle-class woman may share some commonalities with white middle-class women, even as her commonalities with these other groups strongly differentiate her from the white bourgeoise. Can this middle-class black woman provide a certain link between the white bourgeoise and the poor black woman, particularly on shared but differently grounded issues such as child care, abortion, sexual violence, and comparable worth? If, as a Native American heterosexual welfare mother I am raped, I am likely to experience that quite differently from a Chicana lesbian attorney, not only because of differences in who we are but also in the experience of the rape itself: the age, race, class of the rapist, the violence and context of the rape, and so forth. But as rape crisis counselors will remind us, there is also much we share.

Postmodern approaches disempower women by preventing any discussion of these similarities, and by doing so they prevent women from creating theories that articulate that experience. As Robert Scholes argues, deconstruction "falters when faced with the need to take action in the ethico-political realm, because it cannot shake its 'de' in order to make constructive moves."[93] And as de Lauretis points out, any "essential difference" of women is "not a difference between woman and man, nor a difference inherent in 'woman's nature' (in woman as nature), but a difference in the feminist conception of woman, women, and the world."

It is what makes the thinking "feminist," and what constitutes certain ways of thinking, certain practices of writing, reading, imagining, relat-

[93]Scholes (1989), p. 94.

ing, acting, etc., into the historically diverse and culturally hetero-geneous social movement which, qualifiers and distinctions not with-standing . . . we continue with good reasons to call feminism. Another way to say this is that the essential difference of feminism lies in its historical specificity—the particular conditions of its emergence and de-velopment . . . the absolute novelty of its radical challenge to social life itself. . . . The term [*essentialism*] serves less the purposes of effective criticism in the ongoing elaboration of feminist theory than those of con-venience, conceptual simplification, or academic legitimation.[94]

It is intellectually unfair, not to mention disingenuous, to accuse *any* kind of feminist theory of the same degree of hegemony, racism, classism, and so forth as the white male western tradition "located at the center of power, at the intersection of three separate axes of privi-lege—race, class, and gender. . . . Feminist theory—even the work of white, upper-class women—is not located at the *center* of cultural power."[95] Such women as a group tend to have more power than women of color as a group, and that is something that feminist theory needs to acknowledge. But they are also, vis-à-vis men of all races and classes, and particularly upper-class white men, oppressed in particular ways related to the fact that they are (socially constructed as) women. Indeed, if my earlier arguments are correct, even white middle-class women should be much more attuned than masculinist post-Enlightenment theorists to claims that they have excluded others. It is not insignificant that the feminist movement as it was originally formulated as a white middle-class movement is readily em-bracing debates about inclusion and exclusion concerning race, class, age, sexual orientation, and so forth, while men's leftist movements of the past several decades—black power, civil rights, antiwar, stu-dent protest, marxist, social democratic—rarely (if ever) accepted or even took seriously issues of gender and sex. Certainly feminism's inclusiveness is far from complete, and feminism is vulnerable to all sorts of hidden biases; but compare this with a "malestream" world, be it politics, academia, or business, where "even" upper-class, young, white, heterosexual women are having extreme difficulties in finding any sort of legitimacy *as women*. The rage that excluded groups have visited on feminism raises questions about the return of the repressed within feminism. Perhaps women feel safer venting their rage against one another than they do expressing it to the real purveyors of power.

The access of the excluded to dominant discourses is an advance that postmodernism has helped feminism realize. But we would be

[94]De Lauretis (1989), pp. 3–4.
[95]Bordo (1990), p. 141.

foolish not to recognize that the issue of difference raised by post-modern theory holds as many dangers for feminism as helpful insights. Too much emphasis on difference can produce "an Other who is an exotic alien, a breed apart,"[96] a being with whom communication is absolutely impossible, almost in a return to the solipsism of Descartes's "cogito," and certainly echoing the oppositional difference of women to men in modern theory. At the same time, as Susan Bordo points out, feminist postmodernism advocates the "dogma that the only 'correct' perspective on race, class, and gender is the affirmation of difference; this dogma reveals itself in criticisms which attack gender generalizations as *in principle* essentialist or totalizing. Surely, such charges should require concrete examples of *actual* differences that are being submerged by any particular 'totality' in question."[97] Feminist postmodernism fails in its own efforts in abstracting the notion of difference beyond the pale of politics and even of theory. Yet by focusing exclusively on the holy trinity of gender, race, and class, feminist postmodernism creates a "coercive, mechanical requirement" for feminist scholarship to be legitimate. What about age, sexual orientation, ethnicity, geography, even species? Certain postmodern feminists attempt to incorporate some of these, but not all by any means, because it is an impossible task. As Bordo asks, "How many axes *can* one include and still preserve analytical focus or argument?"[98] That is the obverse of the difference dilemma: a focus on difference seems to deconstruct itself into the impossibility of writing theory.

Feminist postmodernism thus threatens to become post-theoretical, if not antitheoretical as well. Those that do attempt to incorporate a multiplicity of dimensions provide predominantly general and often vague criticisms of essentialism and exclusion and little by means of concrete suggestions as to *how* inclusion is to be carried out through theory. This may lead us to the conclusion that theory should be abandoned altogether, but I for one am not ready to accept that conclusion; nor, would it appear, are the writers of these criticisms.

Thus a feminist postmodernism evaporates before our eyes; but this is due more to the dynamics of postmodernism than to those of feminism. Postmodern theory cannot be as long as it is *post* modern rather than *pre* something else.[99] And one of the something elses is feminism. By focusing exclusively on deconstructing the past, postmodernism provides no possibility for the future. As in reactive autonomy, the self that is constituted through reactions to others, through

---

[96]Ibid., p. 140.
[97]Ibid., pp. 139–40.
[98]Ibid., p. 139.
[99]I owe this phrasing to James Kurth.

being not-other, is fragile and unstable, failing its own definition of autonomy. The self needs a more positive, constructive conception of autonomy as relational, attending to the ways in which a self becomes a self through relationships with others. Feminism, with relationship and the interdependent self at its core, provides a means for constructing the new something elses that will emerge from the deconstructive rubble of the postmodern era.

A Feminist Method for Political Theory or a Political-Theoretical Method for Feminism?

As Mary Poovey argues, "If deconstruction took feminism seriously, it wouldn't look like deconstruction anymore"; hence there can be no feminist postmodernism. But "if feminism took deconstruction at its word, we could begin to dismantle the system that assigns to all women a single identity and a marginal place"[100] as we say yes to a postmodern feminism. But it should be clear from the foregoing remarks that postmodern feminism must be understood as something very different from feminist postmodernism and from "malestream" postmodern theory. For it must in a sense betray part of its name— the "postmodern" part—in the attempt to achieve goals that satisfactorily address both postmodern and feminist enterprises. In struggling to find the meaning of woman, feminists must embrace postmodern ideals of difference, heterogeneity, and multiplicity without letting go of the goal of constructing theory.

The primary such betrayal required to salvage postmodernism for feminist obligation is to reclaim the subject as a viable category of analysis. Liberalism is to some degree correct in its fundamental assertion that obligation requires agents and subjects, even if it defines those terms problematically. A participatory politics of mutual recognition wherein the content of obligations is worked out and negotiated similarly requires flesh-and-blood people who can converse, deliberate, provide recognition, help others articulate their views, make decisions, and act on them. A collective cannot exist if its constituent parts do not. But liberalism simultaneously denies that women *are* subjects. Similarly, the denial of subjectivity is probably the single characteristic of postmodernism that makes a feminist postmodernism impossible. Postmodernism's key insight that the liberal, Enlightenment subject of natural man is an oppressive fiction helps empower feminism to demand inclusion in political theory. But "to deny the

[100]Poovey (1988), p. 63.

unity and stability of identity is one thing. The epistemological fantasy of *becoming* multiplicity—the dream of limitless multiple embodiments, allowing one to dance from place to place and self to self—is another."[101] Indeed, Flax argues that it is not only impossible but dangerous; "borderline syndrome," in which the self has no "core," is a serious pathology. "Those who celebrate or call for a 'decentered' self seem self-deceptively naive and unaware of the basic cohesion within themselves that makes the fragmentation of experiences something other than a terrifying slide into psychosis."[102] The strength of applying object relations to political theory lies in its recognition of the self as socially constructed, and in its simultaneous search for "healthier" such constructions. It helps reveal that what makes fragmenting and volatile identities "sick" is not just the attitudes of modern society toward them nor the institutional responses to such people (though both may contribute to the problem) but the fragmentation itself. And to respond that of course the person feels tormented by the condition itself because language constructs the condition as illness and then determines this feeling and reaction is horrifically to deny such pain.

Although the notion of subjectivity utilized throughout my study is not a unified totality but one of multiple selves, these selves are not fragmented and fractured but rather synthesized in a concrete person. In liberal obligation theory our identities are fractured by the very fiction that defines us as unified, and by the denial of individual multiplicity. If I have only one central identity, that one must have different parts to accommodate my experiences: for instance, a public self and a private self. But if we embrace a notion of subjectivity as a gathering together within one person of a multiplicity of identities created and influenced by and through relations with a variety of other persons, each of whom has relations with a variety of still other persons in a web of interrelationship and identity, we get a concept of subjectivity that exists—that does not evaporate in a postmodern deconstruction of self—but is not falsely coherent or unified.

A feminist subjectivity, while allowing for core identities and varying degrees of authenticity, need not be reduced to the totally unified subject of the Enlightenment. Diana Fuss suggests that we can view "subjectivity as a nexus of possibilities" rather than an essentialized, unitary entity; not an "I/not I" but rather a continuum of existence.[103] This notion is interesting and illuminating, for at once it allows the myriad possibilities that any individual person can be—if institutional structures such as patriarchy do not discipline her to be one particular

---

[101]Bordo (1990), pp. 144–45.
[102]Flax (1990), pp. 218–19.
[103]Fuss (1989), p. 87.

way—but at the same time recognizes that it is a flesh-and-blood person who has these possibilities. To say that this person is a subject is not to define her for eternity but precisely to recognize the ways in which she can change: partly through choice, partly through chance, and partly through response to external factors, which comprises both choice and nonchoice. This subject always has the potential for more change; but that does not mean that subjectivity evaporates. Just because someone I love may die next week, sending me into a tailspin depression that leads me to institutionalize myself; or just because a financial windfall allows me to quit my job and pursue a lifelong dream of moving to Paris and writing poetry; or just because reading Foucault or even a particularly intense visit with a psychotherapist may enable me to see how the meaning I have attributed to certain of my behaviors is really an illusion, thus causing me to recast my entire self-understanding: these possibilities do not mean that I cannot define myself as I am, here and now, with the conscious recognition that this description is neither timeless nor unchanging nor exhaustively complete. Nor is this new sense of self completely discontinuous with my former sense. Indeed, it can be fully understood and appreciated only in the context of my entire personal history.

Within this context of possibility, the concept of essentialism becomes transformed, more acceptable and even useful for postmodern feminism. As Gayatri Spivak points out, "When put into practice by the dispossessed themselves, essentialism can be powerfully displacing and disruptive."[104] De Lauretis similarly highlights the strategic and political importance of incorporating a notion of essentialism into postmodern feminism: "If feminist theory remains unwilling to take the risk of essentialism seriously while continuing to gesture toward it from a respectable distance, call it poststructuralist/deconstructionist or communist or simply anti-essentialist, it will remain unable to be both feminist and poststructuralist, both feminist and communist, or both feminist and radical at once. And the question is, in that case, can it remain feminist?"[105] Postmodernism's negative methodology is obviously extremely useful; but given the fact that we operate in our language and understand concepts through the dominant ontology and epistemology, even as we try to build them anew, then the tearing down can go only so far. Once we deconstruct to the limits of language, we are left with no means of communicating and even of formulating our ideas.[106] Wittgenstein's maxim that all meaning occurs

[104]Quoted in Fuss (1989), p. 85.
[105]De Lauretis (1989), p. 32.
[106]Indeed, in *Philosophical Investigations* Wittgenstein derides philosophy as "the bumps that the understanding has got by running its head up against the limits of language" (p. 43).

in language does not mean that we cannot critique or pull apart existing structures of thought, nor does it mean that new concepts and words cannot be introduced and utilized effectively. But it does mean that our deconstruction can go only so far before it loses meaning; and that even if we decompose as far as we are able, we are still left with part of the old structure. This, however, is not bad, as the more radical feminist postmoderns might claim; it just *is*. Just as it is pointless to say that gravity limits my freedom to fly, so is it meaningless to say that language as such limits our expression. Language is constituent of our ability to express and communicate ideas and experience. To go beyond this and completely deconstruct language itself leaves us with only "an inarticulate sound."[107]

Or does it? Do I perhaps overstate the case? Although language is a constituent feature of our social being, it is also, unlike gravity, manmade, and hence can and does contain many sexist, racist, and classist elements which can be highly inhibitive of expression. So it both is and is not pointless to say that language limits us, inhibits our ability to formulate and express ideas. The entities or ideas that words express have meaning only insofar as those meanings can be expressed in language. But those meanings can be perverted by language as well, and we may try to achieve a truer expression of our meaning. For instance, mothering as a practice or as a language game contains a variety of meanings in daily actions and expression, and these meanings constitute themselves through language. But there is also a great deal of nonverbal communication between mother and infant, the meaning of which may be hidden from the observer and even from the practitioners themselves, because such meaning is actively obscured by the larger, dominant language game—patriarchal society—within which mothering takes place. That is, the dominant male nonmaternal discourse to a large degree controls and dominates the language of maternal practice, and this is because maternal practice, while supporting and making possible the dominant discourse, is in many ways at odds with it. According to object relations theory, mother-only child rearing creates men who need to dominate women, which in turn ensures that women will continue to mother children.

It is thus, we can argue, that part of the dominant language game *depends* on an obfuscation of maternal practice and a subversion of its meaning. Ruddick suggests that in a society in which morality is defined in terms of rights and separated individuals and values of connection and relationship are devalued, maternal thinking will likely be subverted into self-denigration with distastrously conflicting re-

[107]Ibid., p. 93.

sults. Values of "preservation" and "holding" within a society defined by competition, property, ownership, comparative value and the denial of self-creation to women except through their children will not surprisingly tend to degenerate into possessiveness or overprotectiveness, with growth stunted as a result. "Acceptability" can become an important or even a primary value in such a society, which will produce results antithetical to the practice, demanding conformity and crushing the creative spirit. It will also result in sons' going to war, a practice in many ways diametrically opposed to maternal practice.[108]

Of course, maternal practice is not a "pure" thing that is merely talked about incorrectly; it is shaped by that language as well. Yet there would seem to be two conflicting meanings within one practice: the meaning of the dominant discourse and the meaning that women experience but cannot articulate because they lack a suitable language. That we tend to deny that such nonverbalized experience has meaning attests not only to the hegemony of masculinist discourse (could the primacy of language as a determinant of meaning be a reflection of empiricism?) but also to the difficulty of building theories within a hostile environment. If it seems in feminist enterprises that we run against the walls of our language, perhaps it is because our language expresses—and can only express—particular perspectives and ideas, particular kinds of theory and ways of developing theory. The challenge embodied in getting beyond this problem is one that needs to be faced, however, not only for the success of feminist theory but also to ensure the future viability of political theory in general.

I have argued that a key to meeting this challenge lies in a concept of plural feminist standpoints: an application of standpoint epistemology to the idea of multiplicity to allow for a variety of standpoints that reflect the variety of women's and men's experiences. By locating it within the modifier *feminist*, we curtail the relativism of postmodernism. Not just *anything* can count as a feminist standpoint. But for a complete picture—or at least a less partial one—other groups excluded and marginalized from the dominant discourses need to develop their stories as well.[109] Various standpoints must be further ex-

---

[108]Ruddick identifies preservation, growth, and acceptability as three central values of maternal practice; her article presents a deeper analysis of them. See Ruddick (1984b) and also Ruddick (1983).

[109]Although this afterword was largely completed before I read sections of the manuscript of Harding (1991), her argument helped clarify several ideas I was struggling with. The arguments expressed here are largely in agreement with hers, particularly the idea that a feminist standpoint is compatible with, and even requires, multiplicity. Of course my entire book's intellectual debt to and affinity with Harding's earlier work as well should be obvious to most readers familiar with her oeuvre.

plored and articulated, even as feminism itself develops and evolves many standpoints of its own. Feminism may share insights and problems with the standpoint of Native Americans, or disabled people, or the urban underclass, but it cannot speak for such groups because their experiences are far from coextensive. Although feminists must be involved in the struggle to help others realize their subjectivity, such others must also articulate their own standpoints. I realize I run the risk of implying the belief that different groups are established entities with distinct characteristics, thus problematizing the positions of, say, black women (are they African-Americans or feminists?). I do not, however, intend to convey this meaning. As I argued in my brief description of caucus democracy, all of us, including white males, belong to varieties of groups because we have various standpoints reflecting different aspects of our experience. These aspects fragment us only in the context of a discourse that demands our identity to be unified; within a context of multiplicity these aspects allow for the individual to engage in an ongoing and continually shifting process of self-definition, self-understanding, and synthesis. Obviously some standpoints will seem to have more power for different people than others, and at different times in their lives. But the continued articulation of different standpoints is vital not only for empowering more groups and experiences and thus for strengthening the conversation but also for helping others realize the ways in which the identities they thought were not important to them really are.

This means that holders of various standpoints must themselves articulate those standpoints. For instance, women of any description (Muslim women, women of color, working-class women, and so forth) are better able than men to articulate a feminist standpoint. But it also means that others can and must help them realize their standpoints: men can and indeed should also be feminists. Although feminists cannot speak for others any more than others can speak for them, feminists can nevertheless listen and respond as they expect others to listen and respond to them. Through others' articulation, feminists of all sorts learn about one another and about themselves. That is, the articulation of, say, black feminism (which itself may leave out further subdivisions—a black heterosexual feminist may have different experiences from a black lesbian feminist and so forth) or of (a potentially broader and hence even more potentially essentializing) African-Americanism will teach white (and perhaps also middle-class or academic-professional or heterosexual) feminists about the experiences of black women and men; but it also provides a tool for understanding their own experiences as white feminists. That is, using a black feminist or African-American standpoint as a starting point for theory can reveal things about white women's experiences that a white feminist standpoint cannot reveal, precisely because of the privilege that adheres to being white. At the same time, white women do experience oppression, and so it makes no sense to ignore the experiences of white women simply because black women are more oppressed. By that logic we would have to ignore African-Americanism altogether because the category includes men. We would have to find the absolutely most oppressed person (who will most likely be a woman, among other things) and use her standpoint as the basis for a new true theory that tells the whole story. Even apart from the incommensurability of certain oppressions (are Chicanas more oppressed in the United States than blacks? Jews more than Muslims?), such a caricature of standpoint epistemology ignores the interdependence of different kinds of oppression and hence the need to articulate a variety of standpoints.

This variety and multiplicity of standpoints is absolutely crucial if we are to achieve the inclusiveness and mutual recognition of a feminist participatory democratic conversation and hence the determination of obligation. Yet pursuing multiplicity within a standpoints approach prevents the slide into relativism, for it provides collective means of evaluating and discriminating between various claims for a standpoint. In particular, it allows for discrimination between a standpoint and an ideology, which can be racist, misogynist, homophobic, classist, ageist, and so forth. For instance, men have insights to contribute to feminists, as do whites to African-Americans, heterosexuals to lesbians and homosexuals, perhaps even capitalists to workers. But this is different from saying that masculinism has something to offer feminism, or classism has something to offer the proletariat. The dangers and likelihood of masking ideology as standpoint is greater from the perspective of the more powerful in each of these pairs, because such ideologies will reinforce their preexisting claims to power.

The methodological advantage of standpoint epistemology lies in its notion that women will have more to say to men, African-Americans more to say to whites, lesbians and homosexuals more to say to heterosexuals, workers more to say to capitalists, because it considers the experience of the oppressed less partial and perverse than that of the more privileged. But the exchange of insights is not unidirectional, exclusively from the bottom up. The articulation of identity is a collaborative enterprise, which is what makes conversation and mutual recognition so crucial to its success. Mutuality, however, is not a principle of relativism. Rather, as a feminist principle it places certain limitations on what can count as a standpoint as opposed to an ideology. The articulation of such standpoints, within the parameters of feminism, ensures that such experiences must be articulated from the perspective of women's or workers' or African-Americans' or lesbians' lives. As Harding points out, standpoint epistemology does not merely limit itself to passively including the standpoints of others; it requires that we begin from others' lives as the basis for theory. Thus, for instance, a liberal justification of rights would have to begin from the perspective of groups who have been excluded from and hurt by the liberal discourse of rights, and not just from the privileged white male perspective that created rights discourse. Such a shift of perspective, I have argued throughout this book, would require a profound shift in the discourse itself. So the invocation to theorize from others' perspectives does not apply just to feminists and other marginalized groups who most obviously have something to gain from such a mutualistic strategy. Those in traditionally privileged positions must also take responsibility for such theorizing, even though it may appear to disempower them, for in reality it empowers us all.

Accordingly, a feminist standpoints method cannot be content merely "adding and stirring" women of color, lesbian women, women factory workers to a basically white, economically privileged feminist standpoint, any more than it holds that political theorists can "add and stir" women to the theories of Hobbes, Locke, or Rousseau. Theory must be developed that starts from all of these different historical experiences. The feminist postmodern call simply to listen to women's experience is a starting point for this process, but it cannot nourish or sustain feminist projects. Women's voices can be interpreted in sexist ways, and there can be non–self-conscious or non–self-critical representation even of one's own experience. The self-conscious dimensions of postmodernism require us to recognize how we may be wrong even as we point out how others may also be wrong: " 'That's not it' and 'that's still not it.' "[110] But ironically, perhaps, this is the advantage of a feminist standpoints method over feminist postmodernism: it helps keep postmodern goals from folding back on themselves and imploding. A standpoints approach reveals why the double-edged character of identity politics as critique of the oppressiveness of social construction and the liberation of empowering choice is so important to a feminist method for conceptualizing politics and political theory. It can help feminists figure out "how to enter struggles over the meaning(s) of woman in ways that do not repress pluralities, without losing sight of the political necessity for fiction and unity."[111] Fictions are dangerous, but they are also helpful.

[110]Kristeva (1980b), p. 137.
[111]Martin (1988), p. 14.

Although a feminist postmodernist might say, "Sure they're helpful—they've helped 'malestream' theorists for centuries," such a response fails to note the crucial distinction between these new unities and fictions and the old hegemonies they seek not to replace but to displace. For these new fictions are born of a recognition of the dangers of hegemony; they evolve out of a self-conscious rejection of sameness and unity; they emerge from an understanding of the importance of difference as the very soul of meaning. Identity politics can help "shift the terms of the struggle" and provide "the ability to see our position within existing structures but to respond from somewhere else."[112] Such new approaches will always, by Enlightenment standards, appear partial, incomplete, even vague, while by postmodern standards they will simultaneously appear hegemonic and totalizing. But the apparent failure by the standards of both of these discourses can provide the most powerful revelation of feminism's strength. In a sense, as long as feminism can keep both of these kinds of masculinist discourses unhappy—even more, as long as it can keep both of them off base, struggling to defend and rearticulate themselves—feminists have to suspect that they are doing something right.

[112]Ibid., p. 10.

Bibliography

Aboulafia, Mitchell. 1984. "From Domination to Recognition." In *Beyond Domination: New Perspectives on Women and Philosophy*, ed. Carol Gould. Totowa, N.J.: Rowman and Allanheld.

Abrams, Kathryn. 1991. "Hearing the Call of Stories." *California Law Review* 79, no. 4: 971–1052.

Abzug, Bella. 1984. *Gender Gap: Bella Abzug's Guide to Political Power for American Women*. Boston: Houghton Mifflin.

Ackerman, Bruce. 1980. *Social Justice in the Liberal State*. New Haven: Yale University Press.

Alcoff, Linda. 1988. "Cultural Feminism versus Post-Structuralism: The Identity Crisis in Feminist Theory." *Signs* 13, no. 3: 405–36.

Arendt, Hannah. 1972. "Civil Disobedience." In *Crises of the Republic*. New York: Harcourt, Brace, Jovanovich.

Ashcraft, Richard. 1986. *Revolutionary Politics and Locke's Two Treatises of Government*. Princeton: Princeton University Press.

Bachrach, Peter. 1967. *The Theory of Democratic Elitism: A Critique*. Boston: Little, Brown.

Baier, Annette C. 1986. "Trust and Antitrust." *Ethics* 96, no. 2: 231–60.

——. 1987. "Hume: The Women's Moral Theorist?" In *Women and Moral Theory*, ed. Eva Feder Kittay and Diana T. Meyer. Totowa, N.J.: Rowman and Littlefield.

Bakan, David. 1966. *The Duality of Human Existence: Isolation and Communion in Western Man*. Boston: Beacon Press.

Balbus, Isaac D. 1982. *Marxism and Domination: A Neo-Hegelian, Feminist, Psychoanalytic Theory of Sexual, Political, and Technological Liberation*. Princeton: Princeton University Press.

——. 1987. "Disciplining Women: Michel Foucault and the Power of Feminist Discourse." In *Feminism as Critique*, ed. Seyla Benhabib and Drucilla Cornell. Minneapolis: University of Minnesota Press.

Barber, Benjamin. 1984. *Strong Democracy: Participatory Politics for a New Age*. Berkeley: University of California Press.

343

Bardige, Betty. 1988. "Things So Finely Human: Moral Sensibilities at Risk in Adolescence." In *Mapping the Moral Domain*, ed. Carol Gilligan et al. Cambridge, Mass.: Harvard University Press.

Barker, Ernest, ed. 1973. *Social Contract: Essays by Locke, Hume, and Rousseau*. London: Oxford University Press.

Barry, Kathleen. 1979. *Female Sexual Slavery*. New York: Avon Books.

Bart, Pauline. 1984. Review of Chodorow, *The Preproduction of Mothering*. In *Mothering: Essays in Feminist Theory*, ed. Joyce Trebilcott. Totowa, N.J.: Rowman and Allanheld.

Bartkowski, Francis. 1988. "Epistemic Drift in Foucault." In *Feminism and Foucault*, ed. Irene Diamond and Lee Quinby. Boston: Northeastern University Press.

Baudrillard, Jean. 1987. *Forget Foucault*. New York: Semiotext(e).

Beauvoir, Simone de. 1974. *The Second Sex*. Trans. H. M. Parshley. New York: Vintage Books.

Belenky, Mary Field, Blythe McVicker Clinchy, Nancy Rule Goldberger, and Jill Mattuck Tarule. 1986. *Women's Ways of Knowing: The Development of Self, Voice, and Mind*. New York: Basic Books.

Benhabib, Seyla. 1986. *Critique, Norm, and Utopia*. New York: Columbia University Press.

———. 1987. "The Generalized and the Concrete Other: The Kohlberg-Gilligan Controversy and Feminist Theory." In *Feminism as Critique: On the Politics of Gender*, ed. Seyla Benhabib and Drucilla Cornell. Minneapolis: University of Minnesota Press.

Benhabib, Seyla, and Drucilla Cornell, eds. 1987. *Feminism as Critique: On the Politics of Gender*. Minneapolis: University of Minnesota Press.

Benjamin, Jessica. 1980. "The Bonds of Love: Rational Violence and Erotic Domination." *Feminist Studies* 6, no. 1: 144–74.

Bension, Mary Sumner. 1935. *Women in Eighteenth-Century America: A Study of Opinion and Social Usage*. New York: Columbia University Press.

Bentham, Jeremy. 1960. *A Fragment on Government and An Introduction to the Principles of Morals and Legislation*. Ed. Wilfrid Harrison. Oxford: Basil Blackwell.

Berlin, Isaiah. 1971. *Four Essays on Liberty*. New York: Oxford University Press.

Blustein, Jeffrey. 1982. *Parents and Children: The Ethics of the Family*. New York: Oxford University Press.

Bordo, Susan. 1986. "The Cartesian Masculinization of Thought." *Signs: Journal of Women in Culture and Society* 11, no. 3: 439–56.

———. 1990. "Feminism, Postmodernism, and Gender-Scepticism." In *Feminism/Postmodernism*, ed. Linda Nicholson. New York: Routledge.

Bordo, Susan, and Alison Jaggar. 1989. *Gender/Body/Knowledge: Feminist Reconstructions of Being and Knowing*. New Brunswick, N.J.

Brown, Wendy. 1987. "Where Is the Sex in Political Theory?" *Women and Politics* 7, no. 1: 3–23.

Brownmiller, Susan. 1975. *Against Our Will: Men, Women, and Rape*. New York: Simon and Schuster.

Bulker, Eloise A. 1987. "Storytelling Power: Personal Narratives and Political Analysis." *Women and Politics* 7, no. 3: 29–46.

Bull, Norman J. 1969. *Moral Judgement from Childhood to Adolescence*. London: Routledge and Kegan Paul.

Bumiller, Kristen. 1988. *The Civil Rights Society: The Social Construction of Victims*. Baltimore: Johns Hopkins University Press.

Burke, Carolyn. 1980. "Introduction to Luce Irigaray's 'When Our Lips Speak Together.'" *Signs: Journal of Women in Culture and Society* 6, no. 1: 66–68.

Burke, Edmund. 1955. *Reflections on the Revolution in France.* Ed. Thomas H. D. Mahoney. New York: Bobbs Merrill.

Butler, Judith. 1987. "Variations on Sex and Gender: Beauvoir, Wittig, and Foucault." In *Feminism as Critique,* ed. Seyla Benhabib and Drucilla Cornell. Minneapolis: University of Minnesota Press.

Butler, Melissa. 1978. "Early Liberal Roots of Feminism: John Locke and the Attack on Patriarchy." *American Political Science Review* 72, no. 1: 135–50.

Carraway, Nancie. 1989. "Identity Politics and Shifting Selves: Black Feminist Coalition Theory." Paper presented at the annual meeting of the American Political Science Association, Atlanta.

Carroll, Susan J. 1985. *Women as Candidates in American Politics.* Bloomington: Indiana University Press.

Chodorow, Nancy. 1974. "Family Structure and Feminine Personality." In *Woman, Culture, and Society,* ed. Michelle Zimbalist Rosaldo and Louise Lamphere. Stanford: Stanford University Press.

———. 1978. *The Reproduction of Mothering: Psychoanalysis and the Sociology of Gender.* Berkeley: University of California Press.

———. 1979a. "Feminism and Difference: Gender, Relation, and Difference in Psychoanalytic Perspective." *Socialist Review* 46: 51–69.

———. 1979b. "Mothering, Male Dominance, and Capitalism." In *Capitalist Patriarchy and the Case for Socialist Feminism,* ed. Zillah Eisenstein. New York: Monthly Review Press.

———. 1980. "Gender, Relation, and Difference in Psychoanalytic Perspective." In *The Future of Difference.* Vol. 1 of *The Scholar and the Feminist: Papers from the Barnard Women's Center Conference,* ed. Hester Eisenstein and Alice Jardine. Boston: G. K. Hall and Co.

———. 1989. *Feminism and Psychoanalytic Theory.* New Haven: Yale University Press.

Chodorow, Nancy J., Dorothy Dinnerstein, and Roger Gottlieb. 1984. "An Exchange: Mothering and the Reproduction of Power." *Socialist Review* 78: 121–30.

Christian, Barbara. 1988. "The Race for Theory." *Feminist Studies* 14, no. 1: 67–79.

Cixous, Hélène. 1980. "Sorties." In *New French Feminisms,* ed. Elaine Marks and Isabelle de Courtivron. Amherst: University of Massachusetts Press.

Clark, Alice. 1982. *The Working Life of Women in the Seventeenth Century.* New York: Routledge and Kegan Paul.

Cohen, Joshua. 1986. "Reflections on Rousseau: Autonomy and Democracy." *Philosophy and Public Affairs* 15, no. 3: 275–97.

Colker, Ruth. 1983. "Pornography and Privacy: Towards the Development of a Group-Based Theory of Sex-Based Invasions of Privacy." *Law and Inequality: A Journal of Theory and Practice* 1, no. 2: 191–237.

Collins, Patricia Hill. 1987. "The Importance of Black Motherhood in Black Culture and Mother/Daughter Relations." *Sage* 4, no. 2: 3–10.

———. 1989. "The Social Construction of Black Feminist Thought." *Signs: Journal of Women in Culture and Society* 14, no. 4: 745–73.

———. 1990. *Black Feminist Thought: Knowledge, Consciousness, and the Politics of Empowerment.* Boston: Unwin Hyman.

Connolly, William. 1985. "Taylor, Foucault, and Otherness." *Political Theory* 13, no. 3: 365–76.

Cooper, Sandi. 1986. "Introduction to the Documents." Also the documents "Offer of Proof Concerning the Testimony of Dr. Rosaline Rosenberg" and "Written Testimony of Alice Kessler-Harris." *Signs: Journal of Women in Culture and Society* 11, no. 4: 753–79.

Coser, Lewis A. 1977. "Georg Simmel's Neglected Contributions to the Sociology of Women." *Signs: Journal of Women in Culture and Society* 2, no. 4: 869–76.

Coser, Rose Laub. 1975. "The Complexity of Roles as a Seedbed of Individual Autonomy." In *The Idea of Social Structure: Papers in Honor of Robert K. Merton*, ed. Lewis A. Coser. New York: Harcourt, Brace, Jovanovich.

Daly, Kathleen. 1987. "Structure and Practice of Familial-Based Justice in a Criminal Court." *Law and Society Review* 21, no. 2: 267–90.

DeCew, Judith Wagner. 1984. "Violent Pornography: Censorship, Morality, and Social Alternatives." *Journal of Applied Philosophy* 1, no. 1: 79–94.

de Lauretis, Teresa. 1989. "The Essence of the Triangle, or Taking the Risk of Essentialism Seriously: Feminist Theory in Italy, the U.S., and Britain." *Differences* 1: 3–37.

Department of Government Tutorial Office, Harvard University. 1989. "Gender and the Harvard Government Department: The Experiences and Concerns of Undergraduate Women," April 10.

Derrida, Jacques. 1972. *Positions*. Trans. Alan Bass. Chicago: University of Chicago Press.

——. 1976. *Of Grammatology*. Trans. Gayatri Chakravorty Spivak. Baltimore: Johns Hopkins University Press.

——. 1978. *Spurs: Nietzsche's Styles*. Trans. Barbara Harlow. Chicago: University of Chicago Press.

——. 1982. *Margins of Philosophy*. Trans. Alan Bass. Chicago: University of Chicago Press.

——. 1985. "Deconstruction in America: An Interview with Jacques Derrida." *Critical Exchange* 17: 1–33.

Diamond, Irene, and Lee Quinby. 1988. *Feminism and Foucault: Reflections on Resistance*. Boston: Northeastern University Press.

Dietz, Mary. 1985. "Citizenship with a Feminist Face: The Problem with Maternal Thinking." *Political Theory* 13, no. 1: 19–37.

Diggins, John. 1984. *The Lost Soul of American Politics: Virtue, Self-Interest, and the Foundations of Liberalism*. New York: Basic Books.

di Leonardo, Micaela. 1984. *The Varieties of Ethnic Experience: Kinship, Class, and Gender among Californian Italian-Americans*. Ithaca: Cornell University Press.

Dill, Bonnie Thornton. 1987. "The Dialectics of Black Womanhood." In *Feminism and Methodology*, ed. Sandra Harding. Bloomington: Indiana University Press.

Dinnerstein, Dorothy. 1976. *The Mermaid and the Minotaur: Sexual Arrangements and Human Malaise*. New York: Harper and Row.

Di Stefano, Christine. 1983. "Masculinity as Ideology in Political Theory: Hobbesian Man Considered." *Women's Studies International Forum* 6, no. 6: 633–44.

——. 1990. "Dilemmas of Difference: Feminism, Modernity, and Postmodernism." In *Feminism/Postmodernism*, ed. Linda Nicholson. New York: Routledge.

———. 1991. *Configurations of Masculinity: A Feminist Perspective on Modern Political Theory*. Ithaca: Cornell University Press.

Dreyfus, Hubert, and Paul Rabinow. 1982. *Michel Foucault: Beyond Structuralism and Hermeneutics*. Chicago: University of Chicago Press.

Dunn, John. 1969. *The Political Thought of John Locke*. Cambridge: Cambridge University Press.

———. 1980. "Consent in the Political Theory of John Locke." In *Political Obligation in Its Historical Context*. Cambridge: Cambridge University Press.

———. 1984. *Locke*. London: Oxford University Press.

———. 1985. "'Trust' in the Politics of John Locke." In *Rethinking Modern Political Theory: Essays, 1979–1983*. Cambridge: Cambridge University Press.

Dworkin, Andrea. 1981. *Pornography: Men Possessing Women*. New York: Putnam.

Ehrensaft, Diane. 1984. "When Women and Men Mother." In *Mothering: Essays in Feminist Theory*, ed. Joyce Trebilcott. Totowa, N.J.: Rowman and Allanheld.

Eisenstein, Zillah. 1981. *The Radical Future of Liberal Feminism*. New York: Longman.

———. 1988. *The Female Body and the Law*. Berkeley: University of California Press.

———. 1990. "Reproductive Rights and the Problem of the Democratic State: Bush and Ceausescu on Abortion." Paper presented at the annual meeting of the American Political Science Association, San Francisco, September 1.

Elshtain, Jean Bethke. 1981. *Public Man, Private Woman: Women in Social and Political Thought*. Princeton: Princeton University Press.

Equal Employment Opportunity Commission v. Sears, Roebuck and Co. 1986. 628 F. Supp. 1264, 39 FEP 1672 (N.D. Illinois).

Estrich, Susan. 1987. *Real Rape*. Cambridge, Mass.: Harvard University Press.

Ferguson, Ann. 1984. "On Conceiving Motherhood and Sexuality: A Feminist Materialist Approach." In *Mothering: Essays in Feminist Theory*, ed. Joyce Trebilcott. Totowa, N.J.: Rowman and Allanheld.

Fishkin, James. 1982. *The Limits of Obligation*. New Haven: Yale University Press.

Flathman, Richard E. 1972. *Political Obligation*. New York: Atheneum.

———. 1980. *The Practice of Political Authority: Authority and the Authoritative*. Chicago: University of Chicago Press.

———. 1987. *The Philosophy and Politics of Freedom*. Chicago: University of Chicago Press.

Flax, Jane. 1978. "The Conflict between Nurturance and Autonomy in Mother-Daughter Relationships and within Feminism." *Feminist Studies* 4, no. 2: 171–89.

———. 1980. "Mother-Daughter Relationships: Psychodynamics, Politics, and Philosophy." In *The Future of Difference*. Vol. 1 of *The Scholar and the Feminist: Papers from the Barnard Women's Center Conference*, ed. Hester Eisenstein and Alice Jardine. Boston: G. K. Hall and Co.

———. 1983. "Political Philosophy and the Patriarchal Unconscious: A Psychoanalytic Perspective on Epistemology and Metaphysics." In *Discovering Reality: Feminist Perspectives on Epistemology, Metaphysics, Methodology, and Philosophy of Science*, ed. Sandra Harding and Merrill B. Hintikka. Dordrecht: D. Reidel.

———. 1986. "Gender as a Problem: In and For Feminist Theory." *American*

Studies/Amerika Studien (journal of the German Association for American Studies) 31: 193–213.

——. 1990. *Thinking Fragments: Psychoanalysis, Feminism, and Postmodernism in the Contemporary West*. Berkeley: University of California Press.

Flexner, Eleanor. 1959. *Century of Struggle: The Women's Rights Movement in the United States*. Cambridge, Mass.: Belknap.

Foucault, Michel. 1979. *Discipline and Punish: The Birth of the Prison*. Trans. Alan Sheridan. New York: Vintage.

——. 1980. *Power/Knowledge: Selected Interviews and Other Writings, 1972–1977*. New York: Pantheon.

——. 1982. "The Subject and Power." In Hubert Dreyfus and Paul Rabinow. *Michel Foucault: Beyond Structuralism and Hermeneutics*. Chicago: University of Chicago Press.

Franklin, John Hope. 1974. *From Slavery to Freedom: A History of Negro Americans*. 4th ed. New York: Knopf.

Fraser, Antonia. 1984. *The Weaker Vessel*. New York: Random House.

Fraser, Nancy. 1991. "Rethinking the Public Sphere: A Contribution to the Critique of Actually Existing Democracy." In *Habermas and the Public Sphere*, ed. Craig Calhoun. Cambridge, Mass.: MIT Press.

Fraser, Nancy, and Linda Nicholson. 1989. "Social Criticism without Philosophy: An Encounter between Feminism and Postmodernism." In *Feminism/Postmodernism*, ed. Linda Nicholson. New York: Routledge.

Freud, Sigmund. 1961. *Three Essays on the Theory of Sexuality*. In *The Standard Edition of the Complete Psychological Works of Sigmund Freud*, ed. James Strachey. London: Hogarth.

Friday, Nancy. 1977. *My Mother, Myself: The Daughter's Search for Identity*. New York: Delacorte Press.

Fried, Barbara. 1982. "Boys Will Be Boys Will Be Boys: The Language of Sex and Gender." In *Biological Woman: The Convenient Myth*, ed. Ruth Hubbard, M. S. Henifin, and Barbara Fried. Cambridge Mass.: Schenkman.

Frye, Marilyn. 1983. *The Politics of Reality: Essays in Feminist Theory*. Trumansburg, N.Y.: The Crossing Press.

Fuss, Diana. 1989. "Reading Like a Feminist." In *Differences* 1: 77–92.

Garrison, Dee. 1981. "Karen Horney and Feminism." *Signs: Journal of Women in Culture and Society* 6, no. 4: 672–91.

Gauthier, David. 1969. *The Logic of Leviathan: The Moral and Political Theory of Thomas Hobbes*. Oxford: Clarendon Press.

——. 1990. *Moral Dealing: Contract, Ethics, and Reason*. Ithaca: Cornell University Press.

Gelles, Richard J. 1976. "Abused Wives: Why Do They Stay?" *Journal of Marriage and the Family* 38, no. 4: 659–68.

Giles-Simms, Jean. 1983. *Wife Battering: A Systems Theory Approach*. New York: Guilford.

Gilligan, Carol. 1982. *In a Different Voice: Psychological Theory and Women's Development*. Cambridge, Mass.: Harvard University Press.

——. 1984. "The Conquistador and the Dark Continent: Reflections on the Psychology of Love." *Daedalus* (Summer): 75–95.

——. 1986. "Remapping Development: The Power of Divergent Data." In *Value Presuppositions in Theories of Human Development*, ed. Leonard Cirillo and Seymour Wapner. Hillside, N.J.: Erlbaum.

——. 1988. "Remapping the Moral Domain: New Images of Self in Relationship." In *Mapping the Moral Domain*, ed. Carol Gilligan et al. Cambridge, Mass.: Harvard University Press.

Gilligan, Carol, Sharry Langdale, Nona Lyons, and J. M. Murphy. 1982. "Contributions of Women's Thinking to Developmental Theory: The Elimination of Sex Bias in Moral Development Theory and Research." Final Report of the National Institute of Education.

Gilligan, Carol, Nona P. Lyons, and Trudy Hanmer, eds. 1990. *Making Connections: The Relational Worlds of Adolescent Girls at Emma Willard School*. Cambridge, Mass.: Harvard University Press.

Gilligan, Carol, Janie Victoria Ward, and Jill McLean Taylor, with Betty Bardige, eds. 1988. *Mapping the Moral Domain*. Cambridge, Mass.: Harvard University Press.

Gilligan, Carol, and Grant Wiggins. 1988. "The Origins of Morality in Early Childhood Relationships." In *Mapping the Moral Domain*, ed. Carol Gilligan et al. Cambridge, Mass.: Harvard University Press.

Ginsburg, Fay. 1989. *Contested Lives: The Abortion Debate in an American Community*. Berkeley: University of California Press.

Godwin, William. 1976. *Enquiry concerning Political Justice and Its Influence on Modern Morals and Happiness*. Ed. I. Kramnick. Middlesex: Penguin.

Gottlieb, Roger. 1984. "Mothering and the Reproduction of Power: Chodorow, Dinnerstein, and Social Theory." *Socialist Review* 77: 93–119.

Gould, Carol. 1984a. "Public Rights and Private Virtues: Women, the Family, and Democracy." In *Beyond Domination: New Perspectives on Women and Philosophy*, ed. Carol Gould. Totowa, N.J.: Rowman and Allanheld.

———, ed. 1984b. *Beyond Domination: New Perspectives on Women and Philosophy*. Totowa, N.J.: Rowman and Allanheld.

Green, Thomas Hill. 1986. *Lectures on the Principles of Political Obligation*, ed. Paul Harris and John Morrow. Cambridge: Cambridge University Press.

Greenberg, Jay R., and Stephen A. Mitchell. 1983. *Object Relations in Psychoanalytic Theory*. Cambridge, Mass.: Harvard University Press.

Griffin, Susan. 1978. *Woman and Nature: The Roaring inside Her*. New York: Harper and Row.

———. 1981. *Pornography and Silence: Culture's Revenge against Nature*. New York: Harper and Row.

Gross, Michael, and Mary Beth Averill. 1983. "Evolution and Patriarchal Myths of Scarcity and Competition." In *Discovering Reality: Feminist Perspectives on Epistemology, Metaphysics, Methodology, and Philosophy of Science*, ed. Sandra Harding and Merrill B. Hintikka. Dordrecht: D. Reidel.

Habermas, Jürgen. 1979. *Communication and the Evolution of Society*. Boston: Beacon.

Hamilton, Victoria. 1982. *Narcissus and Oedipus: The Children of Psychoanalysis*. London: Routledge and Kegan Paul.

Haraway, Donna. 1988. "Situated Knowledges: The Science Question in Feminism and the Privilege of Partial Perspective." *Feminist Studies* 14, no. 3: 575–99.

———. 1990. "A Manifesto for Cyborgs: Science, Technology, and Socialist Feminism in the 1980s." In *Feminism/Postmodernism*, ed. Linda Nicholson. New York: Routledge.

Harding, Sandra. 1981. "What Is the Real Material Base of Patriarchy and Capital?" In *Women and Revolution*, ed. Lydia Sargent. Boston: South End Press.

——. 1982. "The Gender Politics of Infancy." *Quest* 5, no. 3: 53–70.
——. 1983a. "Why Has the Sex/Gender System Become Visible Only Now?" In *Discovering Reality: Feminist Perspectives on Epistemology, Metaphysics, Methodology, and Philosophy of Science,* ed. Sandra Harding and Merrill B. Hintikka. Dordrecht: D. Reidel.
——. 1983b. "Common Causes: Toward a *Reflexive* Feminist Theory." *Women and Politics* 3, no. 4: 27–42.
——. 1984. "Is Gender a Variable in Conceptions of Rationality? A Survey of Issues." In *Beyond Domination: New Perspectives on Women and Philosophy,* ed. Carol Gould. Totowa, N.J.: Rowman and Allanheld.
——. 1986. *The Science Question in Feminism.* Ithaca: Cornell University Press.
——. 1987a. "The Instability of the Analytical Categories of Feminist Theory." *Signs: Journal of Women in Culture and Society* 11, no. 4: 645–64.
——, ed. 1987b. *Feminism and Methodology.* Bloomington: Indiana University Press.
——. 1991. *Whose Science? Whose Knowledge? Thinking from Women's Lives.* Ithaca: Cornell University Press.
Harding, Sandra, and Merrill B. Hintikka, eds. 1983. *Discovering Reality: Feminist Perspectives on Epistemology, Metaphysics, Methodology, and Philosophy of Science.* Dordrecht: D. Reidel.
Hare-Mustin, Rachel T., and Jeanne Marecek. 1986. "Autonomy and Gender: Some Questions for Therapists." *Psychotherapy* 23: 205–12.
——. 1990. "Beyond Difference." In *Making a Difference: Psychology and the Construction of Gender,* ed. R. T. Hare-Mustin and J. Marecek. New Haven: Yale University Press.
Hart, H. L. A. 1961. *The Concept of Law.* Oxford: Clarendon.
Hartman, Heidi. 1987. "The Family as the Locus of Gender, Class, and Political Struggle: The Example of Housework." In *Feminism and Methodology,* ed. Sandra Harding. Bloomington: Indiana University Press.
Hartsock, Nancy C. M. 1979. "Feminist Theory and Revolutionary Strategy." In *Capitalist Patriarchy and the Case for Socialist Feminism,* ed. Zillah Eisenstein. New York: Monthly Review Press.
——. 1983. "The Feminist Standpoint: Developing the Ground for a Specifically Feminist Historical Materialism." In *Discovering Reality: Feminist Perspectives on Epistemology, Metaphysics, Methodology, and Philosophy of Science,* ed. Sandra Harding and Merrill B. Hintikka. Dordrecht: D. Reidel.
——. 1984. *Money, Sex, and Power: Towards a Feminist Historical Materialism.* Boston: Northeastern University Press.
——. 1987. "Rethinking Modernism: Majority vs. Minority Theories." *Cultural Critique* 7: 187–206.
——. 1990. "Foucault on Power: A Theory for Women?" In *Feminism/Postmodernism,* ed. Linda Nicholson. New York: Routledge.
Hawksworth, Mary. 1989. "Knowers, Knowing, Known: Feminist Theory and Claims of Truth." *Signs: Journal of Women in Culture and Society* 14, no. 3: 533–57.
Hegel, G. W. F. 1977. *The Phenomenology of Spirit.* Trans. A. V. Miller. New York: Oxford University Press.
Hekman, Susan. 1989. "Derrida, Feminism and Epistemology." Paper presented at the annual meeting of the American Political Science Association, Atlanta.

——. 1990. *Gender and Knowledge*. Boston: Northeastern University Press.

Hirschman, Albert O. 1977. *The Passions and the Interests: Political Arguments for Capitalism before Its Triumph*. Princeton: Princeton University Press.

Hirschmann, Nancy J. 1987. "Political Obligation and Feminist Theory." Ph. D. diss., Johns Hopkins University.

——. 1989a. "Freedom, Recognition, and Obligation: A Feminist Approach to Political Theory." *American Political Science Review* 83, no. 4: 1228–44.

——. 1989b. "Hume's Social Thesis of Obligation." Paper presented to the annual meeting of the American Political Science Association, Atlanta.

——. 1990. Review of Carole Pateman, *The Sexual Contract*. *Political Theory* 18, no. 1: 170–74.

——. 1991. "Feminism and Liberal Theory." *American Political Science Review* 85, no. 1: 225–33.

Hobbes, Thomas. 1949. *De Cive or The Citizen*. Ed. Sterling P. Lamprecht. New York: Appleton-Century-Crofts.

hooks, bell. 1984. *Feminist Theory from Margin to Center*. Boston: South End Press.

Horowitz, Gad. 1987. "The Foucaultian Impasse: No Sex, No Self, No Revolution." *Political Theory* 15, no. 1: 61–80.

Hull, Gloria T., Patricia Bell Scott, and Barbara Smith, eds. 1982. *All the Women Are White, All the Blacks Are Men, but Some of Us Are Brave: Black Women's Studies*. Old Westbury, N.Y.: Feminist Press.

Hume, David. 1948. *Hume's Moral and Political Philosophy*. Ed. Henry D. Aiken. New York: Hafner.

——. 1953. *Political Essays*. Ed. Charles W. Hendel. Indianapolis: Bobbs Merrill.

——. 1957. *An Inquiry concerning the Principles of Morals*. Ed. Charles W. Hendel. New York: Liberal Arts Press.

——. 1978. *A Treatise of Human Nature*. Oxford: Oxford University Press.

Irigaray, Luce. 1980. "When Our Lips Speak Together." *Signs: Journal of Women in Culture and Society* 6, no. 1: 69–79.

——. 1981. "And the One Doesn't Stir without the Other." *Signs: Journal of Women in Culture and Society* 7, no. 1: 60–67.

——. 1985. *This Sex Which Is Not One*. Ithaca: Cornell University Press.

Jackson, Jesse. 1989. *Keep Hope Alive: Jesse Jackson's Presidential Campaign: A Collection of Major Speeches, Issue Papers, Photographs, and Campaign Analyses*, ed. Frank Clemente with Frank Watkins. Boston: South End Press.

Jaggar, Alison. 1983. *Feminist Politics and Human Nature*. Totowa, N.J.: Rowman and Allanheld.

Jefferson, Thomas. 1926. *The Best Letters of Thomas Jefferson*. Ed. J. G. de-Roulhac Hamilton. Boston: Riverside.

Johnstone, Donna Kay. 1988. "Adolescents' Solutions to Dilemmas in Fables: Two Moral Orientations—Two Problem Solving Strategies." In *Mapping the Moral Domain*, ed. Carol Gilligan et al. Cambridge, Mass.: Harvard University Press.

Jones, Ann Rosalind. 1981. "Toward an Understanding of L'Écriture Féminine." *Feminist Studies* 7, no. 2: 247–63.

Kathleen, Lyn. 1986. "The Impact of Gender Difference on Public Policy Formation." Discussion paper, Center for Public Policy Research, Boulder.

Keenan, Tom. 1987. "The 'Paradox' of Knowledge and Power: Reading Foucault on a Bias." *Political Theory* 15, no. 1: 5–37.

Keller, Catherine. 1986. *From a Broken Web: Separation, Sexism, and Self*. Boston: Beacon.

Keller, Evelyn Fox. 1983. "Gender and Science." In *Discovering Reality: Feminist Perspectives on Epistemology, Metaphysics, Methodology, and Philosophy of Science*, ed. Sandra Harding and Merrill B. Hintikka. Dordrecht: D. Reidel.

———. 1985. *Reflections on Gender and Science*. New Haven: Yale University Press.

Kelly, Rita Mae. 1989. "Gender and the Meaning of Politics and Power." *Women and Politics* 9, no. 1: 47–82.

Kerber, Linda, et al. 1986. "On *In a Different Voice*: An Interdisciplinary Forum." *Signs: Journal of Women in Culture and Society* 11, no. 2: 304–33.

Kessler, Suzanne J. 1990. "The Medical Construction of Gender: Case Management of Intersexed Infants." *Signs* 16, no. 1: 3–26.

King, Martin Luther, Jr. 1969. "Letter from Birmingham City Jail." In *Civil Disobedience: Theory and Practice*, ed. Hugo A. Bedau. New York: Pegasus.

Klein, Ethel. 1984. *Gender Politics: From Consciousness to Mass Politics*. Cambridge, Mass.: Harvard University Press.

Klein, Melanie. 1950. *Contributions to Psychoanalysis, 1921–1945*. London: Hogarth.

———. 1975. *The Psychoanalysis of Children*. London: Hogarth.

Kohlberg, Lawrence. 1979. "Justice as Reversibility." In *Philosophy, Politics, and Society*, ed. Peter Laslett and James Fishkin. 5th ser., Oxford: Blackwell.

———. 1984. *The Psychology of Moral Development*. Vol. 2 of *Essays on Moral Development: The Nature and Validity of Moral Stages*. San Francisco: Harper and Row.

Kramnick, Isaac. 1990. *Republicanism and Bourgeois Radicalism*. Ithaca: Cornell University Press.

Kristeva, Julia. 1980a. "Oscillation between Power and Denial." In *New French Feminisms*, ed. Elaine Marks and Isabelle de Courtivron. Amherst: University of Massachusetts Press.

———. 1980b. "Woman Can Never Be Defined." In *New French Feminisms*, ed. Elaine Marks and Isabelle de Courtivron. Amherst: University of Massachusetts Press.

———. 1986. *The Kristeva Reader*. Ed. Toril Moi. Oxford: Blackwell.

Kuykendall, Eleanor. 1984. "Towards an Ethic of Nurturance: Luce Irigaray on Mothering and Power." In *Mothering: Essays in Feminist Theory*, ed. Joyce Trebilcott. Totowa, N.J.: Rowman and Allanheld.

Lacan, Jacques. 1985. *Feminine Sexuality*. Ed. Juliet Mitchell and Jacqueline Rose. New York: W. W. Norton.

Langdale, Sherry. 1983. "Moral Orientations and Moral Development: The Analysis of Care and Justice Reasoning across Different Dilemmas in Females and Males from Childhood to Adulthood." Ph.D. diss., Harvard University.

Lasch, Christopher. 1977. *Haven in a Heartless World: The Family Besieged*. New York: Basic Books.

Lederer, Laura, ed. 1980. *Take Back the Night: Women on Pornography*. New York: William Morrow.

Levine, Andrew. 1976. *The Politics of Autonomy: A Kantian Reading of Rousseau's Social Contract*. Amherst: University of Massachusetts Press.

Locke, John. 1950. *A Letter concerning Toleration*. Indianapolis: Bobbs Merrill.
——. 1965. *Two Treatises of Government*. Ed. Peter Laslett. New York: New American Library.
——. 1975. *An Essay concerning Human Understanding*. Ed. P. H. Nidditch. Oxford: Oxford University Press.
——. 1990. *Questions concerning the Law of Nature*. Ed. Robert Horwitz, Jenny Strauss Clay, and Diskin Clay. Ithaca: Cornell University Press.
Lockridge, Kenneth. 1968. "Land, Population, and the Evolution of New England Society, 1630–1790." *Past and Present* 39 (April): 62–80.
Longino, Helen, and Ruth Doell. 1983. "Body, Bias, and Behavior: A Comparative Analysis of Reasoning in Two Areas of Biological Science." *Signs: Journal of Women in Culture and Society* 9, no. 2: 206–27.
Lorber, Judith, Rose Laub Coser, Alice S. Rossi, and Nancy Chodorow. 1981. "On *The Reproduction of Mothering*: A Methodological Debate." *Signs: Journal of Women in Culture and Society* 6, no. 3: 482–514.
Love, Barbara, and Elizabeth Shanklin. 1984. "The Answer Is Matriarchy." In *Mothering: Essays in Feminist Theory*, ed. Joyce Trebilcott. Totowa, N.J.: Rowman and Allanheld.
Love, Nancy. 1989. "Foucault and Habermas on Discourse and Democracy." *Polity* 22: 269–93.
Lugones, Maria C., and Elizabeth V. Spelman. 1983. "Have We Got a Theory for You! Feminist Theory, Cultural Imperialism, and the Demand for the Women's Voice." *Women's Studies International Forum* 6, no. 6: 573–81.
Lukes, Steven. 1973. *Individualism*. New York: Harper Torchbooks.
Lyons, Nona. 1988. "Two Perspectives: On Self, Relationships, and Morality." In *Mapping the Moral Domain*, ed. Carol Gilligan et al. Cambridge, Mass.: Harvard University Press.
——. 1990. "Listening to Voices We Have Not Heard: Emma Willard Girls' Ideas about Self, Relationships, and Morality." In *Making Connections: The Relational Worlds of Adolescent Girls at Emma Willard School*, ed. Carol Gilligan et al. Cambridge, Mass.: Harvard University Press.
Lyotard, Jean-François. 1979. *The Postmodern Condition: A Report on Knowledge*. Minneapolis: University of Minnesota Press.
MacDermott, Patrice. 1978. "Post-Lacanian French Feminist Theory: Luce Irigaray." *Women and Politics* 7, no. 3: 47–65.
Macdonald, Margaret. 1960. "The Language of Political Theory." In *Logic and Language*, ed. Anthony Flew. Oxford: Basil Blackwell.
MacFarlane, Leslie J. 1974. Review of *Political Obligation* by Richard E. Flathman. *American Political Science Review* 68, no. 3 (September): 1305–6.
MacIntyre, Alisdair. 1981. *After Virtue: A Study in Moral Theory*. Notre Dame: University of Notre Dame Press.
MacKinnon, Catherine A. 1982. "Feminism, Marxism, Method, and the State: An Agenda for Theory." *Signs: Journal of Women in Culture and Society* 7, no. 3: 515–544.
——. 1983. "Feminism, Marxism, Method, and the State: Toward Feminist Jurisprudence." *Signs: Journal of Women in Culture and Society* 8, no. 4: 635–58.
——. 1989. *Toward a Feminist Theory of the State*. Cambridge, Mass.: Harvard University Press.
Macoby, Eleanor, and Carol Jacklin. 1975. *The Psychology of Sex Difference*. Stanford: Stanford University Press.

Macpherson, C. B. 1962. *The Political Theory of Possessive Individualism: Hobbes to Locke*. London: Oxford University Press.

Mahler, Margaret. 1968. *On Human Symbiosis and the Vicissitudes of Individuation*. New York: International University Press.

Mahler, Margaret, Fred Pine, and Anni Bergman. 1975. *The Psychological Birth of the Human Infant*. London: Maresfield Libary.

Mandel, Ruth. 1983. *In the Running: The New Woman Candidate*. Boston: Beacon Press.

Mansbridge, Jane. 1980. *Beyond Adversary Democracy*. Chicago: University of Chicago Press.

Marcil-Lacoste, Louise. 1983. "The Trivialization of the Notion of Equality." In *Discovering Reality: Feminist Perspectives on Epistemology, Metaphysics, Methodology, and Philosophy of Science*, ed. Sandra Harding and Merrill B. Hintikka. Dordrecht: D. Reidel.

Marks, Elaine. 1978. "Women and Literature in France." *Signs: Journal of Women in Culture and Society* 3, no. 4: 832–42.

Marks, Elaine, and Isabelle de Courtivron, eds. 1980. *New French Feminisms*. Amherst: University of Massachusetts Press.

Martin, Biddy. 1988. "Feminism, Criticism, and Foucault." In *Feminism and Foucault*, ed. Irene Diamond and Lee Quinby. Boston: Northeastern University Press.

Martin, D. 1976. *Battered Wives*. San Francisco: Glide Publications.

Masters, Roger D. 1968. *The Political Philosophy of Rousseau*. Princeton: Princeton University Press.

Mezcy, Susan Gluck. 1980. "The Effects of Sex on Recruitment for Connecticut Local Offices." In *Women in Local Politics*, ed. Debra Stewart. Metuchen, N.J.: Scarecrow Press.

Miller, Jean Baker. 1976. *Toward a New Psychology of Women*. Boston: Beacon.

Millet, Kate. 1970. *Sexual Politics*. Garden City, N.Y.: Doubleday.

Money, John, and Anke Ehrhardt. 1972. *Man and Woman, Boy and Girl: The Differentiation and Dimorphism of Gender Identity from Conception to Maturity*. Baltimore: Johns Hopkins University Press.

Moore, Kristin A., and Martha R. Burt. 1982. *Private Crisis, Public Cost: Policy Perspectives on Teenage Childbearing*. Washington, D.C.: The Urban Institute Press.

Morris, Richard B. 1959. *Studies in the History of American Law*. Philadelphia: Joseph M. Mitchell.

Mostov, Julie. Forthcoming. *Power, Process, and Popular Sovereignty*. Philadelphia: Temple University Press.

Murdoch, Iris. 1970. *The Sovereignty of Good*. London: Routledge and Kegan Paul.

Nelson, Barbara J. 1984. "Women's Poverty and Women's Citizenship: Some Political Consequences of Economic Marginality." *Signs: Journal of Women in Culture and Society* 10, no. 2: 209–31.

Nicholson, Linda, ed. 1990. *Feminism/Postmodernism*. New York: Routledge.

Noone, John B., Jr. 1980. *Rousseau's "Social Contract": A Conceptual Analysis*. Athens: University of Georgia Press.

Oakeshott, Michael. 1962. *Rationalism in Politics, and Other Essays*. New York: Basic Books.

O'Brien, Mary. 1981. *The Politics of Reproduction*. Boston: Routledge and Kegan Paul.

Okin, Susan Mahler. 1979. *Women in Western Political Thought*. Princeton: Princeton University Press.

——. 1989. *Justice, Gender, and the Family*. New York: Basic Books.

——. 1990. "Reason and Feeling when Thinking about Justice." In *Feminism and Political Theory*, ed. Cass Sunstein. Chicago: University of Chicago Press.

Olson, Mancur. 1971. *The Logic of Collective Action: Public Goods and the Theory of Groups*. Cambridge, Mass.: Harvard University Press.

O'Neill, William L. 1969. *Everyone Was Brave: The Rise and Fall of Feminism in America*. Chicago: Quadrangle Books.

Ortner, Sherry B. 1974. "Is Female to Male as Nature Is to Culture?" In *Woman, Culture, and Society*, ed. Michelle Zimbalist Rosaldo and Louise Lamphere. Stanford: Stanford University Press.

Paine, Thomas. 1951. *The Rights of Man*. New York: Dutton.

Pankhurst, Emmeline. [1914.] 1985. *My Own Story*. Westport, Conn.: Greenwood.

Parenti, Michael. 1974. *Democracy for the Few*. New York: St. Martin's.

Pateman, Carole. 1979. *The Problem of Political Obligation: A Critical Analysis of Liberal Theory*. New York: John Wiley and Sons.

——. 1980. "Women and Consent." *Political Theory* 8, no. 2: 149–68.

——. 1983. "Feminism and Democracy." In *Democratic Theory and Practice*, ed. Graeme Duncan. Cambridge: Cambridge University Press.

——. 1984. "The Shame of the Marriage Contract." In *Women's Views of the Political World of Men*, ed. Judith Stiehm. New York: Transnational.

——. 1985. "Afterword." In *The Problem of Political Obligation: A Critique of Liberal Theory*. Reprint. Berkeley: University of California Press.

——. 1988. *The Sexual Contract*. Stanford: Stanford University Press.

——. 1989. *The Disorder of Women*. Stanford: Stanford University Press.

Pateman, Carole, and Nancy J. Hirschmann. 1992. "Political Obligation, Freedom, and Feminism." *American Political Science Review* 86, no. 1: 179–88.

Petchesky, Rosalind Pollack. 1980. "Reproductive Freedom: Beyond 'A Woman's Right to Choose.'" *Signs: Journal of Women and Culture in Society* 5, no. 4: 661–85.

Piaget, Jean. 1965. *The Moral Judgment of the Child*. New York: Free Press.

Pitkin, Hanna. 1965. "Obligation and Consent: I." *American Political Science Review* 59, no. 4: 990–99.

——. 1966. "Obligation and Consent: II." *American Political Science Review* 60, no. 1: 39–52.

——. 1972. *Wittgenstein and Justice: The Significance of Ludwig Wittgenstein for Social and Political Thought*. Berkeley: University of California Press.

——. 1984. *Fortune Is a Woman: Gender and Politics in the Thought of Niccolò Machiavelli*. Berkeley: University of California Press.

Piven, Frances Fox, and Richard A. Cloward. 1988. *Why Americans Don't Vote*. New York: Pantheon.

Pocock, J. G. A. 1975. *The Machiavellian Moment: Florentine Political Thought and the Atlantic Republican Tradition*. Princeton: Princeton University Press.

Poovey, Mary. 1988. "Feminism and Deconstruction." *Feminist Studies* 14, no. 1: 51–65.

Presston, Larry M. 1984. "Freedom, Markets, and Voluntary Exchange." *American Political Science Review* 78, no. 4: 959–70.

Prior, Mary, ed. 1985. *Women in English Society, 1500–1800*. London: Methuen.

Randall, Vicky. 1982. *Women and Politics*. New York: St. Martin's.

Rawls, John. 1964. "Legal Obligation and the Duty of Fair Play." In *Law and Philosophy*, ed. Sidney Hook. New York: New York University Press.

——. 1971. *A Theory of Justice*. Cambridge, Mass.: Harvard University Press.

Reagan, Maureen. 1984. "In Support of the ERA." In *Feminist Frameworks: Alternative Theoretical Accounts of the Relations between Men and Women*, ed. Alison Jaggar and Paula Rothenberger. New York: McGraw Hill.

Rhode, Debra, ed. 1990. *Theoretical Perspectives on Sexual Difference*. New Haven: Yale University Press.

Rich, Adrienne. 1976. *Of Woman Born: Motherhood as Experience and Institution*. New York: W. W. Norton.

Riley, Denise. 1988. *"Am I That Name?" Feminism and the Category "Woman" in History*. Minneapolis: University of Minnesota Press.

Riley, Patrick. 1970. "A Possible Explanation of Rousseau's General Will." *American Political Science Review* 64, no. 1: 86–97.

Ringelheim, Joan. 1985. "Women and the Holocaust: A Reconsideration of Research." *Signs: Journal of Women in Culture and Society* 10, no. 4: 741–61.

Rorty, Richard. 1979. *Philosophy and the Mirror of Nature*. Princeton: Princeton University Press.

——. 1990. *Objectivity, Relativism, and Truth*. New York: Cambridge University Press.

Rosaldo, Michelle Zimbalist. 1974. "Woman, Culture, and Society: A Theoretical Overview." In *Woman, Culture, and Society*, ed. Michelle Rosaldo and Louise Lamphere. Stanford: Stanford University Press.

Rosaldo, Michelle Zimbalist, and Louise Lamphere, eds. 1974. *Woman, Culture and Society*. Stanford: Stanford University Press.

Rousseau, Jean-Jacques. 1962. *Du contrat social ou Principes du droit politique* Paris: Édition Garnier Frères.

——. 1973. *The Social Contract and Discourses*. Trans. G. D. H. Cole. London: J. M. Dent and Son.

——. 1979. *Emile: Or, On Education*. Trans. Harold Bloom. New York: Basic Books.

——. 1987. *The Basic Political Writings*. Ed. Donald Cress. Indianapolis: Hackett.

——. 1988. *Rousseau's Political Writings*. Ed. Alan Ritter and Julia Conaway Bondanella. New York: W. W. Norton.

Rubin, Gayle. 1975. "The Traffic in Women." In *Towards a New Anthropology of Women*, ed. Rayna Reiter. New York: Monthly Review Press.

Rubin, Jeffrey, F. J. Provenzano, and Z. Luria. 1974. "The Eye of the Beholder: Parents' Views on Sex of Newborns." *American Journal of Orthopsychiatry* 44, no. 4: 512–19.

Ruddick, Sara. 1983. "Pacifying the Forces: Drafting Women in the Interests of Peace." *Signs: Journal of Women in Culture and Society* 8, no. 3: 471–89.

——. 1984a. "Maternal Thinking." In *Mothering: Essays in Feminist Theory*, ed. Joyce Trebilcott. Totowa, N.J.: Rowman and Allanheld.

——. 1984b. "Preservative Love and Military Destruction: Some Reflections on Mothering and Peace." In *Mothering: Essays in Feminist Theory*, ed. Joyce Trebilcott. Totowa, N.J.: Rowman and Allanheld.

——. 1989. *Maternal Thinking: Toward a Politics of Peace*. Boston: Beacon.

Russell, Diana E. H. 1975. *The Politics of Rape: The Victim's Perspective*. New York: Stein and Day.

Ryan, Alan, ed. 1979. *The Idea of Freedom*. London: Oxford University Press.

Sargent, Lydia, ed. 1981. *Women and Revolution: A Discussion of the Unhappy Marriage of Marxism and Feminism*. Montreal: Black Rose Books.

Scales, Ann. 1989. "Militarism, Male Dominance, and Law: Feminist Jurisprudence as Oxymoron?" *Harvard Women's Law Journal* 12: 25–73.

Scholes, Robert. 1989. "Eperon Strings." *Differences* 1: 93–104.

Schor, Naomi. 1987. "Dreaming Dissymmetry: Barthes, Foucault, and Sexual Difference." In *Men in Feminism*, ed. Alice Jardine and Paul Smith. New York: Methuen.

——. 1989. "This Essentialism Which Is Not One: Coming to Grips with Irigaray." *Differences* 1: 38–58.

Schuck, Peter H., and Rogers M. Smith. 1985. *Citizenship without Consent: Illegal Aliens in the American Polity*. New Haven: Yale University Press.

Schwartz, Felice N. 1989. "Management Women and the New Facts of Life." *Harvard Business Review* 67: 65–76.

Schwartz, Joel. 1984. *The Sexual Politics of Jean-Jacques Rousseau*. Chicago: University of Chicago Press.

Schwendinger, Julia, and Herman Schwendinger. 1983. *Rape and Inequality*. Beverly Hills: Sage.

Scott, Hilda. 1974. *Does Socialism Liberate Women?* Boston: Beacon.

Scott, Joan. 1988. "Deconstructing Equality-versus-Difference: Or, the Uses of Poststructuralist Theory for Feminism." *Feminist Studies* 14, no. 1: 33–50.

Shanley, Mary, and Carole Pateman, eds. 1990. *Feminist Interpretations and Political Theory*. University Park: Pennsylvania State University Press.

Shapiro, Ian. 1988. "A Conditional Theory of Natural Obligation." Paper presented at the annual meeting of the American Political Science Association, Washington, D.C.

Shklar, Judith N. 1969. *Men and Citizens: A Study of Rousseau's Social Theory*. Cambridge: Cambridge University Press.

Simmons, A. John. 1979. *Moral Principles and Political Obligation*. Princeton: Princeton University Press.

——. 1981. "The Obligations of Citizens and the Justification of Conscription." Working Paper, Center for Philosophy and Public Policy, College Park, Md.

Singer, Peter. 1973. *Democracy and Disobedience*. Oxford: Oxford University Press.

——. 1979. "Famine, Affluence, and Morality." In *Philosophy, Politics, and Society*, ed. Peter Laslett and James Fishkin. 5th ser. New Haven: Yale University Press.

Skinner, Quentin. 1985. *The Return of Grand Theory to the Human Sciences*. Cambridge: Cambridge University Press.

Slater, Philip E. 1961. "Toward a Dualistic Theory of Identification." *Merrill-Palmer Quarterly of Behavior and Development* 7, no. 2: 113–26.

Smith, Janet Farrell. 1984. "Parenting and Property." In *Mothering: Essays in Feminist Theory*, ed. Joyce Trebilcott. Totowa, N.J.: Rowman and Allanheld.

Smith, Joseph H., ed. 1961. *Colonial Justice in Western Massachusetts (1639–1702): The Pynchon Court Record*. Cambridge, Mass.: William Nelson Foundation, Harvard University Press.

Smith, Rogers M. 1985. *Liberalism in American Constitutional Law*. Cambridge, Mass.: Harvard University Press.

Spelman, E. V. 1988. *Inessential Woman: Problems of Exclusion in Feminist Thought.* Boston: Beacon.

Spivak, Gayatri. 1988. *In Other Worlds: Essays in Cultural Politics.* New York: Routledge.

Steinberg, Jules. 1978. *Locke, Rousseau, and the Idea of Consent: An Inquiry into the Liberal-Democratic Theory of Political Obligation.* Contributions in Political Science no. 6. Westport, Conn.: Greenwood.

Stoller, Robert J. 1973. "The Sense of Femaleness." In *Psychoanalysis and Women: Contributions to New Theory and Therapy,* ed. Jean Baker Miller. New York: Brunner-Mazel.

Taylor, Charles. 1979a. "Atomism." In *Powers, Possessions, and Freedom,* ed. A. Kontos. Toronto: University of Toronto Press.

———. 1979b. *Hegel and Modern Society.* London: Cambridge University Press.

———. 1979c. "What's Wrong with Negative Liberty?" In *The Idea of Freedom,* ed. Alan Ryan. London: Oxford University Press.

———. 1984. "Foucault on Freedom and Truth." *Political Theory* 12, no. 2: 152–83.

———. 1985. "Connolly, Foucault, and Truth." *Political Theory* 13, no. 3: 377–85.

Thoreau, Henry David. 1981. *Civil Disobedience.* In *Works of Henry David Thoreau,* ed. Lily Owens. New York: Crown.

Tinder, Glen. 1983. "What Should Political Theory Be Now?" In *What Should Political Theory Be Now: Essays from the Stambaugh Conference on Political Theory,* ed. John S. Nelson. Albany: State University of New York Press.

Trebilcott, Joyce, ed. 1984. *Mothering: Essays in Feminist Theory.* Totowa, N.J.: Rowman and Allanheld.

Tronto, Joan. 1987. "Beyond Gender Difference to a Theory of Care." *Signs: Journal of Women in Culture and Society* 12: 644–63.

Truman, David. 1959. *The Governmental Process.* New York: Knopf.

Tussman, Joseph. 1960. *Obligation and the Body Politic.* Oxford: Oxford University Press.

Walker, Lenore. 1979. *The Battered Woman.* New York: Harper and Row.

———. 1984. *The Battered Woman Syndrome.* New York: Springer.

Walzer, Michael. 1970. *Obligations: Essays on Disobedience, War, and Citizenship.* Cambridge, Mass.: Harvard University Press,

———. 1983. *Spheres of Justice.* New York: Basic Books.

———. 1984. "Liberalism and the Art of Separation." *Political Theory* 12, no. 3: 315–330.

Wenzel, Helene V. 1981. "Introduction to Luce Irigaray's 'And the One Doesn't Stir without the Other.'" *Signs: Journal of Women in Culture and Society* 7, no. 1: 56–59.

Whitbeck, Caroline. 1984. "A Different Reality: Feminist Ontology." In *Beyond Domination: New Perspectives on Women and Philosophy,* ed. Carol Gould. Totowa, N.J.: Rowman and Allanheld.

Whyte, William H. 1956. *The Organization Man.* New York: Simon and Schuster.

Winch, Peter. 1958. *The Idea of a Social Science and Its Relation to Philosophy.* London: Routledge and Kegan Paul.

Winch, Robert F. 1962. *Identification and Its Familial Determinants.* New York: Bobbs Merrill.

Winnicott, D. W. 1965. *The Maturational Processes and the Facilitating Environment: Studies in the Theory of Emotional Development.* New York: International Universities Press.

——. 1971. *Playing and Reality*. New York: Basic Books.

Wittgenstein, Ludwig. 1968. *Philosophical Investigations*. Trans. G. E. M. Anscombe. New York: Macmillan.

——. 1972. *On Certainty*. New York: Harper and Row.

Wolff, Robert Paul. 1970. *In Defense of Anarchism*. New York: Harper and Row.

Wolfinger, Raymond, and Steven Rosenstone. 1980. *Who Votes?* New Haven: Yale University Press.

Young, Iris. 1984. "Is Male Gender Identity the Cause of Male Dominance?" In *Mothering: Essays in Feminist Theory*, ed. Joyce Trebilcott. Totowa, N.J.: Rowman and Allanheld.

——. 1987. "Impartiality and the Civic Public." In *Feminism as Critique*, ed. Seyla Benhabib and Drucilla Cornell. Minneapolis: University of Minnesota Press.

——. 1990. "The Ideal of Community and the Politics of Difference." In *Feminism/Postmodernism*, ed. Linda Nicholson. New York: Routledge.

Index

Library of Congress Cataloging-in-Publication Data

Hirschmann, Nancy J.
    Rethinking obligation : a feminist method for political theory / Nancy J.
Hirschmann.
        p.   cm.
    "Portions of this book appeared earlier in article form in the American political
science review"—Pref.
    Includes bibliographical references and index.
    ISBN 0-8014-2309-0 (cloth : alk. paper). — ISBN 0-8014-9567-9 (paper : alk. paper)
        1. Political obligation.   2. Social contract.   3. Feminist theory—Political
aspects.   I. Title.
JC329.5.H57   1992
320'.01'1—dc20   91-55540

1512